Cassell and Company

The Gold Standard

A Selection from the Papers Issued by the Gold Standard Defence Association in

1895-1898

Cassell and Company

The Gold Standard
A Selection from the Papers Issued by the Gold Standard Defence Association in 1895-1898

ISBN/EAN: 9783337280864

Printed in Europe, USA, Canada, Australia, Japan

Cover: Foto ©Suzi / pixelio.de

More available books at **www.hansebooks.com**

THE GOLD STANDARD.

A Selection from the Papers

ISSUED BY THE

GOLD STANDARD DEFENCE ASSOCIATION

IN 1895–1898.

CASSELL AND COMPANY, LIMITED:

LONDON, PARIS, NEW YORK & MELBOURNE.

1898.

PREFACE.

— ◦◀ —

THE Committee of the Gold Standard Defence Association, in issuing this volume, has felt that some explanation should be given of its origin and purport.

In the year 1895, many of the leading men of business in the City of London considered, with a foresight amply justified by subsequent events, that a formidable attempt was to be made upon the established monetary system of Great Britain, and they accordingly decided to organise the Gold Standard Defence Association with the object of maintaining that system and of opposing bimetallism. Those who favoured the unlimited coinage of silver were at that date full of hope; they had possessed for many years an active organisation in the Bimetallic League, they had recently collected a large fund of money, and they could reckon many names of distinction among the list of their supporters. Hitherto no step had been taken to counteract this movement. Those who were familiar with sound monetary principles had not co-operated, and now they realised that the public mind was confused upon the matter of currency, and, so to speak, lost in the maze of bimetallic literature.

It was the demand of the bimetallic party that government should fix the relation between two commodities, gold and silver. Similar attempts had uniformly failed, for the simple reason that the forces of demand and supply are beyond the province of legal authority. But the bimetallists hoped to succeed this time by ordaining that each of the two metals was to be unlimited legal tender at a given ratio, not only in this country, but by international agreement in all the chief commercial countries of the world. Thus, when silver fell, owing to the natural action of the market, to a price lower than that proclaimed by law, it was argued that all debtors would hasten to discharge their obligations in that metal, and that, owing to the demand for silver thus created, silver would rise again to the point whence it had fallen. Such an assumption, as Sir Robert Giffen has shown in his paper entitled " The Scientific Theory of Bimetallism," is most improbable. But even if it is correct, it is the condemnation of bimetallism. For the plan is thus based on the existence of those very market fluctuations which bimetallism itself is supposed to abolish. Yet there were even more serious objections than these. Viewed in another light, it is a scheme for granting to all debtors the option of paying in the cheaper of two metals, and thus would be a blow struck at the very basis of mutual confidence. If the ratio to be established between gold and silver is 1 to $15\frac{1}{2}$ or 16, as many bimetallists appear to desire, it would be, in the words of the present Chancellor of the Exchequer, " an act of absolute dishonesty to creditors."

It may be thought that bimetallists, however wrong in their specific proposals, have had some well-grounded and substantial causes of complaint against the gold standard. This, however, is not the case. It may be said of our system that it is founded upon the popular choice, that it is built up in accordance with the established principles of science, and that it has won the admiration and the confidence of the world. In the words of the French law of 1876 :—" Great Britain has laid down principles which have attracted " round her an ever-increasing circle of nations," and the best proof of the truth of that statement is that we have become, thanks, no doubt, in a large measure to the world's confidence in our financial stability, the monetary centre of the world. It was by popular choice that towards the close of the seventeenth century we began to adopt gold as our measure of value, and, as Lord Farrer has shown in his paper entitled " England's Adoption of the Gold Standard," the movement proceeded actually in spite of the opposition of the Government. For our people reposed more confidence in gold, and less in silver, than did other nations, and thus silver left our markets for the better markets of the Continent. Finally came the legislation of 1816, which, by the simple device of token coinage, has reconciled with the legal adoption of the single metal, gold, as the sole standard of value, the free use of as much silver coin as we need for a medium of daily exchange.

Bimetallists in claiming bimetallism to be "international" have perhaps felt that they would render it more attractive to superior minds. To such let the experience of the past serve as a warning. In the paper entitled "Bimetallism in France" Mr. Macleod has traced the "the crowning example of the Latin Union. No sooner was it established than it began to break up." The wider the ring of governments who pledge themselves to the impracticable task of fixing the relation between two commodities, the more numerous will be the peoples involved in the failure of such an attempt. Equally doomed to failure are such schemes as those put forward last year under which, for example, this country was to pledge herself to the annual purchase of £10,000,000 of silver. It would be almost as sensible to enter into an international agreement to fix the volume of our annual imports, and we can buy £10,000,000 of silver annually at any time in the market if, and when, we need it.

The true international agreement is the practice by all peoples of sound finance. The monetary difficulties of the world are mainly rooted in national extravagance and unbalanced budgets. It is the nation that does not pay its way which has a bad currency, for the same reason that an individual who cannot meet his obligations has bad credit. Meanwhile Great Britain does what she can, by adopting sound principles herself, to create a world-wide standard, and thus it has come to pass that a bill of exchange drawn on London has become in large measure the best medium of international trade.

It often happens during the progress of some revolution in human affairs, that many honest, and even some superior minds, puzzled and alarmed at the change around them, are driven to adopt strange remedies. Of such are those who, upset by the economic change in operation during the last quarter of a century, have had resort to bimetallism. With that period began a rapid fall in the price of silver, which profoundly affected, sooner or later, the currencies of the foremost countries of the world. There was one main exception—Great Britain—whose monetary system, organised with profound foresight, was entirely proof against the shock. Within our borders a transformation began, ' painful no doubt to many interests, but beneficial to the general body of our people. There was a rise in the wages paid to labour, and there was a fall in the prices of many staple commodities ; the artisan got more shillings a week, and each shilling purchased more goods than before ; while, conversely, the manufacturer and the farmer paid more to their employés at the same time that the prices of their goods declined. For detailed illustrations reference must here be made to the remarkable papers of Mr. Shaw-Lefevre on agriculture, and of Mr. H. H. Spencer on the woollen and worsted industry. Only one fact made all this possible ; it was that labour had become more fruitful and more efficient, and that the labourer was worthy of his increased hire. But there were many sufferers who could not, or did not, accommodate themselves to the times. The landowner found his rents declining with the decline of wheat ; the manufacturer thought that his wages bill had become a burden, and that an alteration of the currency, which would enable him, without altering the nominal amount of his wages, to pay his men less than before, would also enable him to compete more easily with his rivals. To some of such persons it appeared that Britain was in imminent danger of being ruined by a continuation of low prices and high wages. There was the remedy of protection, but that was out of date and impossible. But would not bimetallism both raise prices and lower wages? So to bimetallism they turned in their distress. Then was witnessed that powerful alliance between the few who seriously wished to fix the relation of silver and gold by an impossible plan, and the many who wished to increase the volume of the currency for a practical purpose. From the grave of protection rose the ghost of bimetallism.

Five great causes, however, during recent years, have undermined the influence and exposed the statements of the advocates of this propaganda. First, there was the extraordinary increase in the production of gold. In 1877, the eminent Austrian geologist, Dr. Suess, in his work "The Future of Gold," had proved that the decrease in the annual output, which had commenced in 1860, was to be continuous, and that Nature herself barred the way to the adoption of the gold standard. But in 1886 the Randt fields were discovered; in Australia, in India, in the Guianas, in the United States, and British Columbia, the gold industry developed by leaps and bounds, and the output of the metal, which was about £22,000,000 in 1887, rose to about £48,000,000 in 1897. Fresh nations adopted the gold standard, and thus the forces that could be mustered in favour of silver inevitably declined. Again, there was the collapse of the Monetary Conference at Brussels in 1892, an account of which is given in the paper entitled "Is it only England that 'Blocks the Way'?" The declarations there made by the delegates of Germany, of Austria-Hungary, of Great Britain, of Italy, of Switzerland, of Russia, and of Sweden, showed very clearly that the opinion of Europe, after an agitation of nearly twenty years, was adverse to the adoption of bimetallism.

In the third place, the defeat of the "Silverites" under Mr. Bryan at the Presidental Election of 1896 in the United States of America, was a blow to bimetallism in Europe. For, during the heat of the conflict, the true issue of the movement became revealed, and many men who had hitherto lent their support to a harmless theoretical opinion, now realised that they were playing with tools edged with repudiation. Besides, the Silverites declared their adherence to a ratio of 16 to 1; and when bimetallism was seen to mean nothing less than an attempt to double the price of silver by law, many of its former adherents shrank from connecting themselves with such a scheme. And, fourthly, there was the failure in 1897, the story of which is given very fully in the paper entitled "The Bimetallic Negotiations and their Result," a paper in which the Committee of the Gold Standard Defence Association has recorded the defeat of a carefully devised attack.

But perhaps it will not be considered a presumption to suggest that not least among the causes of the decay of bimetallism has been the work of the Gold Standard Defence Association itself. It has been the policy of the Committee to furnish a complete answer to the bimetallists, and to oppose to their assertions the authority of facts and figures. Nor has this duty to the public solely engaged the attention of the Committee, which has provided in the following pages an explanation of the principles of a sound currency and the accordance of our system with those principles. The papers numbered I., XIII., XXVII., and XXVIII. in this volume represent fully the views of the Committee as a whole, and have been discussed and agreed to by them in detail. The other papers are published on the responsibility of the authors, so far as their details are concerned. But they have received the general approval of the Committee.

In the last paper of this series there is printed a recent speech of Lord George Hamilton, who, speaking as one of the originators of the movement, confesses that the world is opposed to bimetallism. If the speaker is correct, and if the movement is dead, it has lived already longer than it deserved. If, in spite of the experience of the past, of the guidance of reason, and of the opinion of the world, it still survives, it will be met by an opposition as uncompromising as before.

July, 1898.   GEORGE PEEL.

CONTENTS.

PAGE

GENERAL STATEMENT.*

By the COMMITTEE   THE GOLD STANDARD DEFENCE ASSOCIATION.

1. THE agitation on behalf of silver, both abroad and at home, has assumed such proportions that it is thought desirable to form an **Association to oppose the policy known as bimetallism, and to unite in defence of the gold standard** all those who believe that an adherence to that standard is essential to the commercial position of our country and to the due discharge of contracts.

2. One leading object of the Association is to explain the principles which should govern a sound currency and a trustworthy standard of value; and to show that whilst our present system is in conformity with those principles, the proposals of the bimetallists are in conflict with them.

3. Though to do this effectually requires a series of papers, the main issue may be made intelligible in a few words by stating the different forms which an obligation to pay money, such as is contained in every contract, must assume under the two systems.

4. Under our present monometallic system, the form of an obligation to pay is, "I am bound to pay one hundred gold sovereigns." Under the bimetallic system the form of an obligation to pay would be, "I am bound to pay either one hundred gold sovereigns, or as much silver as is equal in weight to some fixed multiple of one hundred gold sovereigns, whichever I find the cheaper." What this fixed multiple should be our **English bimetallists refuse to answer,** though the question is one of the most vital importance.

5. But the mere statement of this difference condemns bimetallism. The monometallic form of obligation is simple, clear, and natural. It is the language now used in all our internal dealings, and in most of the international dealings of the world. The bimetallic form of obligation is artificial and forced. Its language is obscure, and its

* *Issued in June,* 1895.

B

operation still more obscure. It is a form which no one would use except under compulsion of law.

6. It is **a fatal objection to bimetallism** that no one can foresee its ultimate results. This only is certain—that at any ratio less than the present market ratio it would entail most serious loss on all gold creditors, and beyond others on the people of the United Kingdom. For it is plain that other nations would take advantage of a bimetallic option to pay us their debts not in gold but in silver. From this point of view, bimetallism is a policy which favours exist-ing debtors at the expense of creditors, and other countries at the expense of the United Kingdom.

7. It is urged on behalf of bimetallism that it would raise prices —for instance, the price of wheat or cotton. **If this be so, bi-metallism is a direct attack upon every artisan and labourer in the country,** since their well-being depends, above all things, on the cheapness of the necessaries of life.

8. Again, it is said that there is not enough gold in the world for currency purposes, and that silver should be added to gold to supply that deficiency. But the facts are otherwise : the new supply of gold in recent years has been enormous, and far beyond any currency demand, whilst the annual output of gold has been the largest in history.

9. Again, bimetallism is recommended on the ground that it would remedy fluctuations in international exchange. It seems more likely, however, that, if each man had the option of paying his neighbour either in gold or in silver, the difficulties of exchange would be imported into the daily operations of our national life.

10. The monetary history of all countries in which the law of dual legal tender has been combined with free mintage of both metals shows a continuous record of failure to maintain both concurrently in circulation. Of this the cases of the Latin Union and of the United States are striking examples. In both instances, the option given to the debtor, and the pressure of silver at the Mints, have rendered the attempt impracticable, and have forced these countries to close their Mints against silver, and to resort to a single gold standard.

11. The Association has no connection whatever with Party politics, for it is clear that **men of all shades of political opinion can unite to prevent a revolution in our currency and to re-sist an attack on our trade and on the well-being of our people.**

Bimetallism Considered.*

By the Rt. Hon. Sir JOHN LUBBOCK, Bart., M.P., etc.

THE BIMETALLIC CASE.

1. THE currency is a subject which has long had a profound interest for me, not only as a practical banker, having been for twenty-five years secretary, and subsequently vice-president, of the London Bankers, but also as having been a member of the International Monetary Commission, and the Gold and Silver Commission, as well as chairman of the committee for the selection of the designs on our present coins. The Bimetallic League rest their case, as I understand, mainly (*a*) on the alleged contraction in the amount of money, (*b*) on the demonetisation of silver, (*c*) on the scarcity of gold, and (*d*) on the supposed appreciation of gold. As regards the first point, the Director of the United States Mint tells us that while the stock of the world's money in 1860 was 3,400 millions of dollars, it had risen in 1894 to no less than 8,021 millions. The average output of gold and silver for 1866–73 was £38,000,000, less than that of gold alone now. **Surely, then, the "artificial famine of money" is a pure fallacy.**

2. Secondly, has silver been demonetised? Certainly not. It is still used as money by the majority of mankind. According to the most recent estimates, the population mainly using silver is 800,000,000, against less than 400,000,000 using gold. No doubt, however, those using gold are the most advanced and energetic. Still, the amount of silver coin in circulation is estimated at over

---

* *An Address delivered before the Liverpool Chamber of Commerce on January 24th, 1896, and issued by the Gold Standard Defence Association in February, 1896.*

B 2

3,100,000,000 ounces, as against 200,000,000 ounces of gold.* The Gold and Silver Commission, after inquiring into the question, reported that—"When all the facts are taken into account it seems doubtful whether there has been, on the whole, any great diminution in the use of silver for currency purposes. **The demonetisation of silver is, then, to a great extent, quite a myth.**

3. I now turn to the supposed scarcity of gold. The chairman of the Institute of Bankers pointed out recently that the amount of gold held by the banks of England, France, Germany, and the Associated Banks of New York was no less than £186,000,000, showing an increase of £65,000,000 in ten years. Moreover, the annual production of gold has risen in the same period from £20,000,000 to £40,000,000. **Certainly, therefore, there is no scarcity of gold.**

4. I next come to the supposed appreciation of gold. No doubt since 1873—the year which is generally taken for comparison—there has been a heavy fall in prices. But 1873 was a year of exceptionally high prices. The *Economist* newspaper began its valuable series of index numbers in 1850, based on the average of six previous years. Since that time there has been a drop of about 10 per cent. After that date prices rose until 1873, and then fell heavily; but is it the commodities which have fallen, or the gold which has risen? When we remember the improvement which has taken place in manufactures, the greater facilities of transport, etc., we are irresistibly driven to the conclusion that the change in prices is mainly due to a cheapening of other commodities, and not to an appreciation of gold. Moreover, there are some important articles which have not declined. Wages, for instance, are distinctly higher. Here, again, I may quote the authority of the Gold and Silver Commission. "We do not think," they say, "that the causes, other than those relating to the standard, which have been operating to produce a fall of price, are far to seek. When we examine the case of individual commodities, we see factors at work which fully account for a fall in their prices, even if the standard had remained, so far as it was itself concerned, stable. Take, for example, the case of wheat. The increase in the supply during recent years in many parts of the world, but especially on the American Continent, has been enormous. This has been due in a great measure to the fact that vast territories, consisting in some cases of virgin soil, have been opened up by the construction of railways, and become the means of creating supplies largely in excess of the needs of those engaged in

* *See, for instance, Probyn : Statistical Journal, 1895.*

their production." In addition to this, the cost of transit from these countries to other parts of the world has very much diminished. **The Commission sum up on this point that "there is no conclusive evidence of a substantial appreciation of gold to be derived either from a review of the variations in prices, or of the circumstances relating to the production and use of that metal."**

BIMETALLISM FAVOURS ONE PARTY TO A CONTRACT.

5. What now is the change proposed? Bimetallists endeavour to whittle down the magnitude of the change. The only difference they say is that under the present system the pound sterling is defined as so much gold ; but under the other, it would be defined as so much gold or so much silver. But there is a condition implied, though not expressed, that it is so much gold or so much silver, "at the option of the debtor." True bimetallism would be payment half in one metal and half in the other. Spurious bimetallism gives an option in favour of one party to the contract. At present no doubt gold may rise or fall. As a fact, the fluctuations are very small, and the chance of a rise or fall is at most times equal; but if you give either the debtor or creditor two metals to choose from, he has twice the chance of a fall—if you give him gold, silver, and copper, he would have three chances in his favour. **The Bimetallic League, however, maintain that the value of gold and silver could never vary. Have they the courage of their opinions ? Would they give the option to the creditor ? Certainly not.** If they made such a proposal they know that their support would disappear. And yet, if their principle is correct, it would be immaterial whether the option rested with the one or the other, because it could never be of any value. Bimetallism is based on the idea that the law can do that which no wise Government would attempt, and which all sound economists condemn—viz. fix the value of one article in terms of another. I believe this is impossible. **What bimetallists really propose is not true bimetallism, but monometallism at the option of one party.** True bimetallism would consist in enacting that the legal pound sterling should consist partly of gold and partly of silver, but what they propose is that the debtor should be authorised to pay at his option either in gold or silver. One cause to which we owe the development of our commerce is the confidence felt in the stability of our standard of value, and we should be very unwise to alter it except under the clearest necessity.

CAN ANY INTERNATIONAL ARRANGEMENT MAINTAIN A FIXED RATIO PERMANENTLY?

6. We are for maintaining our gold coinage and standard, but it does not follow that we would wish other countries to abandon silver. At present, speaking roughly, half the world use gold and half silver. That is a convenient arrangement, and one which it would be undesirable under existing arrangements to disturb. But could any ratio of value be maintained? Let me quote you the figures for the production of silver :—In 1871, 52,500,000 ounces; in 1875, 62,262,000 ounces ; in 1880, 74,791,000 ounces ; in 1885, 91,652,000 ounces ; in 1890, 126,095,000 ounces ; in 1894, 166,000,000 ounces. **With such an enormous increase in production, I ask you confidently, as business men, whether you think that any possible arrangement could prevent a fall in the value of silver?** The supporters of bimetallism argue as if gold and silver were used in coinage only. But that is not so; the use of the precious metals for other purposes is enormous. Out of the total annual production of gold, it was estimated by Dr. Soetbeer, some years ago, that over £12,000,000 was used in arts. Probably the amount of silver annually absorbed for ornaments, etc., is at least as great. Does anyone suppose that we could maintain a fixed ratio between gold and silver used in the arts? But, if not, it is clear that the ratio for coinage purposes could not be maintained either. One metal or the other would go out of circulation.

7. We are told that up to 1873 France maintained a ratio. What were the facts? The history of the French coinage is very instructive. Before 1873 France was a reservoir into which other countries could pour either of the precious metals which they did not want, and from which they could draw whichever they might require. That, of course, tended to keep a stable ratio, but it did not prevent an agio on gold coins in France, and led to extraordinary fluctuations in the coinage—evils from which we have been free, but which the adoption of bimetallism would tend to introduce here. Before the gold discoveries of 1850 the coinage of gold in France had almost ceased, and gold was at a premium. If you travelled in France you either had to load yourself with a great weight of silver, or to pay a premium on gold, which, when you came to use it, you were almost sure to lose. After the gold discoveries, on the contrary, the coinage of silver immensely decreased. The coinage of gold, which had fallen from £4,000,000 in 1831-5 to £800,000 in 1841-5, rose to no less than £108,000,000 in 1856-60 ; while the coinage of silver, which had been £15,000,000 in 1841-5 and

£21,000,000 in 1846-50, fell to £875,000 in 1861-5. Thus under bimetallism France was at one time flooded with silver, and almost denuded of gold; while at another the silver was exported, and there was an enormous coinage of gold.

8. **It has been often said that up to 1873 the ratio of silver to gold remained stationary. But that is not so.** The fluctuations were, no doubt, smaller than they have been since, but they were considerable. The Director of the United States Mint has shown that even the averages for different years varied as much as 5 per cent. The extremes were, of course, larger. These fluctuations caused great inconvenience, from which our system protected us. Moreover, our own experience is almost as instructive. In the eighteenth century we tried, and tried in vain, to maintain a fixed ratio between gold and silver. Professor Thorold Rogers, in a paper read before the London Chamber of Commerce, gave the nominal mint and real market prices for twenty-three years, and during that time there were only two months in which they coincided. The attempt, in fact, was a total failure.

9. Bimetallists affirm that the divergence between the price of gold and silver is primarily due "to the abandonment of the bi-metallic system which had prevailed in certain countries prior to 1873." But why did these countries abandon this system? They did so on account of that very divergence. The divergence was obviously not primarily due to the abandonment of bimetallism, because the abandonment of bimetallism succeeded and was due to that very divergence; though, of course, I do not deny that the closing of the mints in the Latin Union tended still further to depress the value of silver. **In fact, it was the fall in silver which compelled the Latin Union to close their mints.**

THE GOLD AND SILVER COMMISSION.

10. But, then, it has been over and over again stated that the Gold and Silver Commission were unanimously of opinion that an agreement between the principal nations of the world would be sufficient to maintain a fixed ratio of value between gold and silver.* This, however, is quite incorrect. In the first place, Mr. Birch and I expressly said "that, having regard to the great uncertainty as to the probable future production of the mines, the large use of the precious metals in the arts, and to the number of countries

---

* e.g. "*The final report of the Royal Commission on Gold and Silver was, however, of a character so favourable to the cause advocated by the League, that the question is now thoroughly rife for settlement.*"—Official Statement of Bimetallic League, *para.* 15.

which would still remain outside the combination, we doubt whether any given ratio could be permanently maintained." As regards four of our other colleagues also the statement seems to me inaccurate. Their language was very guarded. They said : " We think that in any conditions fairly to be contemplated in the future, so far as we can forecast them from the experience of the past, a stable ratio might be maintained if the nations we have alluded to were to accept and strictly adhere to bimetallism, at the suggested ratio." I understand this to be no more than the expression of opinion as to the probable results of such an arrangement, and by no means as a decisive statement that such a result would necessarily follow.

11. Moreover, they go on to say : "It will be observed that from 1830 to 1845 the coinage of gold (in the Latin Union) was almost replaced by that of silver, and from 1846 to 1865 that of silver again, to a great extent, by that of gold. The continuance for a few years longer of the conditions which prevailed up to 1845 would apparently have resulted practically in the entire cessation of a gold coinage in France. Even as things were, the result led to the existence of an agio on gold coins ; and it seems probable that the most extended international agreement would lead from time to time, in some of the countries included in it, to the existence of a premium on either the gold or silver coins ; and it cannot be denied that an agio on any part of the coinage would be a serious evil." **So far, then, from admitting that a stable ratio could be secured, they state that even under the most extended international agreement there would probably be an agio either on the gold or on the silver.**

SOME ASPECTS OF BIMETALLISM.

12. The members of the Liverpool Stock Exchange have pointed out, in an able memorial to the Chancellor of the Exchequer, that ten years ago 100 classes of currency bonds and 40 classes of gold bonds of the United States railway companies were officially quoted by the London Stock Exchange. The quotations of currency bonds have now shrunk to 28 classes, whilst those of gold bonds have increased to 190 classes, a conclusive evidence of the distrust of currency securities entertained by investors. Messrs. Virtue & Co. tell me that since this was written the gold bonds have still further increased to over 200. This shows the importance attached by investors to the right to payment in gold. Bimetallist advocates constantly express themselves as if the maintenance of the ratio

was the same as the maintenance of the value. What would probably happen would be that, sooner or later, one of the metals would become dearer than the other; it would no longer be taken to the mints; the coins of it would be melted down; and it would pass out of circulation, or would go to a premium. The cheaper metal would thus become practically the standard, and, if the fall continued, the standard would sink. **The mercantile community are certainly not in favour of the proposed change. It was brought before the Associated Chambers a few years ago, and out of 170 delegates, representing fifty-four chambers, only eleven voted for it.** Since then I believe it has not been raised again. It is obviously very improbable that Australia and South Africa would adopt bimetallism. We are assured officially by the Bimetallic League "that it is not the object of international bimetallism to raise prices." But assuredly the support which the League has received has been given mainly under the belief that it would do so.

WANTED—A RATIO.

13. Bimetallists have always declined to commit themselves to any ratio. But it is obvious that the results of the change would, to a great extent, depend on the ratio which was adopted. At present we may say roughly that gold is more than thirty times the value of silver. There are, I know, some bimetallists who would insist on a ratio approaching the market values. Practically, however, we may at once dismiss any such idea. In France the legal ratio is still 15½ to 1, and no French authority has shown any disposition to accept any material change. America would, I believe, take a similar view. **Practically, then, bimetallism means a ratio of 15 or 16 to 1—*i.e.* that foreign countries should be permitted to send us any quantity of silver at double its present price.** No doubt bimetallists tell us that if there was any practical probability of the adoption of bimetallism, the value of silver would rapidly rise. I doubt, however, whether this would be the result. We should rather, I think, see a great stimulus given to silver mines, a great increase of production of silver, and all creditors would do their best to call in their debts while they could still claim payment in gold.

ARE WE BEING RUINED?

14. But is there any real reason for a change? As regards India, the exports and imports, excluding Government stores and treasure, amounted in 1873 (in tens of rupees) to £57,000,000, and in 1893-4 to £110,000,000. And, after all, how do we

stand at home? As regards the working classes, while in
1873 there were 38 paupers in every thousand, the numbers are
now only 23. The average rate of wages has risen from £43 8s.
in 1873 to £53 16s. in 1891. Agriculture no doubt is suffering,
but we should not benefit our farmers by taking 10s. and calling it
£1. How about trade? The Clearing House transactions in 1868
amounted to £3,400,000,000, in 1873 they were £6,000,000,000,
an exceptionally large amount, but in 1895 they were £7,600,000,000.
The averages of exports and imports for the ten years ending in 1873
were £560,000,000 : in 1896 they were £680,000,000. There
has been a fall of prices. If we take this at only 25 per cent., and
it is no doubt more, it will bring up the amount to £850,000,000,
showing an increase of no less than £290,000,000 in twenty-two
years. But we are told that our trade with silver-using countries has
suffered. So far from this being the case, in 1873 the amount of our
exports to silver-using countries was 14·3 of the whole; it was in
1894 20·1 per cent. I admit the depression in agriculture and in
certain trades, but this only makes the general progress all the more
remarkable. The total amount on which income tax was paid in
1873 was £514,000,000 ; in 1894 it was £706,000,000, showing
**an increase of no less than £192,000,000 in twenty-one
years.**

THE SUPPOSED NECESSITY FOR A CHANGE DOES NOT EXIST.

15. In conclusion, then, I have attempted to show that while
the necessaries of life have fallen in price, say 25 per cent., wages, on
the contrary, have not diminished, so that the interests of the great
wage-earning class are opposed to the change ; that those who have
any of their savings invested in foreign countries would be unfavourably affected by the change ; that our great Australian Colonies are
not likely to concur; that we cannot expect to prevent fluctuations
in value between two great articles of commerce such as gold
and silver ; that the mercantile community are opposed to it ; and
that the supposed necessity for a change does not exist. I see no
**reason then to change the opinion which I have always
held; and submit that we should be very unwise to
introduce any fundamental change in the standard of
value and system of currency under which our trade and
commerce have attained a magnitude and prosperity un-
exampled in the history of the world.**

The Measure of Value and the Metallic Currency.*

By the Rt. Hon. LORD FARRER.

---

1. IT is a function of every civilised State to settle the terms
in which trading transactions are carried on. The State does
this in two ways. First, it prescribes certain measures of weight and
size in which the quantities of articles bought and sold are to be described, and it gives the means of ascertaining that these measures
are accurate. Secondly, it both determines and stamps and issues the
coin in which the value of all goods bought and sold is measured,
and by means of which, as a medium, they may be exchanged. The
utility of this function is obvious. In the simplest and rudest form of
trading, one article would be exchanged against another, without any
description or definition except such as would arise out of the direct
impression made by the particular articles on the senses of the two
parties. An apronful of corn would be exchanged against an armful
of meat or against a hewn tree or stone, or a day's labour would
be exchanged against some handfuls of wheat : but there would be
nothing by which the quantities of any of these articles could be
known, or by which, in the absence of the articles themselves, any of

* *Issued in August,* 1895.

the parties could tell what he was giving or getting. Nor would there be any common measure of value to which each could be referred. The person possessing the corn, and wanting meat, wood, or stone, must wait until he could find a person possessing the requisite piece of meat, or wood, or stone, and at the same time wanting corn ; or the person able to labour and wanting corn must wait until he could find a person possessing corn and wanting labour ; and then the two parties must come together, and compare their respective articles by the use of their unassisted senses.

2. Contrast this with the sale of 100 quarters of corn at so many pounds sterling a quarter ; or the purchase of so many pounds of beef at so many pence a pound ; or the wages for an eight-hour day's labour at 2s. 6d. per hour. The facilities of dealing in the latter cases, as compared with the former, are obvious. But these facilities would be impossible if we did not know accurately and universally what was meant by a quarter, and by a pound weight, and by a £ sterling, and by a shilling, and by a penny ; and in order that they may be accurately and universally known, they must be determined in such a way that all persons must accept them ; and this can only be done by the authority of the State. It has therefore been admitted in all civilised societies that the State must determine measures of weight, size, and value. **The State accordingly provides certain standards of weight and size**—viz. a standard pound weight and a standard yard measure—which are kept at Westminster ; and by reference to these standards all the measures of weight, length, and capacity used in ordinary dealings are, under carefully prepared regulations, verified and tested.

3. The determination of the standard or measure of value is a less simple affair than the determination of the standard pound weight or yard. The value of any given thing is the quantity of other things for which it will exchange ; and that quantity is, of course, constantly changing, and changing differently in the case of different things. It is, of course, in such a case impossible to have any fixed standard or measure of value such as are the standard pound weight and the standard yard measure of length.

The only thing which can be done is to select some object which varies as little as may be in its relation to other things, and to make a given quantity of this the standard by which the value of other things is measured. For this purpose mankind has for ages used gold and silver. Out of these metals have been fashioned the coins in which payments have been made, and by means of which exchanges have been effected. In other words, **gold and silver coins have not only been standards of value, but means of exchange;** and their true position and character as standards of value have been secured by making them also the actual media by which purchases and sales have been effected. For instance, suppose that a quarter of wheat, a coat, and a day's labour will all exchange one for the other, and that each will also exchange for the quantity of gold contained in an English sovereign. Then the gold contained in the sovereign or pound sterling will be the measure of value of the quarter of wheat, of the coat, and of the day's labour; and an actual gold sovereign may also be the medium by the use of which these things are exchanged for one another.

4. But though standard coins are thus both measures of value and media of exchange, it is very important to distinguish between the two functions. In any sound system of currency the metal coin which is the measure of value must also be *a* medium of exchange: but there are many media of exchange besides the standard coin. Indeed, in this country, and in the greater part of the civilised world, **the standard coin plays an insignificant part as a medium of exchange compared with other more convenient media,** such as subsidiary token-coins, bank-notes, bills of exchange, bankers' cheques, and other forms of credit. It is from a neglect of this important distinction, and of the actual facts of common business, that many errors and much confusion arise. We find, for instance, the word "money" used—even by accurate writers like Lord Liverpool— as synonymous with standard coin; whereas, in the daily language of the market, of the press, and of common life, "money" means and includes not only gold sovereigns, but silver, shillings, and pence, as well as all the various instruments of credit with which we buy

and sell, and which are probably at least a hundred times as great at any given moment as all the gold sovereigns in the country.*

5. Of the coins used in our currency, the pound sterling or gold sovereign is the real standard of value, and gold sovereigns are the only coin which are legal tender for debts exceeding forty shillings.† The gold sovereign consists of a certain fixed fraction of an ounce of pure gold combined with a certain quantity of alloy.‡ **The essential function of the Mint consists in ascertaining that its weight and purity are what the law requires, and in stamping and issuing it so that it may be known everywhere as certified by the Government to possess these qualities. Beyond this the Government does nothing to determine its value, which is simply the value of that quantity of gold in the open market.** But, it may be said,

---

* The following passage from Lord Liverpool's well-known treatise on the "Coins of the Realm" contains so good a descript on of the standard coin that I quote it here, merely adding the correct expression "standard coin" where Lord Liverpool uses the word "money" :—

"The [money] standard coin of a country is the measure by which the value of all things bought and sold is regulated and ascertained, and it is itself, at the same time, the value, or equivalent, for which goods are exchanged, and in which contracts are generally made payable. In this last respect, the [money] standard coin, as a measure, differs from all others, and to the combination of the two qualities before defined, which constitute the essence of this [money] standard coin, the principal difficulties that attend it in speculation and practice, both as a measure and an equivalent, are to be ascribed. These two qualities can never be brought perfectly to unite and agree; for if the [money] standard coin were a measure alone, and made, like all other measures, of a material of little or no value, it would not answer the purpose of an equivalent. And if it is made, in order to answer the purpose of an equivalent, of a material of value, subject to frequent variations, according to the price at which such material sells at the market, it fails on that account in the quality of a standard or measure, and will not continue to be perfectly uniform and at all times the same. Civilised nations have generally adopted gold and silver as the material of their [money] standard coin, because these metals are costly and difficult to procure, little subject to variation in value, durable, divisible, and easily stamped or marked."

† 33 *Vict. cap.* 10, *s.* 4.

‡ 123·27447 *grains in weight:* 11/12*ths fine gold*, 1/12*th alloy* (33 *Vict. cap.* 10, *first schedu'e*). *The reason for this special quantity is historical, and is founded on the quantity of gold contained in the guinea.*

how can this be the case when the Mint price of an ounce of gold is fixed by law at £3 17s. 10½d. ? The answer is, that by the *Mint price* of gold is only meant the quantity of sovereigns and fractions of a sovereign into which the Mint divides an ounce of gold which is brought to it for coinage; and it is important to remember that by the shillings and pence which form part of the *Mint price* are meant, not given quantities of silver or bronze, but the fractions of a gold sovereign which are known by these names. An ounce of gold is divided into three whole sovereigns and 17/20ths and 10/240ths and 1/480th of a gold sovereign; and this is what is meant when it is said that the *Mint price* of gold is £3 17s. 10½d. So long, therefore, as the gold currency is in a sound condition, there can be no permanent or important variation between the market price and what is called the Mint price.

6. But we could not be sure that the gold sovereign would be of the value of the gold contained in it, if the Government had the power to increase or diminish the quantity of coined sovereigns at their own discretion, and thus to determine what quantity of currency the people shall use. It is therefore made incumbent on the Mint to coin into sovereigns all the gold which is brought to it for coinage. The quantity of coins in circulation must, therefore, depend entirely on the demand for them, and not on the action of the Government. If more coins are needed, gold is brought to the Mint and turned into coins. If fewer coins are needed, existing sovereigns are melted down, and exported or otherwise used. The value of the coin must therefore be that of the gold used in making it, with nothing added but the value of the Government certificate of its weight and purity. **It is this self-acting character of the Mint which is the great safeguard of the coinage.** If it were, in the power of the Government to refuse to coin, they would be able to restrict the coinage, and thus to add to its exchangeable value. If they were able to alter the quantity and purity of the metal contained in the sovereign, they would be able to depreciate its value, as has in former times often been done. In either case they would be able to derange markets and alter existing contracts, which are

made in terms of the sovereign or pound sterling. The self-acting character of the Mint operations reduces the function of the State in issuing money to that of a verifier in weights and measures.

7. With regard to the silver coinage the case is different. The gold sovereign, it is obvious, or even the gold half-sovereign, is not suited for small payments; and attempts to issue a smaller gold coin, such as the gold 5-franc piece in France, have not been attended with success. In many countries paper money is largely used for the purpose of small payments, *e.g.* the paper dollar in the United States. But it is less convenient—or, at any rate, less suited to English habits—than metallic coin; and there is an advantage in having a subsidiary coin made of a substance which has some value of its own. For these reasons, amongst others, it has been found desirable to use a metal of larger bulk and smaller value than gold; and silver is the metal used for the purpose.

8. By royal proclamation the gold sovereign is equivalent to twenty shillings, or, in other words, is divided into twenty parts called shillings. Previously to 1816 the weight of standard silver con-tained in a shilling was 92·90 grains, making the relative value of a given weight of silver to the same weight of gold as 15·21 to 1. In 1816 the weight of standard silver contained in a shilling was reduced to 87·27272 grains—a reduction of about 6 per cent.*

9. The effect of this alteration was, at the then market value be-tween gold and silver, to make the value of the shilling measured in gold rather more than the value of the silver of which it was composed. In other words, the shilling became a token-coin, the currency value of which was no longer the value of the silver contained in it, but the value of 1/20th of a gold sovereign. There could, therefore, be no longer any motive for melting it down or exporting it. But since with free mintage of silver it would have been greatly to the advant-age of the owners of silver to bring it to the Mint—to get it coined into shillings—and to pay their debts with the shillings so coined,

* *See the present Coinage Act, 33 Vict. cap. 10, s. 3, first schedule. According to this Act, the weight of silver in a shilling is, as above stated, 87·27272 grains; the fineness 37/40ths of fine silver to 3/40ths of alloy.*

two precautions were taken. The right of private persons to have silver freely minted for them, which had been actually suspended for many years, was finally put an end to, and **the right to mint silver coins was confined to the Government.** The second precaution was to limit the operation of the law of legal tender. Under that law, as it formerly existed, either gold or silver coined by the king's authority could be offered in payment to any amount. But under the Act of 1816 silver was allowed to be legal tender for the amount of 40s., but for no greater amount. Under this state of law new supplies of silver coin cannot be procured except with the consent and by the act of the Government, and silver coin cannot be used for the purposes of large payments.

10. **The immediate effect of the Act of 1816 was the resumption of the coinage of silver, which it had been found necessary to suspend under the mischievous operation of the old Bimetallic Law,** and thus to provide the country with an adequate supply of small change, the want of which under that law had proved to be a very serious evil. Very large amounts of silver were coined in 1816 and the years immediately following, and there has been a fairly steady coinage ever since; in fact, just as much as was wanted to supply the needs of the people for small coin.*

11. Since 1816 the gold value of silver has declined, and the ratio —which was then about 15½ to 1—is now above 30 to 1 : so that the difference between the value of the silver contained in a shilling and the value of 1/20th of a gold sovereign, is far greater than it was at the time when silver was first made into a token-coin. One consequence of this is that the Government makes a very large profit on the coinage of silver, since every ounce of silver—which they now

---

* *Continued by the present Coinage Act,* 33 *Vict. cap.* 10, *s.* 4. *Under the operation of the Bimetallic Law, which permitted free coinage of both metals, very little silver was coined during the eighteenth century. The coinage of silver was suspended by law in* 1798, *and was not resumed till* 1816. *Since* 1816 *the aggregate coinage of silver has been about* £41,000,000, *or, on an average, over* £500,000 *a year.*

C

buy for less than 2s. 6d. an ounce—they issue, when turned into silver coins, at 5s. 6d.

12. The silver coins are not, therefore, a measure of value at all ; they are a token-coinage, only used for small transactions. And when a silver coin is spoken of as denoting the price of any article, what is meant by it is the fraction of the gold sovereign to which it corresponds. If we say that mutton is worth a shilling a pound, we mean that a pound of mutton is worth 1/20th of a gold sovereign. If we say that wheat is 50s. a quarter, we mean that a quarter of wheat is worth two gold sovereigns and a half. Under this system the action of the Government in respect to silver coins differs entirely from its action in respect to gold coins. **In the case of gold coins the Mint is obliged to coin all the gold which is brought to it; in short, to turn all the gold brought to it into gold coins. In the case of silver it is not under any such obligation.**

13. The supply of silver coins needed for the retail dealings of the country is easily effected through the banks. When they find that their customers want silver, they demand it through the Bank of England from the Mint, and pay for it in gold coins. They have no motive to ask for more than is really wanted by the country as silver currency ; for the silver in the coins would be worth less if melted down for use in the arts or for exportation than it is worth as silver coin. The Mint buys the silver needed to make the required coin, and gains a profit by the difference between the market value of the silver and the price in gold given for it. But, as they only issue it in accordance with the demands made for it by the bankers, they do not issue more silver coins than the people need.

14. In order that the Mint may perform its function of verifying the quality of the gold and silver used in coinage, there must be a standard of quality. This is found in certain plates of gold and silver which are kept with other standards by the Board of Trade, and which are produced annually on what is known as the Trial of the Pyx, when a jury of the Goldsmiths' Company compares samples of the metals used by the Mint in coinage with the standard plates.

These standard plates were formerly kept in a chapel opening into the cloisters of Westminster Abbey, called the Chapel of the Pyx, in which the king's treasures used to be stored, and on the door of which is still to be seen a trace of the skin of a malefactor flayed alive for trying to rob the king's treasury. The Board of Trade wished to hand this chapel over to the Dean and Chapter, within whose precincts it lies; but the late Dean Stanley characteristically refused to receive it, on the ground that the retention of this interesting spot in the precincts of the Abbey by a department of the State which has to do with the regulation of trade was a symbolic link in the relations of the State to the Church.

15. What is true of silver is also generally true of the copper —or, rather, the bronze—coinage. The metal employed in the bronze coin is worth less than the fraction of the gold sovereign which it is used to express, and it is not a legal tender for more than 12d. The Mint issues it from time to time in different districts, and contracts the issue when it is found to be superabundant.

16. It will therefore be seen that **gold is the sole ultimate measure of value in this country,** and that its value as compared with other commodities is determined precisely in the same way as that of other commodities, viz. by supply and demand; in other words, its value is the value which people will give for it. The sole function of the Government is to ascertain the quality and weight of the gold, and to give it a stamp denoting that quality and weight. Other coins are measured in gold, and do not pass according to their own intrinsic or market value ; they are tokens, not articles of commerce. The function of the Government with respect to them is to supply any number for which the corresponding price in gold is given ; to verify the quantity and quality of the metal they contain, and to stamp them accordingly. **The system of currency thus described has solved two great difficulties.** First, it has adopted as material of the coin which is freely minted and which forms our measure of value one and not two metals—so that the evils of a constant alternation between gold and silver, and of the frequent expulsion of the one by

C 2

the other, under what is known as Gresham's law,* have been put an end to. How great were these evils may be easily learned by those who will read history, not through bimetallist spectacles, but by the light of the facts themselves.† In adopting this standard it does nothing but stamp the coin with a certificate denoting the quantity and quality of the gold which it contains, and it says that the coin so stamped shall be accepted as being what the Government state it to be. It says nothing of the value of the coin, but leaves that to be determined—as all other values are determined—by the higgling of the market.

17. Secondly, **it has reconciled with the adoption of the single metal, gold, as the sole standard of value, the free use of as much silver coin as men need for use as a medium of daily exchange.** It is clear, as above stated, that gold coins are not suited for small daily payments—wages, travelling fares, and the like; and very great inconvenience has often been felt in bimetallic countries when, in consequence of the operation of the Gresham law, silver coins have been melted down or have left the country. Since the reform of the coinage in 1816 no such inconvenience has been felt, or, if felt, it has been promptly remedied.

18. To make the system theoretically perfect, two things ought, perhaps, to be done. It is conceivable that the Government, which has the coinage of silver in its own control, might refuse to coin silver when really needed. It is not likely so to refuse, because, so long as silver is overvalued in the coins, the Government makes a large profit by the coinage of silver. But there would seem to be no reason why, so long as silver is thus overvalued, the Mint should not be obliged to give twenty shillings in silver for every gold sovereign brought to it. There would be no fear of an over-issue, for no one would give a gold sovereign for twenty shillings—the silver in which

* *"Bad money drives out good," is the popular statement of Gresham's law. In other words, if you give people the alternative of paying in either of two things, they will pay in the cheaper.*

† *Those who care to see what bimetallism has done for the nations which have adopted it may be referred to Mr. Shaw's "History of Currency" (Wilsons and Milne, 1895).*

is worth much less than a sovereign—unless ne meant to use them as change. A more probable danger might arise from an over-issue of silver coins, if we could imagine that our Government were disposed to make money by such a device. Such an abuse might be checked by making the token-coins what they really are, viz. promises to pay gold, and by compelling the Government to redeem them in gold at their face-value. Supposing these two additional precautions to be adopted, the principle on which our token-coinage is founded would be carried out completely, and the action of the Government with respect to it would be, as it is with respect to our gold coinage, purely automatic.

19. **Our present system possesses a further convenience.** The gold sovereign, or pound sterling, unites in itself three characters : It is the measure of value ; it is also the current coin ordinarily used by the people as pocket-money ; and it is the unit ot account in which all the dealings of the country, and most of the dealings of the commercial world, are carried on. This is an advantage not possessed by other nations with a gold standard—*e.g.* the United States, where a gold dollar is rarely, if ever, seen ; and France, where there is no such thing as a gold franc.

20. From the above account of our coinage, it will be seen how inaccurate it is to speak of our law of 1816 as having "de-monetised" silver. In fact, it had the opposite effect. It finally took from it the possibility of ever becoming the standard metal, or measure of value, or of being used compulsorily in large payments. But in so doing, it made the use of silver in the form of subsidiary and token coins convenient and secure by placing them under conditions which offered no inducement to melt them down or export them ; so that, as a matter of fact, silver—which was scarce and little used in this country before 1816—has since the change in the law been largely coined and used. **The importance of the principle of a subsidiary silver token-coinage, first embodied in the English currency reforms completed by the Act of 1816, may be illustrated by the great extension which the principle has received in other countries in later years.** It

was estimated by the Gold and Silver Commission (Final Report, Part II., par. 56) that out of £392,150,000 of silver in use as money in Europe and America in 1885, more than three-fourths was subsidiary silver currency maintained at an artificial gold value. In the Report of the Indian Currency Committee (pars. 67 to 96) is contained an analysis of the currencies of the principal countries of the world. This analysis shows how comparatively small is the actual quantity of gold coin in the currencies of nations which successfully maintain a gold standard at par; and how large is the part successfully played by silver token-coins and other subsidiary forms of currency.

21. The particular cases are too long to be described at length here, but special reference may be made to the enormous quantity of silver kept in circulation at a gold value in Germany, France, and the United States, and to the case of Holland and its colonies, where there is a successful gold standard with a circulation of paper and of silver—inconvertible except for export. It is also worthy of notice that these subsidiary currencies are maintained at a gold value by closing the Mints to the free coinage of silver and without the further precautions taken in our own case. Experience drawn from these cases suggests that the future development of the currencies of different nations, and the remedy for any difficulties which may arise either from increased demands on the standard metal or from the growing need of a single standard of value throughout the world, may be found in the extension of credit and in a free use of token and subsidiary currencies coupled with the single gold standard, rather than in a **hopeless attempt to tie gold and silver together by a marriage of which Nature has forbidden the Banns.**

Gresham's Law.*

By Mr. HENRY DUNNING MACLEOD.

1. THE whole of the controversy between the bimetallists and the monometallists may be reduced to a single, simple and definite issue. Supposing that gold and silver are coined in unlimited quantities, and a fixed legal ratio is enacted between them :—

(*a*) Is it the fixed legal ratio enacted between the coins which governs the relative value of the metals in bullion?

(*b*) Or is it the relative value of the metals in bullion which governs the relative value of the coins?

(*c*) And if it be found impossible for any single and separate country to maintain gold and silver coined in unlimited quantities in circulation together, at a fixed legal ratio, is it possible for any number of countries combined to do so by international agreement?

The bimetallists maintain the first of these issues, and the monometallists maintain the second. With respect to the third question, the bimetallists maintain the affirmative, and the monometallists the negative. **The purport of the following remarks is to explain why the European States, having vainly attempted to**

* *Issued in September,* 1895.

maintain bimetallism for 500 years, and having found it a
hopeless failure, have been constrained to abandon it and
adopt monometallism.

2. Charlemagne established the system of coinage which was
adopted throughout Western Europe. He made the pound weight
of silver the standard, and coined it into 240 pennies. For some
centuries these were the only coins issued by the Sovereigns of
France, and for a considerable time they coined these pennies at
their full weight and fineness. But about the beginning of the
twelfth century they began not only to diminish their weight, but
to debase their purity. They considered it part of their inalienable
divine right to declare that their subjects should accept the diminished
and debased coin at the same value as the good coins of full weight.
They further complicated matters by issuing gold coins, and they
considered it as part of their divine right to change the rating of the
coins with respect to each other as often as they pleased. These
constant tamperings with the coin produced commotions and disturbances for centuries, and drove away foreign trade from the
country. At length that great sovereign Charles V., surnamed the
Wise, perceived that the only way to restore prosperity to the
country was to reform the coinage. He referred the matter to one
of his wisest and most trusted councillors, Nicolas Oresme, afterwards Count Bishop of Lisieux, who, in answer to the appeal of his
Sovereign, drew up, in 1366, his now famous *Traictie de la première
invention des Monnoies* in twenty-six chapters, which has only recently
been brought to the notice of economists. After explaining the true
nature and uses of money, he laid down the following principles :—

a. That the Sovereign has no right to diminish the weight,
debase the purity, or change the denomination of the coin.
To do so is robbery.

b. That the Sovereign, or the law, can in no case fix the value,
i.e. the purchasing power of the coins. If he could do so,
he could fix the value of all commodities.

c. That the legal ratio of the coins must strictly conform to
the relative market value of the metals.

d. That if the fixed legal ratio of the coins differs from the
natural, or market value of the metals, the coin which is

underrated disappears entirely from circulation, and the coin which is overrated alone remains current.

    e. That if degraded and debased coin is allowed to circulate along with good and full-weighted coin all the good coin disappears from circulation, and the base coin alone remains current, to the ruin of commerce.

This great treatise, which may justly be said to stand at the head of modern economic literature, laid the foundations of monetary science. As it was written long before the days of printing, it never got into public circulation. It is merely a report addressed to Charles V. The same evils existed all through Europe, and were called *morbus numericus.*

    3. Poland, which then comprehended the modern Prussia, was, among other countries, afflicted with these evils. Sigismund I., King of Poland, who was fully sensible of the injury they inflicted upon the country, sought the advice of Copernicus, who was a member of the Prussian diet. At the instance of Sigismund, Copernicus in 1526 drew up a masterly treatise on money which he entitled *Ratio monetæ cudendæ,* which has only been discovered within the present century, and is included in the magnificent edition of his works printed at Warsaw in 1854. Copernicus had no knowledge of the treatise of Oresme written 160 years before his time, but he came to exactly the same conclusions. He said :—

    (*a*) That the four principal causes of the decadence of States are civil discord, pestilence, the barrenness of the land, and the debasement of the coin.

    (*b*) That it is impossible for the prince, or the law, to regulate the value of the coins, or of any other commodities.

    (*c*) That all the prince, or the law, can do, is to maintain the coin at a fixed denomination, weight and purity.

    (*d*) That it is robbery for the prince to change the denomination, diminish the weight, or debase the purity of the coin.

    (*e*) That it is impossible for good full-weighted coin and for degraded and debased coin to circulate together ; but that all the good coin is hoarded, or melted down, or exported, and the degraded and debased coin alone remains in circulation.

(*f*) That the coins of gold and silver must bear the same ratio to each other as the metals in bullion do in the market, and that this ratio must never be changed, except in consequence of a change in the market ratio of the metals.

(*g*) That when good coins are issued from the mint, all the base and degraded coins must be withdrawn from circulation, or else all the good coins will disappear, to the ruin of commerce.

(*h*) That it is impossible to have two measures of value in the same country, just as it is impossible to have two measures of length, or weight, or capacity.*

4. As in all the rest of Europe, the standard in England was the pound weight of silver, coined into 240 pennies. Except during the turbulent reign of Stephen, the early English kings did not diminish the weight or debase the purity of their coins. But immense numbers of false coiners sprang up, and notwithstanding the severest penalties of mutilation denounced against them, it was found impossible to suppress them. Moreover, vast quantities of base money were imported from abroad. All the good money disappeared from circulation as soon as it was issued from the Mint. Edward I. was the first to debase the coinage, by coining 243 pennies out of the pound weight of silver and yet to call the diminished coins by the same name. In 1344 Edward III. coined gold money, and thus bimetallism was established in this country, and for 470 years the futile attempt was made to keep gold and silver coins in unlimited quantities in circulation together, at a fixed legal ratio. Henry VIII. was the first, not only to diminish the weight, but to debase the purity of the coins, and this practice continued during the reigns of Mary and Edward VI. During all this time repeated debates were held in Parliament in consequence of the disturbances and misery caused

* *Mr. Gibbs has impugned the accuracy of this summary from the works of Oresme and Copernicus. It would be too long to give the original passages to justify them, but I have given in my* Bimetallism *careful extracts of these works.*

by the bad state of the coinage, and the instant disappearance of the good coin as soon as it was issued from the Mint. No measures were taken to demonetise and withdraw from circulation the clipped, degraded, and debased coin, as Oresme and Copernicus had pointed out ought to be done. The statesmen and financiers of the day were utterly perplexed at the extraordinary disappearance of all the good coin. They seemed to think that the people were inspired by the Evil One to prefer the degraded and base coin, and to reject the good coin. They had no Oresme or Copernicus to explain to them that it is an assured law of nature that bad coin always drives good coin out of circulation. The only remedies they could devise were to denounce penalties of death and mutilation against all persons who exported the good coin, which were wholly ineffectual.

5. The shameful state of the coinage caused so much public distress, and gave rise to so many disturbances, that the council of Edward VI. saw the necessity of reforming it, and had taken measures for that purpose when the boy-King died. No sooner had Elizabeth acceded to the throne than she turned her attention to complete the reform of the coinage which had been begun by her brother, being moved thereto by the illustrious Gresham, who was the first in this country to point out to her that good and bad coin cannot circulate together, but that the bad coin always drives the good coin out of circulation. The **facts** were only too familiar by the experience of centuries, but no one in this country had previously discerned the necessary relation between these facts before Gresham. He addressed a letter to the Queen explaining that the debasement of the coinage by Henry VIII. was the **cause** of the disappearance of all the good coin. Thus for the first time in this country he showed that the two facts were necessarily related as cause and effect. In 1858 I suggested that this great fundamental law of the coinage should be known by the name of "Gresham's Law," and this has now been universally accepted. But at that time I was not aware that this great law had been demonstrated by Oresme 192 years, and by Copernicus 32 years, previously, as their treatises were not published by my friend M. Wolowski for general circulation till 1864. Nor is there any reason to suppose that Gresham had any knowledge of these treatises, as they were merely memorials drawn up for the information of their respective Sovereigns, and were never published for general circulation. These three illustrious men were, therefore, independent discoverers, and the law ought, therefore,

rightfully to be called the Law of Oresme, Copernicus, and Gresham. This law, however, soon became a matter of common knowledge. In a pamphlet in 1696 it is thus stated : "When two sorts of coin are current in the same nation of like value by denomination, but not intrinsically (*i.e.* in market value), that which has the least value will be current and the other as much as possible will be hoarded ; " or melted down or exported, we may add. Or we may express it in these terms : "**The worst form of currency in circulation regulates the value of the whole currency, and drives all other forms of currency out of circulation.**"

6. This great law applies in the following cases :—

(*a*) If the coinage consists only of a single metal, as in the early coinage of England, and clipped, degraded and debased coin is allowed to circulate along with the good coin, all the good coin disappears from circulation. It is either hoarded away, or it is melted down, or it is exported. All laws are ineffectual to prevent this, and the clipped, degraded and debased coin alone remains current.

(*b*) If coins of two metals, such as gold and silver, are allowed to circulate together in unlimited quantities, and if a legal ratio be attempted to be enforced between them which differs from the natural value of the metal in the market of the world, the coin which is underrated disappears from circulation—it is either hoarded away, or it is melted down, or it is exported ; and the coin which is over-rated alone remains current.

(*c*) And as a necessary corollary, it follows that it is impossible to establish and maintain a fixed par of exchange between countries which use different metals as their standard coin. This law is not confined to single and separate states, it is not limited in time and space ; it is absolutely universal ; it is as universal as the law of gravitation ; and it is equally impossible for the whole world to maintain coins of two or more metals in circulation in unlimited quantities at a fixed legal ratio, which differs from the natural or market ratio of the metals, as it is for single and separate countries to do so. The explanation of this problem which was such an inscrutable mystery to statesmen and financiers for so many ages is extremely simple. If shillings are allowed to circulate together in

unlimited quantities, some of which are worth twelvepence and some
only ninepence, and all persons are allowed to pay their debts in
whichever coin they please, they will naturally pay their debts with
the shillings worth ninepence and keep the shillings worth twelvepence
in their pockets. Or if the shillings worth twelvepence have no more
value than the shillings worth ninepence, bullion dealers will collect
all the heavy coins they can and either melt them down into bullion,
in which form they have more value than in coin, or they will export
them to foreign countries where they have their full value. Thus the
underrated coins have always been found to disappear in one or other
of these three ways.

7. It is exactly the same in all cases in which persons are allowed
to pay their debts in things which have nominally the same value, but
are in reality of different value. When persons are allowed to pay
their rents in kind, they naturally select the worst portion of their
produce to pay their landlord, and keep the best portion for themselves. If the law allowed two different yard measures to be used,
one of three feet and one of two feet, and merchants received an
order for so many yards of cloth, they would naturally fulfil their
orders in yards of two feet rather than in yards of three feet. If the
law allowed two measures of capacity—a pint and a quart—and
called them both by the same name, and a person ordered so much
beer or wine from the merchant, he would naturally pay in pints
rather than in quarts. If the law allowed a mile of two different
lengths, one of 1,000 yards and one of 1,760 yards, and a cabman
were ordered to drive so many miles, he would naturally drive so
many miles of 1,000 yards rather than so many miles of 1,760 yards.
It is only natural that all persons should pay their debts in the
cheapest form to themselves. So if the law allows debtors to pay
their debts in coins of different metals which are rated equally in
law, but whose value differs in the markets of the world, they will
naturally pay their debts in the coins which are rated too highly, and
keep those which are rated too low at home. Thus inevitably the coin
which is rated too low according to its natural, or market value, disappears from circulation; and the one which is rated above its natural
or market value, alone remains current. And this is true whether
the whole world does so, or only single and separate countries. **If,
then, the whole world were to agree to rate a coin below its
market value it would entirely disappear from circulation;**

because, if the whole world were to agree to such a system, it would, for the purposes of coinage, become one country, and the whole world can no more by international agreement make 9 equal to 12 than any separate country can. For the very same reason it is impossible to maintain a fixed rate of exchange between countries which use different metals as their standard unit, because coins are only received in foreign countries according to their market value as bullion : and as the value of the metals is constantly changing in the market of the world, the value of the coins must equally do so too. When a legal ratio is fixed between the coins, which differs from the market ratio of the metals in bullion, the coin which is underrated, or whose market value exceeds the legal ratio, is said to go to a *Premium*, and whichever coin goes to a premium disappears from circulation by one of the three methods described above ; moreover no one brings metal of that coin to the mint to be coined, because by doing so he would reduce the value of his metal which is worth twelvepence in bullion to ninepence in coin.

8. It has been shown that Oresme and Copernicus both laid down that the prince, or the law, has no power to impose at will an arbitrary value on the coins ; they must strictly conform to the relative value of the metals in bullion. Accordingly in several states they did attempt to conform to this rule. But it was found to be absolutely impracticable. The relative market value of the metals kept constantly changing, and it was impossible that the legal ratio should follow these perpetual changes. **The practical result was that while the legal ratio remained fixed, the relative market value of gold and silver bullion rose above and sometimes fell below the legal ratio. The consequence was that gold and silver coins alternately drove each other out of circulation, as the market value of either metal rose above or fell below the legal ratio.** This caused perpetual disturbance in the coinage of England, and all attempts to rectify it wholly failed. The rule of Oresme and Copernicus was found to be wholly inoperative ; and experience showed that it was utterly impossible to keep coins of both metals in circulation together in unlimited quantities at a legal ratio differing from the market value of the metals in bullion. Sir William Petty, the greatest financial statesman of the age, at last hit upon the true remedy. In a posthumous work named the *Political Anatomy of Ireland*, published in 1691, he said that money is under-

stood to be the uniform measure of the value of commodities : that the proportion of value between pure gold and fine silver alters, as the earth and industry of men produce more of one than the other. That gold had been worth but twelve times its own weight of silver, but that of late it had been worth fourteen. "**So there can be but one of the two metals of gold and silver to be a fit matter for money.**" This is, so far as I am aware, the first enunciation of the great principle that only one metal should be adopted for the standard coin and measure of value. I am not aware of what amount of attention it received when it was announced. But it was speedily recognised by the highest authorities on monetary science as the true remedy for the disturbances of the coinage which had prevailed for centuries, and has now been adopted by all the European States, as well as by others.

9. In 1692, the silver coinage had fallen into a most disgraceful state. Bags of silver coin collected from all parts of the kingdom showed that the silver coins were clipped down to little more than half their weight. As a necessary consequence guineas which had been coined to be equal in value to twenty shillings in silver, had risen to thirty shillings, and the foreign exchanges, which were then reckoned in silver, had fallen 25 per cent. It was shown to a committee of the House of Commons that the profit of melting down the milled money for exportation was more than £25 per £1,000. The evils caused by this flagrant state of the coinage could no longer be neglected. The Treasury ordered their secretary, Mr. Lowndes, to make a report on the subject. He proposed that the ounce of silver bullion should be coined into seventy-five pence instead of sixty pence; and gravely maintained that doing this would raise the value of the coin. Locke replied to this proposal in a treatise, showing in the most scathing terms its utter folly. This treatise is far too long to be quoted entire here, but I have given long extracts from it in my *Bimetallism*. But I may give a short abstract of his argument. He said that raising the denomination of the coin was a pure delusion and fraud; that it added no real value to the coin; that it was only the quantity of silver in the coin which was the measure of its value ; that it was just as rational to hope to lengthen a foot by dividing it into fifteen parts instead of twelve, as to hope to increase the value of the silver by dividing it into fifteen pieces instead of twelve, and calling them pennies; that raising the denomination of the coin was as

gross a fraud as to coin silver pieces of the same name and to debase them with more alloy. Nothing could make clipping unprofitable but making all light money go only by weight : this stops all clipping at once ; brings out all the milled and weighty money ; deprives us not of any part of our clipped money for the use of trade, and brings it orderly and by degrees and without force into the mint to be re-coined.

10. At that time silver was the standard coin of England and the rest of the world. Locke says, " I have spoken of silver coin alone because that makes the money of account and measure of trade all through the world. For all contracts are, I think, everywhere made and accounts kept in silver coin. Silver, therefore, and silver alone is the measure of commerce. **Two metals, as gold and silver, cannot be both together the measure of commerce in any country** : because the measure of commerce must be perpetually the same, invariable, and keeping the same proportion in value in all its parts. But so only one metal does, or can do, to itself : so silver is to silver, and gold to gold. An ounce of silver is always of equal value to an ounce of silver, and an ounce of gold to an ounce of gold, and two ounces of the one or the other double the value to an ounce of the same. But gold and silver change their value to one another ; for suppose them to be in value as sixteen to one now, perhaps the next month they may be as fifteen and three-quarters, or fifteen and seven-eighths, to one. And one may as well make a measure, *e.g.* a yard, whose parts lengthen and shrink, as a measure of trade of materials that have not always a settled invariable value to one another. **One metal, therefore, alone can be the money of account and contract, and the measure of commerce in any country.** Money differs from uncoined silver only in this, that the quantity of silver in each piece of money is ascertained by the stamp it bears, which is set there to be a public voucher of its weight and fineness. To Lowndes's allegation that raising the coin by making it more in tale would make it more abundant for general use, Locke replied, " Just as the boy cut his leather into five quarters, as he called them, to cover his ball, when cut into four quarters it fell short, but after all his pains as much of his ball lay bare as before. If the quantity of coined silver employed in England fall short, the arbitrary denomination of a greater number of pence given to it will not make it commensurate to the size of our

trade, or the greatness of our occasions. This is as certain as if the quantity of a board, which is to stop a leak fifteen inches square, it will not be made to do it by being measured by a foot, which is divided into fifteen inches instead of twelve, and so having a larger tale, or number of inches in denomination, given to it. The increase of denomination does, or can, do nothing in the case, for it is silver by its quantity, and not denomination, that is the price of things and measure of commerce ; and it is the weight of silver in it, and not the name of the pieces, that men estimate commodities by, and exchange them for.

11. Locke shows that if the law can raise the value of one coin with respect to the other in any degree whatever above its natural or market value, it can do so to any extent, and might make gold and silver equal in value weight for weight. The simple facts detailed above, and the arguments founded upon them by Oresme, Copernicus, Gresham and Locke establish the Law, which I have termed Gresham's Law, beyond cavil or dispute. It is as clearly demonstrated and universal as the law of gravitation. And it will be as well to recapitulate the principles established by these illustrious writers. They are :—

a. The prince's, or the law's, sole power and duty is to maintain the denomination, the weight and the purity of the coin unchanged.

b. If different metals are coined in unlimited quantities, the law has no power to regulate the value of the coins with respect to each other, or with respect to other commodities.

c. Coins are only pieces of bullion stamped with a certificate to denote their weight and purity, and if no charge be made for changing the metal in bullion into coins, there can be no difference in value between the metal in bullion and in coin.

d. It is the relative market value of the metals in bullion which determines the relative value of the coins, and not the fixed legal ratio of the coins which regulates the relative market value of the metals in bullion.

e. If clipped, degraded and debased coins are allowed to circulate

D

together along with good, full-weighted coins, all the good coins disappear from circulation, and the base and degraded coins alone remain current.

f. If coins of different metals be allowed to circulate together in unlimited quantities at a fixed legal ratio differing from the relative market value of the metals in bullion, that is the same in effect as allowing base and degraded coins to circulate together with good coin, and the coin which is underrated disappears from circulation, and the coin which is overrated alone remains in circulation.

g. There cannot be any par, or fixed rate of exchange between countries which use different metals as their standard coin.

h. When the relative market value of the metals in bullion rises above or falls below the legal ratio of the coins, the metals alternately displace one another from circulation—the one which is underrated disappears from circulation, and the one which is overrated alone remains current.

***i.* If the whole world, or any number of mercantile countries, were to combine and adopt a common legal ratio for the coins, they would become one country for the purposes of coinage. Gresham's Law would operate in the more extended space exactly in the same way as it operates in single countries. The coin which was underrated would entirely disappear from circulation; and the coin which was overrated would alone remain current.**

12. These principles, founded on the experience of centuries, have been found to be true in every country and in every age. They are the principles which dominate the whole controversy between the bimetallists and the monometallists.

The Scientific Theory of Bimetallism.*

By Sir ROBERT GIFFEN, K.C.B., F.R.S.

---

1. Some bimetallists, especially Professor Foxwell and Mr. Courtney, make a great boast of the scientific theory of bimetallism. It is impossible, they admit, for Legislatures generally by mere fiat to cause any two commodities to exchange at a given ratio. But in coinage and money, by exception, they affirm that the thing can be done. The reason is that by the act of Legislature in coining two metals at a ratio, and making them legal tender at a ratio, an automatic process is set up by which the undervalued metal goes out of use as standard money, and so becomes less in demand, and the overvalued metal comes into use as standard money, and so becomes more in demand. Until the one metal goes wholly out of use and the other metal displaces it, this automatic process goes on, and there is no need to change the ratio until the process is complete. As it is inconceivable, moreover, from the quantity now in circulation that either gold or silver can go wholly out of use as money within any short period, a ratio to be fixed by common agreement of all civilised Governments can be indefinitely maintained. **This is the scientific theory of bimetallism; the theory from which it is held that Governments can do for gold and silver what they cannot do for other commodities, and upon which the great commercial communities of the world are asked to revolutionise their monetary systems and the principles upon which they have been founded.**

2. Is the theory scientific or true? Let us look first at the major premiss. Suppose an automatic process could be set up between any two articles—say, potatoes and wheat—by which as the one became undervalued, as compared with a given ratio, the demand for it was diminished, and as the other became overvalued, as compared with a given ratio, the demand for it was increased, would the effect necessarily be that the given ratio would be maintained? Is it not obvious that all that could be

* *Issued in October, 1895.*

D 2

affirmed would be that *some* ratio would come to exist as the resultant of the diminished demand in the one case and the increased demand in the other at which business would take place, but not necessarily the given ratio? Always in all markets there is a price at which business is done, the resultant of all the higgling that takes place and of all the causes acting on the demand and supply; but this price at which business is done is never the same in any one place for any length of time, and never the same in any two places if they are at all apart. The fact that there is an automatic process for diminishing the demand for one article when it tends to rise in relative value and increasing the demand for the other article when it tends to fall in relative value would not tend to fix the ratio at any one point, however near the actual point at which business was really done might be to that fixed point. The market would never be the same as the legal ratio. We make this affirmation on the ground of market experience. **If Nature abhors a vacuum, so do markets abhor fixed points. In theory, then, to prove that two commodities will approximate more or less closely to a fixed ratio because one will be in less demand, and the other more in demand if the ratio is departed from, is not the same thing as proof that the ratio itself will be maintained. The propositions are not identical, and the assumption that they are so is the first error in the scientific theory.**

3. The case between potatoes and wheat, we may add, is not supposititious. As wheat becomes dearer relatively to potatoes it tends to become less in demand as a rule, and as wheat becomes cheap relatively to potatoes it tends to become more in demand. A force is always at work making them approximate towards a particular ratio at which they would be naturally equivalent one to the other. But no one supposes that a ratio between wheat and potatoes could be fixed; still less a ratio for long periods and many distant places. It is the same for beef and mutton, or any other commodities which can be named that become more or less in demand automatically as substitutes one for the other. There may be some approximation as the result, round or near to a fixed point, for a length of time, until some great change of conditions occurs, but there is never any possibility of fixing a ratio.

4. The major premiss of the scientific theory being thus disposed of, we may look at the minor premisses. Are gold and silver commodities the demand for which can be made to change automatically to any material extent by the coinage of both at a ratio, and making them full legal tender at a ratio? This question involves consideration of the statistical position of gold and silver as commodities, and of the nature of the demands for them as standard or token money, which we are not aware of any bimetallist having ever written about. The assumption constantly is that the joint use of the two metals as standard money will involve a large replacement

of one by the other when the market differs continuously in one direction from the legal ratio. The assumption is, moreover, entirely unfounded. The main demands for gold and silver do not arise from their being used as standard money. They are required for hoarding ; for use in the arts (gold much more largely than silver in both cases), and for use as currency, and not as standard money ; and these uses far exceed any common use they might have as standard money only. We should say that not less than nine-tenths of the stocks of gold and gold coinage in the world at any one moment are employed irrespectively of the fact that gold is "standard" money, and the same of silver, and what is true of the stocks and coinages in existence is also true of the annual production of the metals. Their chief uses are for the arts, for hoarding, for currency, each metal in differing degrees and for different purposes in detail, and not for the common purpose of standard money at all. How then can their coinage at a ratio, and their being made legal tender at a ratio which is intended to unite them for standard money, set up the automatic process which the bimetallic theory assumes? Clearly there would be no difficulty in changing from the one metal to the other as standard in a moment without the automatic process having much room to play.

5. There is a further difficulty in the matter. Gold and silver are unlike potatoes and wheat, or beef and mutton, or iron and copper, or any other two commodities which can be more or less substituted one for the other, in this respect—that, whereas in all these cases there is a ratio at which the one commodity is really the equivalent of the other, there is no such natural fixed point between gold and silver as standard money. They can perform that function as well at a ratio of 1 to 1, or 10 to 1, or 20 to 1, or 100 to 1, as at the bimetallic par of $15\frac{1}{2}$ to 1. The fixed point has thus no real support in nature as it has in the case of wheat and potatoes or any other of the groups of commodities above named. **A fixed ratio between gold and silver through the automatic process suggested is thus more inconceivable than a fixed ratio for potatoes and wheat,** even if the demand for gold and silver were likely to be more affected by the automatic process than they possibly can be.

6. The wisdom of Locke and the other great authorities on money, in laying down that there could not be a fixed ratio between gold and silver, because, if the law laid down 15 to 1 one day, the market might stand at $14\frac{7}{8}$ to 1 the next, is thus apparent when we examine the new and crude scientific theory which is so much vaunted. Not only have those who put forward the theory confounded the proposition that an automatic process varying the demand and supply of two articles as they changed from a fixed ratio between them would tend to cause varying approximations to that ratio to exist with the proposition that the fixed ratio would itself be maintained, but they have mistaken altogether the extent to which

demand is likely to vary in the case of gold and silver even if the automatic process were set up. Professor Foxwell seems conscious of some defect in the theory, as he supplements it by a proposal to suppress the special uses of gold and silver for currency, and to replace them both by paper—a startling innovation in practice of whose full import he does not seem to be aware. Whatever it is, his proposal is not that of the Bimetallic League, nor would it mend the case for bimetallists in any way if they were generally to accept it. Novelties of that sort, however ingenious academically, are out of place in practice. **It is significant that the practical proposals of bimetallists are not thoroughly supported by their advocates, but are replaced in discussion by daring and impracticable fancies.**

7. We have been discussing the "scientific" theory only as a theory, and this is not the place consequently to discuss the assertions of bimetallists as to the fixed ratio having actually been maintained in past times. We may state, however, that when the facts of past times are referred to in detail, it is found that in no country at any time was the market ratio between gold and silver ever the same as the legal ratio. There were always variations, as Locke said there would be, and bimetallists, when pressed, do not deny this. What they affirm is, that the variations are not so great as to prevent the law of legal ratio continuing. But this is a different thing, again, from the affirmation that bimetallic practice will continue. What Locke pointed out was, that even a variation of the market from the legal ratio to the extent of substituting $14\frac{7}{8}$ to 1 for 15 to 1 made the use of two metals at the legal ratio impossible, and compelled the countries interested to select the overvalued metal as their sole standard money, whatever the law about coining both at a ratio and making them legal tender at a ratio might be. Consequently there is never bimetallism, the employment of two standards, in practice, but only monometallism, the employment of one standard, and the price of the other metal in the standard is fixed by the market, and not by the legal ratio.

8. As a matter of fact also, although in past times, when bimetallic practice existed, there have been long periods when the ratio between gold and silver ranged between points like 14 to 1 and 16 to 1, yet there have been other periods when great changes took place—as, for instance, at the beginning of the seventeenth century—showing that **bimetallism in practice never prevents changes in the ratio, small as a rule in ordinary times, but great when occasion arises.** There is nothing in the facts of experience, therefore, to conflict with the theoretical conclusion we have come to that the scientific theory of bimetallism is untrue. We are only discussing the theory here, but we put in this *caveat*, lest bimetallists should allege, when their theory gives way, that we have not discussed their facts.

The Quantitative Theory of Money and Prices.*

By the Rt. Hon. LORD FARRER.

---

1. Is it true that the rise and fall of prices depend on the quantity of money? And if true, in what sense is it true, and to what extent? The question assumes practical importance at the present time, because one of the complaints of the bimetallists is that prices have fallen in consequence of what they call the demonetisation of silver, and the consequent scarcity of money. Whether this allegation is well founded; whether all prices have fallen; whether a fall in the prices of necessaries is a bad or a good thing; whether a general rise in all prices would do good or harm; and whether it is desirable to try to raise prices by tampering with the currency, are questions on which, though differing entirely from the bimetallists, I do not propose now to say anything. **My object is to discuss the theoretical question, " What, if any, is the relation between the quantity of money and prices ? "**

2. The *primâ facie* view of the quantitative theory of money and prices is very simple. It may be stated in the following form :
" Every sale or purchase consists of an exchange of a certain quantity
"of a particular kind of goods for a certain amount of money,
"which amount of money is called price. Let the quantity of goods
"remain constant; then, if the amount of money available for the
"exchange also remains constant, prices will remain unchanged; if
"it increases, prices will rise; if it decreases, prices will fall. What
"is true of a single sale or purchase is true of two or more sales or

* *Issued in January,* 1898.

"purchases ; and what is true of two or more sales or purchases is true
"of all sales and purchases. If, therefore, we could at any given
"moment know the quantity of goods which are being sold or pur-
"chased, and the amount of money for which they are exchanged,
"we might conclude that, so long as the quantity of goods remains
"the same, any increase in the amount of available money would
"raise prices, and any decrease in the amount of available money
"would lower prices." The formula thus stated is logically correct ;
but, *dolus latet in generalibus.*

3. We must know the exact significance of the terms we use, and
their application to the existing circumstances of the market, before
we can derive any useful information from the above formula. In
that formula we have used the word money, and "money" is a
word which has several different meanings. Indeed, it is to the
ambiguous use of the word "money" that many of the errors and
confusions of thought, so prevalent in currency discussions, have
arisen. In the present controversy arguments for a great practical
change in the relations between gold and silver are constantly based
on the quantitative theory expressed in the above formula, and it
will be found that those who use such arguments make a serious
misuse or misapplication of the word "money" by treating it as if it
meant gold or silver coin. We shall see presently what a confusion
there is here, and what dangerous consequences flow from it.

4. For our purpose the most important distinction between the
different meanings of the word "money" is the distinction between
"money" signifying the coin which constitutes the "standard of
value" and "money" signifying the "media or means of exchange."
The money which is the standard of value is always one of the
"means of exchange," but it is only one of many means of exchange.
The distinction is of the highest importance, and it is one which,
with the progress of modern business, becomes more and more
important every day, because every day sees a greater and greater
use of "means of exchange" which are not in any sense standards of
value. **Coins of the standard precious metal or metals,
which formerly constituted a very large proportion of the
"means of exchange," now constitute among us a very small
proportion of them.**

5. **Let us first consider "money" as the "standard of
value."** Taken in this sense, it is used to signify the coins or pieces
of precious metal which we have agreed to adopt as our measure or
unit of value—in other words, gold sovereigns. It is to the
quantity of standard gold contained in a sovereign that we refer in

determining the values of all other things. It is the number of gold
sovereigns for which things will exchange which constitutes their
price, which settles the terms of every bargain, and which enables
us to compare the value of one thing with that of another. The gold
sovereign itself is only a piece of gold of a given weight and fineness,
stamped with the Queen's head in order to show that its weight and
fineness have been officially tested. The quantity of sovereigns in
actual use depends solely on the demand for them, since anyone can
take gold to the mint and have it turned into sovereigns. Under
these circumstances the value of the sovereign is simply the market
value of the gold which is contained in it.

6. But gold itself varies in value. If the aggregate demand of
the world for gold increases in a greater proportion than the supply of
gold in the world, the value of the gold sovereign increases, and gold
prices fall. If the supply of gold in the world increases in a greater
proportion than the demand, the value of the gold sovereign
decreases, and prices rise. To this extent, therefore, the available
quantity of gold in the world, or, in other words, the supply of gold,
does, by affecting the value of the standard unit of value, influence
all gold prices. But this is a very different proposition from that
with which we started, and does not bear out the proposition that
prices depend on the quantity of money. It should rather be stated
as follows :—

**The market value of the gold contained in a sovereign
depends on the market value of gold; that value depends
on the supply (or, in other words, the available quantity) of
gold, and the demand for gold. Quantity of gold does
therefore affect the standard or unit of value, and in that
way affects all prices.**

7. But in considering the question whether at any given time
variations in the quantity of gold have or have not affected prices, we
have to deal with a complicated set of facts, many of which are very
difficult to ascertain. We have to determine what are the relations
between the whole supply of gold in the world, including all accumulated stocks, whether of gold coin or gold bullion or gold articles of
any kind, and including also the production of gold for the time
being, on the one hand, and the demands for gold, whether for
purposes of current coin or of reserves, or of hoarding, or of the
Arts, on the other. It is scarcely possible to arrive at an exhaustive
and exact solution of this problem. **But it is for those who
allege that demand has exceeded supply, and that consequently the value of the gold in a sovereign has risen**

and has caused a fall of prices, to prove their case upon
these data, and this they certainly have not done. On the
contrary, considering that stocks of gold accumulate ; that the annual
production of gold is increasing enormously ; that the demands upon
gold caused by the so-called demonetisation of silver were, at the
commencement of the bimetallic agitation, trifling compared with
the stocks of gold, and are still far from sufficient to exhaust the
supply ; and, above all, as we shall see below, that banking facilities
and changes in habits are constantly reducing the proportion of gold
money needed for carrying on business, and the consequent demand
for gold used as a medium of exchange, the strong probability seems
to be that, considered as a whole, the supply of gold in the world has
increased, or is increasing, faster than the demand. Consequently
there is not at the present moment any reason to suppose that the
quantity of gold contained in a sovereign has increased, or is increasing, in exchange value, much less to conclude that it is a deficiency
in the supply of the metal of our standard coin which is responsible
for the fall of prices which has taken place in certain articles of
general consumption.

8. This does not profess to be a statistical paper, and I do not
propose to deal with the figures here. Those who wish for further
and more detailed information may be referred to Soetbeer's
"Materialien" ; to the Report of the Gold and Silver Commission ;
to the evidence given to the Agricultural Commission ; to the
Annual Reports of the Director of the United States Mint ; to
the paper in this series by M. Ottomar Haupt, entitled " Is Gold
Scarce ?" ; and to the tables of the production of gold and silver,
given in the *Statist* of 25th September and 2nd October, 1897.

9. We have been hitherto considering "money" in the
sense of the "standard of value." But, as we have seen, the
word "money" also signifies "means or media of exchange;"
and it is in this sense that the word " money " is used in the formula
I have placed at the beginning of this leaflet. Used in this sense,
" money " does not mean simply gold sovereigns. It is not true that
every sale and purchase is effected by the use of gold sovereigns.
On the contrary, it is notorious that out of the whole number of
wholesale transactions, those in which gold sovereigns are used as a
means of exchange are so few and small as scarcely to deserve
notice. It is also notorious that in retail transactions the use of
gold is already much restricted, and is daily becoming smaller
and smaller. It is by different forms of credit that our dealings are
actually carried on. Whilst the gold sovereign is the unit or measure

of value in terms of which contracts are made, **the real medium of exchange is not gold sovereigns, but a promise to pay gold sovereigns ; a promise the actual performance of which is seldom exacted unless in the case of panic.**

10. Money in the sense of " means of exchange"—the "money" of the quantitative formula given above; the "money" of the market; the "money" of the Press ; the "money" of common speech and conversation, consists not wholly or principally of coin, but of bank notes, of cheques, of bills, of bank credits, and of all the different forms of orders to pay and promises to pay by which in practice men settle their dealings with one another. It has been estimated that in 98 per cent. of the commercial transactions of this country credit in one form or another is the only medium of exchange. Let anyone, whether in business or not, consider his own practice. In how many cases of ordinary retail transactions does he make a payment with gold, or even with notes? How many debts has he which he does not pay by cheques ? The banking deposits of the country have been estimated at nearly £800,000,000, whilst the whole gold coin of the country, including what is called waistcoat-pocket money, has been roughly estimated at £100,000,000. The amount of settlements effected through public clearing houses in which neither coins nor notes are used is enormous. In the London Clearing House alone payments were made in 1896 to the extent of £7,575,000,000, the average for the ten years 1868–77 having been only £4,941,000,000. Gold sovereigns are now scarcely used except in payments across the counters of retail shops, in refreshment houses, in travelling fares, and perhaps above all in payment of daily and weekly wages. **Indeed, it is one of the ironies of the situation that whilst the recent fall in prices is attributed by bimetallists to scarcity of gold, the cases on which they rely as proving a general fall of prices—viz. the cases of wholesale prices of goods collected by Mr. Sauerbeck and others—are cases in which gold is seldom or never used as a means of payment, whilst in the principal case in which gold is used—viz. in payment of wages—prices have risen.**

11. Gold coins, whilst remaining our sole "standard of value," have long ceased to be our ordinary "medium of exchange." To say that gold has been economised is a very inadequate statement of the fact. Gold has been supplanted and replaced by other forms of currency, infinitely more economical, because in themselves they cost little or nothing ; infinitely more safe, because they cannot be

stolen ; infinitely more convenient, because they expand and contract
automatically with the need for them.

12. **In short, it is the whole mass of credit currency, and
not the number of gold sovereigns in use, which constitutes
the great factor in price, and which gives its tone and real
meaning to the word "money" in the quantitative formula
set out above.**

13. I have said that these media of exchange expand and contract with the demand for them. This is a most important consideration, in view of the quantitative theory of prices, because it
shows that so long as business is in a healthy condition and there is
no panic, there cannot .possibly be any deficiency of means of
exchange in the transactions which are carried on by these
media, or any lowering of price in consequence of such deficiency.
As sound business increases—business, that is, which does not over-
estimate production or consumption—credit increases with it, and
with credit, bills, bankers' credits, cheques, and other forms of
promises to pay, which form our real media of exchange.

14. As business increases credit money increases, and if the
effect of increasing business is to raise prices, and thus to require an
additional quantity of media of exchange, credit increases in proportion, and the additional media are at once forthcoming. **Thus the
quantity of money in use at any given time depends on
business, and not business on money. It is business which
creates money, and not money which creates business.**

It is only in those dealings in which coin is still used that a
scarcity of coin can restrict business or lower prices, and how few
and small these are we have seen above.

15. But it may be asked, "Upon what is all this credit money
"based? If it consists of promises to pay gold, how are those
"promises secured? Must not there be somewhere a reserve of
"gold out of which to pay them if required? Must not this reserve
"increase with the business founded on it? And must not the mass
"of credit money founded on it be proportioned to the amount of
"the gold reserve?" The answer to this is that so long as business
is properly and safely conducted, the promises to pay will never be
presented for payment in gold. They will be set off against one
another. It is only when expectations have been falsified that men
are asked to pay in gold. To provide against such falsifications—
which, of course, cannot be avoided altogether—there must be some
security, and this is found in an ultimate liability to make payment
in gold. To meet such liability, and also to provide for the payment

of international balances—which, however, are now constantly settled in other ways—sufficient stocks or reserves of gold are no doubt required, and are, or ought to be, kept by the banks. It is the all-important business of bankers to know what stocks are necessary for this purpose, and it is their duty to keep whatever may be necessary. What this amount should be in each case is a matter of opinion and of habit. But it may be safely stated that it bears no definite proportion whatever to the business of which it is the basis and the ultimate security. If there is any element in business to which it really bears a proportion, that element is only the ultimate liability to pay in gold which is so seldom enforced; in other words, the apprehension of men that contracts may not be performed, that expectations may be falsified, and that the material products of industrial undertakings may be less than is anticipated. If all promises to pay were presented for payment no possible amount of gold would prevent insolvency, and uncertainty on this point is the cause of every panic. On the other hand, when there is no alarm, any addition to the gold reserve beyond the amount which habit and sound practice has shown to be necessary, is superfluous and remains idle in the banks. So far as reserves are concerned there is no unlimited demand for gold, a fact which has been sufficiently obvious in recent years.

16. No doubt there are circumstances in which the subtraction from the reserves of a substantial quantity of gold might injure credit, and thus lower prices. If, for instance, in a state of incipient panic or of strain, when men were beginning to be alarmed and were inclined to present promises for payment in gold, a large amount of gold were withdrawn from the banks, it would aggravate the strain, contract credit, and lower prices. But there is no evidence whatever that any such thing has happened. On the contrary, the rate of discount, which is the barometer of the state of credit, has been lower, and the reserves of the banks have been greater since the so-called demonetisation of silver than they were before. Again, if, at such a time of strain, a large amount of gold were suddenly added to the stores of the banks, it might create confidence in their ability to pay, might prevent a run on the banks, and might thus raise or maintain prices. But if the same amount of gold were added to the reserves of the banks at a period when there was no such strain, it would probably have very little or no effect; it would certainly not alter prices more than an addition of the same amount of credit money would have altered them. In such a case the effect of this addition of gold, considered as a constituent of price, would be proportioned, not to the increase in the amount of the gold reserve, but to the increase in

the whole amount of money, whether metallic money or credit money, in existence for the time being, and its effects on prices would therefore be infinitesimal. **This is probably what has happened during the recent years in which the supply of gold money from the mines and in the banks has largely increased without any apparent effect in raising prices.**

17. Let me guard against a possible misconception. I do not say that gold discoveries do not increase business and raise prices. I do not say that men bringing home quantities of gold, or, which is the same thing, large profits made out of gold mining, may not spend their gains in such a way as to expand trade, raise wages, and increase circulation. Still less do I deny that the demand for necessaries to supply the wants of highly-paid gold-miners creates a demand for manufactured goods and for agricultural products which is satisfied by the gold they produce, and which has immense and far-reaching effects on the development both of the countries in which the mining takes place and of other countries. All this is true of the fresh production of gold, just as it is true of the fresh production of wheat or iron or any other useful commodity. My present argument is confined to showing that the addition of a fresh quantity of gold to the reserves of gold on which our vast mass of credit money is based is simply an addition of so many pounds sterling to the whole mass of money in existence, whether metallic money or credit money ; and is consequently comparatively insignificant as a factor in prices.

18. It will be obvious how important a bearing this view of credit money as a medium of exchange has upon the value of the gold standard coin considered as a standard of value. That value, as we have seen, depends on the relation between the aggregate supply of gold in the world and the aggregate demand for gold in the world. Although the aggregate demand for gold in the world is a different thing from the demand for gold as a means of exchange in civilised countries like Great Britain, yet these two are intimately connected. If it is true that in such countries the use of gold coin as a medium of exchange is constantly more and more dispensed with, and that it is replaced by a credit currency which expands and contracts with the demand for it, **we may put aside any notion that the demand for gold as a means of exchange increases in proportion to the increase of population and business, and any apprehension that growing trade is likely to be crippled and stunted for want of gold coin to be used as a means of exchange.** More than this. Taking the above view of the use of credit money, and coupling with it the great recent increase in the supply of gold, we may regard with perfect equanimity the accession of one civilised country after another to the gold

standard, and may devote our attention to the development of banking facilities throughout the world, and to the gradual acquisition by all civilised nations of one single standard of value, with its settled par of exchange. Such a consummation, however distant, is well worth fighting for.

19. **Let us now sum up. In asking the question whether prices depend on the quantity of money, we must first determine what we mean by "money."** Money may mean the gold coin or sovereign which is our standard of value, and the unit of which all prices are multiples. The value in exchange of the sovereign is the value of the gold which it contains ; the value of gold depends, as in all other cases, on demand and supply ; and since quantity is the most important element in supply, the quantity of gold in existence affects the value of the sovereign, and through the sovereign affects prices. But it is the quantity of available gold in existence, not the quantity of coined money, which has this effect ; and the question of the moment is whether the whole quantity—in other words, the supply of gold— has increased or diminished when compared with the demand. The answer to this question is that there is much more reason for thinking that it has increased than for thinking that it has diminished. **Prices have not fallen in consequence of any diminution in the supply of gold.**

20. "Money," again, may mean, and in general language does mean, the "media" or "means of exchange" ; and in this sense it includes gold sovereigns, coined silver and copper money, bank notes, cheques, bills, bank credits, and all the different forms of credit and promises to pay by means of which payments are effected. To the quantity of these means of exchange, taken as a whole, prices no doubt bear some fixed relation. But these means of exchange or credit money are indefinitely greater in amount than the gold coin ; they bear no definite proportion to the gold coin ; they expand and contract according to the demands of business, and do not, unless in the special and exceptional cases above referred to, depend on the supply or quantity of gold coin. An addition of gold coin to the currency, consequently, has not, unless in these exceptional cases, any effect on prices beyond that which the addition of a similar quantity of "credit" money would have, and is, therefore, in general, considering the small proportion it bears to the mass of credit money, infinitesimally small—in fact, a negligible quantity.

21. **How do these conclusions affect the bimetallist proposal ?** That proposal is, by opening our mints to the free coinage of silver, in addition to gold, to add silver to gold and thus increase the quantity of metallic money, whilst at the same time attempting the task of making both metals circulate at a given ratio.

Will this addition to the quantity of money in the world, suppose it could be made, raise prices?

22. First. What will be the effect on the standard of value? It will add largely to the quantity of the metal available for mintage into the standard coins, and to this extent, supposing the sovereign still to exist as the standard coin, and to consist for the future either of its present weight in gold or of fifteen and a half times its weight in silver, it ought to reduce the value in exchange of the sovereign and to alter all contracts and all arrangements made in sovereigns and all gold pieces. To what extent it would have this effect, and whether any such effect would be just and honest, are questions I do not enter upon here.

23. Secondly. What would be the effect of the bimetallist proposal on "money," considered as including all the different media of exchange? The first answer is that, in point of quantity, the addition of the new coined silver money to the whole mass of money, metallic or otherwise, would be so small as to make no perceptible difference in prices. But there might very well be an effect of another kind which would enormously diminish the quantity of credit money in existence, and thus diminish prices far more than any diminution of value of the standard coin would increase them. If men of business were to apprehend that they were to be paid in silver at an artificial value instead of in gold; if they should, under such apprehensions, determine to make all their contracts in gold, to the exclusion of legal tender silver; or if, at the present or at any future time, they should apprehend that the artificial ratio between gold and silver could not be maintained, the result might very well be a run on gold, a commercial panic, and a contraction of credit money, which would cause such a collapse of prices as we have never seen, and which would far more than counterbalance any increase of prices due to the proposed diminution in value of the standard coin.

24. But these are matters of speculation on which I do not wish to dogmatise. **My object is to show that the relation between the quantity of money and prices is a very complex one, and depends on the meaning we give to "money"; that any alteration in money considered as the standard of value is a very serious matter, and not to be undertaken on the evidence before us; and, finally, that there is no ground whatever for any apprehension of deficiency in "money" considered as a means of exchange, and no reason for attempting to add silver to gold as a means of remedying such supposed deficiency.**

The Old Bimetallism and the New.*

By Sir ROBERT GIFFEN, K.C.B., F.R.S.

1. INTERNATIONAL Bimetallism, such as the Bimetallic League now advocate, is a wholly new thing both in theory and practice.

2. Bimetallic theory of any sort is itself almost entirely novel. When there was much bimetallic practice in the world there was no bimetallic theory. Governments had bimetallic laws because the expedient of token money with which we are now so familiar had not then been devised. Two, and even three, metals are required for currency purposes, according to the magnitude of the payments which have to be made. For some purposes gold is the most convenient metal, for others silver, for others copper, just as for other purposes again, paper, *i.e.* promises to pay, is more convenient than any metal. It has been found by experience that for these purposes it is best not to make the tokens other than representative. Token coins, in other words, are not full valued, but are promises to pay in which the medium on which the promise is made is also worth a large part of the value promised; but in the days when bimetallic practice prevailed, before the plan of token money had been devised, the only way in which it was thought two metals could be used in coinage was to rate the one to the other, and to use both at the ratio as long as market conditions rendered that course possible. A new ratio was applied when market conditions changed. The coins of two metals were full-valued at the ratio, because the idea

* *Issued in August,* 1895.

E

of charging a heavy seigniorage on the one and giving a monopoly of its coinage to Government, which has since been found so convenient in practice, had not then occurred to men's minds. **Such was the practice of bimetallism in ancient times.** There was no theory as to the desirability or practicability of maintaining a fixed ratio by the method of rating the one metal to the other, and having full-valued coins of both. In fact, down to recent times, legislatures and Governments were occupied with incessant changes in the ratio, and had no idea that there could be fixity.

3. During the long period, also, when there was bimetallic practice, the monometallic theory of money arose, and received the assent of Oresme, Copernicus, Sir William Petty, Locke, Newton, Adam Smith, Ricardo, the Bullion Committee, Sir Robert Peel and many more, and was embodied explicitly in the English Monetary system, viz. that a standard for money could only be composed of one metal, because there could not be a fixed ratio between two, and the expedient of token money was devised in order to employ and use two or more metals in coinage consistently with this principle.

4. When any theory of bimetallism such as we now have began it is difficult to say; but even as late as the French Law of 1803 the only reasons assigned for rating one metal to the other were the convenience to business of having two metals available for the different payments required, the object now perfectly accomplished by token coins, and the desirability of having plenty of money in a country which it was thought would be hindered by coining one metal only. **A system of standard and token money such as we now have thus fulfils all the objects intended by the practical bimetallism of those times when bimetallism existed in practice.**

5. In the present century a theory grew up which M. Wolowski and other economists of some repute advocated, viz. that the system of having full-valued coins of two metals had some effect in making the legal ratio established effective in the market, and that it was worth while keeping up the system for that reason, although it was recognised that any country attempting to maintain it would have to submit to alternations in the use of the one metal and the other, according to changes in the market ratio from the legal ratio. It was argued, however, that such alternation was not

Injurious to the countries submitting to it, and was, indeed, rather a good thing. It was not denied, however, that there might and would be alternations.

6. The new bimetallism for which arguments are now employed is of an entirely different nature. It is now maintained in theory that although bimetallism was not good for any one nation, and no one nation could make it effective, yet if all Governments were to agree upon a ratio within certain limits not stated that ratio would be effective. Governments are accordingly called upon to agree upon international bimetallism, and to fix upon a ratio by mutual agreement, on the ground not merely that such an agreement might have some effect in making the market ratio conform—the argument of the first bimetallic theorists—and that alternations, though they would be inevitable, would not be very injurious; but on the ground that Government action would necessarily make the ratio effective, and that alternations are not to be feared.

7. **The new bimetallism is thus entirely different from the old, and was unheard of in the world either in theory or in practice until now. The new theory may be right, but surely its extreme novelty should be recognised, and strict proof of the validity of so novel a theory called for, before people stake the fortunes of their monetary systems upon it.**

8. The significance of the fact that since any bimetallic theory was constructed its form has changed so rapidly is also very great. bimetallic theory, as distinguished from bimetallic practice, is hardly half a century old, but already its advocates have advanced from the position that the legal ratio would have some effect (of un-known degree) in making the market ratio conform, and that inevitable alternations would not be injurious to the nations en-during them, to the position that if all nations agree the legal ratio will be certainly effective, and that there will be no alternations. That the latter arguments began to be used because the former arguments were found unconvincing, and for no other reason, is also a matter of history. Bimetallists proper, before the exigencies of controversy forced them to resort to the idea of international bi-metallism and the certainty of maintaining a ratio, were all for particular bimetallism and not merely international bimetallism; and their special arguments for the latter, including the assertion of

the certainty of maintaining a ratio, are for the gallery only, and not for those who have made any study of the subject. No economist of any repute, except Professors Nicholson and Foxwell—perhaps we should now include Mr. Courtney with them—has ever gone so far as to maintain that a fixed ratio between gold and silver can be established by one or more nations.

9. It is not proposed to discuss here the theory of the new bimetallism. That is done elsewhere. **But the importance of the history of the theory is obvious, and goes a long way to discredit the theory itself.**

IS GOLD SCARCE?*

By Mr. Ottomar Haupt,

Author of " The Monetary Question," " Arbitrages et Parités," etc.

---

1. At the present moment, when the question of the scarcity of gold is raised, it is important to submit it to a fresh investigation, be it only for the sake of ascertaining whether the bimetallists are entitled to adduce from it, should it be answered in the affirmative, an argument in favour of their theory. As is well known, **the bimetallic theory culminates in the idea that the actual volume of metallic money is not sufficient** for the trade of the civilised nations, and that for this reason, and in the absence of the necessary quantity of gold, silver should be coined in unlimited amount.

2. The following are extracts from recent statements upon this point by leading English bimetallists. The Bimetallic League gives its "serious doubts as to the sufficiency of future supplies" of gold as making the "necessity strikingly apparent" for establishing international bimetallism.† The Hon. H. C. Gibbs says :—"In

---

* *Issued in January,* 1897. *The figures for* 1897 *have since been included.*

† *Official Statement of Bimetallic League, para. 10.*

" truth, the bimetallic argument is that gold is relatively scarce,
" taking into account the increased demand."* On the other
side of the Atlantic, Mr. Bryan, in accepting the nomination for
the Presidency of the United States, said : " So long as the scramble
" for gold continues prices must fall." **Is gold relatively scarce?
Is there a scramble for gold ?**

3. Before dealing further with the subject, let me ask whether
gold is really scarce in the leading countries of the world after
the enormous output of the South African and Australian mines has
been turned to account either by the respective mints or by the
national banks, which have received the metal in the shape of bars
as cover for the issue of notes or certificates in the ordinary course
of business. To ask the question is to answer it at the same time.
**There cannot be the least doubt that a regular flow of the
precious metal has taken place during the last seven years,
such as the world has never previously seen.** To give an
idea to what an extent there has been an increase in the stocks of
gold in the leading banks from the end of 1890 to the end of
1897, I have constructed the following table, based on official data
at different periods :—

Banks.	End of 1890.	End of 1895.	End of 1897.
	£	£	£
Bank of England	23,120,000	43,400,000	30,400,000
,, ,, France	45,040,000	78,520,000	78,100,000
,, ,, Russia	38,600,000	76,840,000	123,900,000
Austro-Hungarian Bank ...	5,400,000	20,480,000	31,000,000
German Reichsbank ...	30,200,000	28,560,000	27,800,000
Bank of Italy	7,120,000	11,960,000	12,000,000
,, ,, Spain ...	6,080,000	8,000,000	9,400,000
Total ...	£155,560,000	£267,760,000	£312,600,000

**As will be seen from the foregoing figures, the stock of
gold in the principal banks has been augmented within the
space of about seven years by more than £157,000,000.** The

---

* *" Bimetallism Considered," p. 4 (1896).*

total stocks of gold held by England, France, and Germany may
be estimated in 1895 at about £120,000,000 for England, against
£100,000,000 in 1885*; at £140,000,000, against £90,000,000
in 1885, for Germany; and at £184,000,000, against £168,000,000
in 1885, for France.

4. As regards the coinages of the precious metal in the world,
the figures are still more astounding, amounting to about
£24,750,000 in 1891, £35,720,000 in 1892, £48,120,000 in 1893,
£47,200,000 in 1894, £45,860,000 in 1895, and £39,000,000 in
1896. From these amounts has to be deducted about £8,000,000
as a yearly average for re-coinage of gold pieces. The balance
represents a total of about £190,000,000. It must not be thought,
however, that the mines of the world alone have furnished gold to
the mints of the leading countries. For instance, the United States
have lost from the end of 1890 to the 30th of September, 1896, not
less than £32,000,000, part of which, however, has been returned.
All things considered, I give the estimates of the production of the
mines, after deduction of the industrial consumption, as follows :—
For 1891, £13,000,000; for 1892, £18,500,000; for 1893,
£20,500,000; for 1894, £25,000,000; for 1895, £28,000,000;
and for 1896, £33,000,000. In other words, the earth has
yielded in the six years, for monetary purposes alone, about

---

*These figures do not agree with the Report of the British Mint, which gives
the following estimate of the stock of gold for 1895 :—*

	£
In the Banks	30,000,000
In actual Circulation	62,000,000
Total	£92,000,000

*This, however, includes sovereigns and half-sovereigns only, while my estimate
for the same year includes bullion as well as gold coin, and is as follows :—*

	£
In the Bank of England	43,400,000
,, other English Banks	8,000,000
,, Scotch Banks	4,900,000
,, Irish Banks	2,900,000
	59,200,000
In active Circulation	62,000,000
Total	£121,200,000

£138,000,0c0 ; while for the year 1897 a net addition of about £40,000,000 sterling may certainly be counted upon—for monetary purposes alone.

5. **Facts and figures of such moment tell their own tale, and need no further comment.** They prove beyond doubt that there exists no scarcity of gold of any kind in any of the leading countries of the world, and that in reality the output of the mines creates rather a feeling that at no distant future we shall have to deal, not with too little, but with too much, of the precious metal. It is this feeling which has already brought about the discussion of the problem by the Economical Society in Paris—What would be the consequence of a glut of gold on the course of prices of commodities in the near future? Opinions were very much divided in this respect, but the fact that such a body has already discussed the subject, and that the discovery of the Transvaal and other mines has caused a revolution in the monetary outlook, denotes the spirit reigning on this score in financial circles. At all events, we have already to deal with the question—What will become of the plethora of gold in future?—at a time when the Bimetallic League feels "serious doubts" about its sufficiency.

6. **Now, it should be mentioned that the bimetallists argue that gold is scarce, in the sense that it is only to be found in the banks—that is to say, it is hoarded and not accessible to the public at large. But this also is a great error.** In the first place, it is a well-known fact that in England, in Germany, and in France, all the channels of business intercourse are overflowing with gold, and that in none of these countries is the slightest inconvenience experienced in getting the paper money exchanged against it. In the United States, it is true, little gold is seen in active circulation; but the practice there is to use notes and certificates, and the precious metal finds, so to say, its own way into the Treasury and the banks. No doubt, of late a certain tendency of hoarding had been developing itself in that country, brought about by the fear of free coinage of silver, and coupled with the hope that later on a substantial premium might be obtained for gold. But this tendency was purely speculative; and when the cause for the alarm had been removed, everybody was glad to get rid of his gold coin, and to exchange it once more for paper money. The banks and the bankers were

flooded with gold, and did not know what to do with it, as the Treasury did not wish to renew the old operation of receiving gold in exchange for certificates. This fact shows clearly that in the United States the public does not care to use metallic money, which in the ordinary course of business is driven into the Treasury and into the banks, and serves as cover for notes and certificates. But this operation by no means indicates that gold is hoarded by these institutions, and that in consequence thereof it is useless and unused by the public. **In point of fact, it is the public who do not want to use gold, and for this very reason only a small part of the coin struck by the United States mints finds its way into actual circulation.**

7. Unfortunately, things are not presented in this light by the bimetallists, and it is, therefore, well to lay stress on the aforesaid fact, that the Treasury refuses gold coin at present in exchange for certificates—a fact which speaks for itself. It is by no means denied that the United States have in the course of the last few years lost gold through withdrawals for Europe. But the country is itself still the biggest producer of the precious metal, and can easily obtain it from abroad at any given moment, as we have seen only recently. In this respect the bimetallists have nothing to gain by citing a struggle for gold in troubled times which did not leave the slightest trace when confidence was restored. On the contrary, events have shown that **there has been rather a struggle to get rid of the gold accumulated so hastily and without any pertinent reason.**

8. What is much more important and conclusive is the fact that gold has been at all times at the disposal of bankers and bullion dealers in the United States who wanted it for export. What do the paltry sums demanded by a few persons anxious to profit by a given situation amount to in presence of the enormous shipments of the precious metal during recent times to Europe? To talk, under the circumstances, of hoardings of unused gold, as has been the wont of the bimetallists—Mr. Bryan at the head of them—is tantamount to a misrepresentation of the real state of things. This much is clear—that these expressions do not at all apply to the system of banking and monetary organisation in the United States. For this reason we may disregard them, all the more so as they have been made use of for a kind of warfare which cannot stand the test of close investigation.

9. In order to show how the case stands in another country which is on the eve of introducing the single gold standard, and which has for years been accused of hoarding millions of pounds sterling, **the example of Russia should be cited.** That country has, in the course of the last few years, amassed an enormous sum of gold in the Bank of Russia amounting to not less than £124,000,000. All that has been done so far (1897) has consisted in fixing the Russian exchange at the parity of $7\frac{1}{2}$ roubles to the half-imperial, at which it has been fixed for good. Although not a single gold coin of the new type has so far been put into circulation, the Government has already commenced to pay part of the salaries of its employees in gold, that is to say, in old half-imperials. **The Imperial Bank of Russia and also the private banks do their best to force gold into circulation, in order that the public may get accustomed to it. But all this is of no avail.** People are so used to paper money that they prefer it to gold, which only very few of them have ever seen. What is the consequence of this strange fact? Simply this: the public keep to their notes, and the Imperial Bank sees the precious metal flowing back into its coffers. Now, in this case the superficial observer might talk of hoarding gold, although it is really a case of endeavouring to force gold on the people.

10. **But perhaps the most inconsistent argument of all is that used by the bimetallists when they say that "the heaping-up of gold is the result of stagnation of trade."** * In the first place, this cuts away their own argument that gold is scarce, for it admits that gold is superabundant. Secondly, it destroys their own argument that bad trade is due to scarcity of gold, for it assumes that bad trade causes accumulations of gold.

11. All things considered, I may state once more that—in the ordinary meaning of the word, at least—no hoarding of gold takes place either in Europe or in the United States. Perhaps the fact that £6,000,000 are hidden by the German Government in the *Juliusthurm* of Spandau might be adduced in order to prove the contrary, but in reality it proves nothing, since a like amount of Treasury notes has been issued against this so-called war fund.

For the sake, however, of leaving nothing out of account, the recent monetary policy of the Bank of France, which for some

---

* *" Colloquy on Currency"* (*p. 220*), *by the President of the Bimetallic League.*

time has given neither gold bars nor foreign gold coin for export, deserves attention. In this case the bimetallists might talk of gold which seems inaccessible to the public. In the first place, however, it should not be forgotten that this establishment has never ceased to exchange its notes against gold for everybody; and, further, that the new policy has simply been dictated by the desire of the council to avoid all operations resembling any trafficking in gold as long as the discussion of the new Bill for the renewal of the bank's charter has not been concluded. Under the circumstances the misgivings of some of our over-anxious bi-metallists may be dismissed, all the more so as the Bank of France a short time ago largely contributed towards the gold shipments to the United States.

12. **As will be seen from the foregoing explanations, the story of the hoarding of gold by the banks, invented by the bimetallists, is a myth and has no reality.** The fluctuating character of these very stocks of the precious metal in the leading countries of the world ought to furnish sufficient proof of the fact that such gold is accessible to the public, and that it plays, in point of fact, an important part in the specie movements from one country to another. As, during the last twenty-five years, gold alone has been used for international payments when the foreign exchanges have reached the so-called specie-point, and as these movements are regularly published by the newspapers, everybody, by paying only a superficial attention to the monetary question, can convince himself that the gold deposited in the banks cannot be termed "useless" or "unused." For this reason it is time that the bi-metallists should cease to attack the gold standard on that score. As to the alleged scarcity of gold, it is, as we have seen, completely out of the question at the present time; and even in the times of the so-called "struggle for gold" it had only a very limited prevalence. **To repeat that "gold is relatively scarce," and that there is a "scramble for gold" at a time when the very contrary fact is perfectly evident, is a policy which may go down with the uneducated masses, but which cannot but produce a painful impression on the initiated student of the Monetary Question.**

(Note.—For Appendix, see over.)

[60]

APPENDIX.

PRODUCTION OF GOLD IN THE WORLD FROM 1873 TO 1897. (From the
Report of the Director of the United States Mint.)

(Converted at £ = $4·867).

	Ounces, Fine.	Value.
		£
1873	4,653,675	19,766,000
1874	4,390,031	18,646,000
1875	4,716,563	20,033,000
1876	5,016,488	21,307,000
1877	5,512,196	23,412,000
1878	5,761,114	24,469,000
1879	5,262,174	22,350,000
1880	5,148,880	21,869,000
1881	4,983,742	21,168,000
1882	4,934,086	20,957,000
1883	4,614,588	19,600,000
1884	4,921,169	20,902,000
1885	5,245,572	22,280,000
1886	5,135,679	21,813,000
1887	5,116,861	21,733,000
1888	5,330,775	22,642,c00
1889	5,973,790	25,373,000
1890	5,749,306	24,419,000
1891	6,320,194	26,844,000
1892	7,094,266	30,123,000
1893	7,618,811	32,360,000
1894	8,764,362	37,225,000
1895	9,641,337	40,950,000
1896	9,817,991	41,700,000
1897	11,300,000*	48,000,000*

* *Estimated roughly.*

The average value of the gold and silver together produced annually in the
years 1866-70 was £38,068,000. The estimated production of gold alone in
1897 was about £48,000,c00. Thus it will be seen that the output of gold alone
in 1897 exceeded by about £10,000,000 the average total value of both the gold
and silver produced annually in the years 1866-70.

Bimetallism and Legal Tender.*

By the Rt. Hon. LORD FARRER.

"The Mint would again be opened to the coinage of gold and silver into LEGAL TENDER money at a defined ratio."—*President of Bimetallic League, Times, 4th September*, 1895.

I. BIMETALLISTS PROPOSE :—

(*a*) THAT every nation shall coin freely both gold and silver.

(*b*) That every nation shall agree to make a law under which either so much gold, or so many times its weight in silver, shall be **legal tender** for every promise to pay ; and that every debtor shall be able to pay a debt at his pleasure in either gold or silver coin at a ratio which the bimetallists themselves, though obviously desiring the ratio of 15½ to 1, do not venture to specify, and which, though the very kernel of their scheme, they relegate to statesmen to wrangle out at an International Conference.   In other words, the law will force people, in the absence of special stipulations to the contrary, to accept unlimited quantities of either one metal or the other in payment of debts, **and will in so doing make a contract for people which they do not make for themselves ; and this they do by means of legal tender.**   It is therefore desirable to understand what legal tender really means—what our law of legal tender is ; what it has done ; and what it can be expected to do with advantage.

* *Issued in September*, 1895.

2. What, then, is the law of legal tender in this country ? It seems
that according to English Common Law as declared by the Courts,
gold and silver coins issued from the Royal Mint were legal tender
to any amount at the rates fixed by Royal Proclamation. Where no
such rates were so fixed, as between 1670 and 1717, silver alone
possessed the full quality of legal tender.* From 1717 to 1816 both
gold and silver were nominally legal tender at the rate of one guinea
to 21s., though gold alone was, in practice, the real standard coin.
By the Coinage Act of 1816, practically re-enacted in the Coinage
Act of 1870, gold sovereigns are legal tender to any amount, whilst
silver coins are legal tender to the amount of 40s., and no more.
Bank of England notes are legal tender everywhere except at the
Bank of England, but as they are always convertible into gold at the
Bank, they are really not legal tender at all. **The privilege or
power of legal tender is therefore in this country, for every-
thing except small payments, confined to gold sovereigns.**

3. The law of legal tender has practically no effect on International
dealings. If a bill is drawn in New York on London, American
dollars are legal tender for the purchase-money of the bill in New
York, and English sovereigns are legal tender for the discharge of
the bill in London. But as there is no international legal tender
law fixing the number of dollars which shall be paid for a sovereign,
the number of dollars or of sovereigns to be paid for a bill is settled
by private contract based upon the number of dollars which the
market will give for a sovereign. The international dealing, therefore, is settled according to market values, and there is no question
of legal tender in the matter.

4. Again, in the bulk of transactions within this country, those,
namely, which are settled by cheques or by set-off of debts, the law
of legal tender has no operation. A cheque is not legal tender ; the
payee may refuse to accept payment until it is cashed by the banker.
A set-off is not touched by the law of legal tender. And yet from
90 to 100 per cent. of all transactions in this country are thus
settled.

---

* *See for the opinions of Adam Smith on this point, " Wealth of Nations,"
9th Edition, Book I., p. 59, and of Ricardo, Works, Ed.* 1876, *p.* 224.

5. If a debt is paid in bank-notes other than those of the Bank of England, they are not legal tender. Where a debt is paid in Bank of England notes, the notes are no doubt legal tender, except at the Bank of England ; but at the Bank of England, to which they can always be taken, they must be paid in gold, so that they are not really or completely legal tender at all. But do they owe such debt-paying power as they have to their limited privilege of legal tender ? Gold sovereigns are legal tender. But do they owe their debt-paying power—their circulating power—to this fact ? Suppose that they ceased to be legal tender to-morrow, would not they—the law of contract remaining what it is—be still the recognised medium in which to pay debts ? Would not people still make their contracts to pay and be paid so many pounds sterling ? And would not the ordinary law enforce these contracts, without any special statute making gold sovereigns legal tender ?

6. There is no doubt one case in which the law of legal tender has a direct and powerful effect, viz., the case of subsidiary silver and copper coins. In this case, since the metal they contain is not as much as their face value in gold—since, for instance, the silver in a shilling is worth much less than the twentieth of a pound sterling— people would not receive them in payment unless the law attached an arbitrary and fictitious value to them by making them legal tender at their face value. And since the law gives them this fictitious value, it very properly limits their issue and also the amount for which they are legal tender, and thus prevents them from becoming the general medium of exchange in ordinary transactions. In fact, their function is a limited and subordinate one. For international transactions, for wholesale transactions, and for large transactions forming the bulk of retail transactions, they are needless and functionless. They are no measure of prices; they have no connection with the standard of value. And yet they are the only form of currency with respect to which our law of legal tender is really operative.

Do not these considerations lead to the conclusion that the law of legal tender is a thing of much less weight and value than is commonly supposed ?

7. What, then, is this law of legal tender? What does it really mean? What does it add to our law of currency? **Legal tender is something which the law specially distinguishes as a thing to be accepted as payment of a debt.** It may be gold, silver, or paper—or indeed anything else. Or it may be all these or any combination of them. It is of course not at all the same thing as the Standard of Value, which like a lb. weight or a yard, is the term or unit in and by which values are stated and measured. In fact, legal tender is essentially different from the Standard of Value. Any nation or group of nations may adopt a standard of value—say a certain unit weight of gold, and may make other things besides that unit legal tender. Indeed, if they make nothing else but the standard unit legal tender, there is no need and no room for the operation of any special law of legal tender. The ordinary law of contract does all that is necessary without any law giving special functions to particular forms of currency. We have adopted a gold sovereign as our unit, or standard of value. If I promise to pay 100 sovereigns, it needs no special currency law of legal tender to say that I am bound to pay 100 sovereigns, and that, if required to pay the 100 sovereigns, I cannot discharge my obligation by paying anything else. It is necessary to keep very clearly in mind the distinction between that function of law, or of government or of international agreement, tacit or expressed, which selects a standard of value, and that function which in creating legal tender professes to state in terms in what substance or substances a promise to pay may be discharged. The latter is a function superadded to the former, and superfluous and unnecessary if a promise to pay in terms of the standard unit is strictly performed.

8. What more, then, does the law of legal tender do? What has it done? What good, or what harm, has it done? And what can it do with advantage? It has enabled kings and governments to put a smaller amount of pure metal into their standard coins, and to say that the coin thus reduced in real value shall be of the same effect in paying a debt as the original coin. Without saying that such debasemen of the coin was always fraudulent, we shall all admit that the practice was, and is, in the highest degree

inexpedient, and that such an application of the law of legal tender is indefensible.

9. Again, the law of legal tender has enabled governments to say that an obligation to pay so many gold or silver units shall be satisfied by the delivery of bank-notes, or other specially sanctioned forms of inconvertible paper. Such a step is occasionally unavoidable under pressure of war or of other necessity, and when managed with skill and prudence, when the body which issues the paper possesses credit, and when care is taken not to over-issue, such a step may be taken for a short time without serious disaster. But these conditions are rare and difficult to secure; where they have been secured, care has always been taken to return to specie payments as soon as possible; and no reasonable man will be found to allege that this form of legal tender is a thing to be desired or encouraged.

10. Again, the law of legal tender has enabled governments to say that the coin in which a promise to pay is discharged, may be either a gold coin of a given weight, or silver coins of (say) $15\frac{1}{2}$ times its weight. And what has been the consequence? In every case one or other of the two—the cheaper for the time being—has become the standard coin in use; promises to pay have really been promises to pay that coin; and if in the course of events the other metal has become the cheaper, so as to make it better for debtors to pay in coins of that metal, the standard in use has altered from one metal to the other; the currency of the country has been exported to the benefit of no one but the money-changers; and contracts have altered by the operation of the law over the heads of those who have made them.

11. Again, the law of legal tender has been operative, as above noticed, in the case of subsidiary coins, and will probably, if we may judge from the present state of the currencies of the world, have a much wider operation with respect to subsidiary coins, than has heretofore been thought probable or possible. But since the metal of which this token coinage consists is in no sense the standard of value, and has no bearing on prices, we may, in considering the effect of legal tender on the standard of value, dismiss it from consideration. In fact, the man who receives a token coin receives, not so much silver,

F

but such or such a fraction of a gold coin; and if the silver coin were endorsed, as it ought to be, with a promise to exchange it for gold at its face value, and were made convertible into gold in the same manner in which bills, cheques, and notes are convertible, its real character would be made obvious.

12. **Looking to the above cases of the use or abuse of the law of legal tender, other than the last, we see that they possess one character in common—viz., that the law in all of them enables a debtor to pay and requires a creditor to receive something different from that which their contract contemplated.** In fact it is a forced and unnatural construction put upon the dealings of men by arbitrary power. If applied to existing contracts, it may work the grossest injustice. If applied only to future dealings, so that men can understand what the construction of their contracts may be, it is less open to the charge of injustice, but cannot fail, if it has any effectual operation at all, to cause much confusion and inconvenience. An arbitrary and non-natural construction of ordinary contracts is a great evil. It either makes men do what they did not intend to do, or it leads them to make special arrangements for the very purpose of evading the law.

13. Under these circumstances we may say that any Law of Legal Tender is in its own nature " suspect." And, as often happens with laws of this kind, it has failed to operate in cases where it has not been in accordance with the habits or inclinations of the people. For instance, in the critical years at the end of the 17th century which ushered in our gold currency silver was the sole legal tender.* Silver was the old and acknowledged standard: both gold and silver were freely coined, but gold was not rated to silver, and, therefore, could not be legal tender. And yet the people preferred gold; brought gold to the Mint to be coined, to the exclusion of silver; and used gold in payment and receipt of debts. Again, during the American Civil War, greenbacks were legal tender throughout the United States. But California steadily refused to use greenbacks; all contracts were made and per-

* *See above, paragraph* 2.

formed in gold; and Un'ted States notes were not used in that State until the resumption by the United States of specie payments.*

14. The above considerations, drawn from past experience, appear to lead to the conclusion **that whilst the bimetallic scheme is founded on the law of legal tender, the law of legal tender, except as regards subsidiary coins, is non-natural and questionable in principle.**

Do the present proposals of the bimetallists alter these conclusions? The only new factor which they add to past bimetallism is the suggestion that the legal tender of an alternative payment either in one metal or the other at a fixed ratio shall be a legal tender for all nations, fixed by international agreement, instead of a legal tender fixed by each nation for itself. But does this really alter the essentially objectionable character of legal tender? That character consists in substituting for the free operation of voluntary contract, and for a law which simply enforces the performance of such contracts, an artificial construction of contracts such as would never occur to the parties unless forced upon them by an arbitrary law. Will this character of legal tender be changed by the fact that governments agree with one another to make the substitution? Will individual men and women be induced thereby to think and deal in terms of alternative gold and silver, at some arbitrary ratio, instead of thinking and dealing, as they now do, in terms of one single and simple standard metal? Does not ordinary human nature rebel against such a suggestion? Is not all experience, in international dealings, in home trade, in domestic and private business, inconsistent with such an hypothesis?

Contrast the two formulæ:

1. I promise to pay 100 gold sovereigns.

2. I promise to pay either 100 gold sovereigns or as many silver dollars as will be equal in weight to $15\frac{1}{2}$ times 100 sovereigns, whichever of the two happen to be cheaper at the time of payment.

Which of these two formulæ will people naturally prefer?

* *Appendix to Final Report of Gold and Silver Commission, No. V., p.* 93.

F 2

Which of them will a seller or borrower, or even a buyer or
lender who looks to certainty and simplicity, select to do business
in? Which of them will be the formula which will best grease the
wheels of trade and promote numerous and profitable dealings?
Can there be a doubt?

15. Is it not probable—nay, almost certain—that any such new
form of legal tender—*i.e.* of an attempt by governments to enforce
a non-natural and objectionable mode of discharging obligations,
would be followed by the same mischiefs and inconveniences which
have followed other forms of legal tender—viz. by injustice and
confusion and probably by special private arrangements which would
evade an arbitrary law by making all promises to pay payable in gold
and in gold only? If so, the new bimetallic law of legal tender
would, like other forms of legal tender, be set aside in favour of
natural dealings; but not without much inconvenience, and not
without a conflict between law and habit which a wise legislator
always endeavours to avoid, and which is happily avoided in our
present monometallic gold system of currency.

16. To sum up. Under our present system the government exercises two functions—it selects, not without reference to habit, the
material of the standard coin, and it stamps the coin with a certificate
of weight and fineness, leaving people to make their own contracts in
terms of that coin—just as they make their contracts in quarts, feet,
or gallons, or in avoirdupois pounds or hundredweights. The bimetallic proposals would add to these functions a third, viz. that of
determining the value of gold in silver, or of silver in gold, and they
would do this by means of **legal tender, a law, which cannot
govern the supply of these metals at all; a law which can
affect only that part of the demand for them which relates
to currency; a law which, so far as the standard coin is
concerned, is quite unnecessary; a law which, as history
shows, has been generally used for fraudulent or questionable purposes, and with mischievous results.**

What is the Appreciation of Gold, and what is its Effect on the Prices of Commodities and Labour?*

By the Rt. Hon. LORD PLAYFAIR, P.C., G.C.B., etc.

"The conclusion is irresistible, that there have been serious changes in the conditions of the production of gold. Gold is harder to get. If it had been as easy to get as before, there would have been an increase in the quantity gotten : this has not increased ; it has not even been stationary ; it has fallen away."—COURTNEY, *Nineteenth Century*, April, 1893.

"When gold becomes appreciated, and precisely in the same proportion in which it does appreciate, so much more of the produce *and the labour* of the country must be given in exchange for the gold which is required to meet these obligations."—CHAPLIN, *Land and Bimetallism*, page 8.

"There is one large force—the appreciation of gold—which operates with equal pressure, everywhere and simultaneously, thrusting the prices of all commodities downwards."—HEBER CLARK, *Secretary Manufacturers' Club, Philadelphia*.

APPRECIATION OF GOLD IS A SYNONYM FOR LOW PRICES.

1. THE appreciation of gold may be admitted as an expression of the prevalency of low prices, and yet its causation of the general decline in the prices of commodities may be strenuously denied. Everyone will agree that there has been a remarkable fall during the

* *Issued in January*, 1896.

last twenty years in the prices chiefly of machine-made commodities, not a universal and equal fall, but one sufficient in extent to excite anxiety and surprise.

The general statement of the case is that a given weight of gold during the last twenty or ten years will buy more machine-made commodities than it could buy before 1873. This may be a simple expression of a fact, or it may be related to low prices as cause and effect. According to my own belief, the appreciation of gold is simply a synonym for low prices ; and the term only narrates a certain truth in regard to a considerable number of commodities, but not to all.

2. Let us look at the purchasing power of gold in terms of wheat. Comparing the period of 1845-50 with the year 1871, we find that both gold and silver actually *depreciated* in terms of wheat—silver by 8 per cent. and gold by 9 per cent.

The depreciation changed into appreciation in the next few years, and by 1875 both metals would buy more wheat for a given weight—silver by 18 per cent. and gold by 27 per cent.—than in 1871. As the years went on, silver still remained appreciated for wheat, but the divergence between it and gold became more considerable : for in the ten years ending 1892, silver, though still appreciated by 9 per cent., was distanced by gold, which had mounted to 35 per cent. in terms of wheat.*

The reason for this change is obvious : wheat and silver were both falling in price, the former more rapidly than the latter ; while the price of gold has either remained stationary, or it may have risen slightly. It is not true, as bimetallists assert, that an ounce of silver will buy "the same quantity of corn, iron, or most articles of the first utility" as it would do before 1873. In 1873 11.9494 ozs. of silver were required to buy one quarter of wheat at London prices : in 1893 the quarter sold for 8.1568 ozs. **If gold be responsible for the fall of wheat by "appreciation," silver must take a degree of the blame, for during these twenty years both of the precious metals were in a state of appreciation in terms of wheat.**

HOW DID APPRECIATION ACT IN TERMS OF LABOUR ?

3. Mr. Chaplin, in the quotation at the head of this leaflet, says gold reduced the wages of labour as well as the prices of commodities. This is notoriously inconsistent with facts as to labour in general, though the sudden changes may have displaced labour and produced want of employment in special districts and in special industries.

In the payment of labour, which is one of the largest functions gold has to perform, it has depreciated. A fixed

* *I take these figures from Faraday's tables in the Memoirs of the Manchester Literary and Philosophical Society, 1893. He is writing in defence of silver.*

weight of gold—say, one ounce—will buy more machine-made commodities than twenty years ago; but it will buy less skilled labour. As a fact, therefore, gold has depreciated in terms of labour. In other words, as regards machine-made commodities, gold will now buy about 30 to 40 per cent. more than it did twenty years ago; but it will buy from 40 to 50 per cent. *less* labour in this country, and from 50 to 60 per cent. *less* in the United States. At the same time the labourers, who get more gold for their work, have the purchasing power of their wages also largely increased. As higher wages and increased purchasing power form the only concrete way in which the great body of the people can become better off, and as their comforts have palpably improved in the last twenty years, these two great facts are not compatible with the existence of a great downward pressure upon industry. Appreciation and depreciation, as terms relating to the money standard, may be useful to denote the prevalency of low prices or high prices, but they are mischievous when they claim to be a force which produces either.

BIMETALLISTS' MEANING OF APPRECIATION.

4. We do not hear so much of the scarcity of gold as formerly, and even the formidable term "appreciation" has retired more modestly to the background, since the rise in the production of gold. It was this apprehension of, and belief in, scarcity that drove Mr. Courtney into the bimetallic camp. In the extract of his article quoted above, Mr. Courtney obviously feared that gold was now "harder to get," that its production showed signs of permanent diminution, and that this would be followed by increasing appreciation. Like all products of mines, the amount of auriferous ores shows considerable fluctuations of production, sometimes remaining low and at other times mounting during periods of years; but during historical times there has been a steady increase of gold production, as new lands became opened up by civilisation. Professor Laughlin has shown that in the last thirty-five years one and one-third times as much gold has been produced as in the 358 years preceding 1850. At the present time production is on the increase, and for a period of years it is likely to continue. **We cannot admit scarcity; comparing the year 1895 with 1885, there has been an increase of 84 per cent. in the production of gold.** In 1885 its value was £22,280,000, and in 1895 it mounted to £40,950,000. During that time the production of silver in ounces had increased 82 per cent. It cannot be called scarcity when production is increasing so much faster than the growing population. If gold were scarce in relation to demand, a given weight of it would buy more commodities than when it is abundant, because gold itself, being a mere commodity, is subject to the laws which govern barter. But where

is the proof that gold bullion or gold coins have been insufficient to meet the demands of the monetary standard? When the theory of scarcity ceases to be believed, how is appreciation to work as an irresistible force, "operating with equal pressure, everywhere and simultaneously, thrusting the prices of all commodities downwards"? Such a pressure, if operative at all, must act uniformly as to price, as to time, and as to degree. But this has not occurred. There has been no uniformity, and it has not lowered the price of skilled labour, or to any material extent the products of hand-made industries, while the prices of a few machine-made commodities have not fallen at all. **It is a delusion to think that low prices like those of the last twenty years are new in the history of commerce. Between 1846 and 1872, during the reign of the silver ratio and the Latin Union, prices were practically as low as they have been between 1884 and 1891.** An extension of Sauerbeck's index of prices, by Professor Falconer, of John Hopkins University, gives the index (1860 being 100) in the first period as 76.4, and in the latter as 75.4. Undoubtedly, however, the fall in prices has been more persistent since 1873, though for various reasons that year was one of abnormally high prices and is not well suited for comparison.

IF APPRECIATION DOES NOT CAUSE LOW PRICES, WHAT DOES?

5. There are very potent causes which have lowered prices during the last quarter of a century, though they have no relation to a money standard. The two main causes I have formulated in my book called "Subjects of Social Welfare."

(*a*) The world has not yet adapted itself to the marvellous progress of science in the last two decades. Science, in its application to machinery for production, and to the agencies for distribution, has altered the whole character of manufactures and agriculture; and has also profoundly changed commerce by the rapid interchange of knowledge and thought through the telegraph and telephone.

(*b*) New chemical inventions and improvements of machinery have augmented industrial products beyond the immediate demand of the world, and by abruptly displacing old forms of labour have caused individual suffering among unskilled labourers. **The words "the rapid development of production and increased economy and facilities of distribution" mean much more than the shibboleth of the bimetallists, "appreciation."**

GENERAL CAUSES OF LOW PRICES.

6. During the last twenty-five years enormous advances have been made in the production and distribution of commodities; these

causes alone are quite sufficient to account for the general fall of prices. Science has advanced so fast that the world has been unable to adapt itself to the rapidly-changing phases of industry. In many industrial processes the changes produced by scientific invention have amounted to revolutions in industrial production. I will give two examples—one of them being an agricultural, the other a metallurgic industry. The chief source of red colours in the dyeing industry used to be madder, a crop grown chiefly in Turkey, Belgium, and Holland. The tinctorial power of madder was due to a chemical principle called "alizarin." Chemists showed how this valuable red dye-stuff could be artificially prepared from one of the products of coal-tar, and the madder industry was nearly destroyed. In 1872 its import into this country was about 29 millions of pounds, but in a few years it fell to 2 millions—while at the same time a much more valuable industry took its place, for the value of the artificial "alizarin" became ten times greater than that of the madder crop. Surely the appreciation of gold had nothing to do with the fall in the price of madder, which was so great as to put an end to its growth, or to the rise of the new industry which took its place.

7. I now take an instance from the metals used in industry—aluminium. The raw material or ore of this most useful metal is clay, but the extraction of the metal was long a costly process. In 1854, when it first became an article of industrial use, the price of aluminium was £18 (or 360 shillings) per pound. New methods of extraction had reduced the price to 32 shillings per pound in 1887; in two years more (1889) the price had dropped to 8 shillings, and now in 1895 aluminium is selling for 2 shillings per pound. **Could the most ardent bimetallist ascribe these tremendous falls in price to any occult power in the appreciation of gold?** Except in degree, however, the fall in the prices of every staple commodity during the last quarter of a century can be shown to depend on the progressive application of science to improved production, and to increasing facilities for distribution,* which open up new sources of supply. The space at my disposal only allows me to indicate the nature of the causes which have lowered prices in the cases of four staple products—wheat, iron, cotton, and wool. They represent food, and the structural, mechanical, and textile industries; they affect the markets certainly to the extent of 400 millions sterling yearly.

CAUSES WHICH HAVE LOWERED THE PRICE OF IRON.

8. Iron—in its various forms of cast-iron, malleable iron, and steel —forms the chief material for strength, and is used in the construction

* *About half a century ago the coal consumption in ocean steamers was 5½ lb. per indicated horse power; now it is reduced to 1½ lb. The capacity for cargo was 1,000 or 2,000 tons; now the "Georgic" can carry 14,000 tons.*

of the machines and structures of nearly all industries. The continuous fall in its price since 1870 has been very remarkable. One reason for this is that the greatly-increased facilities of distribution have opened up many new fields of ore, and have induced other countries to undertake the manufacture of the metal. Between 1870 and 1884 the world's production rose 237 per cent., and that of the United Kingdom by 131 per cent. The price of Scotch pig-iron in 1873 was 127 shillings per ton : in 1885 it was 41s. 9d. The fall in price was a good deal the effect of more economical production. Thus in 1873 the average annual product for each workman was 173 tons ; in 1885 it had increased to 261 tons, or 51 per cent. But the fall in price was still more due to the progress of chemistry. The " Bessemer " process of making steel direct from pig-iron lowered its price exceedingly, but at the same time largely extended its area of utility. In 1874 the price of steel was 240s. per ton : in 1885 it had fallen to 80s. **In the face of these great changes a fall in price was a necessity, and requires no occult influence of gold to explain it.**

CAUSES WHICH HAVE LOWERED THE PRICE OF COTTON.

9. In former times cotton was picked and cleaned by slave labour, and the daily product per man was $4\frac{1}{2}$ lb. The cotton-gin, which is still being constantly improved, picks and cleans daily 4,000 lb. per man. The residue after picking was thrown away or burned as fuel : it now yields, in the United States alone, annual products of the value of six millions sterling. When the picked cotton reached the mills in 1874, the spindles which spun it into thread used to make 4,000 revolutions per minute : now they make from nine to ten thousand. The best mills in the United States enable each weaver to produce annually 30,000 yards of cloth, an amount more than double the produce of the weaver in 1873. Since that year, which the bimetallists select as the downfall of our industries by the break in the ratio of gold and silver, the world has grown sixteen per cent. in population, but cotton industries have augmented by eighty-six per cent. The chief object of the cotton mills is to cover the bare backs of men with cotton shirts, and the average demand of a working man is 40 yards of shirting yearly ; he will not take more, because he cannot persuade his wife to wash seven shirts weekly ; so it is easy to see that largely-increased supply may overreach demand. The world's demand for American cotton for the years 1890 and 1891 was about 15 millions of bales, while its production in these two years was about 18 millions. Increased cheapness in transportation has opened up new sources of supply to the markets of the world. Cotton grown on the prairies of America, 5,000 miles away, is now brought to Liverpool at a cost for transport of one farthing per pound. **When the palpable cause of fall in price is so obvious, why look for an occult cause ?**

CAUSES WHICH HAVE LOWERED THE PRICE OF WOOL.

10. The causes of the fall in price of wool and its fabrics are various and complex. Sudden changes in fashion and the operation of hostile tariffs are factors requiring consideration, as well as the enlargement of the area of supply and the increasing economies in production. The woollen industry is also attacked by a spurious imitation called shoddy, which consists of old woollen rags torn up and manufactured into new cloth. In addition to these lowering influences on prices, the increase of the raw material through new fields of supply is well known. Since 1860 to the present year the increase of the world's supply is generally estimated in excess of 100 per cent. England now meets with much foreign wool in her markets. Thus in 1864 a standard English wool called "Lincoln Hogs" was 2s. 6d. per pound; but in 1889 it was only 10½d. : in the former year the import of all foreign wools into England was only 211 millions of pounds, while in 1888 it was 650 millions. England was at one time the great producer of wools, but she has had to meet the opened markets of the world. The increase of wool grown in Australia from 1872 to 1887 is estimated at 80 per cent. and that of the United States from 1880 to 1885 at 25 per cent. The cost of transport of wool from Australia, 10,000 miles distant, is only one halfpenny per pound. **It is clear, therefore, that there are abundant causes for the lowering of prices in woollens, without reference to the appreciation of gold.**

CAUSES WHICH HAVE LOWERED THE PRICE OF WHEAT.

11. No commodity has fallen so continuously and heavily in price as wheat, and unhappily the farmers in this country have been taught to look for the chief cause of the fall to the rupture of the bimetallic ratio in 1873. The farmers in the United States met the decline in price by combining to use machinery for ploughing the land, harvesting the crop, milling and handling the produce, in a way that could only be done by co-operation ; while our farmers, continuing to farm independently, either sold at ruinous prices or abandoned the cultivation of the crop. In consequence of the economies of production, which I have not space to give in detail, and to the cheapening of transport by land and sea, the American farmer gets more profit out of wheat sold in England at 34s. per quarter than he did at 54s. per quarter from 1870 to 1873 inclusive. Other countries, like India, the Argentine Republic, Russia, and Austria-Hungary, became exporters of wheat after 1873 ; and although science was not applied in these countries to the economies of production as in the case of North America, yet the cost of transport had become so greatly reduced through the invention of triplex steam-engines to ocean navigation, that foreign wheat poured into our markets to be sold at a price that was scarcely profitable to the senders and almost

impossible for competition by the English farmer on the old system of farming. Of the American flour in a four pound loaf made exclusively of it, the cost for transport does not exceed one half-penny. I trust that farmers will no longer believe that the rupture of the bimetallic ratio in 1873 is the one cause swallowing up all other causes, as Aaron's rod swallowed up the rods of all the other magicians. In former times prices were dependent on local markets. Even a hill intervening between two contiguous market towns influenced the price of wheat. **Now the world has a common market, and prices are no longer determined by local conditions.**

KNOWN CAUSES SUFFICIENT TO ACCOUNT FOR FALL IN PRICES WITHOUT CURRENCY THEORIES.

12. **I have taken four staple industries to show that the changes in production and distribution since 1873 are abundantly sufficient to account for their fall in prices, and that appreciation of gold is not requisite for the explanation of low prices.** In civilised nations natural selection has determined the use of gold as a standard. Its actual use as a metal for carrying on trade is diminishing, though its use as a measure or in verification of values is increasing. From 1864 to 1873 the international trade of the United States was carried on by one dollar in gold sufficing to complete the transactions of about 14 dollars foreign trade ; while from 1883 to 1892 one dollar of gold sufficed for 31·83 dollars. In banking business less than one-tenth of one per cent. of coin is sufficient for the transactions of our banks. As civilisation progresses, the actual use of gold will lessen, if we do not interfere with the standard.

In the last quarter of the century the destructive and constructive influences of science, acting on the whole beneficently, have lowered the prices of commodities, and are likely to continue to do so for the future. The changes thus produced often injure individuals, or even large groups of working men, who from want of adaptability to changed conditions of labour have been unable to fit themselves to the new conditions of production ; still in their result they greatly benefit humanity, for they ameliorate the lives of the people, who find that the fall in prices is accompanied by a rise in the wages of efficient labour and in the increase of their purchasing power.

England's Adoption of the Gold Standard.*

By the Rt. Hon. LORD FARRER.†

1. THE character and operation of our present metallic currency have been explained earlier in this series. The following is an account of the steps by which we arrived at our present gold standard. **The story begins with the coinage of the guinea in the second half of the seventeenth century.** Previous to that time the history of English coinage is a record of arbitrary changes made by kings and governments in the weight and fineness of the coins, or in their relation to one another, or in the rate at which they were to be received in payment : changes made for various purposes, *e.g.* to cheat creditors ; to provide sufficient currency ; or

* *Issued in September,* 1895.

† *For the facts and extracts given I am indebted to Lord Liverpool's letter on the Coins of the Realm, ed.* 1880; *to the Appendix to Dana Horton's " Silver Pound " ; to the Appendix to Gibbs' " Colloquy on Currency " ; to Shaw's " History of Currency,"* 1895 ; *and to Kalkman's " England's Übergang zur Goldwährung im* 18th *Jahrhundert,"* Strassburg, 1895. *I am also indebted to Mr. Edward Rigg, of the Royal Mint, for the figures relating to coinage, and for valuable criticisms.*

to meet and counteract the constant fluctuations in the relative outside or market values of gold and silver.*

2. Subsequently to the coinage of the guinea wiser counsels prevailed under the advice of Locke and others, and no arbitrary change in the weight of the guinea was made from 1670 until the guinea was replaced by the sovereign in 1816. When that was done, the sovereign, or £ sterling—which, as the unit of account, had long been $\frac{20}{21}$ of a guinea—was coined so as to contain $\frac{20}{21}$ weight of the gold which a guinea had previously contained. **The guinea is therefore the foundation of our present gold system.**

3. At the time when it was first coined the king had the right to fix, by proclamation, the weight, fineness, and denomination of all coins, and all gold and silver coins issued by the royal mint were receivable in payment to any amount. But though both gold and silver coins were thus current, silver was the sole legal tender;† and was also in common opinion, as it had originally been in fact, the standard metal; and this opinion, as we shall see, exercised great influence on the course of events.

4. In 1666 an Act‡ was passed, under which the mint was made open to both metals and everyone was entitled to have any quantity either of gold or silver turned into coin. This law continued in force until 1798, with the exception of a few months in 1696. The weight of the guinea was, under the Mint Indenture of 1670, to be at the rate of $44\frac{1}{2}$ to a pound troy of gold. Its value in silver was to be 20s., apparently on the ground that this ratio represented the relative value of gold and silver in the two coins, which, as a matter of fact, it never did.§ The mint rate was not acted on or enforced. It appears to have been the policy of the government to treat gold as subsidiary to silver, and to leave the guinea to find its own value in silver money. At any rate, the public were allowed, without interference by the government, to put their own rate upon the

* *Shaw, p.* 160.
† *Adam Smith, 9th Ed., b. I., p.* 59. *Ricardo Ed.* 1876, *p.* 224. *Jevons, Money, p.* 98,
‡ 18 *Charles II., ch.* 5. *Dana Horton, p.* 230.
§ *Liverpool, p.* 78. *Dana Horton, ch.* 6.

guinea, and it rapidly rose in value—becoming in 1695-6 worth
as much as 30s.* For this rise there were various reasons. The
most important was the state of the silver coin, which by clipping
and waste had become so bad as to lose half its original weight
and value. But this was not the only reason. Gold was becoming
more abundant and cheaper in the markets of the world, and
possibly on this account, and possibly also, as Lord Liverpool
thought,† on account of its greater convenience, people preferred gold.
It is probable that there was also unhealthy speculation in guineas.
**Speculation in the price of gold and silver, disastrous to
all but money changers, has always been the result of past
bimetallism.‡** The consequence of this state of things was
that there was a great import of gold; that all good silver
coins were melted down, hoarded or exported; that there was
a terrible scarcity of silver coin; that no one knew what was the
value of the current silver coin; that all ordinary dealings were
plunged into confusion; and that the value of English money abroad
—in other words, the Foreign exchanges—fell heavily. The first
remedy proposed and adopted was to call in and re-coin the bad
silver money, which, as above stated, was still regarded by the
public, as well as by the highest authorities, as the standard
money of the country. This step, as is known to every reader of
Macaulay, was a step of first rate importance. It was taken on the
advice of very able men, and is said to have cost the country
£2,700,000, a vast sum for those days.§ Nor was this the only step
taken. Orders were made from time to time by the Treasury
fixing and gradually reducing the MAXIMUM amount in silver at
which the guinea should be taken at the public treasuries;‖ and
statutes were passed reducing the MAXIMUM rate in silver at which
guineas should be taken by the public. In 1696 the MAXIMUM silver

* *Dana Horton, App., p.* 238. *Liverpool, pp.* 89, 157.
† *Liverpool, pp.* 92, 154.
‡ *Shaw,* passim.
§ *Lord Liverpool, pp.* 85, 92. *The whole National Revenue in the reign of
Charles II. did not amount to a million and a half.* (*Macaulay, i.* 298.) *The
Revenue from taxes in* 1688 *was between* £1,600,000 *and* £1,700,000. (*Dowell,*
"*History of Taxation," ii., p.* 43.)
‖ *Dana Horton, pp.* 240, 248, 249, 253.

price of the guinea was reduced by statute to 26s., and afterwards to 22s.* In the same year a still more stringent measure was taken. The importation of guineas was forbidden by statute, and the mint was closed against gold.† This statute was, as has been noticed above, only in operation for a few months and was repealed in the following year.‡ In 1697 the Treasury gave notice that they would not receive guineas at more than 21s. 6d., but no guineas were brought in, and in a few days the Treasury directed them to be again received at 22s.§ In 1698 a report of the Commissioners of Trade, signed amongst other persons by Locke, was issued, which, after recommending a further reduction of the rate, sustained that recommendation by the following instructive passage:—"This appears to us the most con- "venient way, because it may at all times be a ready and easy "remedy upon any variation that shall happen in the price of gold, "or even in case this now proposed coining of guineas should not "prove sufficient: **For it being impossible that more than** "**one metal should be the true measure of commerce; and** "**the world by common consent and convenience having** "**settled that measure in silver, gold as well as other** "**metals is to be looked upon as a commodity which,** "**varying in its price as other commodities do, its value** "**will always be changeable; and the fixing of its value in** "**any country, so that it cannot be readily accommodated to** "**the course it has in other neighbouring countries, will be** "**always prejudicial to the country which does so."** ‖

5. The report then proposes to reduce the rate of the guinea to 21s. 6d., which, though not quite so low as the rate in neighbouring countries, will, the commissioners think, "with the addition of costs of coinage, etc., be sufficient to stop the excessive importation of gold." The MAXIMUM rate was accordingly reduced to 21s. 6d., and so continued. But gold was still imported and coined into guineas; and the price which could be obtained for a given weight of silver

---

* 7 and 8 *William III.*, c. 10 and 19. *Dana Horton, pp.* 243, 245.
† 7 and 8 *William III.*, c. 13. *Dana Horton, p.* 244.
‡ 8 and 9 *William III.*, c. 1. *Dana Horton, p.* 247.
§ *Dana Horton, pp.* 248, 249.
‖ *Dana Horton, p.* 252.

bullion continued to be greater than the sum in silver coins into which it was coined at the mint; or, in other words, the market price exceeded the mint price. No private person brought to the mint silver for which he could get a larger price elsewhere ; and the new silver coins, which were more valuable as bullion than as coins, were melted down and exported. **England was stripped of her good silver and the cost of the new coinage was entirely thrown away. Such were the results of the bimetallic system.** This state of things continued till 1717, when Sir Isaac Newton made his celebrated report, in which he pointed out that whilst the guinea passed for 21s. 6d. in England, it was in the market—that is to say, in foreign countries—worth only 20s. 8d., and recommended that 6d. should be taken off and that it should be rated at 21s.* This was accordingly done. In 1718 the guinea was rated by proclamation and by a new mint indenture at 21s., and appears to have been so received by the public.† But the steps thus taken had little or no effect on the state of the currency. Gold was still freely brought to the mint and coined into guineas ; little, if any, silver was brought to the mint ; and there was throughout the last century and down to 1816 a great dearth of silver coin in this country.‡

The coinage of gold and silver in the various reigns from Charles II. to 1816 was as follows :—

	GOLD. £	SILVER. £
Charles II. (1660—1685)	4,672,768 (1667—1685 only in Mint Records.)	... 3,272,311
James II. (1686—1688)	1,659,026	... 386,675
William and Mary (1689—1694) ...	482,342	... 115,895
William III. (1695—1701) ...	3,044,428	... 7,014,047
Anne (1702—1714)	3,128,710	... 530,608§
George I. (1715—1727)	8,115,152	... 229,905
George II. (1728—1759)	11,034,979	... 304,288
George III. (1760—1815)	67,970,181	... 64,625

* *Liverpool, p. 93. See for other reports by Sir Isaac Newton, Dana Horton, pp. 261-271.*

† *Liverpool, p. 95.*

‡ *Liverpool, p. 206 ; Shaw, p. 231 ; Kalkman, p. 64.*

§ *Of this amount, £320,373 was struck at the Edinburgh Mint, in pursuance of the Treaty of Union.*

G

Appended to this paper is a return giving the coinage of gold and silver in each year from 1700 to 1816, when the present system was introduced. It will be seen from these figures that with the exception of the new coinage in William the Third's reign, amounting to £7,000,000, all, or almost all, of which disappeared, there was little or no silver coined from 1700 down to the introduction of the token silver coinage in 1817.

6. Shortly after the middle of the eighteenth century the gold coin, which had become abundant, and was in fact the current coin of the country, had fallen into a very defective condition; the market price of gold bullion exceeded the price in sovereigns given for it at the mint, and the Foreign exchanges fell. In 1774 the defective gold coins were called in and re-issued, a step which was followed by complete success.* The mint price became equal to the market price; the Foreign exchanges rose, and the gold coin remained in the Kingdom. At the same time an Act was passed providing that, for sums above £25, silver should be legal tender not according to the face value of the coin, but according to its actual weight or contents—viz. at 5s. 2d. per ounce.† This Act, important as it has been considered in a theoretical point of view, was probably intended, not so much to depose silver from its rank as the standard metal, as to obviate the defects of the silver coins. It had little practical effect, since little silver coin was current, and all large payments were already made in gold. But in or about 1797 a change occurred in the relative market or outside values of gold and silver. From the time of the introduction of the guinea down to the close of the last century the value set upon gold in England was higher, and that set upon silver was lower than in the outside markets of the world, and the consequence was that gold flowed into England and that silver flowed out of England. But towards the close of the century the production of silver increased, and the balance was changed. According to Soetbeer, the market ratio of gold to silver was 15·27 in the decade 1701–1710, and fell steadily

---

* *Liverpool, p.* 194 ; *Shaw, p.* 233 ; *Kalkman, chap. iv.*
† 14 *Geo. III., c.* 42. *Shaw, p.* 235.

to 14·64 in 1771–1778. From that time it began to rise, and in 1801–1810 reached 15·61, which was considerably higher than the 15·2 which corresponded to the ratio of the guinea at 21s.*

7. Measured by the English standard, silver was becoming the cheaper metal, and if the English law had remained unaltered gold would have flowed out of England and silver would have flowed in. Consequently, and no doubt for the purpose of preventing such a change, the Act of 1774, limiting the character of silver as legal tender (which had been allowed to drop) was revived in 1798–9: the free coinage of silver was suspended,† and remained so suspended until 1816, when our present system was finally established. Under that system **gold became the sole legal standard metal as it had previously been the actual standard.** The sovereign, containing in weight $\frac{40}{41}$ parts of a guinea, became at once both the standard of value, the gold coin in current use, and the unit of account. The mint was and remained freely open to gold; and gold sovereigns were, and remained still, legal tender to any amount. On the other hand, the right to coin silver was confined to the government. The bullion contents of the silver coin were purposely made less in value than · the face value of the coin; and silver coins were made legal tender for forty shillings, but for no more. The provisions of the Act of 1816 were re-enacted by the Coinage Act of 1870.‡ From 1816 silver has been regularly coined, in pursuance of the public demand for silver token coin, at an average amount of half a million sterling a year. During the same period £307,000,000 of gold has been coined, an average annual amount of £3,886,000. It must be remembered, in considering the figures, that whilst the mintage of the standard coin—in this case gold—does not necessarily represent a demand for currency, since gold coins, being equivalent to bullion, are constantly melted down and exported,

---

* *Report of Gold and Silver Commission, Vol. II., App., p. 162.*
† 38 *Geo. III. c.* 59, *continued by* 39 *Geo. III. c.* 75.
‡ 33 *Vict. c.* 10.

G 2

the mintage of token silver coins does represent a real permanent demand for silver currency, since those coins, being more valuable as coin than as bullion, remain in use as coin, and are not melted down or exported.

8. The above are the facts. The lesson they teach has been so much misrepresented that it is worth while to make a few observations on them. **To read bimetallic literature one would suppose that the free coinage of Silver was an inestimable blessing, that the English people really enjoyed it until 1816, or at any rate until 1798 ; and that it was then taken from them by the arbitrary action of gold currency faddists, of whom Lord Liverpool was the chief.* There cannot be a greater travesty of history.** The merit of Lord Liverpool was not that he invented a new Currency Theory; but that he had a true insight into what had long been the actual fact, and that the course he advised adapted legislation to the facts. It is true that by law the mint was open to silver until 1798, but it was open to silver under conditions which in the then state of the market prevented silver from being brought to it. The metal which the people freely bring to the mint to be coined is the metal which constitutes the standard coin, and is the measure of value. A metal which may by law be coined, but which nobody desires to have coined, is as little the standard as a metal which the law forbids to be coined. Gold became our standard because people brought it to the mint to be coined. Silver ceased to be the standard because they did not. This process began at a time when the law favoured neither metal, silver was the acknowledged standard, and the sole legal tender, and when the people were free to put what silver value they pleased upon gold guineas. It is not the fact, as Mr. Gibbs says,† "that the alterations of the Rates which caused the banishment of the silver coin were made from time to time by Orders-in-Council addressed to the mint." The exact

---

* *See Dana Horton's Silver Pound*, passim ; *Gibbs' " Colloquy on Currency,"* p. 271.

† *" Colloquy on Currency,"* p. 273. *See also Foxwell, evidence before Agricultural Commission*, 23, 8267.

opposite was the case. **The over-valuation of the guinea which caused the banishment of the silver coin was the act of the people.** The various acts of the government prior to and including the proclamation of 1717 were all in the direction of reducing that over-valuation. They all placed a MAXIMUM limit on its value ; and it was not till the order of 1717 issued on the advice of Sir Isaac Newton, that a minimum as well as maximum value was placed on it, and that the guinea was actually rated at a fixed amount. The people no doubt placed an extremely high value on the gold coin ; the chief reason for which was probably the bad state of the silver coin. But this was not the only reason. When the silver coins were called in and recoined, at their full weight in silver, people still preferred the gold coins, and the new silver coins were melted down and exported. "But," say the bimetallists, "this would not have been the case had the gold coins been properly rated down to the silver coins." Well, the experiment of rating *down* the gold coin was tried, and the guinea was actually reduced from 30s. or 31s., its highest silver price, first to 21s. 6d., and afterwards, on Sir Isaac Newton's well-known report, to 21s. Still people preferred the guinea ; the guinea was worth more here than it was worth abroad ; silver was worth less here than it was worth abroad ; no silver was brought to the mint and good silver coin still left the country. "Ah ! " say the bimetallists, "this was all the fault of the government. Had they but rated the guinea lower still, they would have succeeded in keeping their silver." But is not this fact the surest evidence that the people would not part with gold? **The authorities wished to keep their silver; but they wished to keep it without losing their gold ; a thing which the operation of the bimetallic law rendered impossible.** The government, advised by the ablest economists, desired to retain silver; they believed silver to be still the standard ; they lowered the rate of the guinea as far as they could ; and they even took the step (but for a few months only) of closing the mint against gold. But further they did not and they dared not go. They either could not or would not put a rate upon the guinea which would deprive people of its use ; a rate which would drive gold abroad and keep silver at home. Whether the government did not wish or did not dare to deprive the people of the use of guineas is really immaterial. The fact remains that they did not take the steps which they knew to be necessary for that purpose, and **gold remained the metal which was the cheaper in the market, which the people preferred, and which consequently became and continued during the whole of the eighteenth century the current coin and the measure of value.**

9. **Gold had thus, before the beginning of the eighteenth century, become the standard coin,** and so far as that coin was concerned no difficulty was felt. The re-coinage of the gold currency in 1774 was completely successful, and was attended by none of the evils which followed the re-coinage of silver in 1695–1699. The inconvenience suffered during the eighteenth century was of a different kind. It was a want of small change due to the fact that under the bimetallic law which opened the mint freely to both metals, silver was not coined, and full-value silver was melted down and exported. Of the real inconvenience thus sustained we who enjoy abundant silver coinage under the law of 1816 can form little conception. For the rich to have no pocket-money with which to pay fares, food, or wages ; for the poor to be deprived of the ready money with which to buy all the necessaries of life, these are evils almost as great as the evils which attend a faulty standard. **And these evils were the inevitable result of the bimetallic law.** The first person who seems to have suggested the true remedy was Sir John Barnard, of Stock Exchange notoriety.* He recommended that the weight of the silver coin should be reduced, so that it should become a token, and that it should not be legal tender. He also proposed that no more silver money should be coined than should be found necessary to make a free circulation of silver coin. Adam Smith, writing in 1776, saw that gold had become the standard, and he saw that it had become the standard in Locke's time, though Locke had never seen it himself. Adam Smith also suggested the over-rating of silver coin as the means of preventing its exportation.†

* " Thoughts on the Scarcity of Silver Coin," 1759   See Kalkman, p. 113.
† See passage quoted in Gibbs' " Colloquy on Currency," App. xxxv.

10. Finally appeared Lord Liverpool's famous letter on the Coins of the Realm.* He had been instrumental in the reform of the gold coinage in 1774, and was a member of the Commission which recommended the suspension of silver coinage in 1798. This letter appeared in 1805, but it was probably written much earlier. It is no doubt the foundation of the reform which was accomplished in 1816. Nor, so far as I can judge, have the bimetallists succeeded in throwing any doubt on the substantial accuracy of his account of the introduction of the gold standard. Whether he does or does not attribute too much importance to the greater convenience of gold as a current coin, and to its greater stability, and whether he gives sufficient weight to the attempts at tariffing gold and silver coin which were made from 1695 to 1717, seem to me immaterial questions. The real point is that when the market was free, gold became over-valued in England, and that the Government, though desirous of retaining silver as the standard, did not venture to stop the free coinage of gold, to under-value gold, or even to rate gold down to the rate which was current abroad. The failure of the attempt to keep both metals in circulation when not rated; the mischievous speculation in gold guineas; the futile attempts at tariffing under the advice of Locke and Newton; the loss of all the newly-coined silver in the seventeenth century; and the dearth of silver money in the eighteenth century; are illustrations of the evils of a double standard. They are also illustrations of the mistakes which Governments make, even when advised by the ablest men, when they attempt a task beyond their proper limits.

The facts given above are undoubted: and what they really show is a steady progress, conscious or unconscious, towards the adoption of a single gold standard, a progress due not solely or chiefly to the arbitrary acts of a Government, but to the wants and habits of the people, and to economical laws which neither Governments nor people can neglect with impunity.

* *See especially Chapter XVII.*

(Note.—For Appendix, see over.)

APPENDIX.

RETURN OF GOLD AND SILVER COINED FROM 1700 TO 1815.

Year.	Gold Coined.	Silver Coined.	Year.	Gold Coined.	Silver Coined.
	£	£		£	£
1700	126,223	14,898	1758	651,814	62,586 ‡
1701	1,249,520	116,179	1759	2,429,010	105
1702	170,172	355	1760	676,231	133
1703	1,596	2,226	1761	550,887	31
1704	Nil.	12,422	1762	553,691	3,162
1705	4,859	1,332	1763	513,041	2,628
1706	25,091	2,889	1764	883,102	15
1707	28,362	{ 3,639 London.	1765	538,272	19
		{ 320,373 Edin. *	1766	820,725	298
1708	47,192	11,628	1767	1,271,808	Nil.
1709	115,317	78,811 †	1768	844,554	Nil.
1710	173,630	2,533	1769	626,582	Nil.
1711	435,663	76,781 †	1770	623,779	68
1712	133,400	5,532	1771	637,796	Nil.
1713	613,826	7,232	1772	843,854	335
1714	1,379,602	4,855	1773	1,317,645	Nil.
1715	1,826,480	5,093	1774	4,685,624	Nil.
1716	1,110,420	5,115	1775	4,901,219	Nil.
1717	709,566	2,939	1776	5,006,350	315
1718	140,632	7,114	1777	3,680,995	Nil.
1719	688,960	5,444	1778	350,438	Nil.
1720	885,859	24,279	1779	1,696,118	254
1721	272,500	7,170	1780	Nil.	Nil.
1722	594,716	6,147	1781	876,795	62
1723	388,098	149,107‡	1782	698,074	Nil.
1724	273,809	5,121	1783	227,083	Nil.
1725	58,360	7,735	1784	822,126	203
1726	872,963	2,592	1785	2,488,106	Nil.
1727	292,779	2,049	1786	1,107,382	Nil.
1728	53,874	2,644	1787	2,890,457	55,459
1729	Nil.	6,370	1788	3,664,174	Nil.
1730	91,628	3,478	1789	1,530,711	Nil.
1731	305,768 -	2,182	1790	2,660,521	Nil.
1732	373,473	2,620	1791	2,456,567	Nil.
1733	833,948	3,580	1792	1,171,863	252
1734	487,108	4,929	1793	2,747,430	Nil.
1735	107,234	3,460	1794	2,558,895	Nil.
1736	330,579	5,310	1795	493,416	295
1737	67,284	3,720	1796	464,680	Nil.
1738	269,837	Nil.	1797	2,000,297	Nil.
1739	283,854	10,528	1798	2,967,505	Nil.
1740	196,245	Nil.	1799	449,962	Nil.
1741	25,231	9,486	1800	189,937	Nil.
1742	Nil.	Nil.	1801	450,242	53
1743	Nil.	7,440	1802	437,019	62
1744	9,812	7,837	1803	596,445	72
1745	292,966	1,860	1804	718,397	78
1746	474,492	136,431 ‡	1805	54,668	183
1747	37,146	4,650	1806	405,106	Nil.
1748	338,523	Nil.	1807	Nil.	108
1749	710,687	Nil.	1808	371,744	Nil.
1750	558,597	Nil.	1809	298,947	115
1751	450,663	8,103	1810	316,936	121
1752	572,657	58	1811	312,263	Nil.
1753	364,876	59	1812	Nil.	53
1754	Nil.	59	1813	519,722	90
1755	224,690	59	1814	Nil.	161
1756	492,983	121	1815	Nil.	Nil
1757	Nil.	16,613			

* Coined in pursuance of the Treaty of Union, Liverpool, p. 91.
† Both coined from plate brought to the mint in pursuance of special arrangements, Liverpool, p. 91.
‡ The exceptionally large silver coinages of 1723, 1746, and 1758, seem, from the records of the mint, to have been also due to exceptional causes.

Is it only England that "Blocks the Way"?*

By the Hon. GEORGE PEEL.

" England, under an erroneous conception of the advantages of a single gold standard, has hitherto stood aloof," *i.e.* from the other Powers who favour international Bimetallism."—*Official Statement of the* BIMETALLIC LEAGUE, para. 14.

"One square mile alone blocks the way," *i.e.* the City of London is alone opposed to International Bimetallism.—Professor F. A. WALKER, *in National Review, August, 1896.*

"I say distinctly that the obstacle in the way of carrying out currency reform does not come from foreign Governments. The obstacle is at home."—Rt. Hon. ARTHUR J. BALFOUR, M.P., *7th February, 1896.*

I. BIMETALLISTS assert, as the above quotations show, that England alone "blocks the way" to the adoption of bimetallism. Even if what they say be accurate, it would not prove that England is wrong. For it may very well be the case that the great statesmen who established us upon a gold standard were right, and that the vast majority of living Englishmen who favour its maintenance are right also. But, passing by this vital question, it remains to enquire whether the bimetallists are correct when they assert as a fact that practically everyone is for bimetallism except ourselves, and that we alone "block the way." One method of testing this is to enquire what happened at the International Monetary Conference held at Brussels in 1892, since that was the last occasion on which

* Issued in January, 1897.

[90]

the European Powers gave official expression to their opinion on this subject. **Is it only England, as bimetallists assert, that "blocks the way"?** It will appear from an examination of the facts that the bimetallists, as so often happens, are in error.

2. The Conference met in the following circumstances :—
" The Government of the United States, having taken measures to
" promote a Conference of the European Powers in order to take into
" consideration the present condition of silver, expressed a wish to
" her Majesty's Government that a ratio might be established by the
" leading nations for the coinage of silver at their several mints. It
" was intimated in reply that her Majesty's Government would not
" be able to accept an invitation couched in such terms."

" The Government of the United States have now proposed a
" Conference of the Powers for the purpose of considering what
" measures, if any, can be taken to increase the use of silver in the
" currency systems of nations. Her Majesty's Government have
" accepted the invitation conveyed in these terms, taking note of the
" statement of the Government of the United States that it does not
" interpose any conditions which will embarrass any Government
" willing to confer generally upon the subject of the proper and most
" advantageous relation of silver to the coinage of the world."*

3. At the opening of the proceedings it might naturally be thought that the Delegation of the United States at once proposed their plan of international bimetallism. Not so. They began by desiring that " the discussion of their own bimetallic " proposal should be postponed till after such subsidiary proposals as " might be brought forward had been considered," and Senator ALLISON concluded his speech by moving as a general resolution, " That in the opinion of this Conference it is desirable that some " measures should be found for increasing the use of silver in the " currency systems of nations." The British Delegation accepted this vague proposal on the ground that it was " merely a recapitu- " lation of the terms of the invitation."

4. **But, in spite of its acceptance by Great Britain, even this abstract resolution had to be dropped, for it aroused at once a storm of opposition. Germany, Austria, and Russia, Roumania, Portugal, Turkey, and Greece would not even vote upon it,** while " the States of the Latin Union, and France " in particular, were, at the outset, at any rate, disposed to criticism

---

* *Instructions for the British Delegates appointed to attend the International Monetary Conference at Brussels (c. 6885).*

" rather than to cordial co-operation with the objects of the Confer-
" ence." * For instance, Count ALVENSLEBEN (Germany) declared
that " Germany, being satisfied with its monetary system, has no in-
" tention of modifying its basis," † while Count KHEVENHÜLLER
METSCH (Austria-Hungary) declared that he could give no opinion
nor take part in a vote.‡ **It was Europe, in fact, which from
the outset was first and foremost to " block the way."**

5. The next important business was to consider the plans of
Mr. MORITZ LEVY and Mr. ALFRED DE ROTHSCHILD. The former
plan, which contemplated the withdrawal from circulation of gold
coins and notes of certain denominations, was not considered important enough to receive really vigorous support, and was finally
abandoned. The latter, after some modifications made by the
Committee to which it was referred, was to the effect that, " The
" European States which agree upon the basis of this proposal will
" buy in each year 30,000,000 ounces of silver, on condition that the
" United States agree to continue their present purchases, and that
" unlimited free coinage be maintained in British India and
" Mexico."§ The Committee, however, declared by a majority,
including all the members of the Latin Union, that even if the
Conference accepted it, they could not recommend the plan to their
respective Governments.

6. During the subsequent discussion of this plan in the Conference Sir RIVERS WILSON summarised the British position on
behalf of himself and Sir CHARLES FREMANTLE as follows :—

" The instructions which we have received from our Government
" require us, before concluding that matters must be left as they are,
" to examine with the greatest care any plan which may be submitted
" for the purpose of extending the monetary use of silver. In order
" to avoid all misunderstanding, I desire, on behalf of Sir Charles
" Fremantle and myself, to make in the face of this assembly our
" profession of faith. Our faith is that of the school of mono-
" metallism, pure and simple. We do not admit that any other
" system than the single gold standard would be applicable in our
" country. The only plans which have as yet been studied by the
" Conference are those of Mr. Moritz Levy and Mr. de Rothschild, and
" we are willing to admit that the adoption whether of one or of both
" these plans would perhaps not be incompatible with the principles
" which we hold. But it is not enough that these schemes would be
" defensible in principle. We have to ask ourselves this question,

---

* *British Report, p. vi.*   † *Proceedings, p. 13.*
‡ *Proceedings, p. 13.*   § *British Report, p. vii.*

" without entering at present upon the discussion of their merits or
" defects—Has either of these plans the least chance of meeting with
" such a preponderance of support as would justify the representatives
" of Great Britain in recommending her Majesty's Government to
" take them into consideration ? So far as concerns Mr. de Roths-
" child's plan, it can hardly be said that it has received such a
" measure of support."*

Finally, Mr. DE ROTHSCHILD stated that he considered it re-
spectful to the Conference to withdraw his plan.

**Thus, here again, it was the general consensus of Europe,
and not England alone, that "blocked the way."**

7. The coast was now clear at last for the bimetallic proposal of
the United States. The first speech was made by Mr. RAFFA-
LOVICH (Russia). He considered, as his countryman Mr. de
Thoerner had stated at the Conference of 1878, that " facts
" have demonstrated that it is contrary to the nature of
" things to attempt to establish a fixed ratio between the value of
" gold and the value of silver." † The monetary history of Russia
had manifested how difficult it was to resist natural forces by laws
and agreements. **"One of the sources of England's strength
" is that she has become the monetary centre of the world,
" the place where you may always be certain of getting
" payment in gold. This is now one of the conditions of her
" greatness; interfere with that certainty, and you will
" break one of the mainsprings of that greatness."** Mr. VAN
DEN BERG (Netherlands), though he was in disagreement with Mr.
Raffalovich concerning the monetary question in general, said that
" As to our foreign credits, I should like to point out, further,
" that they consist almost entirely of drafts on London and Berlin.
" Paper drawn on Paris and Brussels only constitutes a very insig-
" nificant amount ; and why? Because we cannot be sure in
" advance that, when our bills on Brussels and Paris fall due, we
" shall be paid in gold, should circumstances induce us to ask for
" it, without submitting to a premium, to which naturally we object.
" It is this special condition of the money markets of France and
" Belgium which only too often disturbs business, and introduces an
" element of instability which interferes seriously with the liquidation
" of international transactions." ‡

8. Mr. CRAMER-FREY (Switzerland) declared that " No measure,
" then, whatever its nature, could succeed in increasing the effective

* *Proceedings, p. 45.*   † *Proceedings, p. 70.*   ‡ *Proceedings, p. 72.*

" use of silver with us, seeing that, on account of the great weight of
" the metal, banknotes are preferred to it for a sum of any magnitude.
" Any addition would only increase the stores in bank vaults and in
" the public treasuries. Pure bimetallism, that is to say, the free
" coinage of silver, would have the disastrous effect of chasing away
" entirely, or in great part, the gold required by the countries of the
" Latin Union to maintain the gold standard."* Mr. ZEPPA (Italy)
stated that "it is astonishing that persons, admittedly of
" high intelligence and genuine culture, are to be found who
" would wish to lead nations backwards, and to re-establish
" pure bimetallism. There is no human force, no inter-
" national agreement, however numerous the contracting
" States, which can re-establish the old relation between
" silver and gold."† Mr. WEBER (Belgium) concluded a powerful
speech against bimetallism by saying that " the forced circulation
of silver appears iniquitous from whatever standpoint the question is
regarded." ‡

9. Since the specific proposals of Mr. Moritz Levy and Mr. de
Rothschild had been abandoned and the debate on the general
proposal of the United States for bimetallism had begun, a number
of speeches had been made. But, though one of the delegates of
Italy had warmly supported a gold standard, and one of the delegates
of Belgium had strongly condemned bimetallism, and both these
States belonged to the Latin Union, much uncertainty existed as to
the attitude of France towards the bimetallic proposal of the United
States. General Strachey (India) at length requested a categorical
declaration from "the great country at the head of the Latin Union."
Much interest was accordingly felt when Mr. TIRARD (France) rose
to speak, and he was listened to with profound attention, more
especially as the attitude of the French delegates had been one of
great reserve, and their precise views were unknown.

10. Mr. TIRARD promptly declared that "France, under
" present circumstances, has no cause to complain of her
" monetary situation, and she does not complain."§ He
explained the reason why France closed her mint to the unlimited
coinage of silver as follows : "If we ceased to coin silver simul-
" taneously with the other States of the Latin Union, it was be-
" cause we were face to face with a continually increasing volume of
" silver, not only from the growth of its production, but also in conse-
" quence of the transformation of the monetary system of Germany

* *Proceedings, p. 73.*   ‡ *Proceedings, p. 84.*
† *Proceedings, p. 77.*   § *Proceedings, p. 99.*

"All the silver extracted from the mines or demonetised
"elsewhere arrived in France and in the mints of the Latin
"Union; and from this superabundance of metal came
"its depreciation. We ceased to coin it, and I think that
"our course was perfectly right. Mr. Boissevain, with a perse-
"verance which does him honour, Mr. Allard and others, persist in
"thinking that France ought to open her mint to the free coinage
"of silver. But why should France permit the free coinage of
"silver when she is already amply provided with it? I believe that
"she alone possesses as much as all the States of Europe put
"together." *

He then proceeded, "We have heard the Minister of Germany
"and the Minister of Austria-Hungary and then Sir Rivers Wilson
"declare that neither Germany, nor Austria-Hungary, nor England
"had any intention of modifying their monetary systems, with which
"they declared themselves satisfied. Under these conditions we
"evidently cannot re-establish free coinage; and I have not the
"vanity to believe that I should succeed in persuading the Govern-
"ments of these great countries and their eminent representatives
"that they are mistaken, that they have taken the wrong road, and
"that they are in error in remaining attached to monometallism. I
"consider, therefore, until some change takes place, that the question
"of free coinage is decided so far as we are concerned. I hope,
"gentlemen, that I have replied clearly so far as France is concerned,
"to the question which was put to me." †

11. In the course of the discussion which followed, Mr.
HANS FORSSELL (Sweden), ex-Minister of Finance for Sweden, made
a remarkable speech. If, as the bimetallists propose, unlimited
international coinage of silver were resorted to, "The basis of all
"exchanges, of all wholesale commerce, and of all financial opera-
"tions, would be undermined, at the moment when the Bank of
"England, the Bank of France, the Bank of Germany, and the
"Banks of the United States, all gorged with silver, would be forced
"into a struggle to keep the gold which is the necessary instrument
"of their operations. Evidently there would be a struggle, and its
"methods and incidents are well known. Each would pay some-
"thing to be quit of the superfluous and relatively useless silver;
"each would pay something to obtain gold which is sought after and
"relatively more necessary. There you have the premium upon
"gold following infallibly from your system. That is how, even if

"bimetallism embraced the universe, the premium upon gold would
"always issue from the international marriage of free coinage and
"the double standard, the excesses of the one fructifying the vices of
"the other. But the premium upon gold is the upheaval of the
"system, the downfall of universal bimetallism. **Each would
"seek to protect himself from incalculable damage and loss;
"the international treaties would be denounced, free coin-
"age would be suspended, an effort made to get rid of the
"double standard, and liquidation would begin. That
"liquidation is the translation into financial prose of
"the monetary poetry of bimetallism**; and if we should
"have to pay in solid gold for the silver fancies of unlimited
"coinage, we should be staggered by the millions and the thousand
"millions. The liquidation would be more difficult, since with the
"*régime* of international free coinage there would have been no
"relation between the financial resources of each State and the
"amount of money coined with its stamp.

"The States of the Latin Union, and especially Belgium, can
"tell us something of the practical side of the question. Those
"States entered one fine day, full of International confidence, under
"the magnificent arches of a bimetallic system, supported by pillars
"of gold and silver, ranged in a pre-established harmony of $15\frac{1}{2}$.
"But the harmony was disturbed, silver fell; the white pillars were
"transformed into walls which barred the outlet, and they were
"imprisoned. In prison tempers are easily soured, and the Latin
"Union States no longer bless the treaty of 1865.

"**How can it be desired that the European States, with
"eyes opened by these experiences, should willingly enter
"into an international engagement from which there would
"be no retreat? The declarations made here by the dele-
"gates of Germany, of Austria-Hungary, of France, of Great
"Britain, of Italy, of Switzerland, and of Russia—with
"which as delegate of Sweden I would join—have sufficiently
"proved that the European States refuse to do so."** *

12. At the ninth session the discussion upon the bimetallic
proposal was brought to a close. After the declarations which had
been made in the course of the debates, it was felt that it was
unnecessary to proceed to a division, and Senator Allison declared,
on behalf of the United States Delegation, that in the circumstances
they would not press for a vote upon it.

* *Proceedings, p.* 116.

13. At the tenth and last session it was proposed to adjourn the Conference. At this point Mr. BERTRAM CURRIE made a speech, in the course of which he said :—" Three times the delegates of " various nations have met at a Monetary Conference ; on each " occasion they have exhausted their ingenuity in devising plans for " the increase of silver money, and thrice they have been compelled " to separate without accomplishing or even advancing the object " which they had in view. Has not the time arrived when, as men of " the world, and some of us men of business, we should recognise the " fact that the task which was set to them was impossible ? Would " it not be wiser, instead of postponing our decision, to declare " plainly to our bimetallic friends that the plan which they advocate " is no cure for the ills of which they complain, so that, abandoning " vain imaginings and illusive visions which can never become " realities, they may turn their attention to some possible alleviations " of their distress." *

It is perhaps needless to say that the Conference subsequently adjourned, and has not again been summoned.

14. The declarations thus made at the Conference of Brussels have since that date been enforced and illustrated by action. Russia has been actively engaged in establishing a gold standard. So has Austria. As regards Germany, the Imperial Chancellor announced, in February, 1896, that "the Federal Governments have unanimously " determined not to comply with the request for a Conference." Among the other nations, Chile, though occasionally hampered by a somewhat imperfect banking system, has made the gold standard an accomplished fact. Even British Honduras and Santo Domingo have forsaken silver for gold. In fact, the inevitable and resistless tendency of events is against bimetallism.

15. **But, even apart from this, the above official declarations, taken from the document which reported the proceedings of the Conference to the British Government, prove as clearly as it is possible to prove, that what blocks the way to the adoption of bimetallism is the common-sense of Europe, and its practical experience of the working of that disastrous policy.**

* *Proceedings, p.* 197.

The House of Commons and Bimetallism.*

By the COMMITTEE OF THE GOLD STANDARD DEFENCE ASSOCIATION.

" The question whether this country should or should not ultimately adopt Bimetallism within the United Kingdom is left by the resolution a matter for later consideration."—*Statement of the* BIMETALLIC LEAGUE *on the Resolution passed by the House of Commons, 17th March, 1896.*

---

1. THE question of bimetallism was discussed on March 17th, 1896, in the House of Commons. The resolution of the bimetallists had originally stood in the following terms :—

> " That this House is of opinion that the establishment of international bimetallism would be beneficial to the best interests of this country, and urges upon the Government the advisability of doing all in their power to secure by international agreement a stable monetary par of exchange between gold and silver."

But, some days previous to the debate, this resolution was withdrawn, and the following was substituted :—

> ' That this House is of opinion that the instability of the relative value of gold and silver since the action of the Latin Union in 1873 has proved injurious to the best interests of this

---

* *Issued in April,* 1896.

II

country, and urges upon the Government the advisability of
doing all in their power to secure by international agreement
a stable monetary par of exchange between gold and silver."

2. It is obvious that there was a considerable difference
between the two resolutions, for while the former declared
in favour of international bimetallism, the latter omitted any
mention of that particular scheme. The explanation of this
change was given in debate by the seconder of the resolution, Sir
William Houldsworth, who declared that the word " bimetallism " was
kept out of the resolution because there were many who loved the
thing and yet seemed to hate the word. He added that it was
precisely the same resolution in different words, and that it must
be considered a bimetallic resolution. "That explanation," said Sir
William Harcourt, "reminds me rather of the inexpert draughts-
man, who, having delineated some animal, is not confident that all
the world will recognise it, and writes under it 'This is a lion.'"
Even if we accept the interpretation placed upon their resolution by
the bimetallists, it is at least satisfactory to observe that
these motions become less " bimetallic " every year.

3. Had the original resolution remained upon the order book,
those in favour of the ʼgold standard would have opposed it.
But, in the altered circumstances of the case, they decided
that to directly oppose so vague and indeterminate a proposal
would be needless. Accordingly, it was resolved to move an
amendment as definite and as precise in its terms as the resolution was shadowy and uncertain. The amendment was as
follows :—

> " Provided that the country shall not be committed to any inter-
> national engagement which might endanger the maintenance
> of the gold standard in the United Kingdom."

4. It was further agreed that it would be superfluous to move
even this amendment should the Government announce in clear
and unmistakable language that they would not abandon the gold
standard in the United Kingdom. This, indeed, was the actual
course of events. Speaking third in the debate, and immediately
following Sir William Houldsworth, the Chancellor of the Exchequer declared that, in view of the statement just made
that the resolution was to be regarded as bimetallic, he was
to announce on behalf of the Government that "we are not

prepared to abandon the gold standard in the United Kingdom." (Loud cheers.) In view of this satisfactory state-ment the supporters of the gold standard did not move their amendment.

SPEECH OF THE CHANCELLOR OF THE EXCHEQUER.*

The Chancellor of the Exchequer (Sir Michael Hicks Beach) :—About a year ago the House of Commons passed a resolution, which has already been alluded to, to the following effect :—" That this house regards with increasing apprehension the constant fluctuations and the growing divergence in the relative value of gold and silver, and heartily concurs in the recent expressions of opinion on the part of the Government of France and the Government and Parliament of Germany as to the serious evils resulting therefrom.   It therefore urges upon her Majesty's Government the desirability of co-operating with other Powers in an international conference for the purpose of considering what measures can be taken to remove and mitigate these evils." That resolution was accepted by the right hon. gentle-man opposite on behalf of the Government of the day.   It was unanimously approved of by the House of Commons, and I do not think that the House of Commons, and I am certain that her Majesty's Government do not, wish in any way to recede from that resolution. (Cheers.)   The resolution which has now been moved—though perhaps I might criticise some of its terms—appears to me to be in its meaning absolutely identical with the resolution passed last year ; and **I should not have intervened thus early in the debate had not my hon. friend who seconded the resolution stated that in his view it was a bimetallic resolution, though it did not necessarily involve the adoption of bimetallism by this country.**

Looking to the enormous importance of this question, it is right that I should lose no time in expressing my own opinion, holding as I do the important office of Chancellor of the Exchequer, and, what is of far more importance, that I should lose no time in stating to the House the policy which her Majesty's Government think it right to pursue in this matter.   I may congratulate my hon. friend who moved this resolution upon the modesty with which he approached the question. I shall endeavour to imitate him, for I have no sympathy with the confidence with which some persons—and those not always the best informed—lay down the law on one side or the other of this question.   (Hear, hear, and laughter.)   You may hear monometallists speak of bimetallists as if they must necessarily be lunatics or idiots (laughter) ; as if the whole theory which they held must be necessarily so impossible and wrong that it is useless even to argue against it.   On the other hand, you may hear bimetallists who cannot believe that anyone can oppose their favourite theory except on the ground of some selfish interest in con-nexion with the existing system of currency in Great Britain. (Hear, hear.)   I confess that the more I have studied this question the more complex and difficult it has appeared to me. (Cheers.)   I will quote to the House some words in con-nexion with this matter which appeared in the report of the Royal Commission. That commission, composed of very able men, many of whom were experts in the matter which they were considering, stated at the outset of the report :—

"There is hardly any fact connected with the subject on which there are not considerable differences of opinion.   Even if the facts were admitted, there would still remain an element of doubt caused by the uncertainty as to whether we have taken into consideration all the factors necessary to enable a conclusion to be formed ; and in addition to this, the influences which affect the prices and the relative value of the precious metals are so subtle and various that it is difficult, if not impossible, to assign to each its true weight."

In my belief those words are absolutely true. (Cheers.)   It would be a very

*"*Times*" Report, *March* 18th, 1896.*

H 2

wise man who could estimate correctly what has been the exact influence of our system of currency in the past upon the fortunes of this country and of the world. It is not in the power of any of us accurately to foretell and gauge what would be the result of a change in that system. · (Hear, hear.)

As far as I am able to understand the matter, it seems quite impossible to fix a ratio—(cheers)—which shall be absolutely independent of the market fluctuations, between two articles like gold and silver, both of them used for other purposes besides the coinage for which that ratio would be fixed, and one of them capable of being produced in almost unlimited quantities. (Cheers.) But, on the other hand, I do not by any means imply that, if an international agreement of the kind suggested by my hon. friend were undertaken by a sufficient number of nations for the purpose of fixing a ratio between gold and silver for coinage purposes, that agreement would not influence the fluctuations between the two metals, and possibly bring those two metals nearer together in value than they are at present. (Hear, hear.) It seems to me that unless any one is bold enough—as I am not bold enough—to dissent from the unanimous opinion of the Royal Commission, they cannot deny that such an agreement would exercise such an influence. For the Royal Commission reported unanimously that "in their opinion the bimetallic system of the Latin Union exercised a material influence over the relative values of the two metals, and kept the market price of silver approximately steady at the ratio of 15½ to 1." And so, again, take the question, the most important question, of the ratio which should be fixed in any such agreement. I am told that the United States would probably desire that the old ratio of 15½ or 16 to 1 should be adopted. In view of the present market price of silver, it seems to me that to fix any such ratio would be an act of absolute dishonesty to creditors. (Cheers.) It would simply mean that kind of financial panic with all its possible results to the credit of the country which has been in previous debates frequently alluded to by some of the highest authorities. Again, it might be possible, as others have suggested, that the ratio to be fixed should be a ratio approximate to the market value of the two metals at the time the ratio was fixed. All I can say is that, if that were done, and it were subject, as I think it would necessarily have to be subject, to variations from time to time in accordance with the variations of the market price, I do not at all see how any such process would fulfil the vague and extravagant hopes which are entertained by the advocates of bimetallism. (Cheers.)

The very fact of entering into an agreement of that kind would be some danger to the States which entered into it. It would be liable to be broken in the event of political convulsions or in the event of war. If it were broken, what would be the result upon the monetary system of the other States which had joined it? And the very fact that there might be such doubt upon its permanence would materially interfere with its success. But really I do not wish to detain the House by argument upon this question. What I really wish to impress upon the House is its extreme difficulty and complexity, its vast importance to the country— I believe no more important subject to the country can be conceived—and the extreme danger of altering the currency without being absolutely sure that the circumstances warrant it. (Cheers.)

What is the present situation? My hon. friend painted a very dark picture of the condition of the country. It is always agreeable to say we are ruined. (Laughter.) I venture to cast some doubt upon the view of my hon. friend. I should hold, from the information I am able to obtain, that, as a whole, the country was singularly prosperous. ("Hear, hear," from Sir W. Harcourt.) If I look to any of the ordinary sources of information, I fail to gather that the last four years have been the most disastrous years that have ever befallen England. The wealth of the country is very great; it is diffused more generally, perhaps, than in any previous period of our history. (Cheers.) The volume of our trade is enormous, and is increasing and improving since last summer. (Ministerial laughter.) The working classes—though of course there is still, as I fear there always will be, poverty and suffering in the land—are, generally speaking, in receipt of higher wages than they have ever been before—wages which purchase for them far more of the comforts and necessaries of life than they ever did before ; and lastly, perhaps, from my own point of view, I may venture to add I believe there never was a time when any country in the world was better able to bear an enormous burden of taxation with less discomfort to the taxpayer. (Cheers.) Therefore I am bound to say that, if I look to the condition of the country generally, I see no reason whatever that would justify a change in our currency system. (Cheers.)

I admit there are two great interests which are specially suffering. There is first the great interest of agriculture. No one will deny, least of all shall I attempt to deny, that that interest is in a most suffering condition. Then I take it from my hon. friends who have moved and seconded the resolution that the great cotton industry of Lancashire is also suffering. Now, what is the cause of their depression ? I take it that the cause in both cases is low prices. Some would say—Never mind that ; low prices are an inestimable benefit to the nation at large, and if any industry suffers by them that cannot be helped. I cannot accept that view without very considerable limitations. I think that even the stern economy of the right hon. gentleman opposite (Sir W. Harcourt) would be softened by more humane views if low prices, in his mind, involved the ruin of the agricultural industry of Great Britain, or the ruin of the great cotton industry of Lancashire. It is essential for the House to inquire to what causes are those low prices due. Are they due to anything that would be cured by the adoption of bimetallism ? Are they, in other words, due to the appreciation of gold, or to the fall in the value of silver ?

Now, it has been constantly suggested that the low prices of agricultural produce are due to the appreciation of gold, and a few years ago it was generally and perhaps almost universally assumed as a fact that gold had appreciated. A good deal has happened since then. It was considered that the demand for gold exceeded the supply ; that the production of gold was insufficient to keep pace with the demand in consequence of the demonetisation of silver by the adoption of a gold coinage by the principal nations ; that, consequently, it was probable that gold had appreciated ; and that the low prices of certain articles prove that gold had appreciated. Well, I think the first of these views is open to very great question. Is the demand for gold in the coinage of the world greater than the supply ? Now, it is quite certain that the production of gold has very largely increased within the last few years. The production of gold in 1895 was double what it was in 1885, and it stands now at a higher point—the annual production—than it ever reached in the most splendid times of California and Australia. But the question may possibly be rather of the relation between the total stock of gold and the existing demands on it than of the annual production. How does that stand ? There never was a time since 1844 when the stock of gold in the banks was so large as now. The Bank of England is, of course, bound to keep a certain reserve of gold against its note issue. That reserve is, I think, more than double now what it was in 1893. And if I were to pursue the inquiry into the great European banks, I think I should be met with the same result. Does that mean that there is a scarcity of gold ? **There is no scarcity of gold.** (Cheers.) **Does it mean that the gold is kept by the banks instead of being diffused through the country and improving trade ?** Well, the rate of discount never was so low. And yet it is a very remarkable fact that the same year which has shown this enormous and unprecedented stock of gold in the vaults of the Bank of England also shows the lowest prices on record. I find that the index number of the *Economist* newspaper, which was 2,235 on January 1, 1890, was reduced to 1,999 on January 1, 1896, showing a fall of 10 per cent. in prices. I doubt very much —but I speak of this with great diffidence, because it is a very obscure subject—whether in such a country as this prices are affected to any extent by the volume of our metallic currency. (Hear, hear.) **I think the effect of metallic currency on prices varies inversely with the banking facilities of any country,** and I agree with the words which were used by the right hon. gentleman opposite last year, when he said that " metal with us is the measure of value. It is not the instrument of trade. We conduct our trade, the greatest in the world, on the smallest metallic basis of any country, because we have the largest trade."

But let me turn to the other aspect of the question. **Can it be proved that the fall in the price of certain articles of agricultural produce is due to the appreciation of gold?** Now I think if it were due to the appreciation of gold, surely the fall of value in the prices of articles would be universal and would be uniform. But that is absolutely contrary to the fact. (Cheers.) There are some articles of agricultural produce which have fallen very largely. Wheat has fallen 50 per cent. comparing the prices of the decade between 1865 and 1875 with the prices between 1891 and 1895. Other articles have fallen less—barley 32 per cent., oats 25 per cent., wool 26 per cent. The best classes of beef and mutton have fallen much less ; mutton has fallen only 8 per cent. Cheese has fallen 15 per cent., butter 10 per cent., hay 16 per cent., straw and poultry not at all—I believe poultry has actually risen. May not there be a reason for this fall in prices which has absolutely nothing whatever to do with any question of the appreciation of gold? Surely the fall has been, as Mr. William Henry Smith said in this House nine years ago, in the articles of which the production is practically unlimited, and not in the articles of which the production is practically limited. **The fact is this— that the fall in these articles is due to foreign competition** (cheers), and foreign competition is due, first, to peace, which has enabled greater industry to be used in their production ; secondly, to the more efficient use of capital ; thirdly, perhaps to the use of the telegraph ; fourthly, to the vast extension of railways in new countries—in America, in the Argentine Republic, in Russia, and in India— which has brought the produce of these countries to the sea ; lastly, and perhaps most of all, to the wonderful improvements in our mercantile marine, in the size of ships, in the cheapness of the working of marine engines, so that in fact the harvests of the world can now be brought from the places where they are produced to the very door of any country that may require them almost as cheaply as if they were produced in that country itself. Let me ask the House to observe that this is true mainly and mostly of certain articles. It is true of corn, because corn is an article which is specially adapted for production by unskilled labour in new countries. It is true of wool because of the enormous increase in the flocks of sheep in Australia and other parts of the world. But it is not so much true by any means of articles which require more skilled labour to produce them, or which are more of a perishable nature. And when you come to articles like, for instance, straw, which is extremely bulky, and the cost of the transport of which would be out of all proportion to its value, there you find an article which has not fallen in value at all. I think I have said something to show that **there are great and important causes to which the fall in the price of agricultural produce, which has been so injurious to the farming industry of this country, is due, rather than to any idea of the appreciation of gold.** But then I turn to what may be due to the fall in the price of silver. It has often been argued that the fall in the price of silver has brought Indian wheat into very serious competition with wheat grown in this country. That may be true to some extent ; but **this is a fact, that the imports of agricultural products from silver-using countries are now only 2 per cent. of the total amount of agricultural produce imported into this country which competes with agricultural produce grown at home,** and the Indian harvests cannot be—both from the varying amount of their exportation and from the total amount that could be exported—anything like as potent a factor in determining the price of wheat in the world as the harvests, for instance, of Russia or of the Argentine Republic. I find that in the year 1894 only half the amount of wheat was exported from British India that was exported in the previous year ; and I find that the amount exported in 1894 was very little higher than the amount exported in 1877, when silver was nearly double the price at which it stood in 1894. (Cheers.)

My hon. friend who seconded this motion said a great deal about the effect of the low price of silver in silver-using countries in the East upon the competition of these countries with Lancashire. I think he referred mainly, if not entirely, to the cotton industry of Lancashire. I very much question whether other trades have complained of this competition, and if they have not I should very much like to know why. Why is it that the cotton industry of Lancashire is the particular trade that complains of this competition—because if there is this great importance attached to the bounty that may be due to the fall in the value of silver, surely it would apply to other trades besides the cotton industry? But this, at any rate, I believe to be the fact, that the cotton industry of Lancashire is not quite expiring. I am informed that the number of spindles and looms is increasing in Lancashire. (Mr. G. Whiteley: It is very much less.) That is the information that has reached me. I am also informed that the wages of the operatives employed in the cotton industry are better than they were. (Mr. G. Whiteley: They are 10 per cent. below the standard list.) I believe the fact is that more of the profits of the industry go into the pockets of the operatives than before, and less into the pockets of the masters. That might be a fact to be regretted if it led masters to abandon the cotton industry. But why should they abandon the cotton industry? Is the trade with silver countries in the Lancashire cotton trade a losing one? If it is, I am curious to know why our exports of cotton goods to these silver-using countries is increasing by a percentage three times as large as the percentage of increase in the trade between Lancashire and other countries that are not silver-using. (Hear, hear.) I do not at all wish to underrate the importance, whatever it may be, of the fall in silver in the competition between Lancashire and the East in this matter, but I believe the danger of the competition—and I believe it to be a very real danger —is more due to other causes. I believe it is due, in the first place, to the fact that the cotton is nearer at hand there; in the second place, to the fact that the market is on the spot ; in the third place—and by far the greatest of all—to the extreme cheapness of the labour. That labour is probably made more cheap by the effect of the bounty on the fall in silver, and therefore the competition becomes harder. I admit to that extent the fall in silver has been an evil.

The fluctuations in the value between silver and gold have also been an evil owing to the difficulties which they have caused in the rate of exchange between gold-using and silver-using countries. We may wish, all of us, that there will be only one standard in the whole civilised world ; but I am afraid that is a dream that is not likely to be realised. But even the influence, injurious though it may be, on commerce of the fluctuations of the rate of exchange has certainly been minimised by the operations of the exchange banks. What, after all, is the great difficulty in this question as it effects ourselves, is the influence of the fall in silver upon the fortunes of our great dependency of India. I think it has always been admitted by all parties in this House that the great fall of silver has been a serious evil and difficulty to the Government of India. A few years ago the Government of India took the step of closing the mints against the free coinage of silver. Since that time, they have, to a great extent, achieved what I imagine was their object in preventing the fall of the rupee. But there was this remarkable result— the price of silver has very largely fallen, and every year there is an increasing divergence between the market value of the coined rupee and the real value of the silver which is in that rupee. In fact, India now has an inconvertible, appreciated currency. (Hear, hear.) That is not a position—however much relief it may have given for a time to the Government of India—which, I think, can be held to be a satisfactory or final solution of this great question. (Cheers.) I therefore do believe that, in the matters which I have alluded to, there are, as this motion states, evils affecting this country and our Indian Empire in the present low value of silver, and we are perfectly ready, as we have always been, to join with foreign countries in a conference as to the best way in which those evils may be alleviated.

But I would wish to say that there is a part of the Empire which is not included in the United Kingdom, and which is not included in India, which has great interests in this matter besides ourselves. I refer to our Colonial Empire. (Hear, hear.) We have in the United Kingdom a population of 38,000,000. Our colonies have a population of 20,500,000. Of these no less than 15,500,000 are on the basis of a gold standard, with imports and exports in 1893 of 227½ millions sterling—four-fifths of the total colonial foreign trade. That includes all the great self-governing colonies and the bulk of the Crown colonies. On the other hand, there are silver currency colonies, containing a population of

1,500,000, and with a trade of 48 millions sterling ; and there are colonies with the peculiar rupee currency of India, containing a population of 3,500,000, and with a trade of 12 millions sterling. It is obvious that in dealing with this question the interests of our gold-standard colonies cannot, and ought not, to be neglected. (Cheers.) And let the House remember that each and every one of these colonies, whether it be a self-governing colony or a Crown colony, is, and I think always has been, perfectly free to choose its own currency for itself. Therefore, vast as the population of India is, great as are the interests of our Indian Empire, you have, I will venture to contend, even apart from the United Kingdom, enormous interests on the other side. (Hear, hear.)

What is the policy which as a Government we intend to pursue ? As I have said, we are willing, we are anxious, seeing that there are evils in the present low value of silver and in the fluctuations in the value of the two metals, to enter into a conference, or into negotiations, which certainly I believe at the present stage would be much better than a conference, with other countries upon this subject, but **we are not prepared to abandon the gold standard in the United Kingdom.** (Loud cheers.) I have expressed, I think, very frankly my own opinions on this important subject to the House, but it is very well known that there are some of my colleagues who do not agree in these opinions, and who, like my right hon. friend the First Lord of the Treasury, are confirmed and pronounced bimetallists. (Hear, hear.) **But we all agree in this, that we should not be justified in proposing or accepting a departure from the gold standard of the United Kingdom.** And why ? Let me read the words which were used by my right hon. friend the leader of the House in 1890. He said :—" Nothing can be done, nothing should be attempted, which is against the views and the wishes of the great practical financiers and bankers of this country. It would be folly and madness in any Government to go in advance of the educated commercial opinion of the country in this matter. **We cannot, therefore, alter the gold standard of the United Kingdom,** but, with that reservation, we are prepared, in the words of the resolution, 'to do all in our power to secure by international agreement a stable monetary par of exchange between gold and silver.' "

What are the prospects of any such agreement ? I fear they are not very brilliant. (Cheers.) **It will be remembered that in the Conference of 1892 the United States proposed a bimetallic resolution. It was opposed by Germany, by the Scandinavian nations, by Switzerland, and by Austria, who declared themselves gold monometallists.** France and the Latin Union were only prepared to accept it if Great Britain, Germany, Austria, and Russia would join the union, so that the resolution fell to the ground, and the vital question of what the ratio should be in the event of such an international agreement was never even touched. (Hear, hear.) We made suggestions for increasing the use of silver. They were discouraged and withdrawn. If it be possible for other nations to be joined in a bimetallic league or in an agreement on this matter, which seemed good to themselves, I have little doubt but that the Indian Government would be prepared to agree with us in reopening the Indian mints to the free coinage of silver, and that we might endeavour by other minor means to promote the increase of silver in coinage to aid in an international agreement on this great question. But we can go no further. (Cheers.) This great capital is the monetary centre of the world. (Cheers.) Our trade and commerce are probably greater than any other country has ever enjoyed. Our wealth is enormous. It arises from investments and enterprise in every quarter of the globe, and **the great majority of the men, able and experienced financiers, who control the working of this gigantic machine, are of opinion that it has been built up on a gold standard, and that its permanence depends upon the maintenance of our monetary system.** (Cheers.) **With that opinion before us no responsible Government of this country could take any other course than that which I have indicated.** (Loud cheers.)

The Probable Effects of Inter= national Bimetallism.*

By the Rt. Hon. G. SHAW - LEFEVRE.

"The aim of the Bimetallic League, as already mentioned, is to secure, by international agreement, the opening of the mints of the leading commercial nations to the unrestricted coinage of silver and gold at such fixed ratio as may be mutually agreed upon amongst those nations."—*Official Statement of the Bimetallic League, para. 11.*

---

1. It will be admitted on all hands that before taking so important a step as that of endeavouring, in concert with other Powers, to fix by international arrangement, having all the force of law, the relation between gold and silver, it will be well carefully and fully to consider :—

(*a*) What is the exact nature of the scheme.

(*b*) How it is to be carried into effect.

(*c*) What the probable results would be.

With respect to (*a*), it is difficult to arrive at any conclusion in the absence of a definite scheme on the part of the bimetallists. **Everything depends on the ratio which it is intended to establish between the two metals. On this point the bimetallic leaders appear to be either hopelessly ambiguous or suspiciously silent.** †

2. The theoretical bimetallists, who have persuaded themselves that the alleged instability of prices of late years is due to the disuse

---

* *This paper has not previously been issued.*

† *See Appendix A.*

of silver by many countries, to the consequent appreciation of gold, and to the difficulties of exchange between the gold-using countries in the West and the silver-using countries in the East, are generally silent, but would possibly be satisfied by adopting the ratio existing between the two metals at the time when the international arrangement is decided upon, and stereotyping that ratio for the future.

3. The practical bimetallists—those who are interested in raising the prices of their commodities, in reducing the value of their gold debts, or in raising the value of silver—are generally in favour of an effort to return to the ratio which existed between gold and silver before the great change in their relative value which began about 1873.*

4. There is a third party, represented by Professor Foxwell and others, who are in favour of what they call "the climbing ratio." They propose to fix the ratio at first at something less than the existing one, and by degrees and at intervals of time, presumably at the discretion of a majority of the Powers concerned in the arrangement, to raise the agreed ratio of silver to gold till after a term of years it should at last reach the point agreed upon.

5. The bimetallists do not tell us how a selection between these three methods is to be made ; whether the determination is to be arrived at by a majority of the Powers who will be parties to the new arrangement ; or whether this country before entering upon a congress for the purpose is to lay down its conditions on this point.

6. **Of the three methods above noticed, it appears that the second is the one which has the approval of a majority of the bimetallists. It is the only one on behalf of which large personal interests are ranged.** It will be well, then, to consider this scheme of bimetallism in the first instance before dealing with the other alternatives.

It will be obvious that there is an immense practical difference between this, the most extreme proposal of bimetallists, and the other extreme of adopting the existing ratio. Silver before 1873 averaged about 60d. per oz. It is now worth about 26d. per oz.† Its value, therefore, must be raised over 100 per cent. in order to revert to the former ratio.

Let us suppose, then, that the principal Powers of the world should come to the conclusion that it will be wise to adopt a general

---

* *See Appendix B.*
† *May, 1898.*

bimetallic system on the basis of the ratio between gold and silver
which existed before 1873, and under which silver will be raised in
value relatively to gold by over 100 per cent. How are they to effect
their object? By what sanction can they secure the arrangement
being carried out effectively and honestly by the different Powers
concerned? How will the arrangement affect past and future
contracts between individuals?

7. It is necessary to consider in the first place the nature and
form of the agreement which would be come to by the Powers. We
must presume that it would take a form somewhat as follows:—

"It is hereby agreed that from and after a certain date an
ounce of gold shall be the equivalent of fifteen ounces of silver,
and an ounce of silver shall be the equivalent of one-fifteenth of
one ounce of gold, and that all the Powers shall agree to maintain by their municipal laws and by their monetary arrangements
this ratio, and for this purpose shall agree to purchase and coin
all gold and silver which may be tendered to them, and to issue
in exchange such coins as full legal tender at the above ratio;
and shall further by law provide that all debts now existing in
any country having a gold standard shall be payable in gold or
silver coins at the option of the debtor; and all debts existing
in countries with a silver standard shall be payable in gold or
silver coins at the option of the debtor; and all contracts in
countries having any form of currency, whether in paper or
coin, which are now payable in gold shall in future be payable
in gold or silver at the option of the debtor; and it is also
agreed that all Powers who are parties hereto will receive in
gold or in silver coins at the agreed ratio any customs dues
or taxes, and that they will enact laws to the effect that any
person now holding a bill of exchange or note of any kind
payable in gold shall be bound to accept in payment
thereof when presented either gold or silver coin, at the
agreed ratio, at the option of the person bound to pay under
such bill or note. And it is further agreed that the Powers
which are parties hereto shall by law enact that all contracts
hereafter to be entered into for payment of any sum or sums
in gold may be payable at the option of the parties thereto in
silver or gold as they may find convenient."

**It is submitted that this, or something closely ap-
proaching it, must be the form of the international
agreement between the various Powers concerned,** in

order to effect the required object—the establishment of an agreed ratio between gold and silver on the basis of their relative value before 1873. **The mere statement of the form of an agreement must, I think, be sufficient to demonstrate the absurdities involved in the attempt and the impossibility of giving effect to it.**

8. Assuming however, that such an agreement could be carried out, let us consider what would be its effect. There cannot be a doubt that the first effect would be to raise the value of silver as measured in gold by over 100 per cent. All silver securities would also be doubled in value. It is difficult to conceive the extent of the speculation to which the mere prospect of such an enhancement of value would give rise. Silver would be bought up in every part of the world. There would be immense importations of Indian rupees and Mexican dollars in prospect of such a change.

9. What, however, will be the effect of the new joint currency of silver and gold? It is most difficult to form any opinion on the subject. Leading bimetallists now say that they do not want or intend to raise prices. If so, they will grievously disappoint the main body of their supporters, who are bimetallists only because they hope to raise the prices of their products. The effect of the change will be that, if gold is not largely withdrawn from circulation for hoarding, there will be a great increase in the metallic currency of the world by just so much silver as is available for the purpose. The great hoard of silver in the United States Treasury, amounting to 100 million pounds in value, will become available as currency more effectively than at present. The same will be the case with the hoards of silver in the banks of France and Germany; and incidentally it may be said that these three great hoards will be doubled in saleable value as measured in gold. Beyond this there must be accumulations of silver in the world which would soon find their way to the banks of Western powers to be turned into currency. To what extent this would be the case it is impossible to predict. Further a great impetus would also be given to the production of silver. Old mines which have ceased to be worked in consequence of the fall in value of the metal would be re-opened; other mines would be extended, and new mines would be opened.

10. **It is by no means clear, however, that the immediate effect would be a rise in prices. What is certain is that there would be vast speculations** in view of a possible ultimate rise of prices due to the increase of currency. There would also be

a run on the banks and savings-banks, in order to obtain gold, and to invest it in the purchase of produce and stocks that would be likely to rise in value. It is to be recollected also that holders of gold stocks or depositors in banks of money now payable in gold would have the prospect of having their interest and principal sums payable in silver. It will be difficult, if not impossible, to persuade them that under the new law the silver will be equal in value to the gold. **There would, therefore, be all the elements of a widespread and most dangerous panic, which might endanger the financial position of the government of this and other countries and their principal banks.**

11. If, as the result of this, gold should be hoarded, and withdrawn from circulation, it is probable that, for a time at least, the rise of prices of other commodities would not only be stemmed, but reversed. The fear of creditors that they would, on the passing of such a law, be paid in silver, instead of in gold, would lead them to make a rush for gold. Credit would be destroyed, and with credit would collapse the largest and most important part of our present medium of exchange. Cheques and bills would be useless, because no one would know what they meant. If this were to happen purchases of all kinds would be suspended, and there is no knowing to what point prices might not fall. **To create a panic is the surest way of stopping demand and lowering prices.**

12. This would be the probable immediate effect of such a scheme of bimetallism as I have described, if it were fully carried out. But bimetallists have not the courage of their opinions.

The prospect of a panic among the savings-bank depositors on the part of the great multitude of people who would be unable to believe the essential principles of bimetallism, and who would dread the prospect of being paid in the future in silver at half the present value of the gold due to them, has apparently been appreciated by the bimetallists, for their principal scientific advocate, Professor Foxwell, in his evidence before the Agricultural Commission, has admitted that it might be necessary to provide that the savings-bank depositors should be paid in gold, if they demand it, even after the new system has come into effect.* But if this be conceded in the case of savings-bank depositors, it must be conceded also in the case of ordinary depositors in other public and private banks ; for the danger of a run on the banks would be nearly as great as in the case of

* *See Appendix C.*

savings-banks. When exceptions of this kind are once made, the essential principle of the scheme is destroyed; for if the State and the banks are bound to pay in one of the two metals, namely, gold, without any option on their part to pay in silver, there must at once arise a demand for gold above that for silver, and it will be impossible to maintain the ratio, whatever it may be, that may be decided on.

13. **The bimetallists appear also to have equally little the courage of their opinions in the case of existing contracts where it is expressly provided that payment of interest or principal shall be in gold,** and also in future contracts of the same kind. Professor Foxwell, in his evidence, has admitted that it would not be possible in the case of such contracts to override them by the bimetallic arrangement, and to provide that they shall be payable in silver at the option of the debtor.* He admits the same with regard to future contracts.† But what difference is there in principle between a contract in a country where the law provides that all payments shall be in gold and a contract in some South American republic where, in order to provide against possible depreciation of the currency, it has been specially provided that payment of interest and principal shall be in gold? The contracts made in a gold-standard country, under the conditions of existing laws, are quite as sacred as contracts made elsewhere in gold, where there is no security at law for payments in gold.

If, however, all contracts past and future specified in gold, and all past contracts in gold-standard countries are to be exempt from the rule of optional payment in silver, the whole scheme of bimetallism practically falls to the ground; for it is clear that future contracts would be made subject to the condition that payment will be in gold and not in silver.

14. It may, indeed, be confidently expected that in such case bankers and merchants would decline to be parties to a bimetallic system. They would refuse to receive anything but gold or its equivalent, and they would pledge themselves to pay only in gold, thus nullifying the law so far as it aimed at putting silver on a par with gold. There is a precedent for this in the action of the bankers and merchants of California during the American

* *See Appendix D.*   † *See Appendix E.*

Civil War in 1862–64, when they refused to receive from their depositors paper or greenbacks of the Washington Government as currency, and continued to make their bargains and carry on their business on a gold basis.* If bankers and merchants in England were to adopt this course, the scheme of bimetallism would practically be inoperative so far as this country is concerned.

15. It is possible, and even probable, that this boycotting of the system by bankers and merchants would take place even if the law provided that all contracts, present and future, should be payable in either silver or gold at the established ratio; although the difficulties and confusion attending such a conflict between law and practice would be far greater. It is certain, however, that in the event of its being made illegal to contract out of the bimetallic system, a vast and dangerous speculation would take place, and that a widespread feeling of want of confidence would result, and that there would be a general run upon the Government in respect of savings-bank and Post Office deposits, and that a monetary crisis would ensue beyond any in the past in its far-reaching effects. **It would probably result in the hoarding of gold on a vast scale.** States would hoard it as a resource in the event of war; for gold would be far more efficient in time of war than silver. Bankers and merchants would hoard it in amounts far beyond their present reserves. Individuals would hoard it through fear of being compelled to receive their deposits in the savings-banks or in private banks in a depreciated metal such as silver. Gold, in fact, as the Gresham law has proved in the past, would disappear from the currency and silver would take its place.

16. Apart from all the other evils attendant on such a state of things, I cannot but think that the effect of this would be not only to neutralise any tendency for prices to rise owing to the addition to currency caused by the rehabilitation of silver, but to make them fall, at all events for a time. **Prices would certainly fall in the case of a general panic; and how far they would ultimately rise again is extremely uncertain.** .

17. If, on the other hand, prices should rise, as many bimetallists hope and desire, the effect will be that labourers and other consumers of articles in which the fall in the past has been greatest will have to pay more for their food and clothing. After a time wages might accommodate themselves to the new conditions

* *This was also the case with ourselves when we were adopting the gold standard in the seventeenth century.*

of currency, and might rise in proportion to the rise in the prices of commodities ; but in the meantime the effect would be that labourers and consumers generally would be taxed for the benefit of profits of all producers and manufacturers and of the rent of agricultural land.

18. After the adjustment of wages had taken place in the new currency, things would be much as they were before the change so far as labourers, producers, and landowners are concerned. The relation of foreign imports to home produce would not ultimately be materially affected or prejudiced. Trade being essentially a matter of barter, means would be found of accommodating it to the new currency ; and to whatever extent low prices have been due to the opening out of new districts by improvements and inven· tions of all kinds, these conditions would still exist, and prices of raw products and food, though nominally higher when expressed in the new bimetallic currency, would still be low in proportion to other prices and to the wages of labour, and profits of farmers and other producers and manufacturers would be no better than at present.

19. I have hitherto considered the alternative of fixing the ratio between gold and silver at that existing before 1873. The other alternative of fixing it at the ratio existing at the time of the change would not be open to so many immediate dangers and difficulties. There would not be the same temptation to gigantic speculation in silver securities in prospect of the change. There would not be so great or so immediate an alarm on the part of depositors in savings-banks and other banks at the prospect of receiving their interest and principal in a depreciated currency. There would not be the same temptation to hoard gold. On the other hand, all the arguments as to the ultimate rise in price of commodities as measured in the new currency would equally apply, and there might be many inducements to great speculation in prospect of this rise.

20. There remains the question which arises both on this and on the previous alternative : whether it would be possible to maintain the ratio agreed upon. There is authority for the view that the ratio could be maintained. In spite of this I venture to hold that it would not be maintained. Gold must always have a greater value for all practical purposes than silver. International balances of trade must eventually be settled on the basis of the metallic currency, and for the purpose of settling these balances gold is and must be, on account of its less weight, far more con· venient than silver. If a merchant can find no other means of

meeting his engagements in another country than that of transmitting coin, he will naturally prefer gold to silver, for the freight of silver will be twenty times that of gold. Bankers also who have to keep a reserve of coin will necessarily prefer a reserve of gold to one of silver. The storing of silver will be twenty times more costly than that of gold ; and all processes of counting and paying gold over the counter will be simpler and easier in the same proportion. States also which contemplate being at war in the future will always prefer to keep their hoards in gold rather than in silver. It may confidently be expected, then, that there will always be a greater demand for gold than for silver, and therefore a premium on it, whatever may be the agreed ratio between the Powers.

If, then, any single State like our own should honestly endeavour to observe the agreement and receive silver equally as gold, and pay out gold when demanded on equal terms with silver, it would soon find itself with silver only, and all its gold would slip away and find its way to those countries and banks where the scheme of bimetallism would not be observed, and where a small premium would be given for gold.

21. Again, what possible sanction is there, or could there be, for the enforcement of the arrangement agreed to by all the Powers upon any Power which might find it its interest to depart therefrom ? Supposing a small State like Holland were to declare that it would only receive or pay in gold at its national bank, and that it would decline to pass municipal laws to compel its citizens to accept silver on the agreed term of liquidation of any contract, how would the other Powers deal with such a case, and how could they enforce their agreement upon the delinquent State ? It is easy to see that such a State might derive enormous advantage from making itself an exception and dealing only in gold.

What, further, is to prevent any State departing from the arrangement in another direction, namely, by issuing inconvertible paper money to an amount which would drive the bimetallic currency out of its country ? There is and could be no international sanction to prevent this.

22. **An objection perhaps even more formidable than those above noticed is to be found in the possible and even probable boycotting of any such scheme by merchants and bankers.** Trade is a matter of habit and convenience. Traders have become accustomed to measure their dealings in gold sovereigns. Will they abandon this custom ? Will they adopt a mixed standard

1

of gold and silver because the law says that so many ounces of silver shall be equivalent to one ounce of gold? Contrast the two formulæ :—

(*a*) I promise to pay 100 gold sovereigns.

(*b*) I promise to pay either 100 gold sovereigns or as many silver coins as will be equal in weight to *x* times 100 sovereigns, whichever of the two may happen to be the cheaper at the time of payment.

Which of these two formulæ will traders naturally prefer? Which of them will a seller or a borrower, or even a buyer or a lender, who looks to certainty and simplicity, seek to do business in? Can there be a doubt? And if traders continue to prefer the simple and convenient form of contract to which they are accustomed will they not cling to it and use it in spite of any law of legal tender to the contrary? If so, the bimetallic scheme will be futile except for the purpose of creating a most mischievous conflict between law and practice.

23. **It is scarcely worth while to consider seriously the intermediate proposal of Professor Foxwell and others of a "climbing ratio,"** starting at the existing ratio between gold and silver, and gradually over a term of years changing so as to return ultimately to the ratio of 1873. It is impossible to conceive a scheme fraught with more confusion, or with more violent causes of speculation. Whether the stages of this climbing ratio are to be determined in advance or to be defined from time to time by the Powers who would be entrusted to make the bimetallic arrangement, the scheme is equally objectionable or impossible, and it is difficult to conceive how such a scheme can commend itself to anyone of sound judgment.

24. The only possible course would be for the Powers to determine on a ratio which should take effect at once, and which should not be departed from except by general consent. This ratio may be fixed at any point between the two extremes, viz. the old ratio existing before 1873 and the ratio existing at about the time of the change. I have argued the question on the two alternatives at the two extremes. Any intermediate ratio would be open to all the objections raised to the proposal of adopting the ratio of 1873, though in lesser degree as the ratio approaches the other end of the scale.

25. It is difficult to believe that any statesman could be so unwise as to submit to the determination of a majority of a congress composed of the representatives of all countries a question so vitally

affecting our own as that of the ratio to be adopted on the suppo-
sition that bimetallism in some form is practically desirable and
possible. If we should agree to accept a scheme of bimetallism to
which all the Powers should give their assent in detail as well as in
principle, we might safely enter into such a congress with the
absolute certainty that it would never, within any conceivable limit
of time, come to any unanimous opinion as to the details of the
scheme, the ratio to be adopted, and the sanction by which the
scheme is to be enforced upon delinquent States.

**But such a congress, though impotent for the purpose for
which bimetallists desire it, would be fraught with much
evil. It would prolong the state of doubt and hesitation
which, as we see in the case of the United States, is a very
serious impediment to trade, industry, and progress.**

APPENDIX A.

The following extracts from the leading bimetallic authorities
illustrate their ambiguity or silence as to the ratio :—

MR. H. H. GIBBS (LORD ALDENHAM), *President of the* BI-
METALLIC LEAGUE, *in reading a paper on May 3rd*, 1894, *upon*
"THE PRINCIPLES UPON WHICH AN INTERNATIONAL RATIO SHOULD
BE FIXED," *said :—*

"I do not mean to tell you more precisely what the ratio should be, because
I do not know."

SIR WILLIAM HOULDSWORTH, BART., M.P., *Vice-President of the*
BIMETALLIC LEAGUE *and Chairman of the* PARLIAMENTARY COM-
MITTEE, *in reading a paper before the* MANCHESTER STATISTICAL
SOCIETY *on April 20th*, 1898, *said :—*

"They (the bimetallists) were willing to accept any ratio that might be
decided upon."

The official statement of the BIMETALLIC LEAGUE *is silent as to the
ratio, and merely says (paragraph* 11) :—

"Such fixed ratio as may be mutually agreed upon."

PROFESSOR F. A. WALKER, *in* "INTERNATIONAL BIMETALLISM"
(*p.* 211), *says :—*

"It is not my purpose to discuss the question of the ratio."

MAJOR LEONARD DARWIN, *at the close of his work on* "BI-
METALLISM " (1897), *says (p.* 337) :—

"This question of the ratio has to be fought out ; and, until it is decided, probably no real advance can be made in the bimetallist cause ; certainly no clear
understanding can be established as to the objects to be striven for."

I 2

APPENDIX B.

The following extracts show that, however vague or reticent most bimetallic authorities may be, bimetallists as a body generally favour the ratio of 16 or 15½ to 1 :—

MR. HENRI CERNUSCHI, *speaking on May 2nd, 1894, at the Mansion House, said :—*

"Either it will be stipulated that in Europe and the United States gold shall be money at the ratio of 1 to 15½ of silver, or nothing will be stipulated."

The *Economist,* July 6th, 1895, states that at a conference of the French and German bimetallists a resolution was passed adopting the ratio of 1 to 15½.

MR. ERNEST SEYD *wrote in the " Times" of August 19th, 1895, that :—*

"With very few exceptions all the older supporters of the double valuation are unanimous in favour of what you will, perhaps, permit me to call the natural market ratio of 15½ to 1."

During the course of the Wolcott negotiations in 1897 it was stated, "that the French Government preferred the ratio of 15½ to 1, and that the United States were inclined to yield this point and accept this as a proper ratio." (C.—8667, p. 3.)

LORD GEORGE HAMILTON, *speaking in the House of Commons on March 29th, 1898, said :—*

"No such arrangement would be worthy of being called international that did not include France, and France would only accept a 15½ ratio."

APPENDIX C.

The following answers were given by PROFESSOR FOXWELL *before the Agricultural Commission on June 29th, 1894 :—*

26,880.—"You have now admitted the possibility that the savings-banks depositors may be paid in gold. Let me take the case of depositors in other banks —private banks ; can you draw a distinction between them and the depositors in the savings-banks?"

"Only to this extent : that the depositors in savings-banks are very ignorant people, and might suppose there was something wrong ; and as it is a small matter, I would be inclined to give them the benefit of the doubt. With regard to others, they would be intelligent enough to see the position."

APPENDIX D.

Answer 26,874.—"It appears to me that if the contracts which have been made stipulate that the payment should be made in gold, the payment would remain payable in gold."

APPENDIX E.

Answer 26,864.—"By the law of this country it is open to anyone to contract in any commodity he pleases, and I do not propose to alter the law of the country in that respect."

Bimetallism and the Woollen and Worsted Trades.*

By Mr. H. H. SPENCER (of Bradford).

———

". . . . a fall in prices of commodities, as measured in gold, which is everywhere visible, and everywhere baneful in its effects upon . . . manufacturing industry, and upon the growth of employment necessary to provide work for our rapidly-increasing population."—*Official Statement of the* BIMETALLIC LEAGUE, para. 9.

———

1. UNTIL the last two years bimetallism has been almost unknown in the West Riding of Yorkshire, but lately a bimetallic Crusade has been attempted, with results almost as disastrous to the crusaders as to the original army raised by Peter the Hermit. The hard-headed Yorkshireman, after listening patiently to the evils of low prices, rises in his place with reminiscences of the time when he paid 5s. a stone for his flour, and "didn't earn so much wages either." Whatever progress the bimetallists may make in other centres, the growth of the industry which is the staple trade of West Yorkshire has been such under the *régime* of falling prices since 1873 that **stronger arguments than we have yet heard will be needed to draw the woollen trade into the bimetallic camp.**

2. A constantly-reiterated assertion is that on account of the fall in silver the purchasing power of the silver-using countries has been

* *Issued in October*, 1896.

lessened, and their value to us as customers thereby so much reduced. The exports of woollen and worsted fabrics to India, China, Japan, and Hong Kong were in 1872 £1,867,116, and in 1895 £1,586,718. The total number of yards shipped to the Eastern market in 1872 amounted to 26,334,651, and in 1895 to 26,012,500. It should be noted, however, that between 1893 and 1895 there was a decrease in the exports to China of 6½ million yards and £288,coo value, owing to the Japanese war; and but for this, there would have been an increase in the Eastern trade of over 6 million yards in quantity and £7,000 in gold value. The woollen trade with the East is, however, but a small part of the total business. As far as it goes, it shows that the Eastern market, taking into account the great fall in prices, uses as many goods as 23 years ago, and those of better quality; and, while paying us almost as much in terms of gold, manages to pay us an amount in terms of silver very much greater than in 1872.

3. The average annual amount of wool, alpaca, and goats' hair imported during the years 1870–1874 was 307 million lbs., of which 180½ million lbs. were retained for home manufacture. **During the five years 1890–1894 the average annual import had risen to 691 million lbs., and the average amount retained for home consumption to 322 millions.**

The average annual value of raw wool imported into Great Britain was :—

1870–1874	1890–1894
£18,000,000	£26,000,000

The consumption of wool for manufacturing purposes per head of the people was :—

1870	1880	1890	1895
10 lbs.	10¾ lbs.	11¼ lbs.	13 lbs.

The number of operatives in woollen and worsted mills was :—

	Men.	Women.	Children (half-time).		Total.
1874 ...	104,600	134,000	38,100	=	276,700
1885 ...	111,100	142,900	23,500	=	277,500
1889 ...	118,300	156,000	22,800	=	297,100

Comparing our own and foreign countries, we find, in periods of 10 years, the estimated wholesale value of the produce in the woollen and worsted industry to have been :—

	1861-1870 £	1881-1890 £
Great Britain ...	412 millions ...	457 millions
France	325 ,, ...	329 ,,
Germany	215 ,, ...	264 ,,

The average value of woollen and worsted goods consumed by each inhabitant in the three countries was :—

	1861-1870	1871-1880	1881-1890
Great Britain ...	16s. 0d. ...	18s. 0d. ...	21s. 6d.
France	13s. 0d. ...	11s. 0d. ...	12s. 0d.
Germany	8s. 0d. ...	8s. 0d. ...	10s. 0d.

Mr. Hooper, of the Bradford Chamber of Commerce, estimates the value of the woollen and worsted industry to have been in 1895 £54,000,000 ; he also estimates that the home consumption, at wholesale value, of woollen and worsted goods was £39,000,000 ; thus showing that our own people in 1895 used goods of a value almost equal to the total value of the industry in the 'Sixties, and a quantity of goods—taking into account their cheapness to-day— far greater than the whole of the production for both the home and export markets together 30 years ago.

Let us now try and draw some conclusions from these figures.

4. The first and most striking inference is that in spite of, or perhaps because of the fall in prices, the imports of wool have increased hugely both in quantity and value, and that one of our "decrepit industries" needs for its use almost twice as much raw material as it did before silver was demonetised! The average price of wool imported was 15·41 pence per lb. in 1875, and 8·01 pence in 1895, thus showing that **we got our wool in England in 1895 for more than 24 millions sterling less than it would have cost us at the price of 20 years ago.** We find also among the workers a satisfactory increase in the number of men and decrease in the number of children employed. Perhaps the best feature of all is the great increase in the amount per head spent by our own people in clothing. Allowing a purchasing power of 50 per cent. more to money, which is fully within the mark, wool having fallen to almost one-half its old value, we find that **the English nation, on the average, consumes twice as much as it did in the 'Sixties,** and that the rate of consumption has increased faster in Great Britain than in either France or Germany; this notwithstanding the prophecy, now often alleged as a fact, that

" England's trade would suffer more than all other interests " by the demonetisation of silver and the consequent fall in prices.

5. The only discouraging feature of these returns, is the proportionately more rapid growth of German trade, caused—as has recently been pointed out by Lord Rosebery—by the greater skill and adaptability of their manufacturers, and also, in the export trade, by the undervaluation of goods, which has enabled Germany in many markets to undersell Great Britain by evading the payment of full duties. It is hard for the bimetallists, however, that **Germany's great progress dates from the time of her adoption of the gold standard.**

6. When judging the true meaning of the foregoing figures it must in all fairness to our English industries be remembered that the years of comparison are exceptionally favourable to the bimetallists. It is their custom to lament the vanished prosperity of the period of 1870–74, without mentioning the wonderful combination of circumstances at that time favourable to British trade. Germany and France, our greatest competitors, gave up to war a great portion of their workers in 1870 and 1871; the manufacturing districts of France were ravaged, and the destruction of the war had to be repaired after 1871. Germany received a war indemnity of £200,000,000, and spent it with a royal hand. Thus England was placed in a fortunate position such as she never was in before, and may never be in again—firstly, in furnishing supplies for the war ; secondly, in selling to or helping France to repair her fortunes; thirdly, in selling goods to Germany; and, lastly, by the temporary withdrawal of France and Germany from the field of the world's markets. In this paper, comparison has been purposely made between this favoured period—the usual example of the bimetallists—and the last few years when England's industry has had no favours. It has been shown that, notwithstanding the wonderful fortune which England experienced in those years, the growth of the industry with which Yorkshire is identified has been greater since that period than it was either then or before.

7. **Perhaps the argument most used of all in these democratic days is that the bimetallist is the friend of the working-man, and there is no argument more utterly fallacious.** The landlord who, under low prices, has seen a greater share of the produce go to the men who make it, may think that the bimetallist is his friend. The friend of the defaulting debtor he undoubtedly is, who, having used the capital of England to make all he needs, now wishes to return that capital

or its interest by the product of less labour than it cost the lender. But, before he can persuade the worker of his friendship, he must show that, under high prices, the share of the produce that goes to Labour is greater than under low prices. He must prove that as prices have fallen, wages have fallen too ; and, conversely, that when prices have risen, wages have risen more quickly. To every practical tradesman the absurdity of this is manifest. In the necessary inquiries made for the purposes of this pamphlet, over and over again have the remarks been made, by men of practical experience, that prices do not affect wages ; that wages have nothing to do with the market ; that the men always get their full share, whether prices rise or fall. If this is so, and if the profit on the larger output at low prices be greater than on the smaller output at high prices, it follows that low prices bring a greater share of the produce to the workers ; and although some employers, the least thoughtful, welcome a boom for the very reason that the workers' proportion is lessened and their own increased for a time, the wiser view it with distrust, knowing that the stoppage in consumption which follows the rise in price costs them more than they made in the boom ; knowing, too, that the large demand for goods which cheapness brings means steady work for the looms, and less severity in competition, than in the time when wages will purchase little.

8. **Nothing in the industrial history of this country is more remarkable than the constantly increasing share in the produce of Labour and Capital, which low prices have given to Labour.** In a steadily falling market the money rate of both day and piece work has been maintained or increased, and the worker has not only got the benefit which results to him from the fall in the price of the finished article, and the greater share of it which his steady money wage represents, but in many cases he has got an extra advantage in piece work by the speeding or other improvements in the machinery.

9. But an ounce of fact is worth a pound of argument, and below are the actual results in various branches of the textile trade. **Three of the principal branches of textile production are spinning, weaving, dyeing and finishing ; and in each branch the increasing share of the product which goes to the worker has kept pace with the constant fall in the price of goods.** One of the leading Bradford spinners has been good enough to furnish information about the wages paid in his works. One solitary instance in the whole of the Bradford trade has been found of a fall in

money wages, the weekly wage of girls in the spinning room having fallen from 10s. in 1876-77 to 9s. in 1896 ; the purchasing power of their wages, however, having increased by far more than the nominal amount. On the other hand, in the same mill, the twisters, who in 1873 were receiving 10s. to 12s. as a maximum, are now averaging over 15s. a week ; and overlookers, then at 24s. and 26s. per week, are now earning 30s. per week. The clerks and ware-housemen are uniformly better paid. And, strange to say, this spinner is quite content with low prices and things as they are for his own sake as well as his workpeople.

10. In the weaving, too, the same result is given. A cloth made in thousands of pieces for the Japanese market has been traced back to 1882, with the following result :—

1882.	s.	d.	1896.	s.	d.
Weft 3¾ gross of Bobbins, at 7s. 6d. per gross	28	2	Weft at 5s. 6d. per gross ...	20	8
Warp 7 lbs. 12 oz., at 20¼d. per lb.	12	11*	Warp at 16½d. per lb.... ...	10	*9
Putting into looms, &c., per piece (known as dressing, &c.)	0	10	Dressing, &c.	0	10
Weaving wages	4	0	Weaving wages	4	0
	45	11		36	3

The high-water mark of this cloth was 58s., and although the manufacturer has not preserved the make particulars at that date, he states that the weaving wages were the same for that price.

The fall in price, therefore, gives the following result :—

At 58s. 0d. per piece weaver received 6⅞ per cent. of product.
,, 45s. 11d. ,, ,, ,, 8¼ ,, ,,
,, 36s. 3d. ,, ,, ,, 11 ,, ,,

In addition to this, any speeding of the loom, or increased power of production, has further added to the wages of the weaver, the price per piece being the same.

11. In dyeing and finishing, it is impossible to find the exact proportion per piece which has gone to the worker. One of the leading firms in this branch of the trade has, however, furnished figures, showing the proportion which wages have borne to their

* *This figure includes the cost of "edging," that is, of making the edges of the pieces.*

total output. **For four weeks in July of 1870 the wages paid amounted to 27·60 per cent. of the turnover ; and for the corresponding period in 1890 the percentage was 36·00 ; the money value of wages also being maintained, while the price of the product fell.** In the merchanting and distribution of the goods the same thing has happened. Wages of warehousemen have been at practically a steady level for the last twenty years ; and as machinery hardly comes in here, the work per piece in handling is almost the same ; while the average value of the goods has been constantly falling.

12. From several sources the report is the same—that the proportion of wages paid for the handling of goods has increased, notwithstanding the fall in their price. To my own knowledge the wage for this handling has been the same in one firm shipping goods to America for thirteen years, while the average price per square yard of goods shipped from Bradford to America fell from 24·2 in 1882 to 16·6 cents in 1893. In addition to this, during the last twenty years, it is a matter of common knowledge that the hours of work in the warehouses have been very greatly shortened ; the Saturday half-holiday now being universal, and the evening hour of closing very much earlier.

13. The kernel of the lament of the bimetallists seems to lie in the following facts :—In silver-using countries raw materials have kept approximately steady in silver ; wages until recently have been the same, and therefore the cost value of the finished article must be about the same. In England raw materials have fallen as much as silver, in proportion to gold, and the merchant who has to sell more goods for a sovereign to give the yellow man as much for his dollar is on a par with his silver-using competitor, because he buys as much more for his sovereign as he has to sell for it. But wages also have been steady in gold, and therefore the English employer who has to give a greater share of the product to his workman is at a disadvantage with the Indians or Chinese, who give only as much as before.

14. There are two courses open. Either the labourer in England must take the same share as he used to do, or his increased share must come out of somebody else. To give the labourer a smaller share is simple enough, if he will take it. He will not consent to money reductions ; and therefore the other way is—**bimetallism ; or, in plain English, the reduction of the value of money wages** by bringing them down to their old value, and by making the Englishman's sovereign worth only as much in goods as it

used to be. That, in short, is the way out of the difficulty which the bimetallists offer. It is a way that would undoubtedly lead to disappointment all round, but it is none the less the bait that is temptingly exposed to lure the unwary, uninformed, and discontented to destruction.

15. There are some Englishmen, however, who cheerfully acquiesce in the present state of things ; who think that the improvement in the lot of the farm-labourer, the withdrawal of the women from the fields, and the education of the children, are a full compensation to the nation for the fall in rents of land which low prices have brought ; who think that the cheap loaf, and plenty in the cottage, the short hours and the high wages of the factory hand, even at the cost of keen competition and small profits, are better than the white slavery of fifty years ago ; who hold, as Thorold Rogers did, that Government can commit no crime against the people greater than the passing of an Act directly or indirectly tending to raise prices.

16. It is these men, who with the example before them of America, and her efforts to raise prices for the benefit of the few ; of our own country and her cruel corn laws ; and of every land which has debased her currency, or otherwise tried to reduce the purchasing power of her people's wages ; it is these men who are determined, by keeping the value of our currency steady, to secure to the toilers the benefits which cheapness and plenty, improvements in our ships, and inventions in our workshops, have brought and will continue to bring to them.

NOTE.—The chief authorities quoted in this paper are :—" Mulhall's Dictionary of Statistics ; " " The 45th Annual Report of the Bradford Chamber of Commerce ; " " The *Bradford Observer* Wool Tables for 1895 ; " " Blue Book, C8211, on British Trade and Production from 1854 to 1895 ; " and " Blue Book, C8097."

The information as to wages has been given privately, but it is at the disposal of anyone who is not satisfied with or in any way disputes its accuracy.

Bimetallism and Agricultural Depression.*

By the Rt. Hon. G. SHAW-LEFEVRE

(CHAIRMAN OF THE ROYAL COMMISSION ON AGRICULTURE).

" I entirely agree with those speakers who think that Agriculture suffers doubly from the present condition of our currency. I believe, in the first place, that the fall of prices has been largely due to the artificial appreciation of gold, which followed upon the demonetisation of silver ; and I believe further that there is an artificial advantage given to the producer in silver-using countries, from which the producer in gold-using countries necessarily suffers."—*Speech by* RT. HON. ARTHUR J. BALFOUR, *the " Times," February 8th, 1896.*

---

1. IT is admitted by everyone who has considered the question that the primary cause of the serious depression of Agriculture during the last sixteen years has been the great, and till lately the progressive, fall of prices of farm products. There have been contributory causes, such as the rise of wages of labourers and the bad seasons, which have specially affected the East and South of England during the last four years, but the main cause has undoubtedly been the fall of prices, which became serious, so far as farmers were concerned, ● in 1878. While all are agreed as to the primary cause, there are great differences of opinion as to the ultimate cause—namely, **the cause of the fall of prices.**

* *Issued in March, 1896.*

2. There are two distinct views on the subject. The first is (A) that the main causes of the fall of prices, and therefore of the depression, have been (1) the appreciation of gold resulting in part from its reduced production from the year 1873 till within the last six years, and in part from the greater demand for it owing to the demonetisation of silver by various countries in Europe ; (2) the stimulus alleged to be given to the export of their products by silver-using countries, such as India, owing to the fall in value of silver as measured in gold. The other view (B) is that the main cause has been the enormous improvements made during the last twenty years in the conveyance of products by land and by sea ; the great facilities given for the distribution of the world's products by telegraphs, and by the opening of the Suez Canal ; and the great accumulation of capital during a period of profound peace. These causes, it is alleged, have resulted in opening out vast districts in both old and new countries, and in bringing their products to our markets, in competition with the products of our farmers—in other words, in what is popularly understood as " foreign competition." Both of these explanations are founded on the deductive, or *à priori*, method of reasoning. They must be carefully compared with experience and results, before either of them can be accepted as affording a true and adequate explanation of the fall of prices. It is proposed to consider which of the two best conforms to all the surrounding facts relating to Agricultural Depression.

3. (A) **On the assumption that the fall of prices has been mainly due to the appreciation of gold,** it would seem necessarily to follow :—

That the fall of prices would be equally observed in all products, subject, of course, to some temporary or local exceptions, for which special explanations could be given.

That there would be a corresponding fall in the money rate of wages of labourers, in the absence of other causes affecting them. This fall in the money rate of wages would probably lag behind the fall in the price of products, but would inevitably take place after a time. Professor Foxwell, on behalf of the bimetallists, has admitted that such a fall could not be delayed more than five or six years.

That there would also be a similar and equal fall in the rent of all agricultural land. This again would probably lag behind the fall of prices, especially where leases prevail ; but where land is let on yearly tenancies as is generally the case in England and Wales, the reduction of rents could not be long delayed. With these adjustments it must be obvious that the relative position of the farmers or cultivators to other classes would be much the same as before the fall of prices. They would be as well able to grow wheat or any other product with a profit. The land-owners also would find that their rents would go as far in purchasing power or in the employment or labour as before the fall of prices.

4. (B) **On the other assumption that the fall of prices has been due to inventions and improvements, which have opened out new districts, and have brought their products into competition with home produce**, it would also seem to follow necessarily :—

That the fall of prices of different products would be very unequal. That those articles which are specially suited to production in new countries would fall most in price. That articles heavy in bulk, where freight for conveyance has in the past formed a large element in their price, would be more affected in price than articles of small bulk in proportion to their value ; and that articles on which a large amount of labour has to be expended in their pro-duction or manufacture, would also fall in price in a less degree than those which are produced with little labour.

That the money wages of labour would not fall ; that the real rate of wages of labourers, as measured in what can be got for their money wages, would be increased in the same proportion as the fall in prices of the main necessaries of life. In other words, that labourers in this country would be the main gainers by inventions common to all mankind, which result in making the most of the world's products, and in bringing those of distant countries into com-petition with home products.

That the general rate of profits in all trades would be lowered by the very fact of great abundance and increased com-petition.

That the rent of land would be affected by the fall of prices very unequally ; that where land in this country is specially suitable to the production of those articles, the import of which has been most stimulated and facili-tated by the improvements and inventions referred to, and of which the fall in price has been greatest, rent would fall in a far greater proportion than in the case of land the products of which are not open to the same competition.

A careful examination of the condition of agriculture in different parts of the United Kingdom affords most ample proof of the conclusions under assumption B, and equally convincing disproof of the conclusions which would necessarily follow on assumption A.

Let us consider these points somewhat more in detail, and test them by actual experience :—

I.—INEQUALITY IN THE FALL OF PRICES.

5. Comparing the last four years with the ten years 1865-75, a period which included some years of exceptionally high prices, the fall of prices of the principal agricultural products has been as follows :—

Wheat, a fall of 50 per cent.	Beef, 1st quality, a fall of 16½ per cent.	
Barley, ,, ,, 32 ,,	,, 2nd ,, ,, ,, 19 ,,	
Oats, ,, ,, 25 ,,	,, 3rd ,, ,, ,, 28 ,,	
Wool, ,, ,, 26 ,,	Mutton, 1st quality, ,, 8 ,,	
Cheese, ,, ,, 15 ,,	,, 2nd ,, ,, ,, 15 ,,	
Butter, ,, ,, 10 ,,	,, 3rd ,, ,, ,, 20 ,,	
Hay, ,, ,, 16 ,,	Poultry, risen in price.	
Straw, ,, ,, Nil.		

6. **It is clear from these figures how very unequal the fall of prices has been. This is only what was to be expected on assumption B.** Wheat is specially suitable as a crop for virgin soils. The newly broken up land in the Western States of America, Argentina, Uruguay, and elsewhere, is almost invariably devoted for some years to the produce of wheat. The certainty also of a market for this article of prime necessity makes it a desirable crop for such districts, and also for old countries such as India and Russia, which are for the first time opened up by railways. There can be little doubt, then, that the successive reductions in the price of wheat have been largely due to the following causes :—

(*a*) The great extension of railways and the great lowering of the freights in the United States. The mileage of railways there was in 1860—30,600, 1870—53,400, 1880—93,670, 1893—176,461. The acreage under wheat increased from an average of 20,160,000 acres in the five years 1869-73 to 37,960,000 acres, the average of the five years 1888-92, and the produce from 25,150,000 tons, to 56,660,000 tons.

(*b*) The extension of railways in Southern Russia, where the mileage was in 1870—7,170, 1880—14,000, 1892—18,670.

(*c*) The similar extension of railways in India, where the mileage was in 1860—840, 1870—4,830, 1894—18,441.

(*d*) The development of the Argentine Republic, mainly by British capital, where the mileage of railways was in 1870—640, 1880—1,540, 1893—8,376, and which in the last five years has sprung into the position of being third on the list of countries exporting wheat. The acreage under cultivation of wheat increased from 271,000 in 1874 to 5,000,000 in 1894.

(*e*) The improvements in marine engines, which have resulted in great economy of fuel and in a large reduction of freight.

These extensions and economies seem to be sufficient to account for the great fall in the price of wheat, without resorting to any theories as to currency and appreciation of gold.

7. In the case of wool, the great fall in price of late years is sufficiently accounted for by the enormous increase in its production, in a proportion far exceeding the growth of population. The production in 1840 was 786,000,000 lbs., in 1860—1,108,000,000 lbs., in 1880 —1,988,000,000 lbs., and in 1895—3,300,000,000 lbs. With respect to meat, the great difference in the fall of price of inferior qualities of beef and mutton, as compared with that of the best qualities, is conspicuous proof that currency causes can have had little effect. The great facilities for the importation of cattle, sheep, and dead meat of all kinds from the United States, Australia, New Zealand, etc., have led to immense importations of the lower qualities of meat, and have affected their price far more than that of the better quality, produced only in this country. It not unfrequently happens, that there is a fall of price of the lower qualities coincident with a rise of price of the better qualities. The fall in price of hay has been small compared with that of other products. It is doubtless due to the great extent of land which has been laid down in grass, and not to foreign competition. The fall in butter also has been comparatively small. It has been due in great part to competition from Denmark, where farmers have given up growing corn and have taken to produce butter for the English market.

8. When we turn to commodities which cannot be produced in our own country we find similar explanations of the fall of prices of the main articles of consumption and manufacture. The great fall

J

in the price of tea is sufficiently accounted for by the fact that the extension of cultivation in India and Ceylon has been enormous and far in excess of the increase of population. It would have been strange indeed if the price of tea had not greatly fallen. The same holds good of cotton and sugar. The world's production of cotton was in 1870—2,775,000,000 lbs., 1880—3,601,000,000, 1888—4,783,000,000 lbs. The world's production of sugar was 2,730,000 tons in 1870, 3,670,000 in 1880, and 7,893,000 tons in 1894. This great increase has been largely due to the bounties given by many European States for the production of beet sugar, which increased from 900,000 tons in 1870 to 4,972,000 tons in 1894. On the other hand, in those cases where the increase of cultivation has not been great, and where the freight is small in proportion to the value, prices have not fallen, and in many cases have risen. Among such products are coffee, tobacco, cocoa, rum, pepper, indiarubber, gutta percha, cane, etc.

All these facts seem to bear out conclusively the conclusions which result from the assumption that improvements and inventions, rather than the scarcity of gold, have been the causes of the fall of prices.

II.—EFFECT OF THE FALL OF PRICES ON AGRICULTURAL LABOURERS.

9. The agricultural labourers form three-fourths of the population in the average of rural districts, and in many districts a still greater proportion. It is important, therefore, to determine how far they have been affected by the fall of prices.

The best epitome of the facts bearing on this subject is to be found in the reports to the Royal Commission on Labour in 1894, and especially in the summary of the reports of the sub-commissioners by Mr. William Little. This gentleman showed that, taking 34 districts in the several counties in England, in which special inquiries were held, the average rate of weekly wages of labourers, irrespective of harvest wages, was in 1867-70, before the great rise took place, 12s. 3d., in 1879-81 13s. 9d., in 1892-3 13s. 3d.

He pointed out, however, that the averages for 1892-3 were taken only from the unions specially inquired into, and which were selected on account of their being purely rural, whereas the averages for 1867-9 and 1879-81, were taken from the whole of the counties, where in some parts the influence of town employment was felt and somewhat increased the average of wages. It is probable, therefore, that the difference between 1867-70 and 1892-3 was some-what greater than that shown by the figures.

10. The figures as given show the averages of weekly wages only, and do not include harvest wages. If these are taken into account, the average weekly earnings of an adult labourer in 1892-3 was, according to Mr. Little, 15s. 11d. He added, "there appears to have been generally an increase of earnings, such increase being most marked in the south and west of England, and in those districts where the rate of wages was lowest, and that the increase has been least in the great corn-growing counties, in some of which it seems doubtful whether there has not been a decline." His figures do not include Scotland and Wales, where money wages have undoubtedly increased considerably during the last fifteen years. The evidence given before the Agricultural Commission fully bears out Mr. Little's conclusions. It shows that in far the greater part of the country the increase of wages achieved by labourers in 1873 has been maintained, and that in some districts it has been improved upon, especially where there is competition for labour from mines and manu-facturing industries. On the other hand, it shows that in some districts in the east and south, where the depression has been most acute, there has been a fall of wages in the last three or four years to about the point at which they stood before the rise of 1873. This reduction in certain districts must be attributed not to a general fall in the rate of money wages throughout the whole country, but to local conditions, and to the fact that, mainly owing to the changes in the system of agriculture and the reduced cultivation of cereals, and the laying down of a large extent of land in grass, there has been a reduced employment for agricultural labourers in those districts, and that the consequent redundancy of labour has not yet been absorbed in other industries. Taking, however, the average money wages of agricultural labourers throughout the whole country, there can be no doubt whatever that they have increased as compared with the years before 1873, when this scarcity of gold is alleged to have been first experienced.

11. **When, however, we take into account not merely the money rate, but the actual value of wages as measured in what the labourers can get for their money, the difference is far greater, and the labourers are unquestionably far better off than they were twenty-five years ago.** Mr. Little showed in his report that the average prices for a sufficiency of flour, butter,

cheese, tea, and sugar, for a week's consumption of an adult male labourer were at different periods as follows :—

1860–67	- *d.* 50·41
1868–75	- 48·4
1876–83	- 36·21
1884–91	- 31·62
1892–4	- 29·2

a reduction of more than 40 per cent. between 1860–67 and 1892–94. It is generally estimated that an average labourer's family, consisting of himself, his wife, and three children, requires the food of three adult males. If this be correct, the average wage of 12s. 3d. between 1860 and 1873 hardly sufficed to provide the require-ments of an average labourer's family for bread, butter, tea, sugar, and cheese, leaving no margin for other things. The harvest wages provided for rent and clothing. In 1892-4, 7s. 3d. only was required for the purchase of the same articles of consumption, leaving a weekly margin of 5s. for other expenditure, besides the harvest wages, equal to 2s. 6d. a week spread over the year. During the same time the prices of clothing, of boots, of petroleum (one of the greatest of benefits to labourers of modern times), and of many other articles, have also been greatly reduced. Labourers have also been relieved of the cost of educating their children, and have further benefited by the great extension of allotments. On the other hand, the age at which their children are allowed by law to earn wages and contribute to the family means has been raised; and, as a rule, their wives have largely given up working in the fields.

12. **There can, then, be no question whatever that the condition of agricultural labourers has greatly improved since 1873, during the period when prices have been falling.** Mr. Little has rightly said, "It is no exaggeration to say that in the last quarter of a century a great economic revolution, accomplished with little aid from legislation, has transferred to the labourers from one-third to one-fourth of the profits which the landowners and farmers previously received from the cultivation of the land."

It is true that during this period there has also been a great reduction in the number of labourers employed in agriculture. This reduction, however, is only in a partial degree due to the depression. The migration of labourers from rural districts to towns and to other employments was in full force before the depression began. It was the cause of the rise of wages which occurred in 1873. There was a greater reduction in the number of labourers between 1870 and 1880, before the depression was sensibly felt, than between 1880 and 1890.

So far, then, as the agricultural labourers are concerned, the facts before us do not bear out the theories and conclusions of those who contend that the depression has been due to monetary causes, or to the appreciation of gold. They confirm, in a most striking manner, the opposite theory.

III.—INEQUALITY IN THE FALL OF RENTS.

13. Let us now turn to the rent of land. If the appreciation of gold were the cause of the fall of prices, it would follow that the reduction of rent would be evenly spread over the whole country. The very opposite has been the case. The reduction in the value of land has been very different in the different parts of the country. It has been far greater in the wheat-growing districts of the east and south of England, which constitute about one-third of the area of England and Wales. In these districts the fall of rent of purely agricultural land has probably averaged over 40 per cent., and has often amounted to 50 or 60 per cent. In another one-third part of England and Wales, where a mixed system of agriculture has prevailed, namely, in the northern counties, in Yorkshire, and in the centre of England, the reduction of rent has been much less, and has averaged from 20 to 25 per cent. The reduction has been least in the remaining third part, in the pastoral districts of the western counties and Wales, including Lancashire and Cheshire, etc., where the average reduction of rent has not much exceeded 10 per cent. In these districts, where little or no corn is grown, the low price of wheat has been a distinct advantage to all classes, and the fall of barley and oats, for the feeding of cattle and horses, has been favourable to the bulk of farmers, and has been some compensation to them for the reduction in the price of cattle and of dairy produce.

14. It is admitted that the profits of farmers have been greatly reduced of late years. In the eastern and southern districts farmers have felt the stress of times most seriously; large numbers of them have incurred losses or have had to succumb to their difficulties. A large extent of land has been thrown out of arable cultivation, and has been laid down in indifferent grass. **This, however, has been due not to any restriction of the currency, nor to the appreciation of gold, but to the great competition of foreign produce resulting from the opening out of new districts in many parts of the world.** Looking broadly at the condition of the whole of our rural districts, the conclusion is forced upon us that the fall of prices has resulted in a far larger share of the proceeds of the

land going to the labourers, and a far less share of it to the farmers in the shape of profit, and to the landowners in the shape of rent.

IV.—ALLEGED DIFFICULTIES DUE TO INCREASED PRODUCTION IN SILVER-USING COUNTRIES.

15. There remains the question whether the depression of agriculture can be considered as in any way due to the difficulties caused by the divergence in the relative value of gold and silver, and the alleged impetus given to the export of wheat and other produce from countries with a silver standard. **This argument is at once dispelled and shown to be baseless, and, indeed, absurd, by a simple table showing the value of imports of agricultural products from Silver-using countries as compared with those imported from other countries.** It appears that the total value of the imports of agricultural products from silver-using countries for the year 1895 was £3,000,000 only, out of a total of over £148,000,000.* It is impossible to suppose that prices have been materially affected by so small an import from silver-using countries. Further, the statistics of the exports of wheat from India show conclusively that there is no relation whatever between the exports of wheat and the price of silver. † The more these figures are studied the more conclusively they prove that the theories of the bimetallists on this subject are without a shadow of proof.

16. **It is further said that the cheap exports of wheat from the Argentine Republic have been caused by the depreciation of its currency. Even were that true, bimetallism would be no remedy,** for the currency of that country is inconvertible paper, nominally on a gold basis, and has no relation to silver. The rise or fall in the value of silver has no effect there. Accordingly, bimetallism could have no effect upon its exports. Close to the Argentine Republic is the Republic of Uruguay, which has a gold standard and a gold currency, and the exports of wheat from which have increased similarly to those from the Argentine Republic. With a stable currency, and good credit, the growth of the Argentine Republic would probably be far greater than at present. If it were really the case that the depreciation of a currency stimulates production and exports, and enriches the country which resorts to it, then the greater the depreci-

* *See Appendix A.*   † *See Appendix B.*

ation the better, and the example of the Argentine Republic should be followed by every other country; a proposition which has only to be stated to expose its absurdity. What, however, is to prevent any state, under any system of currency, monometallic or bimetallic, and with any amount of international agreement, from issuing notes in excess of its credit and depreciating its currency?

17. If we are right in the above, it follows that, whether we or other countries had a gold standard, or a silver standard, or a bimetallic standard, the results of the past twenty years in the great increase in the cultivation of wheat and the production of cattle, sheep, wool, etc., would probably have taken place much as they have done. **The popular view, then, that low prices and depression of agriculture are due to foreign competition is the true one, and the explanation offered by the Bimetallic League that they are due to currency difficulties, and to appreciation of gold is unsound, and is neither based on, nor confirmed by, experience, or by any of the surrounding facts.**

APPENDIX A.

VALUE of principal imports into United Kingdom for 1895, which competed with British agricultural produce, also proportion of same coming from silver-using countries. (Compiled from "Trade and Navigation of United Kingdom," 3—xi.)

PRINCIPAL AGRICULTURAL IMPORTS.

	£
Animals (living, for food) ...	8,966,252
Meat (for food)...	23,769,638
Wheat, Flour, and other Cereals	49,718,252
Butter, Cheese, and Eggs ...	25,480,021
Lard and Milk	4,026,500
Fruit* and Hops	2,033,572
Potatoes and Onions	1,866,730
Other Vegetables	1,277,058
Poultry and Game	605,166
Yeast	491,351
Wool (Sheep and Lamb) ...	26,031,550
Other Articles	4,010,612
Total £148,276,702	

[Continued over.

* *Comprising Apples, Cherries, Plums and Pears.*

FROM SILVER USING COUNTRIES.

	£
Wheat from India	2,342,132
,, from other countries (say)	500,000
Other Cereals (say)	250,000
	£3,092.132

(Say) £148,000,000 was value of principal foreign produce imported in 1895 which competed with British agriculture. Of this (say) £3,000,000 came from silver using countries; or about two per cent.

APPENDIX B.

Board of Trade Return showing the aggregate Imports of Wheat and Wheat Flour into the United Kingdom in each year from 1872 to 1895 inclusive, with the Imports of Wheat from British India, the total quantity of Wheat Exported from British India, the average Gazette price of British Wheat, and the average price of Bar Silver in the United Kingdom during each of the same years.

Years.	Aggregate Imports into the United Kingdom of Wheat and Wheat Flour.	Imports of Wheat into the United Kingdom from British India.	Total Export of Wheat from British India.	Average Gazette Price of British Wheat.		Price of Bar Silver according to Messrs. Pixley and Abell's Circular.
				Per Imperial quarter.		Per ounce.
	cwts.	cwts.	cwts.	s.	d.	d.
1872	47,612,896	156,665	394,010	57	0	60 5/16
1873	51,631,197	740,934	1,755,954	58	8	59 1/4
1874	49,322,693	1,073,940	1,073,655	55	8	58 5/16
1875	59,546,621	1,334,366	2,510,768	45	2	56 7/8
1876	51,904,433	3,287,236	5,586,604	46	2	52 3/4
1877	63,491,429	6,104,985	6,373,168	56	9	54 13/16
1878	59,691,583	1,820,881	1,056,720	46	5	52 9/16
1879	73,002,110	887,006	2,201,515	43	10	51 1/4
1880	68,459,814	3,229,050	7,444,375	44	4	52 1/4
1881	71,344,659	7,334,616	19,901,005	45	4	51 11/16
1882	80,769,107	8,461,004	14,193,763	45	1	51 5/8
1883	85,073,646	11,248,988	21,001,412	41	7	50 9/16
1884	66,910,443	7,980,831	15,850,881	35	8	50 5/8
1885	82,331,552	12,170,251	21,068,924	32	10	48 5/8
1886	67,021,886	11,023,949	22,263,624	31	0	45 3/8
1887	80,212,293	8,511,512	13,538,169	32	6	44 5/8
1888	80,426,352	8,166,254	17,611,408	31	10	42 7/8
1889	78,929,778	9,218,204	13,802,209	29	9	42 11/16
1890	82,381,591	9,111,582	14,320,496	31	11	47 11/16
1891	89,539,355	13,005,785	30,306,700	37	0	45 1/16
1892	95,604,589	12,495,442	14,973,453	30	3	39 13/16
1893	93,806,666	6,196,096	12,156,851	26	4	35 5/8
1894	96,702,072	5,349,056	6,903,769	22	10	28 15/16
1895	100,118,365	8,802,950	10,002,912	23	1	29 7/8

Has the Gold Standard made the Rich Richer and the Industrious Poorer?*

By the Rt. Hon. LORD FARRER.

1. It is the commonplace of bimetallists that the Demonetisation of Silver (as they call it) has enriched the creditor at the expense of the debtor ; the banker and financier at the expense of the agriculturist and the manufacturer ; Capital at the expense of Labour ; the drones of society at the expense of the working bees.

2. For instance, the following are extracts from English bimetallist leaflets :—

"REASONS WHY WORKING MEN SHOULD SUPPORT BIMETALLISM.

" Because the restrictions put upon the employment of silver as money have considerably increased the exchangeable value of gold, thereby augmenting the burden of Imperial and local taxation, ground-rents, royalties, and conventional and customary charges upon the industrial classes, causing great loss to those who live by industry, and bringing unfair gain to those who live upon it, such as the bond-holding and pensioned classes.

"BIMETALLISM AND JUSTICE TO THE INDUSTRIOUS.

"THE CRUELTY OF THE SINGLE GOLD STANDARD.

" Our National Debt in 1842 was	£839,000,000
"In 52 years we paid off	175,000,000
"Leaving, in 1894 ...	£664,000,000

* *Issued in March,* 1898.

"But in consequence of the increased value of gold the burden of the debt to-day is heavier than it was in 1842, although in the meantime we have paid off such a large sum to the national creditors.

"Gold prices of commodities have fallen so much that fifty per cent. more commodities must be given to pay the present gold debt, or £996,000,000 at the rate of the former purchasing power of gold.

"The true test of a measure of value like gold is what it will procure in commodities; how much wheat, cotton, coal or iron you must give in exchange for a given quantity of it.

"Tested in this way, the English people must give £332,000,000 worth more of their commodities to pay off their present National Debt than they need have given in 1842, although in the meantime they have paid off £175,000,000.

"The Australian gold debt is stated at £200,000,000, but measured in commodities it is now equal to £300,000,000 if compared with the prices current twenty years ago.

"The Indian gold debt is £107,000,000, but that means at the present rate of gold £160,000,000 worth of commodities, if compared with the prices current twenty years ago.

"Is this fair to the industrious workers? Think what this increase of obligations means in human endeavours and human labour! How many human beings must earn this extra tribute to be paid to non-producers by the sweat of their brows!

"This is the cruelty of an appreciating standard, and the injustice of it.

"The value of the mortgages on human labour have been increased by fifty per cent. because governments have refused to allow the legal use of the bimetallic standard which was the measure of human labour when these debts were incurred."

3. We have all of us heard enough, and more than enough, of Mr. Bryan's Cross of Gold. And in a pamphlet which has been sent me by M. Allard,* who holds a respectable position in Belgium —a pamphlet which attacks monometallism with a ferocity and extravagance happily unknown to most English bimetallists—I find the following passage concerning the so-called Demonetisation of Silver :—

"Faithful to this duty—the duty of keeping and increasing their fortunes—the financiers of our age have found the means, hitherto unknown, of increasing their riches. They have betaken themselves to our mints and have falsified the currency, like the ancient King, Philippe le Bel, and others of disastrous memory. Let us see how. They said to themselves, about 1850, that it would be easy to produce a fall in prices if they could persuade governments to exclude from monetary circulation one of the two precious metals, either gold or silver. In this way all capitalists who had sums to receive in metal would profit, since the metal remaining

* *Démocratie Rurale, par Alphonse Allard. Brussels, 1897.*

in circulation would become scarcer and would appreciate in value, thus pro-
curing them more luxuries than before. This falsification of the money was
worthy of the ancient Jews and of Philippe le Bel ; but our modern financiers are
fully resolved not to be behind them in a single respect."

Here not only is it alleged that the effect of closing the
French and German mints to silver has been to rob debtors; but
that it was the intention of the statesmen and financiers who
carried those measures that it should have that effect. This passes
most perversions of history, even those made by bimetallists.

4. But I am not sure that it is essentially stronger than the
following passages in a letter from Professor Foxwell, read at a
bimetallist meeting at Manchester on the 12th October, 1897. In
this letter the Professor, whilst pouring unmeasured praise on the
managers of the Bank of England for their recent action about
silver, denounces in equally unmeasured terms the whole banking
community of London. He says of them :—

"Lombard Street represents, or, as I think, misrepresents, the interest of the
creditor."

And again—

"There is only one thread of consistency to be found in the action of the
monometallist bankers. Now, as often before in English history, their aim is to
aggrandise the creditor by increasing the real value of the money in which his
debt is expressed."

Such charges as these ought not to be made, especially by
persons holding responsible positions, against the statesmen and
financiers of France and the banking community of London without sound and serious reasons. Let us proceed to inquire what the
reasons are.

5. **The most important point in the above quotations is
the charge that the changes in currency effected by what
is called the Demonetisation of Silver have materially
altered the relative positions of debtor and creditor to the
injury of the debtor and the gain of the creditor. I propose
therefore to deal with this point in the first instance, and
afterwards to consider the bearing of the argument on the
general relations between rich and poor.**
6. The charge that the so-called Demonetisation of Silver has
injured debtors and benefited creditors is founded on the well-
known economic doctrine that an alteration in the value of the

standard metal alters all contracts made in terms of that standard. In this country gold is the standard metal, and all contracts are made in terms of gold sovereigns. If, therefore, after a contract is made, the gold contained in a sovereign becomes more valuable, and if in consequence all prices fall, the debtor, who has contracted to repay a certain number of sovereigns, has to repay in goods more than he received, and *vice versâ*. But here we must be on our guard against a prevalent error. A fall in price may be due either to the comparative scarcity of the gold in a sovereign or to the comparative abundance of the article exchanged for a sovereign. If it is due to the former cause, the debtor is undoubtedly injured by the change ; if it is due to the latter cause he is not injured, because if he has to pay back more articles than he received, he has more articles with which to pay. Having regard to these principles let us now consider the facts of our case.

7. **When asked for the real explanation of some extraordinary statement, it is wise to ask whether the statement is true. The statement in the present case is, that since the so-called Demonetisation of Silver, creditors have been enriched, and that they have been so enriched at the expense of debtors.** Before going into the question of "How" and "Why," we shall do well to inquire whether it is the fact that they have been so enriched—in other words, whether it is the fact that a man who is repaid, say, in 1898, a sum of money which he borrowed in 1870, gets back in actual value more than he lent.

8. Let us take a simple case. Let us suppose that one of these much abused financiers possessed in 1870 a sum of gold coins, or an amount at a bank, which he could have converted into gold coins, and let us suppose that the same man has at his command the same sum in 1898. Is he a richer man than he was ? For our present purpose it does not signify what he has done with the money in the interval. He may have locked it up, or he may have lent it, or have otherwise invested it. The material point is to compare the real values to him of a given number of gold sovereigns in 1870, and in 1898. Nor does it much matter what sum we take, provided it be sufficient to bring him within the class of "bloated capitalists" and "intriguing financiers," of whom we hear so much. It may be £1,000,000, or £100,000, or £10,000. Let us take £100,000, and ascertain whether the possessor can get more out of £100,000 in 1898 than he could have done in 1870.

9. This question is commonly settled in a very summary fashion by an appeal to Mr. Sauerbeck's figures, which, valuable and useful as they are when properly used and applied, are made to do a great deal of duty for which they are quite inadequate. The argument founded on them may be stated as follows :—"The wholesale prices of a cer- "tain number of articles of general consumption and commerce have "fallen heavily in the largest consuming market—so heavily that the "average, or, as it is called, the index number, which was 100 in the "decade ending 1877, is little more than 60 in 1898, a fall of 40 per "cent. Therefore all prices have fallen ; therefore 100,000 gold "sovereigns will buy 40 per cent. more of everything than it would "have bought in 1870 ; and therefore, of course, our crafty financier "is 40 per cent. richer than he was in 1870."

10. Charming reasoning, indeed ! I pass over, for the moment, the question whether Mr. Sauerbeck's articles are well chosen ; I pass over the fact that his prices are taken in one great market and at the place of consumption, not that of production ; I pass over the question whether averages and index numbers in such a case are not delusive, and whether the fact that some important articles in his list have actually risen in price, and that those which have fallen have fallen most unequally, does not point to special causes which affect each article, rather than to an increased demand for gold which ought to affect all equally. I pass over, I say, considerations such as these, in order to point out that Mr. Sauerbeck's list does not pretend to include, first, any retail prices ; secondly, any prices of ships or of shares, or of land, or of houses, or of any of the different forms of saleable property which are attached to land, and all of which are just as much sold for gold as any articles in his list ; thirdly, which is the most important omission of all, any prices of labour, or of human services of any kind, from the salary of the prima donna to the earn- ings of the costermonger or of the street sweeper—all of which are gold prices, and ought to be affected by the value of gold just as much as the prices of corn, of meat, of cotton, or of iron. **And yet Mr. Sauerbeck's figures are quoted by bimetallists, and even by economists and statesmen, as if they were an epitome of all human dealings, and an infallible key to the infinite mysteries of price.** Poor Mr. Sauerbeck ! It makes me shudder to think what he has been made answerable for.

11. Let us now—duly using Mr. Sauerbeck—consider carefully what our bloated financier could have done with his hundred thousand gold sovereigns in 1870, and what he can do with them in 1898.

12. **He may wish to spend his money on perishable com-modities.** In that case he may undoubtedly buy more wheat, more bread, more meat, more cheese, more tea, more sugar, more cotton, more iron, more common clothes, and so on through the articles which make up the lowered prices in Mr. Sauerbeck's list, than he could have bought in 1870. But would he ever do so? What can he do with them? He cannot by himself or his family, or his household servants consume more than a very moderate quantity of such articles, and any small saving on such consumption which he may make by their reduced price will be far less than the increase of money wages he has to pay to his servants in 1898.

13. **Or he may wish to spend money on expensive luxuries** —on good pictures, on good wines, on handsome clothes, on jewels, and all the paraphernalia of luxurious modern life. All or almost all of these things he will find cost more now than they did in 1870.

Or he may wish to keep carriages and carriage horses, hunters, race-horses. All these he will find dearer than in 1870, and though the forage they consume may be cheaper, the whole cost of keeping them, and of paying the servants and grooms who tend them, will also be greater.

Or he may wish to buy a beautiful house in the best part of London, or a desirable country residence, or a deer forest or grouse moor and excellent shootings. For all these he will have to pay at least as much as, and probably much more than, he would have paid in 1870.

14. Or he may wish to build a handsome house. This, he will find, will cost him twenty per cent. more in pounds sterling than it did in 1870.

Or he may wish to have a charming garden with hot-houses and conservatories; with flowers, shrubberies, and plantations, such as make so many Paradises in this beautiful country of ours. The cost to him of these will depend on the cost of labour, much of it skilled labour, and this he will find costs more than it did in 1870.

15. **Or he may wish to give his children the best possible education.** Here he will find that public schools and universities, good tutors and governesses, cost as much as and even more than they did in 1870. If the new schools for girls enable him to give them a good education more cheaply than in 1870, it is not from any general fall in prices, but because such schools have only been created and organised in recent years.

16. **Or he may wish to employ his £100,000 in some business which will give him a return for his money**—in agriculture, in manufacture, in shipping, or in trade. Here he will find that his chief outlay is in labour and in services; in the hand that works, or in the brain that manages and superintends; and for such hands and such brains he will have to pay more gold sovereigns than he would have paid in 1870. Labour has no doubt become more productive in cases where its efficiency has been increased by improvements in machinery; but though the output may have been increased, the capitalist gets a smaller share of the net product in 1898 than he did in 1870.

17. **Or, finally, he may wish to re-invest his £100,000 on some good security.** In that case he will find that whilst he could have got five or four and a half per cent. for his money in 1870, he can only get three and a half or three for it now. It would be easy to bring figures to prove this, but it is not necessary. It is notorious that the rate of interest on capital is much lower than it was.

18. **In short, there is no use, or hardly any use, to which our rich man can put his 100,000 gold sovereigns which will not cost him more, or bring him in a smaller return in 1898 than in 1870. Is it not, therefore, the very height of absurdity to quote Mr. Sauerbeck's figures and to say that because corn, cotton, and iron are cheaper, a man who lent £100,000 in 1870 and receives it back in 1898 is richer now than he was then?**

19. But there is another side to the picture, another end of the scale. We have hitherto spoken of the financier or large investor, because he is the object of such attacks as those quoted from M. Allard and Professor Foxwell. But investment is fortunately not confined to large capitalists. Through the medium of joint stock enterprises, of insurance companies, and of savings banks the savings of people of all classes; of the professional classes, of the lower middle classes, and of the labouring classes, find their way into the investment market, and these sums vary indefinitely in amount. Let us take an investment at the lower end of the scale—say of £100, the investment it may be of a mechanic, or of a poor clerk, or of a domestic servant, put aside to form a support in old age as a small provision for widow or orphan children. How will the owner of such a sum of gold stand in 1898 as compared with 1870? If he wishes to re-invest, or even to keep it invested, he will, like

the richer investor, lose something in interest. Instead of, say, five
per cent. or four and a half per cent., he will have to put up with
three and a half or three or even two and a half per cent. But
suppose he wishes to spend the money, how will he stand? His
outlay is very unlike that of the rich man. Of the things which he
uses, house-rent alone has increased since 1870. The education of
his children is provided for him at the public expense. The rest of
his outlay is upon those articles comprised in Mr. Sauerbeck's
list which have fallen most in value—upon bread and meat, upon tea
and sugar, upon common clothing and common furniture. So that
as regards all these things his £100 or the proceeds of it go a great
deal farther than they did in 1870, and these things constitute by far
the largest part of the objects of his expenditure. Upon them
he will save considerably, probably from twenty to forty per cent.
His £100 or the annual proceeds of it will then go much farther
than they did in 1870. **In other words, if there are any
creditors whom the loan or investment of a given sum in
gold will make richer in 1898 than the same sum would
have made them in 1870, it is not the wealthy capitalist,
the banker, or the financier, but the worn-out workman, the
destitute widow, and the orphans of the poor.** These are
the gold creditors who, according to M. Allard and our bimetallic
Professor, are fattening on prices lowered by the crusade against
silver.

20. We have been hitherto considering the case of the creditor.
Let us now consider the case of the debtor. So far as the wealthy
creditor is concerned, we have seen that he has not been made
richer by the fall in prices, and it is clear therefore that if the debtor
has suffered it is not the wealthy creditor who has robbed him. But
has he suffered at all, and if so, to what extent?

21. One remarkable feature of the period under consideration has
been, as we have already seen, the fall in the rate of interest. Money
can be borrowed now at a much lower rate than in 1870. Capital
is more abundant and is seeking investment. Consequently in all
cases in which there is no special undertaking not to pay off debt,
the debtor can pay it off and re-borrow or can convert it so as to
hold and enjoy his loan on much easier terms. This has, as we
know, been done to an enormous extent both with public debts and
private mortgages. The only cases in which it cannot be done are
those in which there is a fixed irredeemable annual charge, and these
are few compared with the vast bulk of debts, public and private.

The fund holder or public creditor is a favourite object of attack with persons such as M. Allard, and the public debtor, or, in other words, the tax-paying public, is an object of their commiseration. **But we all know how the burden of our own debt has been lightened by conversion; and he would be a bold man who could assert that its burden is felt by the mass of the people to be greater than it was thirty years ago. What is true of the public debt is also true of the great majority of mortgages and debenture charges.**

22. Take again the case of productive industries which are carried on with borrowed money. In these cases it is said that the fall in prices, whilst it benefits the creditor, necessarily injures the debtor, because, whilst his outgoings remain, his incomings from what he sells decrease. But this is not the case ; or if it is the case, is so to a limited extent only. How far the creditor has benefited we have seen above. But the debtor, too, reaps his advantages from the fall in prices. His raw materials and implements are cheaper, improvements in manufacture and transport enable him to produce an equal quantity of goods at smaller cost, and the lowered price of his products encourages and increases consumption. If he loses in the price of his products he gains in other ways. **So far as he may have subjected himself to permanent charges which he cannot pay off or reduce, he may suffer, but not so much on account of falling prices as because he cannot take advantage of the lower rate of interest which now prevails.**

23. There is, however, one item, and an important one, in which his outgoings may and often have increased, viz. the item of wages, which have increased in nominal, and much more in real amount. Even against this there has to be set the greater productiveness of labour arising from improvements in processes and in machinery. And if after balancing these items the manufacturers' profits are now less than they were, it is due to the fact that labour gets a larger share of the products of industry than it did in 1870.

24. Finally, let us consider the case of the landowner, the most crucial case of all, and a case in which there is no doubt a large class of debtors who at the present time are worse off—often much worse off—than they were in 1870. Even here we must not exaggerate. The class in question are the owners of agricultural land, and there is a large proportion of the land of Great Britain which is not agricultural. The owner of land in and near towns has not

K

suffered at all; if he has fixed burdens his rents have increased in a much greater proportion. The agricultural landowner has no doubt suffered heavily from lowered prices for agricultural produce. As regards mortgages, the interest he has to pay has in most cases been reduced. But there are many charges, such as jointures, annuities, rates, etc., which cannot be reduced, whilst his rents are largely reduced.

Again, the farmer—if he happens to have fixed charges—may have suffered in like manner; but he ultimately finds relief in the reduction of rent.

25. Let us admit, however, that the debtor who depends on agriculture is, in consequence of the fall in the prices of agricultural produce, worse off than he was in 1870. Is this due to currency? Surely there are two obvious causes which sufficiently account for this fall without bringing in the imaginary scarcity of the pound sterling. **The first cause is the increase of foreign competition caused by improvements in transport, which bring the produce of newer and more productive lands to our shores at a much lower cost. The other is the notorious fact that the agricultural labourer receives out of the aggregate produce of the land a much larger proportionate share than before.** His nominal wages have not fallen, or have fallen very little; whilst his real wages, or what he buys with them —his food, clothing, and necessaries—have largely increased and improved.

26. It is said that before 1870 the money produce of agricultural land might be divided into three equal shares : one for the landowner, one for the farmer, and one for the labourers. Assuming this to be true, it follows that the loss caused by the fall in agricultural prices is no longer shared as before. The general demand for labour enables the labourer to exact an increased share of the whole produce, and whatever reduction there may be in it in consequence of the fall in prices falls wholly on the employer. The labourer's gain is the landowner's loss.*

27. To sum up the case of the debtor—is it true that the man who owed a given number of pounds sterling in 1870, and who owes the same sum now, is worse off, in consequence of the fall in prices, than he was? The answer is no, with two exceptions, viz. the case

* See Mr. Little's Report, Appendix to Final Report of Commission on Labour, pp. 204-217 ; see also the paper in this series, entitled "The Bimetallic Report of the Agricultural Commission," by the Rt. Hon. G. Shaw-Lefevre.

of a debtor subject to a fixed annual charge which cannot be reduced, and the case of the agricultural landowner or farmer, for both of which there are special reasons unconnected with currency. Where the debtor is an employer of labour, whether of agricultural labour or of other kinds of labour, the labourer gets now a larger share of the aggregate product than he did at the earlier date.

28. We have hitherto been considering the effect of the alleged fall in prices on the relative position of different classes, considered as creditors on the one hand and as debtors on the other; since it is on the supposed increase in the burden of debt, consequent on a fall in prices, that the bimetallists are so fond of insisting; and we have found that whilst **such change in their relative positions as has taken place is very different from that which bimetallists have imagined, such change as has taken place is due to causes other than currency.**

29. But the examination of this question, as it affects creditors and debtors, does point to more general conclusions of very great interest concerning the changes which have taken place in the relative conditions of different classes and interests of rich and poor, of capital and industry, of interest and wages. Let us continue the inquiry by eliminating all question of debtor and creditor, and let us consider only the relative position of different classes of society at the two periods—1870 and 1890-98. Let us compare incomes of different amounts at the two periods, from whatever source derived, whether from investments, or from trades or professions, or from services or from labour, and consider what are the relative positions of persons enjoying large incomes and persons possessing small incomes or earnings at the two periods in question. In order to do this it will not be necessary to repeat what has been already said about incomes from invested capital, since they have been dealt with; or about expenditure, since what has been said about the expenditure of rich and poor applies equally to all expenditures whatever be the nature of the income out of which it is paid. We only need to add in a few words what are the salient facts concerning incomes derived from sources other than invested capital; viz. trade and business incomes, professional incomes, salaries and wages—in other words, concerning the prices given for services and labour at the two periods in question.

30. First of all then as regards the incomes of the richer classes which are derived from services of any kind—from business, from professions, and from salaried places. On this subject there are no

K 2

general statistics which I can quote with confidence. But common experience teaches us, I think, that payments for services rendered have not diminished in the last twenty-five years. The remuneration of the manager, of the lawyer, of the medical man, of the artist, has not diminished ; and the salaries of clerks, especially of the lower and more numerous classes of clerks, have notoriously increased.

31. As regards the prices of weekly paid labour, or wages, there can be no doubt that they increased very largely between 1870 and 1891.* Of the general fact there can be no doubt. It is difficult to give the result in a few figures, but it may be mentioned that the careful inquiry made in the article referred to below, gives the average annual wages per man as £43 4s. in 1870, and £53 8s. in 1891. Corrected by Mr. Sauerbeck's figures, so as to show the effect of the cheapening of the articles which the labourer consumes on the real value of his earnings, the figures would be 130 for 1870, as against 202 for 1891.

32. The following extracts from the leaflet written by Mr. Shaw-Lefevre in reply to the bimetallic report of the Agricultural Commission, and issued by this Association, relate to the wages of the agricultural labourer. They are of great importance, because, if wages have risen in agriculture, the most distressed of all our industries, we may be sure that they have risen as much or more in other industries. Mr. Shaw-Lefevre says :—

" It is absolutely certain that in agriculture, equally as in other " industries of the country, in the twenty-four years which have " elapsed since the alleged deficiency of gold commenced, there has " been no general adjustment of the wages of labourers in proportion " to and consequent upon the fall of prices from the year 1873. On " the contrary, money wages generally have risen since the fall of " prices began ; and as the fall of prices has been greatest in articles " of prime necessity, which form the main consumption of the " labouring classes—such as bread, sugar, tea, cheese, the inferior " classes of beef and mutton, and cheap clothing and boots— **" it is certain that, when measured by what the labourers " can get for their money, their real remuneration for their " work has very considerably improved."**

╵

* *See an article by A. L. Bowley on the change of wages in the United Kingdom between 1861 and 1891, in the Journal of the Statistical Society, for June, 1895, and the various authorities there quoted, who, though they may differ in details, agree in general conclusions.*

" Another way of estimating the change is this : Before 1873
" two-thirds of the weekly wages of an agricultural labourer were
" expended in purchasing a sufficiency of bread alone for himself and
" his family.   In 1892-4 less than one-third of his wages sufficed for
" this purpose."

33. It appears, therefore, (a) that the money prices of
human services have increased since 1870; (b) that the
money prices of those forms of service which are paid by
weekly wages have probably increased more than the
prices of more highly paid services; (c) that the real wages
of the lower forms of service, i.e. what is commonly called
labour, have increased much more than the nominal
wages.

Comparing the more highly paid forms of service with the less
highly paid, the real value of the wages of the less highly paid has
increased much more than the real value of the salaries of the more
highly paid, because a much larger proportion of their income is
spent on articles which have fallen heavily in price.

We are now in a position to compare the position in 1870 and
1898 respectively, of persons with large incomes and of persons
with small incomes from whatever source they may be derived.
Let us take for the comparison a rich man enjoying, say, an income
of £10,000 a year, and a poor man earning his livelihood by weekly
wages.

34. First, then, as regards income. The nominal income of the
rich man will have diminished if it depends on invested
capital, because the interest on capital has fallen; the
nominal income of the poor man has certainly risen.

When we turn to expenditure, the income of the rich man
goes less far than it did, because the prices which have fallen are
prices of things of which he consumes only a moderate quantity,
whilst the prices of what he requires, viz. of luxuries and of human
services, have increased.   The income of the poorer man goes
farther than it did, because the things of which the prices have
fallen are things which constitute by far the greater part of his
consumption.

35. So far, therefore, from its being the fact that the last
twenty-five or thirty years has favoured the bloated
capitalist at the expense of industry, the drone at the
expense of the worker, the men of large property at the
expense of those who depend on their hands or their brains

for subsistence, the exact opposite is the case. The rich have not been made richer or the poor poorer, but the contrary. There is one exception—the case of the agricultural land-owner. As a capitalist he shares in the lowered value of his capital with other capitalists, but as a producer he suffers exceptionally because in consequence of foreign competition the price of his produce has fallen exceptionally, and because he still has to pay as much for labour as before.

36. If these are the real features of the situation, is it not in the highest degree absurd to treat the fall of prices as an unmixed evil, to attribute that fall to currency, and to suppose that it is either desirable or possible, by adding to the number of counters in circulation, to raise prices and to reverse the current of industrial progress ? If the changes which have happened were changes due to a want of currency they would affect all prices equally, which has not been the case ; and if all prices were now to be raised equally and simultaneously by adding to currency, everyone's relative position would remain as before. But it is clear that the changes which have taken place are not due to currency, but to factors of a very different kind, which have altered and which, we may hope, will continue to alter the relative position of different classes. These factors may be stated as follows :—

1. Improvements in production and transport, which have lowered prices, especially of those things which form a large proportion of the consumption of the poorer classes.

2. Foreign competition, which, taking advantage of improved transport, has specially reduced the price of agricultural products.

3. Increase of capital and consequently of demand for labour, which has either increased the nominal wages of labour or has prevented them from falling.

The results are a better distribution of wealth and a higher remuneration to labour, results for which we cannot be too thankful.

There is one class, viz. agricultural producers, who really suffer actual loss. But of this loss, some falls on the farmer, still more on the land owner, and little or none on the labourer.

37. Recurring to the question with which we began, we find :

    1. That it is not the fact that debtors as a class have become richer at the expense of creditors.

    2. That it is not the fact that the rich have become richer and the poor poorer.

    3. That it is not the fact that idle capital is increasing its gains at the cost of industry.

    4. That during the period in question the prices of the necessaries of life have fallen, whilst the prices of human services, and especially the prices of labour, have risen, the effect of which is to make the rich poorer and the poor richer, because human services are what the rich man requires and the necessaries of life are what the poor man consumes.

38. In conclusion, let us consider what bearing these facts have on our standard of value. All sensible men desire a standard of value which shall be as stable as possible in respect of all the different things which it is employed to measure. **The foregoing considerations show that when all prices are taken into account, there is nothing whatever in the recent history of prices to show that our present standard of value is unstable.** Again, the foregoing considerations also show that the changes which have taken place in the prices of the necessaries of life and of human services have been changes for the better in the general conditions of society. If, under these circumstances, we were, at the bidding of persons like M. Allard and Professor Foxwell, to depreciate our standard of value, we should be taking a step which is wholly uncalled for. But we should be doing something more and something worse. **We should in all probability check or reverse the wholesome process which is now going on ; and, we should, for a time, at any rate, by causing prices to rise more and to rise faster than wages, increase the profits of capital and diminish the remuneration of human services and labour.**

Bimetallism in France

(From 1803 to 1874).*

By Mr. HENRY DUNNING MACLEOD.

" Until the year 1873 the ratio at which gold and silver were interchangeable was steady, because the Mints of France and other European countries were open to all the world for the unlimited coinage of both metals on the fixed basis of $15\frac{1}{2}$ ozs. of silver to 1 oz. of gold."—*Official Statement of* BIMETALLIC LEAGUE, para. 1.

"The French law adopted in 1803 . . . . its provisions are entirely approved by modern Bimetallists."—*A Bimetallic Primer*, by Mr. HERBERT C. GIBBS, p. 13.

---

1. THE bimetallists claim the period 1803–74, in France, as the golden age of bimetallism : and persistently assert that the ratio of $15\frac{1}{2}$ to 1 kept the exchanges steady throughout the world : and that it was the closing of the French Mints in 1874 to the free coinage of silver that caused the very serious fall in its value.   But the following statement of historical facts will show that there is no foundation for these assertions, and that **it was the fall in the value of silver which caused the closing of the French Mints.**   And on the subject of this paper I can speak from personal experience.

In 1726, after six centuries of innumerable changes in the Mint prices of gold and silver, and the rating of the coins with respect to each other, the ratio was at length fixed at $14\frac{1}{2}$ to 1.   But as gold was underrated by this ratio, by the operation of Gresham's Law, it

* *Issued in November*, 1895.

disappeared from circulation, and silver became the standard in France : just as by the operation of the same law, gold became the standard in England since 1718. No change was made till 1785, when Calonne changed the ratio to $15\frac{1}{2}$; and this was confirmed in 1803, because it was very near the market price.

Nevertheless this ratio wholly failed to keep gold and silver in circulation in unlimited quantities in France during any part of the period 1803-74.

2. The French liberating armies plundered the sanctuaries of the countries they came to liberate. Immense quantities of silver were sent to the Mint to be coined, and the market ratio of silver became 17, while the legal ratio was $15\frac{1}{2}$.* From 1803 to 1850, with two or three exceptions, gold was constantly at a premium in France. As a necessary consequence during that period gold coin was not in general circulation. In 1839-40 I resided in France, and travelled through it, and I can testify that there was no gold to be seen in common use. Everyone who lived in France in those days can testify to the same effect. I remember on one occasion being shown a gold twenty-franc piece as a curiosity. Of course there was abundance of gold coin to be had at the Bank of France, but those who wanted it had to pay a premium for it, and therefore no one applied for it except those who wanted it to settle their foreign obligations.

3. But after 1850 vast quantities of gold began to come in from California and Australia, and then the market ratio of gold and silver began to change. In 1850, while the legal ratio was $15\frac{1}{2}$, the market ratio was $15\frac{3}{4}$, and that slight difference kept gold entirely out of circulation—because, while gold was only worth $15\frac{1}{2}$ as coin, it was worth $15\frac{3}{4}$ as bullion. But in the course of a few years the market ratio rose to $15\frac{1}{3}$, and that slight change in the market ratio drove nearly £200,000,000 of silver out of circulation, and substituted an equal quantity of gold for it—because gold was then worth $15\frac{1}{2}$ in coin, while it was only worth $15\frac{1}{3}$ as bullion. Thus the apparently slight change of the market ratio of gold and silver from $15\frac{3}{4}$ to $15\frac{1}{3}$, while the legal ratio remained fixed at $15\frac{1}{2}$, was sufficient to change the whole metallic currency of France from silver to gold.

* *Lord Liverpool's Treatise on the Coins of the Realm, p.* 180.

[155]

In 1857 I was residing at a French seaport town, and every steamer that came in was laden with casks of Scotch whisky going to be transmuted into French brandy, and every steamer that went out had its decks piled with bags of silver five-franc pieces. It was the same at every seaport town in France. Every steamer and every diligence that left France was loaded with bags of silver five-franc pieces. **Silver departed from France in a flood,** and at last it became so scarce that it became necessary to coin those detestable five-franc gold pieces.

Mr. Shaw says that during the period 1820-50, when the ratio remained below the legal ratio of 15½ to 1, and there was a profit on the import of silver, the total silver coined at the French Mint amounted to £127,458,322, while that of gold was £19,333,854. In the succeeding period, 1850-66, when the market ratio changed and remained for fifteen or sixteen years in favour of gold, the total gold coinage reached £292,416,951, while the total silver coinage was only £1,315,532.*

4. **What, then, becomes of the multitudinous assertions of the bimetallists that a fixed legal ratio between the coins can maintain a steady market ratio between the metals?** What becomes of their assertions that if a legal ratio be enacted, gold and silver will circulate together in unlimited quantities? There never was a more triumphant vindication of the truth of Gresham's Law and its supreme importance.

In 1865 the Latin Union was formed between France, Italy, Switzerland, and Belgium, to unify their coinages, and coin gold and silver in unlimited quantities at the ratio of 15½ to 1, which was to come into operation in 1867. Even then Italy declared itself in favour of a single gold standard. This unification of their coinages was a blessing to those countries and to all persons who travelled in them. But it was founded on the fatal principle of bimetallism, and any sagacious economist could see that it could not last. My distinguished friend, M. Michel Chevalier, and the ablest French economists were always opposed to bimetallism.

5. In 1867, when the Latin Union first came into operation, the

* Shaw's " History of the Currency," pp. 185-6.

ratio of gold to silver had already begun to change, and the most keen-sighted economists foresaw that the principle of the Latin Union would break down. A Commission in that year speaks thus of the situation :—

"It is well-known by all that this ratio (of 1803) by the simple reason of its being fixed could not remain correct. There was quickly a premium on gold, and silver remained almost alone in circulation until near 1850. The discovery of the mines of California and Australia suddenly changed this situation by throwing into the European market a very considerable quantity of gold. By the side of this force, which tended to create a divergence from the legal ratio by lowering gold, there was another which occasioned a rise of silver. Under the influence of various circumstances, too long to enumerate, the needs of the extreme East had grown in unusual proportions, and as silver is alone in favour there, it was exported in enormous masses. There was a premium on silver to the extent of 8 per mille, and it disappeared almost completely from circulation, yielding place to gold.

" Preoccupied by the situation, the Government charged a Com-mission to study the measures to be taken. Its labours are summed up in the report of M. de Bosredon (1857). After examining the system tending to preserve silver money intact by lowering the value of gold money, and conversely the system tending to the adoption of the gold standard by reducing the silver money to the state of billon, the Commission did not decide between them. It confined itself, in fact, to counselling the Government to a transitory step—the raising of the export duties on silver . . . . . The exportation of silver, therefore, continued ; and if the disappearance of five-franc pieces was not remarked, because they were replaced by gold, it was not the same with the scarcity of pieces of a smaller value employed in petty payments.

" Being informed of the obstructions to retail commerce by complaints carried before the Senate, and instructed by the example of Switzerland, which had in 1860 reduced the standard of its divisional money, the Minister of Finance appointed a Commission (1861) to study the remedy to be applied to the evil. This Commission counselled the reduction of the standard of pieces of less than five francs to .834 fine. It did this in complete knowledge of the cause, fully recognising that in so doing the monetary unity of silver, characteristic of our system, would be thereby broken, at any rate for its circulating form ; for while the franc no longer existed in law, the five-franc was disappearing in fact, so that the change was equivalent to the establishment of a gold standard."

This advice of the Commission was, however, by the law of 1864, applied only to pieces of 50 or 20 centimes.

6. But in 1868 the fall in the silver became more accentuated, and a Commission in that year, by a majority, recommended the adoption of a single gold standard. In 1869-70 another Commission, again by a majority, repeated this recommendation in still stronger terms. In June, 1870, the Prussian Parliament appointed a Commission to consider the expediency of adopting a single gold standard for Prussia. But a few weeks after that the Franco-Prussian war broke out, which put a stop to all such discussions.

By Acts of November, 1871, and May, 1873, **the new German Empire adopted a single gold standard** with a subsidiary currency of silver. It is commonly asserted that Germany obtained the gold to effect this by the payment of the French indemnity. Most persons who do not understand exchange operations affirm that the whole of the £200,000,000 levied as a fine on unfortunate France was paid in gold. But this is an utter delusion. In my "Theory and Practice of Banking," and in my "Theory of Credit," I have given authentic details of the payment of the French indemnity from the official report of M. Léon Say, by which it appears that 160 millions of it were paid in paper of different sorts. And of the remainder £10,904,000 was paid in French gold, £25,493,993 in English gold, and the balance in silver.

7. In December, 1872, Belgium adopted a single gold standard with silver as subsidiary. I have seen it stated, but I cannot say on what authority, that Belgium threatened to secede from the Latin Union unless France closed her Mints to the free coinage of silver. But, at all events, the fall in the value of silver continued rapidly to increase; and in January, 1874, a Monetary

Conference was held in Paris. M. Dumas, of the Paris Mint, presided ; M. de Parieu, as representing the French Government, was vice-president. The *Economist* said : "This was the adhesion to the theory of a single gold standard on the part of the French Government, and their appointment of M. de Parieu as one of the Commissioners to represent them, is a fresh sign of their being in favour of the gradual abolition of **a law which, after seventy years' experience, is found to be effete in theory and prejudicial in action."**

The result of this Monetary Conference was that the French Mints were closed to the free coinage of silver.

8. In 1876 the French Government resolved to suspend the coining of five-franc pieces entirely. Accordingly, on the 21st March, 1876, M. Léon Say, Minister of Finance, submitted to the Senate a Bill to that effect. It was followed, eight days later, by a proposition of a law suspending the emission of "bons" for the coining of silver money $\frac{9}{10}$ fine. The *exposé des motifs* of this act is most remarkable * :—

"The events which have happened for some time past in the relations of the precious metals have brought to a head the monetary question among us, although **from 1815 Great Britain has laid down principles which have attracted round her an ever-increasing circle of nations.**

"The theory of the double standard, on which our monetary law of the year XI. reposes, has been called in question since its origin.

"It is, to our conception, less a theory than the result of the primitive inability of the legislators to combine together the two precious metals otherwise than by way of an unlimited concurrence — metals, both of which are destined to enter into the monetary system, but which recent legislators have learned to co-ordinate by leaving the unlimited function to gold alone and reducing silver to the *rôle* of divisional money. From 1857 the French Government has studied the question, and it may be stated that since that date the

* *Shaw's " History of the Currency," pp.* 196–7.

principle of the gold standard has won increasing favour through our several administrations."

Then follows an account of the monetary history of France during the period. "If," the preamble continues, "from 1874, certain precautions had not been taken to arrest the effects of that great perturbation in the ratio, France and her monetary allies would have seen their monetary circulation invaded by silver and correspondingly drained of gold." Hence the Conventions of 1874–75–76, limiting the mintings of the members of the Latin Union, although, "according to us, the fall of silver in 1875 prescribed a complete cessation even for that year rather than a simple limitation."

9. **Thus the persistent assertions of the bimetallists that the closing of the French Mints to the free coinage of silver in 1874 was the original cause of the serious fall in the value of silver since then are utterly confuted.** No one of common sense could suppose that the French Government would have taken the very serious step of closing the Mints to the free coinage of silver without the most cogent reasons. It is now clearly demonstrated that it was the continuous fall in the value of silver that necessitated the closing of the Mints; and it is now shown that the necessity for this had been foreseen by the most sagacious economists for seven years before it took place, and it was only done after the fullest discussion, and by the advice of the most experienced authorities.

10. As a matter of fact, the value of silver had been continuously falling since 1867. I am not called upon to investigate the causes of this fall here, but I must say that one of the main causes of this has been entirely overlooked by European economists. It is impossible to say what effect the changes in the relative production of gold and silver had in producing it. But the ablest financial writers in the United States have pointed out that the stupendous issues of paper money by the Government of the United States were one of the main, if not the most potent cause of the unprecedented fall in the value of silver, and that there is no hope of any material rise in its value until some effectual measures are taken to place the paper issues of the United States on a sounder footing.

It was simply a matter of self-preservation for France to close her

Mints to the free coinage of silver in 1874: just as it was with the Government of India in 1893. I am in no way concerned to deny that the closing of the European and Indian Mints has aggravated the fall in the value of silver. But if the Mints had been kept open much longer, it would have destroyed the stability of the French monetary system.

11. The whole of the facts of this period are the most triumphant vindication of the truth of Gresham's Law. All the most sagacious economists for five centuries had demonstrated that it is impossible to keep gold and silver together in circulation in unlimited quantities at a fixed legal ratio differing from the market ratio of the metals. The Government of India in 1806, after ample and bitter experience of the consequences of bimetallism, gave its official adhesion to this doctrine; the British Government did the same in 1816, and then established our present system of coinage, the most perfect ever devised by the ingenuity of man. **And then came the crowning example of the Latin Union. No sooner was it established than it began to break up**; and its final catastrophe in 1874 demonstrates that no human laws or institutions can contend against the laws of Nature.

12. It has now been shown that it is impossible for gold and silver to circulate together in unlimited quantities at a legal ratio differing from the market ratio of the metals; that the coin which is under-rated invariably disappears from circulation, and the coin that is overrated alone remains current; that as the market ratio rises above or falls below the legal ratio, gold and silver alternately drive each other out of circulation according as the one or the other is underrated or overrated; that it is the relative market value of the metals which regulates the relative value of the coins, and not the reverse; and that **the whole theory of the bimetallists is a vain chimera.**

The Working of Bimetallism in the United States.*

By the Rt. Hon. LORD PLAYFAIR, P.C., G.C.B., etc.

"The Bimetallism which we advocate is that which has been in successful operation in France from the commencement of this century, and in the United States from the foundation of the Union, until 1873."—*Preface to "Silver and Gold"* (*Prize Bimetallic Essay*), *by* SIR GUILDFORD L. MOLESWORTH, 1894.

"There is every encouragement to press the matter, seeing that the United States of America . . . . are willing to co-operate."—*Official statement of* BIMETALLIC LEAGUE, para. 13.

-----

1. WE have heard so much of the working of a bimetallic ratio in France, as being sufficient to keep gold and silver at the ratio of $15\frac{1}{2}$ to 1, that it is desirable to know the effects of other ratios established by law in the United States. Originally bimetallists claimed the experience of both these countries as conclusive that a legal ratio between gold and silver did actually produce proportional parity when there was free and indiscriminate coinage of both metals; though now General Walker and other leading bimetallists are inclined to limit the claim to alternating and not

* *Issued in November*, 1895.

L

to concurrent coinage, the parity being maintained by lessening or relinquishing the coinage of one metal until the quantities in the market adjust themselves to the legal ratio. France certainly made a gallant effort to maintain her ratio, but even she changed the ratio, though within comparatively small limits, 150 times in a single century.

THE RATIOS OF THE UNITED STATES.

2. The United States in the last one hundred years has only had two ratios, and the results are worthy of study. In 1792 the legal ratio between gold and silver was declared to be 15 to 1. That is, 15 lbs. of silver were to buy 1 lb. of gold. The real commercial value was more nearly the French ratio of $15\frac{1}{2}$ to 1. The United States started the new national coinage by overvaluing silver and undervaluing gold. The necessary and invariable consequence followed that **gold, the undervalued metal, rapidly disappeared from the currency**; and by 1812 the United States had practically become monometallic on a silver basis. President Jefferson tried to arrest this result in 1806 by stopping the coinage of silver dollars, and for 31 years not a single standard silver dollar was coined in the United States. The subsidiary coinage of full weight remained, and there was a mongrel currency of Spanish dollars, French crowns, and other silver coins. Gold, however, refused to come back into currency, as the bimetallic ratio of 1792 still prevailed, and another ratio was enacted in 1834 and repeated in 1837.

SECOND RATIO OF 16 to 1.

3. To tempt gold back into currency, the ratio was declared to be 16 to 1; that is, 16 lbs. of silver were to be given for 1 lb. of gold. The Congress was quite aware that it was slightly overvaluing gold, but deemed that to be necessary to bring it back to the country. The bimetallists contended that, as silver had only to rise three per cent. to bridge over the gap between the market and legal ratio of the two metals, the declaration of law would certainly produce a concurrent parity between silver and gold. As a fact, **gold did rush back into the currency, but silver with equal celerity rushed out of it.** Even the fractional or subsidiary currency, as well as the silver dollars, were rapidly disappearing ; but the exodus was stopped by debasing

the former and limiting its legal tender to five dollars. The practical action of the Act of 1834 was to reverse the operation of that of 1792, which created a currency based on silver; while the new ratio converted it as surely into a gold basis as if that had been specially enacted. The overvalued gold returned to America; while the undervalued silver emigrated to other lands which gave a higher market price for it.

GENERAL OPERATION OF THE TWO RATIOS.

4. Both the ratio of 15 to 1 and that of 16 to 1 gave admirable experience of the working of the Gresham Law.

From 1792 to 1834 the ratio of 15 to 1 overvalued silver and undervalued gold, so the consequence was that gold was driven out of the country and the currency became entirely one of silver.

From 1834 to 1873, on a ratio of 16 to 1, the current was reversed, for now gold was overvalued, and the currency became based on gold, without silver dollars, but with much subsidiary or token silver coins.

It is specially to be noted that during the eighty-one years which covered these two experiments on legal ratios, differing very little from the market ratios, **coinage under statute had not the slightest effect in restraining the operation of the Gresham Law,** because in the first period silver was overvalued, and in the second period gold was overvalued. Trade, by its markets, regulates these movements, and no statutory law can prevent them.

THE ACT OF 1873 GAVE LEGAL RECOGNITION TO THE GOLD
BASIS.

5. Practically, since 1834, the currency of the United States has been on a gold basis, and the Act of 1873, repeating an Act of 1853, simply gave recognition to that fact, but it prevented the future coinage of full legal tender silver dollars. Gold had become the standard of value. A new Currency Act of 1878, confirming this recognition, tried to restore silver to parity in the currency by pledging the Government to accept any silver dollars which it might coin as redeemable in gold. There was no bimetallic ratio in this pledge of the credit of the Government, but Secretary Windom in 1889 construed the parity clause in Sherman's Act to mean that all Sherman

notes issued against the bullion were redeemable in gold, and the Treasury since then has concurred in this interpretation.

The market value of silver in the coined silver dollars, as compared with the gold dollars, is not 16 to 1, but more nearly as 32 to 1. For State purposes, England issues a small amount of token silver money and exchanges it for gold to a limited amount, but the United States goes much further, because it backs every silver dollar by a gold dollar in order to make both metals keep in concurrent circulation. As long as the credit of the United States is beyond suspicion, a dollar in silver will remain at par with a dollar in gold. **Can any nation, however great, support such a burden on its credit without rupture?** Let us look at the actual and fictitious differences between the silver and the gold dollar.

RELATIVE VALUES OF HAMMERED OR MELTED DOLLARS

6. If a silver dollar is defaced as a coin, either by being hammered or melted, the market value for the 371.25 grains of pure silver in it is only about half a dollar in gold.

If a gold dollar is subjected to similar treatment it will sell as metal for the same value as it fetched in the form of coin. The silver in the coined dollar is on a par with the gold dollar, not through any inherent virtue of bimetallism, but simply because the Government gives an artificial support to silver coinage by doubling the market value when it is redeemed in gold. The overvalued silver does not expel gold as quickly as the old ratio of 1792, for two reasons: first, because coinage is no longer free; and second, on account of each silver dollar being redeemable by a gold dollar. There is no motive to export coined silver to Europe, where it would only have a commodity value of half its face value in the United States.

SILVER AND GOLD COINAGE IN THE UNITED STATES.

7. **The actual silver dollars are unpopular** on account of their weight and size, and only about 56 millions of them are in circulation, or less than one dollar *per capita* to the 69 millions of population. Under the Bland and Sherman Acts the Government had to buy 460 million ounces of silver. The present silver currency in metal, and paper representing the metal, is about 665 millions of dollars, while the actual demand of silver currency for the purposes of trade is certainly

not above 100 millions of dollars. The surplus as well as that amount is a heavy burden on the Treasury, and, in case of a run due to a distrust of the Government, could not be met except by a large increase of the National Debt. It is true that the gold coin in the country is estimated at 676 million dollars, but the great bulk is circulating in trade, although some also becomes hoarded when Government credit shows weakness. The actual silver coin does not circulate freely, but is stored in the cellars of the Treasury, greatly diminishing in value as the market price of silver falls.

THE EFFECT OF RECENT DISTRUST ON THE TREASURY.

8. There is no law, but there is a general understanding that the Treasury should always keep 100 million dollars of gold coinage in its till to meet sudden calls of silver coins brought in for redemption in gold. Certainly recent experience proves that a larger reserve would be desirable to maintain parity between the silver and gold coinage. In 1894, had there been no distrust abroad, there ought not to have been an excessive exportation of gold. The exports of merchandise from the United States exceeded the imports by 186 million dollars, and yet 81 million dollars in gold left the country in excess of the amount imported. This proved that foreign nations were distrusting American securities by sending them back for realisation. Then the general public also showed distrust by paying silver instead of gold into the Treasury. In 1889, before any distrust as to the coinage arose, the tariff duties were paid by 90 per cent. of gold. The free coinage agitation became strong, the bimetallists being aggressive, and by January 1st, 1893, the gold payments into the Customs had dwindled to 8 per cent. ; by April 1st of the same year it had gone down to 2 per cent. ; and as the year progressed no gold at all was paid for Customs duties. Suspicion being thus thrown on public credit, private credit also became impaired, and in the first month of 1895 a great financial crisis seemed imminent. The reserve of gold in the Treasury, requisite for the redemption of silver coin, had gone down to less than one-half of the minimum considered essential for ordinary times. No one who knows the resources of the United States could apprehend national bankruptcy or repudiation, but it was obvious that the time was approaching when the Government would be placed in a position of great difficulty to fulfil its obligations on

demand. A syndicate of bankers, of whom Mr. Pierpoint Morgan was the leading spirit, and Rothschilds the powerful ally, came to its aid by offering to sell European exchange at a cheaper rate than gold could be taken out of the Treasury and shipped abroad. The Government issued bonds to be bought in gold, and succeeded in maintaining the reserve of 100 million dollars, although sometimes falling below this sum.

The 62 million dollar bonds issued are, however, a simple addition to the National Debt, and prove the present inability of the Treasury to pay in gold out of ordinary revenue on the presentation of legal tender for redemption.

CONCLUSIONS FROM THE EXPERIENCE.

9. **This short history of bimetallism in the United States conclusively shows that no ratios between silver and gold have been able to maintain a parity of value between silver and gold, or to lessen the operation of the Gresham law, that undervalued and overvalued money cannot remain in concurrent circulation—at least, in parity.** The fact that at present each silver dollar, worth in the market only half a gold dollar, is redeemable in the Treasury for a whole gold dollar has nothing to do with bimetallism, but depends on the credit of a promise made by the Government. The danger of such a promise has been manifested by the unsettled state of the money market and the depression of trade since 1890, and came to a climax in the beginning of 1895. Formerly Governments which debased the currency were punished by lack of confidence and lessened trade, and it is interesting to observe that like effects follow the action of a Government that tries to force a circulation of a depreciated coin by pledging itself to redeem it as legal tender at double its real value. Governments when they use their mints merely to indicate the standard quantity and purity of gold and silver coinage are on safe grounds, but a Government like the United States, which gives double value to a token silver dollar, that can only circulate as commodity at half the value in other countries, undertakes a responsibility dangerous to its financial position and demoralising to its population.

Germany and the Gold Standard.*

By Dr. KARL HELFFERICH.

"Germany did a foolish thing in 1872, and she has seen cause to regret it."—
A Colloquy on Currency, by MR. H. H. GIBBS (*President of the Bimetallic
League*), p. 194.

"There is every encouragement to press the matter, seeing that . . . . .
Germany [is] willing to co-operate."—*Official Statement of* BIMETALLIC LEAGUE,
para. 13.

"The Federal Governments have unanimously determined not to comply with
the request for a Conference."—PRINCE HOHENLOHE, Imperial Chancellor,
February 8th, 1896.

INTRODUCTION OF A GOLD STANDARD.

1. One of the most important tasks incumbent on the German
Empire after the completion of the Franco-German War was the due
ordering of the monetary system. Endeavour to bring about a
uniform German monetary standard were almost as old as the diversity of German coinage systems. At the very time when the Franco-
German War broke out, the German Governments were preparing
for a monetary reform. Early in the 'sixties the question arose
whether Germany should adhere to the silver standard which existed
in all the German States except Bremen, or whether she should
proceed to a change in the monetary standard.

2. **The silver standard hitherto in use had entailed
material evils.** Experience had shown that while a silver standard
was in force a circulation of gold could not be maintained. But
silver was too inconvenient for any payment of a large amount, and
consequently the public was inclined to use, instead of coin, paper
money of all descriptions. This circumstance was taken advantage
of by numerous small banks to issue inadequately secured bank notes
for small amounts, which, for want of a gold circulation, the public

---

* *Issued in February*, 1896.

allowed to be thrust upon them. This evil could only be remedied by a sufficient gold circulation.

3. **The question as to whether these evils could be remedied by a transition to a bimetallic standard was scarcely discussed. France had not had the best experience with her bimetallic union,** and French public opinion decidedly inclined towards a gold standard. At the International Conference of 1867, and in the Committee of Inquiry of 1868, the great majority had pronounced in favour of a gold standard ; also the great Council of Commerce, which was sitting at the time when the Franco-German War broke out, had proposed the transition to a gold standard. Germany, therefore, had to reckon with the probability that France, as well as the other States comprised in the Latin Union, would sooner or later exchange their bimetallic for a gold standard. Thus, especially after Germany had come into the possession of two hundred millions of pounds by way of war indemnity, **there was in the German Empire a general consensus of opinion that the only expedient measure would be a transition to a gold standard. A few theoreticians only spoke in favour of a bimetallic standard ; commerce and industry were unanimously in favour of a gold standard.**

4. In the autumn of 1871 the project of a provisional Coinage Act was submitted to the Federal Council and the Imperial Diet. The deliberations were pushed forward, and in December, 1871, the Act was promulgated. It authorised the coinage of Imperial gold coins of 10 and 20 marks value,* and the making of these coins a legal tender side by side with the silver coins hitherto in use in a proportion of 15½ to 1 as between silver and gold. The further coinage of silver was prohibited.

5. This measure was followed by the Coinage Act of July, 1873, which ordered the gradual withdrawal from circulation of the old silver coinage, and the coining of silver token coins of the new system, while the amount of silver constituting a legal tender was limited to 20 marks. The coinage of gold for private account was authorised, and this provision was subsequently supplemented by the Bank Act, by which the duty was imposed on the Imperial Bank of buying any quantity of gold offered to it at the rate of 1,392 marks per lb.

THE ACCOMPLISHMENT OF THE MONETARY REFORM.

6. When Germany decided to adopt a gold standard she had a circulation of silver to the amount of about 1,535 millions of marks. Of this amount, even after the adoption of the gold standard,

* *A mark is nearly equivalent to a shilling.*

from 400 to 450 millions of marks could still be used as small change (10 marks per head of the population). There remained to withdraw from circulation the balance of about 1,100 millions of marks, to melt it down and sell it against gold. Of course, this enormous quantity of silver could not be either withdrawn from circulation at once, or thrown all at once upon the market. On the contrary, this operation had to be divided over a number of years. The German sales of silver commenced in 1873, hesitatingly and cautiously, and steadily increased up to the year 1877.

7. Meanwhile the price of silver fell. Since about the end of the 'sixties the demand for India had been steadily decreasing, and had finally fallen to one-third of the average for the years 1855 to 1865. Moreover, a number of countries effected changes in their monetary systems either simultaneously with, or immediately after, Germany. The Scandinavian kingdoms and the United States of America adopted a gold standard, the Netherlands discontinued their coining of silver, and the countries belonging to the Latin Union first limited their issue of silver coin and then discontinued it. This twofold cause of diminution of the demand coincided with an increase in the production of silver. These circumstances led to a considerable fall in the price of silver, and the melting down and sale of the German silver coin could only be continued with great loss. In May, 1879, it became known that the German Government had discontinued its sales of silver, and since that time they have not been resumed.

8. The consequence of the cessation of the sales of silver is that to this day there are in circulation in Germany, besides the new silver token coins, about 380 millions of marks in old silver thalers * which still remain a legal tender to an unlimited amount. About one-half of this amount is always in the hands of the Imperial Bank, while the other half is in circulation. Hitherto the Imperial Bank has never made use of its right to redeem its notes in silver thalers, but has always paid in gold when gold is demanded. In the bullion stock of the bank there figures, side by side with the 200 millions of marks in thalers, an amount of about 600 millions of marks in gold. Altogether Germany possesses, including the stock of uncoined gold in the bank cellars, a monetary stock of gold to the amount of about 3,000 millions of marks. Under these circumstances, the 380 millions of marks in thalers cannot be held to endanger the German monetary system. Hence, notwithstanding the cessation of the sales of silver, **the transition to a gold standard has been carried out with complete success.**

* *A thaler is equivalent to three marks.*

9. The bimetallic movement has not originated on German soil, but has been imported there from abroad. Dr. Arendt, the leader of the bimetallic agitation, wrote on one occasion as follows : "Before the German Government in May, 1879, suspended the sales of silver the monetary standard question was looked upon as disposed of in Germany." Germany was the only great power that did not participate in the Paris Monetary Conference of 1878.

10. **It was not until the Government showed signs of stopping on the road towards a complete carrying through of the gold standard that bimetallism succeeded in gaining ground in Germany.** About the end of the 'seventies Mr. Cernuschi, a Frenchman, and Mr. Kelley, an American, travelled over Germany in order to agitate for bimetallism. Mr. von Kardorff, a Protectionist and agrarian, was the first representative of bimetallism in Germany, and up to the present day he champions the cause of bimetallism. He was soon joined by Mr. Leuschner, Director of the Mansfeld Copper Mining Association, which had been seriously affected by the fall of silver. Somewhat later these gentlemen found a partisan of great dialectical ability and activity in the person of Dr. Arendt, who since that time has been the intellectual head of the bimetallic movement in Germany. At that time, that is to say, early in the 'eighties, **the arguments of the German bimetallists against the gold standard were as follows :**

(a) Either the sales of silver must be resumed and completely carried through, or the gold standard must be abandoned and a bimetallic standard adopted.

(b) Through the fall of the price of silver the German silver-mining industry has been injured ; and, further, the German income from securities made out for an amount in silver (especially Austrian ones) has greatly fallen off.

(c) A continued decrease of the production of gold, and hence a rise in the value of gold, is imminent.

A number of professors were inclined in favour of bimetallism—thus, for instance, Wagner, Schäffle, Lexis, Neuwirth, and subsequently Conrad.

11. Great stress was laid upon the predictions of Professor Suess of Vienna, that the gold mines of the world were nearly exhausted. When a demand for gold arose in consequence of the United States and Italy adopting cash payments in gold, and when consequently the great banks of Europe increased their rates of discount, these transient disturbances were represented as permanent, and it was asserted that the prophesied scarcity of

gold had arrived. People spoke of "the folly of pulling up the gold blanket which is too short for the bed" and of "paralysing trade by high discounts."

12. **The arguments thus brought forward on the part of the bimetallists were soon proved to be fallacious.** It appeared that the situation created with regard to the German monetary system through the cessation of the silver sales was not serious. The stock of thalers still in existence was not capable of unfavourably influencing the German money market. From the year 1883 the production of gold commenced to increase. The drain of gold to America ceased, and soon America commenced to pass gold to Europe in considerable quantities, and consequently the rates of discount fell to a normal level. In short, facts afforded a striking refutation of the arguments advanced at that time by the bimetallists. But the bimetallists did not for this reason abandon their agitation. They soon availed themselves of the decline in the general level of prices in order to demonstrate thereby an alleged increase in the value of gold. The fall of the prices of agricultural products was attributed by them to the gold standard ; and by holding out a prospect of an increase of prices, they endeavoured to gain over to their side those interested in agriculture. **By such an agitation the peasantry, who could not possibly form an opinion of their own on the monetary standard question, were stirred up against the gold standard.** When about the middle of the 'eighties the Indian exportation of wheat increased very considerably, the bimetallists at once took advantage of this fact for their agitation. It was then that the assertion first cropped up that the depreciation of silver favoured the exportation of grain from silver-using countries, that it was swamping Europe with cereals and thereby destroying home agriculture. The bimetallists upheld their new argument even when the Indian wheat exports, notwithstanding the continued depreciation of silver, ceased to make any further advance, and even when at last a distinct decline set in. When Russia, and more recently the Argentine, appeared in the grain market as competitors, this too was laid to the charge of the gold standard and the silver depreciation, although these two countries do not possess a silver but a paper standard. In view of this ignorance of the most important facts, agitators had an easy task among the rural population.

13. On the other hand, German bimetallists have not hitherto been able to secure any success among people concerned in industry and commerce. For years past they have been untiring in prophesying the destruction of German trade with silver-using countries, yet the exports to silver-using countries are steadily increasing, while the exports to

gold standard countries have somewhat declined. **Accordingly the entire mercantile community in the Hanseatic towns, which are chiefly interested in the trade with silver-using countries, adhere with full energy to the gold standard. Similarly, with none but most insignificant exceptions, the whole of the German Chambers of Commerce advocate the maintenance of the gold standard.** Nor have bimetallists been more successful in their continued endeavours to gain over the working classes. They hold out to them a prospect of increased employment and of an improvement in their general condition, and have been asserting for as long as about fifteen years past that the gold standard leads to a decline of wages. **But German working men possess sufficient intelligence to see that during the twenty-five years of the existence of the German gold standard wages have not only not declined but have actually risen,** and that, on the other hand, it is just the working men, whose wages are very slow in accommodating themselves to the altered value of money, who would have to suffer most through a diminution of the purchasing power of money.

Thus, the bimetallic movement has remained essentially confined, in Germany, to the agricultural classes.

THE MONETARY POLICY HITHERTO PURSUED BY THE GERMAN GOVERNMENT.

14. The German Government has rarely assumed a position calculated to encourage bimetallists, though it is true that the Government has not always been uniformly firm in this respect. We have already mentioned above that the German Government abstained from attending the Paris Monetary Conference of 1878. Prince Bismarck, Imperial Chancellor, caused the Conference which was held in Paris in 1881 to be attended by two German delegates. But their proposals were so little of a nature to be considered concessions to bimetallism that they virtually tended towards the full carrying through of the German gold standard system.

15. Early in the 'eighties the bimetallists repeatedly moved resolutions in the Reichstag, but the Government did not receive them in a friendly spirit. Gradually, however, the resistance on the part of the government relaxed. In 1885, during the debate on the monetary question, the Government avoided taking either side, and a rumour was spread to the effect that Prince Bismarck was ready to change his monetary policy; consequently the bimetallic agitation increased to fever heat. No less than 1,161 petitions, all identically

worded, were submitted to the Reichstag, most of them being signed
by agricultural associations.

16. The Government now considered it advisable to give up
their position of reserve. Quite unexpectedly, in January, 1886,
Mr. Scholz, the Minister of Finance, rose in the Prussian Diet to
give vent to a scathing condemnation of the bimetallic agitation,
and pronounced himself most decidedly in favour of the gold
standard. As soon as the bimetallists had encountered this decided
check on the part of the Government, their agitation fell off considerably. Besides, notwithstanding all predictions, the German
monetary situation improved more and more. How much this
was the case is illustrated by the following figures :—In 1880 the
bullion stock of the German Imperial Bank consisted of 185 millions
of marks in gold and 340 millions of marks in silver ; whereas the
average amount possessed by the Bank in the last two years was 600
millions of marks in gold and only 285 millions of marks in silver.
**The number of adherents of the bimetallic party fell off
visibly ; and a number of professors who, about fifteen
years previously, had inclined towards bimetallism now
sided in favour of the gold standard.**

17. The Government maintained their position even when, after
the retirement of Bismarck, Caprivi conducted the policy of the
Empire. It was not until the spring of 1894 that the new Chancellor
made a concession which, in itself, was not prejudicial. His object
was to break the resistance of the agrarians to the conclusion of a
commercial treaty with Russia, and he convoked the "Silver Commission " in order to gain over, by this concession in the field of
monetary policy, a portion of his opponents in the domain of
commercial policy. But the transactions of the "Silver Commission " had no practical results and German monetary policy continued
in the same course as heretofore.

THE PRESENT SITUATION.

18. After the retirement of Caprivi, Prince Hohenlohe came to
the head of affairs and the bimetallists made a fresh attempt.
This new attack was made in the hope that something might be
expected from the new government, and it was hoped that
a favourable vote might be obtained in the Reichstag. In fact,
the majority of the Reichstag, on the 16th of February, 1895,
voted in favour of a resolution requesting the Government to convoke
an international monetary conference for the purpose of an international regulation of the monetary standard question. **The
Reichstag did not vote in favour of bimetallism ; on the**

contrary, the demand for bimetallism had been purposely eliminated from the resolution in order to secure for it a majority. On this occasion the Imperial Chancellor made a declaration, holding out a remote prospect of negotiations with foreign Governments with a view to raising the price of silver.

19. The bimetallists now used every means in order to urge the Government to convoke an international monetary conference, and adopt a double standard. When, during the last weeks of Lord Rosebery's government, any discussions on the monetary question took place in the Prussian Diet, Dr. Arendt pointed to Mr. Balfour as the coming man, and asserted that very shortly the English government, led by him and Mr. Chaplin, would take the lead in the bimetallic movement.

20. The friends of a gold standard in Germany considered it necessary to oppose the bimetallic assault by an organised resistance. After the most important Chambers of Commerce had passed resolutions in favour of the gold standard, early in April of last year **a Society for the Defence of the German Gold Standard** was founded, the committee of which comprised the leading manufacturers and commercial men, politicians and savants. The president of the Society is the former president of the Imperial Chancellor's Office, Mr. von Delbrück, and one of the members of the Board is Doctor Ludwig Bamberger, who, with Mr. Delbrück, was the originator of the German gold standard. Professor Huber, of Stuttgart, edits the papers of the Association.

21. The activity of the Society has not remained without influence on the position taken by the public press as well as by the German Federal Governments. When an inquiry was made by the Imperial Chancellor, not a single State pronounced in favour of bimetallism, while many decidedly sided against it. On the 8th of February, 1896, Prince Hohenlohe, the Imperial Chancellor, gave the official reply of the Bundesrath to the resolution of the 16th of February, 1895, which has been previously mentioned. **Prince Hohenlohe declared that all the German Governments had unanimously decided not to conform to the resolution of the Reichstag inviting them to convoke an international monetary conference. This declaration was expressed with some diplomatic reserve in order to render it as palatable as possible to the agrarian bimetallists; but the real and practical effect of it is to defeat the bimetallic movement in Germany.**

Our Colonies against Bimetallism.*

" There is a part of the Empire which is not included in the United Kingdom, and which is not included in India, which has great interests in this matter besides ourselves. I refer to our Colonial Empire."—*Speech of* THE CHANCELLOR OF THE EXCHEQUER, *17th March, 1896.*

---

1. THERE is no part of the currency question so little studied or understood as the facts of the currency of Greater Britain. Yet no Imperial view of the monetary situation can exclude Canada, Australasia, South Africa, and the other British Possessions which are under the charge of the Secretary of State for the Colonies. The Colonies, eleven of whom enjoy responsible self-government, contain a total population exceeding half that of the United Kingdom, whilst the total of their exports and imports approaches half that of the United Kingdom. **Obviously, therefore, in considering the monetary policy of the British Empire, the Colonies cannot be disregarded.** The object of this paper is to show the lines on which currency evolution has proceeded, and is proceeding, in our Colonies.

CURRENCY HISTORY OF THE COLONIES.

2. For this purpose it is unnecessary to go back beyond the

---

* *Issued in February, 1897. The facts are drawn, unless it is otherwise stated, from " A History of Currency in the British Colonies," by Mr. Robert Chalmers, of Her Majesty's Treasury (London : Eyre & Spottiswoode, 1893).*

present century. **It will be sufficient to mention that, prior to the year 1825, "the currency of the Colonies consisted principally of Spanish and Portuguese coins, current at nominal rates established by law or custom.** In the application of these rates to British and foreign coins the monetary denominations of the parent state were adopted. They were, however, differently applied in different colonies. In Canada, for example, the rate assigned to the British shilling was 1s. 1d.; to the Spanish dollar, 5s.; and to the Spanish doubloon, £3 4s.; while in Jamaica the same coins were rated as follows: British shilling, 1s. 8d.; Spanish dollar, 6s. 8d.; Spanish doubloon, £5 6s. 8d. It thus appears that not only were different rates assigned to the same coins in different Colonies, but the rates assigned were proportionately different with reference to the intrinsic value of the different coins." *

3. **To put an end to these inconvenient anomalies, and to extend to the Colonies the monometallic principles formally adopted for the United Kingdom in 1816, the Imperial Government essayed in 1825 to establish sterling as the circulatory medium for the Colonies as for the United Kingdom. The attempt of 1825 failed;** (1) because the Spanish silver dollar was admitted to concurrent tender as the equivalent of 52d. instead of its real value of 50d.; and (2) because the Imperial Government of the day left out of account the foreign gold coins (Spanish doubloon and Portuguese Johannes) which had been the real standard of value of the West Indies and other Colonies since the middle of the 18th century. In 1838, having recognised these shortcomings in the legislation of 1825, the Imperial Government passed an Order in Council rating the gold doubloon at 64s. and the silver dollar at 50d. for concurrent tender with the sterling coins which it was still hoped to make the uniform standard of value throughout the Empire, for the East as for the West. In 1852, moreover, the Imperial Government prescribed by Order in Council that the 40s. limit of tender for British silver, hitherto legal tender without limit in all the Colonies, should be enforced not only in Australasia but also in such silver-using Colonies as Ceylon, Mauritius and Hong Kong. But, though the Imperial Government still cherished the belief that sterling was the best standard for our Colonies as for the United Kingdom, **a perfectly fair field continued to be given to silver,** which was rated, in the case of the silver dollar

---

* *"The Currency of the British Colonies," written by an anonymous official (London, 1848)*

and the rupee, at its market value. **Thenceforth it has not been the Imperial Government, but the wish of the Colonies themselves, which in practice has decided for nearly half a century the course of events.**

4. Thus, it is certainly not to any hostile action of the Imperial Government that we can attribute the success in 1864 of the colony of Hong Kong in casting off their nominal gold standard and in obtaining the legal recognition of the silver standard which had always obtained in practice in that colony. A similar step was taken by the Straits Settlements in 1867, and by Ceylon in 1869. All three changes, it will be observed, had been effected before Germany adopted a gold standard and before the French Mints were closed to the "free coinage" of silver. Whatever may have been the influence of the gold discoveries of the middle of the century in diverting these three Eastern Colonies, and Mauritius in 1876, from legal bimetallism to a purely silver standard, there can be no doubt that it was those gold discoveries which impelled Canada in 1853 and Newfoundland in 1863 to discard silver from concurrent tender and to establish a single gold standard with a subsidiary currency of token silver coins. **Thus before the collapse of the Latin Union, the Colonies, of their own initiative, had broken away in opposite directions from the Imperial Government's arrangement of 1838, whereby a fair field had been given to silver for concurrent circulation with gold in the British Colonies. They abandoned bimetallism.**

5. But what had been a fair field in 1838 had become an unfair field (for gold) in 1876. For a quarter of a century the West Indian and West African Colonies had been unfamiliar with the silver dollar, though the coin was still by law a legal tender as the equivalent of 50d. sterling. But in 1876, finding it possible to lay down dollars in the West Indies at 3s. 10d. each, an astute firm proceeded to exploit these colonies by flooding them with the legal but now unwelcome coins. In self-defence the West Indian Islands proceeded to demonetise the silver dollar, as did the West African colonies and St. Helena some three years later under like stress of speculative importations. Alone among our colonies British Honduras, which then did the bulk of its foreign trade with the neighbouring silver-using republics, declined to cut its currency adrift from the dollar, with the result that by 1887 it had passed to, and had legally recognised, a silver standard. **Seven years' experience, however, of a silver standard drove British Honduras in 1894 to revert to**

M

gold, the standard coin adopted being the United States eagle, with a local subsidiary coinage, as in Canada and Newfoundland.

6. The case of Malta is similar in many respects to that of the West Indies. Here individual speculators took advantage of popular ratings to flood the island with Sicilian silver dollars at 50d. When these coins were finally decried by the Italian Government in 1885, the mercantile community of Malta appealed to the Colonial Government for the aid which they did not deserve, and nearly three millions of these coins were paid in to the Italian Government for exchange. Thus Malta purged her currency of silver dollars, and the currency was placed in practice, as in law, on a sterling basis. Gibraltar on the other hand, which geographically forms part of Spain, has since 1872 adopted the Spanish currency. **Such, in its main outlines, has been the currency history of the British Colonies.**

7. CLASSIFICATION OF THE CURRENCY SYSTEMS OF BRITISH COLONIES.*

		Population (Census 1891).	Total of Imports and Exports for 1893. £
I. GOLD STANDARD.			
Sterling	Australasia	4,296,721	119,399,027
	Cape Colony, Natal, West Africa, &c.	4,164,067	34,596,793
	West Indies (with the Bermudas, British Guiana, and the Falkland Islands)	1,651,927	18,843,369
	Malta and Cyprus	374,323	1,474,750
	Total Sterling-using Colonies	10,487,038	174,313,939
	Gibraltar	19,100	751,803
U.S. Eagle with local subsidiary coinage	Canada	4,823,239	49,056,120
	Newfoundland	202,040	2,886,141
	British Honduras	31,471	449,507
	TOTAL FOR GOLD STANDARD COLONIES	15,562,888	227,457,510
II. SILVER STANDARD.			
Hong Kong, the Straits, &c.		1,526,556	48,192,972
III. RUPEE STANDARD.			
Ceylon		3,008,468	8,832,402
Mauritius and Seychelles		387,191	3,171,956
Total for Rupee Colonies		3,395,659	12,004,358
TOTAL FOR ALL COLONIES		20,485,103	£287,654,840

Figures taken from the Table of General Statistics in the "Colonial Office List, 1895."

THE PRESENT SITUATION.

8. The foregoing table shows (1) that in 1891, according to the census of that year, the British Colonies had a total enumerated population of nearly 20½ millions, as against under 38 millions of people in the United Kingdom at the same date ; and (2) that the total of Colonial imports and exports for 1893 amounted to 288 millions sterling, as against a corresponding total of 682 millions for the United Kingdom at the same date. In other words, the Colonies have exceeded in numbers, and are approaching in foreign trade, half the corresponding United Kingdom figures. **Of the 20½ millions of Colonial population no less than 15½ millions (or about 76 per cent.) maintain a gold standard, and on a gold standard conduct a total export and import trade amounting to 227½ millions sterling, or nearly four-fifths of the whole Colonial trade.** A purely silver standard, on the other hand, is in force in the Far East only among a Colonial population of a million and a half of people, doing a total foreign trade of 48 millions sterling, or under 17 per cent. of the whole colonial total. Compared with the gold standard trade, the purely silver standard trade of the Colonies is little more than a fifth.

9. Intermediate between silver and gold come the rupee-using Colonies of Ceylon and Mauritius, with a combined population of under 3½ millions (16 per cent. of the whole Colonial total) and with a foreign trade of 12 millions sterling, or about 4 per cent. of the whole Colonial total of exports and imports. The question of the rupee does not fall within the scope of this paper. For present purposes it will suffice to point out that at the price of silver in the London market the rupee is intrinsically worth about 11d., while its exchange value is now about 1s. 4d. Attention has not hitherto been directed, it is believed, to the analogous position held by the present rupee and the 5-peseta piece of Spain. The latter coin, which is of unlimited tender in Spain (and Gibraltar), is identical in weight and fineness with the 5-franc piece of the Latin Union, but, having little or no gold behind it, passes in exchange at about Ps. 30 to the pound, instead of Ps. 25·22. In other words, the 5-peseta piece (which is intrinsically worth about 2s. at the present gold price of silver, and which cannot exceed the gold par of about 4s.) stands now at an exchange value of 3s. 4d., and therefore holds the same relative position as the rupee.

10. Such being the statistics of the Colonies when classified

M 2

according to their monetary systems, this analysis of the present
situation may be concluded by pointing out that, **great as is the
preponderance of gold as a colonial standard of currency,
that preponderance is still greater if regard be had to the
importance of the Colonies which maintain a gold standard.
For, apart from important Crown Colonies, the gold-standard
Colonies include every single Colony of self-governing rank.**
Gold is the standard of the Dominion of Canada and Newfoundland,
of the Cape and Natal in South Africa, and of New South Wales,
Victoria, New Zealand and the four other great Colonies which
are included in Australasia. Gold is the standard of these eleven
self-governing Colonies; and it is not on record that a single one of
them has manifested any official disposition whatsoever to tamper
with the gold standard under which their commerce has grown up.
Can the untruth of a " scarcity of gold " be preached with any hope
of success to New South Wales, to Victoria, to New Zealand, to
West Australia, or to South Africa ?

11. Canada, on the other hand, has until recently had no gold
mines, nor has silver been discovered there in the large quantities
which Mr. Goschen and Mr. H. H. Gibbs (now Lord Aldenham,
President of the Bimetallic League) suspected in 1878 of
having converted the United States to bimetallism since 1867.*

---

* *See p. 5 of the Report, dated 27th November, 1878, as presented to
Parliament by Mr. Goschen, Mr. Henry H. Gibbs, and Sir T. L. Seccombe, the
Commissioners appointed to represent Her Majesty's Government at the Monetary Conference held in Paris in August, 1878 :*—" Without the explanations
which he [Mr. Groesbeck] gave, it would not have been unreasonable to infer
that the *locus standi* of the United States, as regards the silver question, was
affected by the circumstance that in 1873 the silver standard was discontinued ;
that since then the Nevada mines have become immensely productive, with the
result of a most serious fall in the price of silver ; that a resumption [of specie
payments] on the basis of silver as well as gold thus offered the double inducement
of a cheaper mode, and of a boon to a most important native interest ; and that
accordingly the policy of 1873 was reversed. However, the statements and explanations of Mr. Groesbeck did not pass unchallenged. M. Feer Herzog
questioned the predilection of the public in the United States for the use of
silver, and Mr. Goschen and others pressed Mr. Groesbeck on the remarkable
allegation that silver could have been discontinued as a legal standard ' by in-
advertence.' "

The completeness of the *volte-face* of the United States between 1867 and 1878
is indicated by the following (translated) extract from the speech of 20th June,
1867, by Mr. Ruggles, the delegate from the United States, at the third Meeting
of the International Monetary Conference of 1867 at Paris :—"The double

Yet Canada, though its commercial interests are necessarily connected, and intimately connected, with the United States, has never manifested any desire to imitate its neighbour in falling between two stools in currency. On the contrary, Canada, while taking the United States gold eagle as its standard coin, has steadfastly declined to recognise the United States silver dollar, and has completed the Dominion currency by a purely subsidiary system of her own silver and bronze tokens. Untroubled by "greenbacks" or by Bland and Sherman Acts, **the Dominion of Canada has steadfastly maintained a purely gold standard,** and has shown how, with a sound standard, it is both possible and safe to economise the metallic basis of "money," in the real or City sense of the term, to an extent which is not dreamed of on the Continent. All the gold in the country is practically held by the Banks or by the Dominion Government. From the published accounts* it appears that the five millions of Canadian population conduct the whole of their enormous commerce, including 49 millions sterling of foreign trade, on a gold basis which, so far as any gold kept in Canada is concerned, has never exceeded 3¼ millions sterling,† supplemented by little over a million sterling additional in the shape of Dominion token coins. **In other words, the whole Dominion currency in the fullest sense of the term rested in 1893 on a metallic basis (including tokens) of 4½ millions sterling, or about 18s. per head of the population.**

---

standard does not exist in fact. . . . The legislators and the people of the United States have sufficiently learned, if not by study yet by experience, that the system of the double standard is not only an imprudence, but also an impossibility, seeing that it implies necessarily a fixed relation between the values of two different commodities, gold and silver. . . . The United States now share, without reserve, the conviction more and more diffused through the civilised world, according to which it is impossible to admit a double standard which presumes the existence of a fixed relation between the values of the two metals." (*See p. 169 of Report of the Royal Commission on International Coinage, 1868.*)

* *See the Table laid before the Royal Commission on Agriculture by Lord Farrer on 13th December, 1894. Question No. 38,410, and Appendix F, therein referred to.*

† *The United States Treasury Report, 1894 (p. 180),* gives an estimate of $14,000,000 in gold and $5,000,000 in silver as the metallic stock of Canada on January 1st, 1894. The United States figures make the comparison *infra* somewhat more unfavourable to the States.

12. With this compare the case of the United States in the same year, 1893, as stated by the Director of the Mint in the United States.* According to the Director, the estimated metallic stock of the United States on July 1st, 1893, was as follows :—

Gold	$597,697,685
Silver	615,861,484
	$1,213,559,169

Taking the population of the United States in 1893 as 67 millions, the above total gives no less a sum than £3 12s. per head as the metallic basis of United States currency, or four times the corresponding figure for the Dominion of Canada. **This is a striking difference, but it does not tell, as, according to the bimetallic doctrine, it should, against the Dominion and in favour of the United States.** Facts do not show that the quantitative theory or any other part of the bimetallic contention receives any support from the four-fold abundance of metallic money in the United States. It is not a fact that United States prices (including wages) are four times as high as they are over the Canadian border. Nor are the United States four times as prosperous as Canada. Nor does the abundance of United States currency, which is replenished according to the favourite simile of bimetallists, from "two cisterns" in about equal volume, give the United States an immunity from crises, in the proportion of one to Canada's four.

All this goes to show that the British Empire, as far as our Colonies are concerned, is against bimetallism.

* *Report of the Secretary to the Treasury for 1894, p. 177.*

Why Canada is against Bimetallism.*

By Mr. B. E. WALKER, of Toronto, Canada,

General Manager of the Canadian Bank of Commerce, and ex-President of the

Canadian Bankers' Association.

---

1. THE southern boundary of Canada and the northern boundary of the United States run together from the Atlantic to the Pacific Ocean for about 3,850 miles. Elsewhere, except in the north, where it meets Alaska, Canada is bounded only by oceans. It is the source from which the United States must procure many of the products of nature, especially those which grow only, or grow best, in a northern climate. On the other hand, because of the greater development of manufactures in the United States, and because they grow certain products which cannot be produced in Canada, the latter country must always buy largely from them. **Although Canada, in common with almost all other countries, settles the final balance of its trading and financial operations in London, the more immediate clearing city for such operations in the case of both Canada and the United States is New York.** If Canada requires to pay London in excess of the bills which are being created by Canadian shipments to Great Britain, or to other countries which settle through London, it buys the bills for such excess in New York. If Canada has more exchange on London than is required by her importers, the surplus is sold in New York. Gold coin is occasionally shipped back and forth between Canada and New York; but this is a less frequent

* *Issued in July,* 1897.

method of settlement than by bills on London. Some of the Canadian banks have branches in New York, Chicago, and other cities of the United States, and both the grain crops of the west and the cotton crops of the south depend largely on these banks for money with which to buy and transport them, while the foreign exchange market of New York would lose one of its most important features were the Canadian banks to withdraw their agencies from that city. Such being the intimate trading and financial relations between the United States and Canada, **I wish to explain why Canada maintains so easily its position as a gold-standard country, and why its great and wealthy neighbour, the United States, also a gold-standard country, has been repeatedly threatened with the degradation of its standard from gold to silver.**

2. When the provinces of British North America entered into the Confederation known as the Dominion of Canada, they resigned their powers in the matters of banking and currency, and these were assumed by the Federal Government. There is, therefore, no conflict of authority on these subjects between the Federal and the Provincial Governments. When the Confederation known as the United States was formed, the original States were anxious to retain as far as possible their sovereign powers. They therefore conferred upon the Federal jurisdiction certain defined powers only, including the power to stamp metal as money. All powers not thus specially conferred on the Federal jurisdiction remained with the States, and under this balance of power the States have the right to create banks. The Federal Government also has power to create a bank as it has to create any business corporation ; but, with the exception of the two semi-state institutions called in each case the "Bank of the United States," the Federal Government did not attempt to exercise this power until driven to do so by the exigencies of the war. **In the United States since the war both Federal and State Governments have continued to create banks, and neither is likely to surrender this power.**

BANKING AND CURRENCY IN THE UNITED STATES.

3. The first bank charters granted in the old province of Canada about 1820 were copied largely from that of the Bank of the United States, and until 1832 the banking systems in the two countries did not differ materially. Neither government had yet issued notes as money, and both left the creation of paper money to the banks, who were of course supposed to redeem in gold. In both countries banks were developing systems of branches, although the granting of charters by the several States instead of by the Federal Government tended to make the banks in the United States local in character instead of national, and the majority of these banks had no branches. There was, however, in the United States one bank, the semi-state institution called the Bank of the United States, which transcended in importance all others. Its relations to the Government on the

one hand and to the mercantile community on the other were not very different from those of the Bank of England or the Bank of France. ,It issued notes, had branches in the chief cities through which it effected a reasonably satisfactory distribution of loanable capital, dealt largely in foreign exchange, borrowed money abroad when necessary to increase its loans at home, and acted as banker for the Government. These were days when the commerce and land settlement of the country were fraught with unusual financial risks. Instead, however, of patiently studying the difficulties and gradually improving the system, the Bank of the United States became a political issue, and in 1832 President Jackson refused to renew its charter. The Bank of the United States continued to exist for some years under a State charter, but the Federal Government, in pursuance of its policy, transferred its banking business, then very considerable in consequence of payments for land, to various State banks. **The Government, however, found before many years that these State banks, individually weak as to capital, were not satisfactory as bankers, and the idea of the Government becoming its own banker, as far as possible, took shape in the present Treasury system.** For many years after this period such banks, working under State laws, as endeavoured to establish systems of branches were met with great animosity by the politicians who reflected the popular feeling that large banks were dangerous to the public welfare. Naturally the branch system did not thrive, and when the war broke out the inland banking business of the country was being done by a vast array of State banks individually weak as to capital, and having little power to cohere for any large financial transaction, while the foreign banking business was mainly carried on by private bankers.

4. Had the legislators of the United States carefully matured the system with which they began there would have been in existence at the outbreak of the war in 1861 great banks of international importance able to procure loans abroad and otherwise serve the Government financially. **But because there were no banks adequate to the situation, and because of the peculiar Treasury system, the Government, for the first time in its history, resorted to the issue of non-interest-bearing promissory notes, intended to circulate as money.** The first issue of these notes was payable on demand in coin, and was so redeemed, but suspension of specie payments followed within a few months, and the Government began a series of experiments in paper money of which the existing residuum is that body of notes sometimes called " war legal-tenders " or "greenbacks," and amounting to about 346,000,000 dollars.

5. **In order to aid in floating its bonds the Federal Government in 1863 and 1864 passed Acts creating the national banking system,** notwithstanding the strong opposition of the banks working under State laws ; and in 1865, in order to

make the new Acts effective for the purpose of the Federal Government, a tax of 10 per cent. was levied upon the circulation of any
bank-notes other than National Bank notes—that is, upon the notes
of banks working under State laws. Under this system any national
bank, upon depositing United States Government bonds with the
Treasury, may issue notes, nominally the promises to pay of the bank,
but of uniform design, guaranteed by the Government, and possessing
such qualities as currency that redemption by the particular bank of
issue is practically not required. Thus the circulation of notes by the
State banks was brought to an end, and there were practically no
bank-note issues left in the United States, the so-called "bank-notes"
of the national banks being merely an enlargement of the paper issues
of the Federal Government. In this manner a nation at one time
accepting the sound principle that the function of the Government
regarding currency was merely to certify to the weight and fineness
of gold, silver, and other coined money, and that all credit instruments intended to pass as money should be issued by banks who
would, by the circumstances of their business, be always able to
issue enough, and yet, by the fact of daily redemption, be unable to
keep in circulation too much, had now passed to the most dangerous
of all theories regarding currency. **Thus the United States had
accepted the theory that it was a proper exercise of power
by a Government to enforce by law the passage of any
instrument as money, and while some only sought to excuse
such action by the necessities of the war, others were ready
to argue that the power to issue paper money should be
enjoyed only by the Government.**

PRESENT RESPONSIBILITIES OF THE UNITED STATES TREASURY.

6. I have no space to follow the subsequent course of events in
the United States, of which the main features are indicated in
this series by Mr. Horace White, the eminent American authority.*
Suffice it to say that by following the incorrect principles stated above,
the United States Treasury now stands deeply involved. The issues
for the redemption of which in gold the Government is directly or
indirectly responsible were at 1st December, 1896, as follows:—

	Dollars.
Legal tenders authorised during the war	346,681,016
Silver certificates issued under the Bland Act, which are legal tender for payments to the Government	367,903,504
Legal tender notes issued for silver purchased under the Sherman Act	121,677,280
United States National Bank Notes	235,398,890
Total	1,071,660,690

From this it would be fair to deduct from one hundred to one
hundred and fifty millions of dollars for cash held in the Treasury.

Against this mass of paper money the Treasury is supposed to

* *See page* 199.

maintain a gold reserve of 100,000,000 dollars, but by repeated experiènce in recent years it has been seen that it cannot do this comfortably when trade relations make it necessary that the country should ship gold. **It is abundantly clear that the currency of the country cannot be placed on a sound basis until the Government redeems at least a portion of the above paper issues, and until a new banking system is devised which will permit the issue by the banks of notes against their general estate**—that is, not secured by the actual pledge of Government or other bonds, and subject to daily redemption, so that the ebb and flow of the aggregate of such notes shall adjust itself automatically to the requirements of trade.

BANKING AND CURRENCY IN CANADA.

7. When in 1792 the merchants of the chief city in Canada endeavoured to establish a bank under legislative authority, they proposed that it should transact the business " usually done by similar establishments "—viz., to receive deposits, ISSUE NOTES, discount bills, and keep cash accounts with customers. It was further proposed to OPEN BRANCHES " to extend the operations of the bank to every part of the two provinces (now known as Quebec and Ontario) where an agent may be judged necessary." Although there was at the time no law preventing the issue by private individuals of notes for circulation as money, the legislature refused to grant such powers to an incorporated bank. No charters were actually granted to joint-stock banks until 1820, but **the two principles of (1) a note issue against the general estate of the bank—that is, not specially secured—and (2) systems of branches for the gathering and distributing of loanable capital were recognised**; and the new joint-stock banks soon opened branches and took their position in the business world as institutions having a national instead of a local character. It has been already stated that much of the detail in these first charters was copied from that of the Bank of the United States, and it is interesting to note that many of these features are retained in the present Act, unaltered except as to the phraseology by which they are described. In the early days, owing to the poverty of the country and to inexperience, banking was subject to many vicissitudes, and the British authorities frequently sought to interfere. Although such suggestions were rarely accepted at the moment, they were often the cause of improved legislation at some later time, but we doubtless owe to the proposals of Lord Sydenham, referred to hereafter, the one serious blemish in our currency system.

8. In 1850, as a result of dissatisfaction in some portions of Western Canada with the facilities extended by the banks, a measure usually called the Free Banking Act was passed. Under it a bank might be organised with a very small capital, and might issue notes

based upon the security of the bonds of the Provincial Government. This was an imitation of the banking system of the State of New York, from which also the National banking system of the United States was largely copied. The old banks in Canada were not, however, forced to adopt the new system, and, as it was unsound in principle, it never gained headway, and in a few years came to an end. Lord Sydenham, as Governor-General in 1841 of the united provinces of Lower and Upper Canada, had suggested a Provincial Bank of Issue, the right to issue notes by the chartered banks to be cancelled, and suitable remuneration paid therefor. This was rejected by the people, and a similar proposal made in 1860 met the same fate. In 1866, however, owing to the pressure of the finances of the Provincial Government, an Act was passed authorising the issue by the Provincial Government of notes payable in specie, and to be a legal tender, to an amount not exceeding eight million dollars.

9. In 1867 the two provinces comprising Old Canada, together with the provinces of Nova Scotia and New Brunswick, were confederated as the Dominion of Canada. The new Federal Government unfortunately did not abandon the issue of legal-tender notes. At the present time the maximum issue permitted of notes partially covered by specie is 20,000,000 dollars, and for all issues in excess gold must be held. Of the 21,600,000 dollars outstanding at 31st October, 1896, 8,200,000 dollars are in the shape of notes of denominations smaller than 5 dollars, bank issues being forbidden for such denominations. The remainder of the issue is mainly in notes of very large denominations held by the banks. The gold held by the Treasury Department at this date amounted to 10,000,000 dollars, nearly 50 per cent. upon the entire issue, or nearly 75 per cent. upon the large issues. The large issues are practically the only notes on which redemption in gold is from time to time required. The banking legislation in Nova Scotia and New Brunswick previous to confederation offered no difficulty to the adoption in 1870 of a General Banking Act following the lines of the system in use in Old Canada. Under the new system the charter of each bank is renewed for periods of ten years, all charters expiring at the same time. The banks all work under the General Banking Act, and at the Parliamentary session immediately before the charters expire this Act is re-enacted with such improvement as time has demonstrated to be necessary.

10. **The features with which we are mainly concerned are the note issue and the branch banking. A Canadian bank is permitted to issue notes intended for circulation as money, in denominations of 5 dollars and upwards, to the extent of its paid-up and unimpaired capital.** No securities are specially pledged for such issues. In the event of the insolvency of a bank each shareholder is liable for the debts of the bank to the extent of a sum equal to the face

value of his shares. This is generally called the double liability.
The note issues of a bank are a first lien upon all the assets of a
bank, including this double liability, and prior to any lien of the
Federal or of a Provincial Government. To avoid a discount on
notes in circulation at a point remote from the establishments of the
issuing bank, every bank must arrange for the redemption of its
notes in certain designated cities of commercial importance throughout Canada. And to avoid discount at the moment of a bank's
suspension, or thereafter, because of doubt as to the sufficiency of
the assets for this particular liability, the banks as a whole maintain
in the hands of the Government a fund equal to 5 per cent. of the
aggregate of notes in circulation, upon which drafts may be made if
the assets of the failed bank are insufficient. The notes of a failed
bank carry interest at 6 per cent. per annum from the date of
suspension until the receiver advertises his ability to redeem. **The
past history of the country shows that, had these features always been in force, no note-holder would have suffered loss,
and since these features were embodied in the Act, no holder
of a Canadian bank note has ever lost anything thereby, and
the people understand the security afforded so well that
the note of a suspended bank passes without difficulty.**
The aggregate capital of the Canadian banks at present is about
61,700,000 dollars; · the highest circulation during 1896 was
36,300,000 dollars, and the lowest 29,400,000 dollars. It will
therefore be seen that should an unusual expansion of the currency
beyond the maximum named be suddenly required—a thing only
theoretically possible in Canada—there is a reserve power to issue
of about 70 per cent. It will also be observed that about 23 per
cent. more notes are required to do the business in the active or
crop-moving period of the year as compared with the dullest period.
The average circulation for the past year was 50·76 per cent. of the
paid-up capital. Not only was the required circulation supplied
with perfect ease, but, what is of equal importance, it was forced out.
of circulation immediately it was not required.

11. **The emission and redemption of these notes, the ab-
sorption of bank deposits and the making of bank advances,
is effected in Canada by 37 banks with about 500 branches.**
There is nothing new in this to the European mind, and it is introduced here only to mark the contrast with the United States. The
result of the branch system is that the loanable capital is directly
gathered where it can be found and directly lent where it is required.
The rate to the borrower is neither subject to violent fluctuations
because of panic nor to widely varying rates for geographical reasons,
and the borrower with good security is able to borrow at fair rates,
while the note issues afford a circulation both elastic and secure.

WHY CANADA IS NOT TROUBLED WITH A BIMETALLIC AGITATION.

12. In conclusion, I wish to emphasise the following points :—

a. The agitation in the United States in favour of the unlimited coinage of silver is simply the form in which the discontent with existing conditions is expressed by those who do not understand currency and banking problems. They see that something is wrong, and accept the suggested remedy largely because nothing else is proposed. The general fall in prices and the demonetisation of silver have been used as arguments for the unlimited coinage of silver ; but had the suggested remedy been unlimited fiat paper money, quite as valid arguments would doubtless have been urged.

b. Existing conditions regarding currency and banking in the United States are wrong mainly because in the past politicians have generally regarded popular or untrained opinion. Had the legislators of the United States followed the old maxim, "hold fast that which is good," and as time passed endeavoured to make the good they possessed better, they would now have had a system of banking and currency not essentially different from those of England, France, Germany, Scotland, and Canada. **But the violent policy of Jackson led to the Treasury system, the ruin of branch banking, and the survival only of the weak State banks ; and these conditions caused the issue during the war of non-interest-bearing notes for use as money, which was followed by an agitation for fiat paper money, and later by an agitation lasting for twenty years, for the free coinage of silver.**

c. Had the early banking methods been retained, and improved from time to time, there would now exist in the United States many large banking institutions with branches, creating an automatic flow of loanable capital from the points where bank deposits accumulate to the points where loans are most required. There would also exist a paper currency issued only by banks, redeemable in gold, and capable of just the measure of expansion and contraction in its volume necessary for the comfort of trade. With an equitable rate of interest to the borrower, and a suitable and elastic currency, the silver-miners could never have caught the ear of the discontented.

d. The history of banking in Canada shows that a country may have a paper currency supported by a very slight percentage of gold provided the other reasons for its issuance are sound. During the seventy-five years of its existence, except for a few months in a time of rebellion (1837), the bank-note currency of Canada has always been redeemable in gold. **With a sound and elastic currency, and a banking system which ensures an equitable rate for borrowed money, Canada naturally has practically no public discussion on the question of bimetallism except in the case of the few who imagine that they find a connection between the general fall in prices and the so-called demonetisation of silver.**

Why Australia Believes in a Single Gold Standard.*

By Mr. R. L. NASH, of Sydney, New South Wales.

The BIMETALLIC LEAGUE, *in its Annual Report, issued on June 2nd, 1897, states that " the growth of interest on the subject of Bimetallism in our Colonies, especially in Australasia, continues to be well maintained." The following paper exposes this particular error, and shows that in this case, as in others, the Bimetallists have been misinformed.*

---

1. THERE are important silver interests in Australia, and undoubtedly we Australians wish well to the metal. To put 50 per cent. more silver into the shilling, and to abolish the half-sovereign (or, internationally, all gold coins below 20 francs in value), would be steps probably meeting with sufficient approval, or, at any rate, acquiescence, in the widespread interests of Broken Hill and Mount Lyell. But at the same time we take the common-sense view that if the Broken Hill mines can pay £550,000 in dividends, as they did in 1896, with silver at 2s. 6d. per ounce, there is not the slightest prospect of the price being forced up to 5s., a figure which would make the profits, not only of Australian mines, but those of the silver

* *Issued in June,* 1897

mines of the world, fabulous, if it were possible to maintain the exchangeable value of silver at that figure. We can see that silver-mining would then be by far the most profitable industry in the world, and its cent. per cent. protection at the expense of all the other industries would inevitably work its own cure, and that after a fashion Australians would be the last to appreciate. The impossibility of the attempt is thoroughly recognised.

2. **We are a sufficiently practical and commercial people to grasp the fact that if a metal, or any other commodity, can be produced at a fair profit, and in practically unlimited quantity at a certain current figure, it could only be forced up to double that figure by "rigging the market" after the most unscrupulous fashion, and then the reaction would be as speedy as it would be inevitable.** Beyond this, though the Australian would rejoice in seeing the silver-lead industry progressing and prosperous—and 3s. an ounce for silver and £12 for lead per ton would mean great prosperity—he would experience far greater consternation at the world taking any step tending to jeopardise the value of gold, or to restrict its production. Gold-mining has progressed substantially in almost all these colonies of late years, and Australasia is now yielding annually £9,000,000 worth of gold to about £2,000,000 worth of silver; and this consideration, selfishly possibly, but no less potent on that account, is of itself sufficient to render us less than lukewarm on the subject of bimetallism. Again, we are a democratic community, and we have probably nearly 100,000 men engaged in gold-mining, as against only 7,000 men engaged in silver-mining; and the welfare of the greater number is our chief consideration. As it is, the silver-miners can hold their own, and earn as good wages as the gold-miners. **There is, therefore, no need to trouble our minds about a passing academic craze that has really never, for any lengthened period, withstood, and could not under modern conditions withstand, the test of practical experience.**

3. Let us take, however, what some enthusiasts may regard as a more workable basis of bimetallism—that is, bimetallism under limitations—because the question has been discussed on this side of the world. What should we gain if it were possible for all nations to unite to limit the production of silver so as to maintain a higher value? It would utterly prohibit expansion in the industry, and would even throw existing labour out of employment. That is not what we want. What we aim at is to cheapen the cost of production,

as new processes and new forms of smelting are continually doing, so
that we shall be better able to compete with the United States, Mexico,
and the Western States of South America, and to extend employment
in our midst. An industry that cannot grow must diminish in the
scale of comparative importance, and with production in Australia
growing upon all sides, we should cease to interest ourselves in an
industry which was artificially paralysed. Far better commercial
freedom than any restrictions such as these.

4. **It is just the same with silver as with wool.** In those
striking years 1872–73, when the markets ran wild after ten years of
war and destruction, and when wages in England in some leading industries ran up to wholly unprecedented levels, average Australian wool
was worth 14d. per pound, whereas it is now selling at only 7½d. But
Australians would not revert to the price of 1873 if they could, if at
the same time it meant that we must restrict our present output of
700,000,000 lbs. to that of 1873, which was only about 220,000,000
lbs. We now export about £21,000,000 worth of wool at the cheaper
price as against £13,000,000 worth at the price of 1873 ; and the cost
of conducting sheep stations is so much less, carriage to and from
up-country districts is so greatly reduced, that we can consequently
afford to sell cheaper than then. We certainly wish to see wool,
even more than we wish to see silver, advance in price, yet it is recognised that an advance can only be attained by practicable means.
As one writer here recently put the matter—we can as readily decree
that 8 ozs. of wool shall be sold for a pound weight without reduction
in price, as that an ounce of silver shall sell for 5/- instead of 2/6; and of
the two, we would far rather see wool enhanced in value by international
agreement than silver. However, even such comment is now dying
out in Australia, though it was rife enough a few years ago, when
Mr. Moreton Frewen conducted his crusade in the interests of the
white-metallists ; because **it has now come to be recognised
that the bimetallic cause is more than hopeless—it is impossible.**

5. In reality, Mr. Moreton Frewen's visit to Australia did good
to the cause of monometallism. We had not paid much attention
to the subject before. Prior to his coming, a well-known Australian
politician asked the writer, "Is it true, as the Bimetallic League
asserts, that, without exception, all the Professors are bimetallists?"
and he added, "If so, there should be something more in the cause
than I had thought there was." When Mr. Moreton Frewen came
he repeated the fallacy over and over again, and I think that, as

N

a bold statement to an average audience, it made more impression than any other argument, or rather declaration, he advanced. Had the statement gone uncontradicted people might have been impressed by the fact that scientific experts, whose avocation it was to study such questions, had pronounced bimetallism to be both feasible and beneficial. But a little research enabled us soon to prove that this sweeping assertion was wholly unjustified, and that various of those Professors who did lend their names to the bimetallic propaganda were professors of something else than economics, though there were admittedly exceptions ; and that most of the Professors who did support bimetallism, did so with qualifications and restrictions, so that bimetallism in their case did not mean the free and unfettered production of both metals and their free and unfettered coinage at 15½ or 16 to 1. Indeed, our inquiries demonstrated the fact that the so-called scientific and economic experts were very chary of committing themselves to any particular ratio. The Australian press took the matter up, and discussed it at the time pretty thoroughly. Some writers wavered, but the succession of facts and figures marshalled by such journals as the *Sydney Daily Telegraph* and the *Melbourne Argus* practically silenced the discussion, as it was clearly shown that the fall in the prices of our products was attributable to greatly increased and cheaper production, to increased and cheaper facilities for carriage, and to increased rivalry and new sources of supply throughout the world. It was shown, moreover, that there was to-day more gold coin and more full tender silver coin per head in the countries of the world than there was at the time when "the crime of 1873 " was perpetrated. Mr. Moreton Frewen utterly failed to carry Sydney with him, and I have good reason for asserting that he failed to carry any other Australian centre.

6. **As far as New South Wales is concerned, bimetallism is practically dead.** True, there is the skeleton of a branch of the Bimetallic League here, and occasionally its President or Hon. Secretary try to keep its bones from crumbling into dust. But the flesh is nowhere ; the body of adherents wholly wanting. At the last annual meeting in Sydney there were about half a dozen people present. A reference was made to the last House of Commons resolution, which has been paraded in the organ of the League for ten times more than it is worth, and the time-honoured declaration was repeated that the great cause was surely progressing. But it would be politeness to describe the proceedings

as "formal." I study most of the leading Australian newspapers, their views and opinions, and it is rare nowadays to come upon even a reference to bimetallism in any of them.

7. **The difficulty is, therefore, to put active life into any recapitulation of the reasons why Australians are adverse to bimetallism. The main reason is that Australians, as a mass, regard the whole affair as a passing craze, and as the interested efforts of the silver States of America.** In this they probably go too far. There are sincere believers in Bimetallism, as there are probably in all the faiths of the universe. bimetallism has lived in one guise or another too long to be wholly ignored, and if little or no refutation of the delusion is now needed on this side the world, it is evident enough from the recent vote in the United States in support of Mr. Bryan's candidature, that elsewhere the question has to be faced. A second reason is that gold constitutes a far more important part of Australian production than silver, and will continue to do so. Gold gave Australia its start in life, and our belief in its paramount importance could not be easily shaken. A third reason is that the bimetallic propagandists hailed us quite on the wrong tack. They tried to make us believe that all the depression which assailed us in 1893–4–5 was due to the appreciation of gold; but we know sufficiently about our own affairs to know better. The Australian boom of 1888–90 came after the fall in silver, and the appreciation of gold—if it be appreciated—did not prevent it. The collapse of 1892–3 was but too plainly due to our own over-commitments and to the excessive prices paid for lands speculatively held, and silver had equally nothing to do with it. As for the fall in wool or tallow, what, it has been asked, has silver to do with our vastly increased production, or with River Plate competition? Would even the rehabilitation of silver in the world's markets raise the value of Argentine paper money? No! We want better reasons than these to prove to us that bimetallism is the panacea for the ills from which we are now slowly recovering. **As for the argument that our indebtedness to the mother country has been doubled by the appreciation of gold, the vast bulk of our debts to the United Kingdom were raised long after the fall in silver had set in. So that bimetallic argument was grounded altogether on a misconception of the Australian position.**

8. What Australians must be shown by the bimetallic fraternity

N 2

before they could be won over to even a passive acquiescence
in their efforts, is that their grand scheme for depreciating gold
would not have the effect of ruining our gold-fields—would not
necessitate the writing off of tens upon tens of millions sterling
invested in those mines. This, however, is a point the Bimetallic
League has never faced. But it would be a preliminary to securing
any adhesion here. Otherwise, we are left to the conclusion that
they are asking us to support a cause which, could it ever win a trial,
would ruin one of the main industries in these colonies, and around
the head of which there hangs a halo of romance, as well as a
crown of reality, such as is not the attribute of any other Australian
pursuit. **That such a suicidal creed as bimetallism could
ever find any footing in England, far less in the City of
London, is to us a marvel.**

9. At one time we were rather interested in that catch-phrase of
the bimetallists—"The yellow man with the white metal," etc.*—
and it was discussed rather freely, because the yellow man, the Malay
and the East Indian, are our nearest neighbours. Were Australia
likely to be overrun with Chinese, Japanese, and Indian goods, and
were the Australian producer likely to be dispossessed, the people
here would undoubtedly take alarm. But it was at once seen that
the contention was ludicrous. We are *par excellence* producers of
raw materials, with superabundant land and few people; the coloured
races of Asia form dense populations who find it difficult to feed
themselves, and have not the space to compete with us in the
products which constitute our wealth. We may advantageously
exchange merchandise ; we cannot compete. It is true that the
protectionist leader of the opposition did produce a pair of Japanese
boots and sought to move Parliament on the subject. But it turned
out that it was about the only pair of boots which had been imported
from thence, and the incident ended in laughter, as did that of the
Colombo chaff. Then it was said the Japanese coal mines would
ruin our coal trade ; but they have not done so, and though Australian coal is cheap, it is selling more largely than ever. Australia
once had a scare about an invasion of Chinese labour, and we put a
poll-tax on him. We were asked to place a penalty upon his wares
also, but a little ridicule was ample to silence the protectionists, who

* "*It has now come to this, that in the throat-cutting competition engendered
by the fall in the exchanges with Asia, the industry of the white man with the
yellow money is being strangled by the yellow man using the white money.*"—
Mr. MORETON FREWEN *at the Athenæum Hall, Melbourne, 5th February, 1895.*

were certainly not bimetallists, and the invasion has not come, though this colony has now adopted the freest of free trade. We are now shipping wool and hides and other products to Japan, and the Japanese have started a line of steamers to these parts with advantage to both countries. It is curious, too, that when we send bullion to China or Japan, it is gold which is shipped rather than silver. The Chinese, especially, are constantly shipping gold in small amounts. **No one now talks about yellow competition; that argument also of the bimetallists has quite died out.**

10. Some of the inquiries instituted here a few years ago, when bimetallism was being discussed, would, I think, have merited a place in English financial literature. It was shown in detail that the gold and silver coin in the countries with which we are connected in business had actually more than doubled per head since the middle of this century; and it was asked how, in the face of this, could it be maintained, with all our increased banking and exchange facilities, which materially reduce the use of coin, there could possibly be a currency famine. This was admittedly a one-sided argument, as we should not measure coin requirements by the numbers of the people, but by the volume of transactions based on that coin. But surely .we possess the best of tests that our coin supplies are adequate in the relative cheapness of money. The rates charged for money depend upon the floating supplies of coin, or its recognised equivalent, available for lending purposes, and the banks of Europe or America, or here in Australia, might have any quantity of deposits, but if they had not adequate supplies of coin, their rates would have to be advanced until business was sufficiently checked and supplies of coin could be sufficiently attracted. Now, it is quite certain that throughout Europe the rates for money have been persistently lower of late years than ever before in the world's history, and at this distance we have marvelled at the comparative ease with which those vast accumulations of gold have been amassed in Russia, Austria, in the Bank of France, and to a less extent in the Bank of Germany and the Bank of England. It is evident beyond denial that floating supplies are relatively adequate, and that recent stores of gold have been far more readily built up than was the case when Germany set about reforming her currency. **It is considered here that it is idle to parade a scarcity of gold, and the direful effects produced by that phantom scarcity, as the bimetallists are always attempting to do. Australia is not suffering from any scarcity of gold, but from a scarcity of**

employment for it. The Australian banks have never been so over-charged with gold as they are at the present time. Apart from their holdings in London, which are never inconsiderable, in the December quarter of 1896 they held £25,770,000 in coin on this side, besides £1,165,000 in gold bullion, with which to meet about £38,000,000 of current accounts and £62,000,000 of deposits at interest having one or more years to run. This for four millions of people is regarded as a preposterously large amount of metal to retain, and we should be glad if a demand arose which would pay for the shipment of a not inconsiderable portion of it. We recently sent £1,600,000 to America on London account, and if twice or thrice that amount had gone it would have paid us better.

11. Australians have recently had a striking example of what havoc can be played with the credit of a country by silver faddists. The whole of the American currency troubles have been watched with keen interest, and they afford an object lesson, which has shown clearly the pitfalls we must be careful to avoid. **Were it necessary to poll these Colonies on the subject, I am convinced that with the example of the United States of America in view, the Gold Standard Defence Association could secure fifty adherents in Australia to each one adherent of the Bimetallic League.** We are content with the sovereign, and with the metal it represents, and would be found far less ready even to admit its appreciation than would some Old Country monometallists. We have one standard to go on which, at any rate, if there has been over-production, has stimulated consumption in nearly an equal degree—and that is population. Now, man's labour, and woman's labour too, have not fallen in value, and that is the best of all tests we can apply to the gold standard, to ascertain whether it is appreciated or depreciated. If the workman be well employed, and his employer fairly remunerated—and the workman would not be employed without the latter following as a natural consequence —the cheapness of commodities is all so much to the advantage of the world in general, and becomes the truest measure of the world's progress. **Australia may have suffered latterly, but no one can look upon her well-dressed, well-fed workmen and their families without being assured that the gold standard has suited them, and that they, on that point, are content to let well alone.**

The Monetary Issue in the United States.*

By Mr. HORACE WHITE,

Editor of the NEW YORK "EVENING POST," *and Author of* "MONEY AND BANKING," *etc.*

---

1. THE silver agitation in the United States took its rise in 1876 in the *débris* of the greenback controversy. There had been a party in favour of paying the nation's interest-bearing debt with Government legal-tender notes (greenbacks), at that time irredeemable and depreciated. Some of the Greenbackers desired to use only the notes actually outstanding; others proposed to issue new notes for this express purpose. The latter were Inflationists. They wished to favour the debtor class, and "make good times."

2. It happened that forty-four million dollars of the notes issued during the War had been redeemed and cancelled. The Inflationists prevailed upon Congress to pass a law to reissue this sum. President Grant vetoed it. There was great excitement over the veto. This happened in 1874. The Republican party was then in control of the Government. It was so badly rent by the veto and the controversy that it lost the Congressional elections of that year. Before it went out of power, however, it pulled itself together and passed a Specie Resumption Act to go into effect four years later. This Act exasperated the Inflationists, who made a political issue of it in the State elections in 1875. They were defeated. The absurdity

* *Issued in October*, 1896.

and dishonesty of paying the Government's interest bearing debt with its non-interest-bearing debt were too palpable.

3. **At this juncture the decline in the gold price of silver had begun to attract attention. The Inflationists, who had been beaten in the elections, seized upon this fact with eagerness.** Silver, they said, was a metal. It was procured by labour. It could not be increased in amount indefinitely. It was the dollar of our fathers. It was the dollar of the poor man, the dollar of the debtor, the dollar of the common people. It was remembered, however, that two years earlier Congress, in an Act revising the coinage laws, had prohibited the coinage of that metal for private persons, and limited its legal-tender faculty to five dollars. At the time when this Act was passed we had no metallic money in circulation, not even for small change, and the silver dollar, if there had been any, would have been worth, in the market, two cents more than the gold dollar. **There had been no American silver dollars in circulation for nearly forty years.**

4. Originally we had the double standard of silver and gold at the legal ratio of 15 to 1. This was under Hamilton's law of 1792. It conformed to the market ratio at that time, but the ratio gradually changed. The relative value of gold rose. That metal passed out of circulation. The weight and bulk of silver became an increasing trouble until Congress took up the subject in 1834, and adopted a new ratio (approximately 16 to 1) in which gold was overvalued about $2\frac{1}{4}$ per cent. The intention was to make the ratio such that gold would supplant silver in the circulation, as it did.

5. There had been no silver dollars coined at the mint for thirty years, but the half-dollars and other smaller coins were of proportional weight and fineness with the dollar, and of full legal tender. President Jefferson had ordered the discontinuance of the coinage of dollars in 1806 for a technical reason, which need not be considered here. **The fact of importance is that the silver dollar was practically an unknown coin in the United States prior to 1873,** for, although some eight millions of them had been coined, they had been used almost exclusively in trade with China and the East Indies. They were seen at home only as curiosities. English crowns were more common in our circulation, and Spanish dollars much more so.

After 1834 our small change consisted principally of foreign silver coins passing at their bullion value, our own silver coins being worth too much to circulate at par with gold. At one time two half-dollars were worth four cents more than a gold dollar.

In 1853 Congress had provided for a subsidiary coinage by reducing the weight of all the silver coins smaller than one dollar 7 per cent., and making them legal tender for only five dollars. The debate in the House shows that the intention of those who brought in the Bill was to adopt the single gold standard.

6. If they had actually done so, they would have spared their posterity much trouble. But they left the silver dollar as a possible, although an unused, coin of full legal tender. Probably the reason why they did so was that it was useful in our trade with Oriental countries, where the trading community was accustomed to it, and because nobody then anticipated the change in the relative value of the two metals which has since taken place. The law was incongruous with the intention of its promoters in this particular. The Act of 1873 was a revision and consolidation of the coinage laws of former years. The incongruity of the Act of 1853 was noticed and corrected, and thus the law was made to conform to the fact. Few persons observed the correction, because the silver dollar was an obsolete coin, almost as scarce as the stater of ancient Greece. Nevertheless, the omission of the silver dollar from the list of authorised coins was publicly discussed in the House, and the reasons given for it were evidently satisfactory, since only 13 votes were cast against it out of a total of 123.

7. **When the Greenback Inflationists found that silver had been demonetised in 1873, and that some of their own party had voted that way, they exclaimed that they had been tricked and deceived, and they started a campaign for remonetisation.** Their opponents were taken by surprise, and were at first at a loss what to say or do. Many fell in with them and joined the hue and cry, considering themselves lucky that they had escaped the greater evil of unlimited paper. The question of bimetallism was new. The demand for more money was vociferous. The public mind had been fatally misled by the greenback itself, having been taught by it to believe that the Government was charged with the duty of making money plenty, or, according to a common saying, " making the volume of money equal to the wants of trade." The result was that the House, in the latter part of 1877, passed the Bland Bill for the free coinage of silver on the same terms as gold at the ratio of 16 to 1. Silver was then about 9 per cent. below parity with gold at that ratio.

8. The opponents of silver were of three varieties—(a) those who

were opposed to it *in toto ;* (*b*) those who were opposed to free coinage except by international agreement; (*c*) those who did not believe that an international agreement was practicable, but who wanted to gain time, hoping that the excitement would blow over. The advocates of silver were likewise of different sorts—(*a*) the silver miners, who wanted to sustain the price of their product; (*b*) the " debtor class " and the Inflationists, who were glad to find a new weapon to their hand in place of the greenback ; (*c*) a multitude of unthinking or misinformed persons, who thought that an injustice, if not a fraud, had been committed in the Demonetisation Act, which Act is still called by the silver party "the crime of 1873."

9. In order to defeat free coinage and gain time, some of its opponents in the Senate said that it would be unfair to give to those who happened to possess silver bullion an advantage of 9 per cent. over everybody else ; that that profit ought to accrue to the Government; since the Government had no silver bullion, it ought to purchase a certain quantity at the market price, coin it, and sell the resulting coins to the people, or use them to pay its expenses or to buy more silver with. This was a plausible fallacy. It neutralised Mr. Bland's fallacy for the time being, and it was probably the only way that free coinage could have been stopped at that time. An amendment, proposed by Senator Allison, to the Bland Bill embodying these views was adopted by the Senate and accepted by the House. The Bill as passed was vetoed by President Hayes, and passed over his veto.* The votes taken in the House were fairly representative of public opinion at that time. There were 73 votes to sustain the veto, *i.e.* against silver in any form, and 196 to pass the Bill over the veto. There were 203 votes for the Allison amendment, and 72 for the original Bland Bill. The party of compromise exceeded the combined votes of the extremists on both sides.

10. **One section of the Allison amendment authorised the President to invite an international monetary conference. The Paris Conference of 1878 was the result. Its futile ending need not be recounted here, but since it is one of three conferences of like character and initiative it is worth remarking that all of them have been political makeshifts**

---

* *Act of February 28th, 1878.*—Sec. I.—The Secretary of the Treasury is authorised and directed to purchase, from time to time, silver bullion, at the market price thereof, not less than two million dollars' worth per month, nor more than four million dollars' worth per month, and cause the same to be coined monthly, as fast as so purchased, *etc.*

—the attempts of politicians to stave off the inevitable, and to prevent the very kind of battle that we are now fighting. Probably Mr. Allison's amendment would not have been accepted in 1878 if it had not held out the hope of an international agreement. Everybody could see that the monthly purchase of 2,000,000 dollars' worth of silver on Government account could not go on for ever. This was not an end in itself, but a stop-gap.

11. If the question be asked, "What proportion of the American people are bimetallists?" we must first define bimetallism. This means the simultaneous use of two metals as money. **If bimetallism means international bimetallism, what proportion of our people are bimetallists in this sense?**

12. If any inference may be drawn from the diversity of views expressed at the beginning of the campaign of 1896 as to the meaning of the words "16 to 1," I should say that only an inconsiderable fraction had any ideas whatever in reference to bimetallism. The contention of the supporters of Mr. Bryan is that we ought to have the "free and unlimited coinage of silver at our present legal ratio of 16 to 1" (the market ratio at present is about 31 to 1). The following varieties of opinion, honestly entertained, have been encountered, since the campaign opened, as to the meaning of these words :—

(*a*) That the Government ought to coin sixteen silver dollars every time it coins one gold dollar.

(*b*) That sixteen silver dollars ought to be worth as much as one gold dollar.

(*c*) That the Government ought to coin sixteen dollars for each person, making a total coinage of sixteen dollars *per capita*.

(*d*) That the Government ought to give sixteen dollars to each one. A newspaper in Alabama published a letter from a man who favoured the policy of 16 to 1 because it would give him eighty dollars, his family consisting of five persons.

(*e*) That it means sixteen dollars to each white man and only one dollar to each coloured man, for which reason the latter was opposed to it. This in North Carolina.

The phrase "free coinage of silver" having been shortened in common parlance to "free silver," many persons have come to understand that it means the free distribution of silver by the Government to the people.

13. Would any other people evince more wisdom *per capita* if thrust suddenly into the labyrinth of finance, banking, coinage, ratios, seigniorage, value, price, demand, supply, etc., and told to find their

way out? I doubt it. However that may be, the demand for information on these subjects now is enormous and insatiable. I venture to think that before the end is reached the American people will know more *per capita* about these things than any other people of ancient or modern times.

It follows from these facts that the mass of the American people are neither for nor against bimetallism. They simply do not understand the subject, but are trying to learn. How is it with the few who do understand it, or think they do?

14. In the first place, the silver men of the Bland and Bryan type are not bimetallists. They are silver monometallists. Mr. Bland makes no concealment of his contempt for international monetary conferences. Directly after the adjournment of the Brussels Conference he wrote an article on "The Boons and Banes of Free Silver," published in the *North American Review* of February, 1893, which began with these words: "The adjournment of the monetary conference recently held at Brussels, without any definite conclusions or agreement on the silver question, is no disappointment or surprise to anyone. The conference was not solicited by our Government with the view of any serious consideration of the matters involved. It was well known here and abroad that the moving cause of the conference on the part of our Government was to defeat or postpone legislation on the silver question, and to amuse and deceive the people pending the Presidential election. Able and affable gentlemen met in debate, suggested vague and impossible plans, had a good time, and finally adjourned, expressing the hope that the junketing farce may be repeated in May."

Referring also to the conferences of 1878 and 1881, he continued: "No definite conclusions were reached or even hoped for at any of these conferences, the main subject of which was to stem the popular tide for the free coinage of silver in this country; to gain time and the opportunity to go back to the demonetisation policy of 1873."

15. It is easy to quote platforms of political parties in favour of bimetallism. These platforms are written by the same men who steer the question into international conferences, and whose motives are not incorrectly delineated by Mr. Bland in the paragraphs here quoted. From one Presidential election to another they have been trying to shelve the question, adopting various devices of legislation to produce a dead-lock and to gain time. To recount all these shifts, devices, and combinations,

including the Sherman Act of 1890,* would fill too much space. Two results have been produced—a confused state of the currency and a confused state of the public mind regarding bimetallism. Having read in their party platforms, year after year, that they were in favour of international bimetallism, without knowing that the real reason (as Mr. Bland says) was to defeat or postpone definite action at home, a great many people have come to believe that they are in favour of it, without having the least idea how it is to be brought about, or what obstacles lie in the way of it. To them bimetallism is a shibboleth. This cannot be considered an effective public opinion, since these people are just as ready to drop it as they were to take it up. Let the silver monometallists of the Bland and Bryan type be once shelved, and they will shelve bimetallism gladly.

16. The scientific bimetallists—those who have fixed opinions and can give reasons for them, like General F. A. Walker and the late S. Dana Horton—were never more than a handful. **But the number of bimetallists of every type is dwindling rapidly now. The issue of the present campaign is not bimetallism, but the Gold standard** *versus* **the Silver standard.**

17. Silver purchasing and coining came to an end in 1893, after a financial panic of great severity. That was also a political make-shift, and is likewise played out. It was more costly, however, than international conferences. We paid out 464,000,000 dollars gold for the purchase of silver bullion that we did not want merely to introduce a new kind of rot into our currency. In order to keep it at par with gold, we have been obliged to borrow nearly $300,000,000 during the past three years, and to issue interest-bearing obligations therefor. **This is a small part of our loss. The larger part has come from the unsettling of credit and the expulsion of capital caused by endangering the gold standard. The financial crisis of 1893 has become chronic since its cause is chronic.** All of this misery and turmoil, this loss of capital and waste of energy, this real danger to our institutions, has its origin in the Government legal-tender notes issued during the War, which taught our people to believe that there was virtue in a cheap dollar. If the Silverites ever achieve their end, the Green-backers will swallow them at a gulp. They are quite ready to be

---

* *Act of July 14th, 1890.*—Sec. I.—The Secretary of the Treasury is hereby directed to purchase, from time to time, silver bullion to the aggregate amount of 4,500,000 ounces, or so much thereof as may be offered, in each month, at the market price thereof, *etc.*

swallowed. Mr. Bryan's nomination was endorsed by the Populists because he was one of them. He made a speech advocating their greenback doctrines in Congress only two years ago.

18. **Probably no words of caution from us are needed by the British public on this subject. We offer you our example, which ought to be sufficient. We have not abandoned the gold standard**; we are not likely to, but we have made the pretence of doing so, and have alarmed people with the notion that we might abandon it designedly or might slip away from it without design. The consequences to trade and industry have been disastrous, and they are capable of repeating themselves on a still larger scale and among any number of nations which may toy with bimetallism, make a pretence of adopting it, and frighten people as we have done.

19. These consequences would follow from any serious attempt to discard, as a medium of exchange and standard of value, something in which everybody has confidence, and to substitute for it something in which nobody has confidence. The silverites in America are just as anxious to get gold for their products, their labour, their investments, as anybody is. Laughable instances of their preference for the yellow metal in their private business abound. Is this universal preference to be neutralised by a resolution or statute of any number of Governments? The public know that all such bonds are loose at best, and that they come to an end some time. Every man of business will know how to insure himself against contingencies, and will avail himself of his privilege to do so. He will indulge his preference for gold after a bimetallic agreement as before, and the preference will upset the agreement—if we can imagine such an agreement possible. I cannot.

20. **That England should abandon the gold standard, either alone or in conjunction with others, while this preference of the commercial world for gold exists, is unimaginable. Much of the uncertainty and prolonged agony that have afflicted us has arisen from concessions indiscreetly made by the friends of sound money, that the decline in the price of silver is a world-wide evil. An evil it is undoubtedly to those who have silver, but not to others. We had none of it, but we took some, to our infinite harm. If our example is worth anything to England, she will continue to shun it.**

The Bimetallic Campaign in France.*

By M. YVES GUYOT,

Ex-Minister of Public Works ; former President of the Société de Statistique de Paris ; Member of the Institut International de Statistique ; Member of the Société d'Économie Politique de Paris ; Hon. Member of the Cobden Club ; Editor of "LE SIÈCLE"; Author of "LA SCIENCE ECONOMIQUE," "L'ÉCONOMIE DE L'EFFORT," and other works.

---

1. **The true theory of money.**—How has bimetallism been able to make any headway in France, the native country of Nicolas Oresme, Councillor to Charles V. ? It was he who insisted on a good and fixed currency for the whole kingdom. He said :—" The " effigy and sign of the prince are put on a coin in order to vouch "for the accuracy of the weight, quality, and standard of the metal." In a word, a coin is an ingot, the standard and weight of which are certified. The legal imprint does not impart any value to it. Here, then, is the truth revealed in the fourteenth century by Nicolas Oresme, who adds :—"Should not any prince be ashamed of coin-"ing base money, when it is his duty to punish counterfeit coiners "with death ?"

2. **A prejudice.**—Bimetallism, however, only exists in France because its promoters, its partisans, and the public are accustomed to.speak of five grammes of silver of a standard of nine-tenths fine as being worth one franc.

* *Issued in October,* 1897.

3. **The terms of the law of 1803.**—Now, the Act of the 7th Germinal of the Year XI. (28th March, 1803) simply says :—" Five "grammes of silver of a standard of nine-tenths fine constitute the "monetary unit, which preserves the name of franc," as instituted by the Act of the 18th Germinal, Year III. Article 6 adds :—"Gold "coins of twenty and forty francs shall be struck." Article 8 states : "Twenty-franc pieces shall be minted at the rate of one hundred "and fifty-five to the kilo, and forty-franc pieces at the rate of "seventy-seven and a half."

4. **The law is not bimetallic. It gives no value to either silver or gold.** It gives a name to a piece of metal of a fixed weight and standard, and it adds that each of the 155 ingots obtained from one kilogramme of gold shall bear the name of a twenty-franc piece. There is no reference to bimetallism either in the preamble or in the body of the statute. The Act was merely based upon the existing ratio of value of 1 to $15\frac{1}{2}$ between gold and silver, which was approximately the rate of exchange at the time. It did not establish this ratio ; but silver and gold francs both possessed legal tender power between private persons and at Government and other public offices (*caisses*). That is what gave rise to the saying that France had a double monetary standard.

5. **A misleading phrase.**—This statement is misleading, for a standard of measurement, of capacity, or weight is invariable, whatever may be the nature of the thing measured or weighed by it; whereas the value of money changes according to the thing which it measures or weighs from time to time. It cannot possess the essential feature of a standard because it is variable. All bimetallic prejudices are based on the confusion caused by these words. Bimetallists assert that the State fixes the value of the pieces of metal stamped at its mint.

6. **The experience of the past.**—As Mr. Henry Dunning Macleod proves in his remarkable leaflet on "Bimetallism in France," * the experience of France has demonstrated the contrary. The relative value of gold and silver has constantly varied. In his report to the Minister of Finance, M. de Foville, Director of the Mint, has published a statement of these variations from 1821 to 1895. The gold premium reached 17 francs per 1,000 francs in 1833 ; in 1851 it fell for the first time to a discount of 1·30 francs, and this continued with fluctuations until 1858. In 1859 gold stood at

* *See page* 153.

par. In 1861 it was again at a premium, and this has been maintained, but the premium is very low; in 1895 it was 0·03 francs. The exchange on silver also varies. From 1821 to 1851 the highest premium was 7·05 francs. From that year it rose, and in 1857 it reached 30·85 francs. Since 1873 there has been a discount on silver, and in 1880 it reached 125·95 francs, and in 1895 503·08 francs. Notwithstanding these variations, bimetallists maintain that the Act of Germinal, Year XI., established a fixed ratio between gold and silver, and that this ratio was invariable up to 1873. Up to 1850, says the Monetary Commission of 1867, silver was almost the only metal circulating in France; the discoveries in California made gold flow into Europe, and diminished its value, while the demand for silver from the Far East increased the value of the latter metal.

7. **The gold standard in France.**—In 1857 the French Government appointed a Commission, who, in their report, examined without arriving at any conclusion the question as to the adoption of a gold standard and the reduction of silver to the position of token coinage. But M. Léon Say, in the preamble of the law, introduced in March, 1876, with the object of suspending the issue of notes against silver deposited for coinage, said that "from 1857 " the principle of the gold standard has won increasing favour through " our several administrations." In 1861 the Minister of Finance appointed a Commission to ascertain whether France ought not to follow the example of Switzerland, who, in 1860, reduced the standard of silver coins under five francs to 834 per 1,000 fine; which was, in fact, the suppression of the monetary unit, viz. the franc of five grammes of silver of nine-tenths fine, and the substitution of the gold standard. Hence arose the monetary Convention of the Latin Union in 1865 between France, Belgium, Switzerland, and Italy, subsequently joined by Greece. Mr. W. A. Shaw has justly said that the Union was a measure of protection against the action of bimetallism in those countries which had adopted the monetary system of France and were exposed to its disastrous fluctuations. This Convention in reality adopted the gold standard, and by reducing the standard of silver coins of under five francs relegated them to the rank of token coins, and limited the coinage thereof in proportion to the population of each country.

8. **The cessation of silver coinage.**—In 1868 France convened a conference, in which eighteen nations took part, with a view to rendering coinage uniform. At that conference gold was declared by the delegates of all the nations, except that of Holland,

O

to be the only international money. They adopted the gold standard and the divisions of the decimal system, the five-franc coin being the unit. On the 9th of November, 1869, the Conseil Supérieur du Commerce, de l'Agriculture et de l'Industrie was instructed to make inquiries, with the result that the gold standard was adopted by a very large majority. Political events prevented this conference from meeting again. Germany adopted the gold standard in 1871.

9. But while the Paris Mint had only coined 58 million francs in five-franc pieces in 1869, in 1873 it coined to the value of 154,649,000 francs ; in 1874 59,996,000 francs ; in 1875 75,000,000, and in 1876 52,661,000 francs. In 1871 and 1872 Belgium coined 34,000,000 francs ; in 1873 111,000,000 francs. In September, 1873, the Belgian Minister was alarmed at this invasion of silver money, and in December the coinage of silver on private account was suspended. Switzerland called a meeting of the members of the Union, which was held in January, 1874, and which fixed a limit to the coinage for each State during 1874. Other treaties were made on the 26th of April, 1875, and the 3rd of February, 1876.

10. **By the Act of the 5th of August, 1876, the French Government obtained authority by decree to stop the manufacture of five-franc pieces, and by the treaty of the 5th of November, 1878, all the States of the Latin Union undertook not to coin any more five-franc pieces.** Article 8 of the treaty of 1885, which was entered into for five years, but which is now renewed from year to year by tacit agreement, lays down the principle of the suspension of the coinage of five-franc pieces, but it admits that any of the States may resume free coinage thereof on condition that they redeem, in gold and at sight, from the other contracting countries the five-franc pieces bearing their own effigy and circulating in the territories of such States. In addition to this, the other States to be at liberty to refuse the coinage of any State which might begin again to mint these coins.

11. **A lesson for France.**—This last clause was introduced by the bimetallists, but no State ever cared to take advantage of it. Article 14 specifies, that in the event of the treaty being denounced, each contracting party is bound to redeem any silver coins issued by them, and which might be in circulation in other States; the condition being that they were to pay to such States an amount equal to the nominal value of the specie redeemed, all the conditions to be stipulated by special arrangement. According to the arrangement made with Belgium, the latter country is exempt from repaying half

of the balance, provided such balance is less than, or equal to, 200 millions of francs. If this balance be over 200 millions, Belgium is exempt from paying 100 millions. The benefit of these concessions was claimed by Italy, who obtained it. **In the event of the Union being dissolved, France runs the risk of losing an amount in Belgian and Italian coinage which might amount to as much as 200 millions of francs. This loss, great as it is under a limited treaty like that of the Latin Union, even when free coinage is stopped, should cause the French bimetallist to reflect upon the difficulty of a liquidation following upon an international treaty for the free coinage of silver.**

12. **International efforts towards Bimetallism.**—In 1878 the United States invited the European Governments to appoint a monetary Conference with a view to resuming the coinage of silver. France responded to the appeal. A Conference consisting of the delegates of twelve nations met in Paris. It proved a failure. In 1881 the French Government arranged with the United States for a new Conference. Nineteen countries were represented thereat. The French and American Governments suggested that a Convention, including England, France, Germany, and the United States, should establish a fixed ratio between gold and silver, and also the free coinage of silver. The Conference adjourned without arriving at any conclusion. The United States again arranged for the meeting of a Conference, which was held in Brussels on the 22nd of November, 1892, and proved to be another failure. From that time the bimetallic agitation has assumed a certain amount of importance in France.

13. **Bimetallism an alternative to Protection.**—The duty on wheat, of 5 francs per 100 kilos, was established by the Act of the 25th of March, 1887. However, the price of wheat continued to fall until 1891, in which year the harvest was bad. It then became necessary to reduce the duty to 3 francs by the Act of the 3rd of July, 1891, which remained effective up to the end of June, 1892. Gold monometallism had not prevented the rise in the price of corn. But the subsequent crops turned out abundant, and the price of wheat began to fall again. Then came the Act of the 27th of February, 1894, which raised the duty on wheat to 7 francs. But the protectionists had lost confidence in the efficacy of the Customs duties. They perceived that, as economists who had studied the past had told them, when the supply was abundant the duties did not produce

O 2

their entire effect. Nevertheless, they were unwilling to admit this simple explanation. They declined to acknowledge that they had been deceived in their predictions when they affirmed that the Custom House tariffs would cause a rise equivalent to their calculations. **The protectionists cast about for an alternative explanation of the fall of prices, and this explanation was that the coinage of silver had been stopped. The remedy, therefore, they concluded, was bimetallism.**

14. **The silver assignats.**—In 1894 the "Société des Agriculteurs de France" expressed an opinion in the above sense. The English Bimetallic League invited them to an international monetary Conference which was held in London in May, 1894. The "Association de l'Agriculture et de l'Industrie Française," a very powerful protectionist organisation, presided over by M. Méline before he was President of the Council, and the "Société d'Encouragement à l'Agriculture," presided over by M. Loubet, now President of the Senate, kept up the agitation on the question of bimetallism during the whole of the summer. It became the universal panacea. If the Custom House duties did not act, if farmers had not derived all the profit that had been promised them, it was because the supply of money had been insufficient. With an extraordinary levity, which nothing but an astounding ignorance could excuse, they pointed out that wheat and cattle would go up in price if France were inundated with five-franc pieces. Economists told them, with justice, that it was not the value of the wheat which would increase, but that the purchasing power of money would diminish. They recalled the good old time of the assignats under the Revolution, in the Year III., when one sack of flour fetched 13,000 louis; and in Pluviose, Year IV., when one gold louis was worth 5,000 francs in paper, and yet the farmer was no better off for it. **Economists pointed out to the bimetallists that once they asserted that the State could attribute a value to any particular metal, they might just as well attribute it to paper, and that, in reality, what they were proposing was a system of silver assignats.**

15. **The bimetallic programme.**—In February, 1895, each of these three societies passed solemn resolutions in which they asserted that gold monometallism was the cause of the universal and constant fall in prices; that it constituted in countries having a single silver standard an enormous premium on the export of their produce, and a no less considerable protection against the imports from countries having a single gold standard; that the fall in the value of the silver

standard, as compared with the gold standard, was only due to the legislative measures taken in favour of gold and to the detriment of silver. These societies invited the Government to take the initiative in an international understanding with a view to settle :—

(1) The establishment of a fixed ratio between the two standards.

(2) The free coinage by all nations of gold and silver at some ratio to be established between them.

The "Société des Agriculteurs de France" added :—"In the "event of this international understanding being recognised as im-"possible, the French Government to be invited to consider what "might be the results on French finance of a return unconditionally "to the free coinage of silver." This society imported into France the policy of Mr. Bryan in the United States. **The members of these agricultural societies who, passing themselves off as the protectors of home agriculture, had objected to see a single hectolitre of wheat come into France, now wanted to open wide our doors to silver, which is not a national product, and constituted themselves the ardent protectors of the American silver mine owners.**

16. **The Bimetallic League.**—These three societies founded in Paris, on the 25th of March, 1895, the National Bimetallic League. It possessed powerful means of action. Among its honorary presidents were MM. Magnin, Governor of the Bank of France, and Méline, ex-Minister, President of the Parliamentary Customs Commission, and now Prime Minister. Its Chairman was M. Loubet, now President of the Senate. Its staff was composed of persons of note. Although a certain number of the Directors of the Bank of France were opposed to this League, the whole organisation of the bank was placed at its disposal. The chief cashier of the bank was the treasurer of the League. In spite of this, however, from 1861 up to 1896, the maximum gold reserve of the Bank of France had always been maintained at a higher figure than the maximum silver reserve, except in 1863, 1879, 1880, 1881, 1882, and 1883—that is to say, for thirty years out of thirty-six. The League conducted a very active press campaign, and called meetings and conferences. The General Secretary, M. Théry, was gifted with the sort of assurance which impresses people. In a discussion before the " Société d'Économie "Industrielle et Commerciale," in March, 1894, he affirmed that within a year an international Conference would decide to undertake

the free coinage of silver and establish a fixed ratio between it and gold. I told him in reply that it was impossible to argue with prophets, but I offered to make him a bet. He was compelled to take it. He lost.

17. **International Parliamentary agitation.—The French Bimetallic League summoned the German and English Bimetallic Leagues to a preliminary Congress on the 10th of December, 1895, for the purpose of mutually determining the terms of a Parliamentary motion, the object of which was to invite their respective Governments to enter at once into negotiations for arriving at the bases of an international bimetallic understanding.** In consequence of this meeting, a motion was brought before the House of Commons, on the 17th of March, 1896, which, however, did not help the bimetallic cause. M. Méline on the same day presented a notice of motion signed by 348 members, constituting a considerable majority in the Chamber of Deputies, which is composed of 581 members. The preamble of the motion merely reiterated the resolutions of the societies, which I have summarised above. The title of this was: "A notice of motion for the re-establishment of a fixed ratio between gold and silver by means of an international agreement." It ran as follows:—
"The Chamber of Deputies, considering that the establishment
"of international bimetallism would be a great benefit to the
"agricultural, industrial, and commercial interests of the country,
"invites the Government to take the necessary steps to establish
"and ensure, by means of an international understanding, a fixed
"ratio between gold and silver." The Chamber evinced no enthusiasm; it resolved that it would decide subsequently as to the declaration of urgency asked for by those who had taken the initiative. The proposal never came up for discussion.

18. **In September, 1896, the _élite_ of the European bimetallists, assembled at Budapest, sent an address to Mr. Bryan, in which they said:—"If you triumph in November, "we undertake to spare no effort and no pains to exert imme- "diate pressure on our respective Governments, so that they "may act in concert with your great nation to restore silver "as the monetary standard."** The election of Mr. McKinley upset the French bimetallists for a moment; but on the following day they declared themselves enchanted, though they looked disgusted all the time, and told people to wait for 1900. If Mr. McKinley did not want the United States alone to resume

the free coinage of silver, that did not mean, they said, that he was opposed to an international understanding. Therefore, all was for the best.

19. When in April, 1897, Mr. McKinley appointed Commissioners to visit Europe in order to consider the possibility of calling an international conference, the French bimetallists again tried to revive a little agitation, but they had lost faith. At the time when the American Commissioners were in Paris, I suggested to M. Théry that we should make another bet. He reduced the amount I offered to him, and postponed the settlement till 1902. This was not a proof of very ardent faith. Immediately after the departure of the American Commissioners, who, in order to ascertain the opinion of France as to bimetallism, declined to communicate with its adversaries, **two facts arose to destroy the bimetallic argument, viz. the coincidence of the fall in the price of silver to 24d. per ounce and the rise in the price of corn to 30 francs per quintal (August, 1897).**

20. **The assertions of the bimetallists and facts.**—If bimetallists are asked how they explain this phenomenon, which contradicts all their assertions, they reply, " Cereals rise in price because the " supply is less than the demand." But then they lose all their authority with those whom they had led away by repeating that if the price of wheat fell it was on account of the stoppage of the silver coinage ; that the increase in its production, and the facility of the means of transport, had nothing to do with it ; and that if free coinage and the unlimited legal tender of silver were not established, all prices would continue to fall.

21. **The adversaries of bimetallism.**—French bimetallists have had against them the leading newspapers in France, such as the *Journal des Débats, Le Temps, Le Siècle, Le Messager de Paris, La Liberté ;* special newspapers like the *Journal des Économistes* and the *Économiste Français.* M. Frédéric Passy, of the Institut de France, who bears such a well-known name, and who is the champion of every good cause, brings his eloquence to the aid of the science of sound money. M. P. Beauregard, Professor of Political Economy to the Faculté de Paris, and editor of *Le Monde Économique*, who was formerly biased in favour of bimetallism, has turned strongly against it, and has published some very trenchant criticisms. M. A. Neymarck, editor of *Le Rentier*, and member of the Institut International de Statistique, is also opposed to bimetallism. Among the latest works of M. Léon Say, whose death is universally lamented, were three long and

powerful articles against the folly of bimetallism. The Académie des Sciences Morales et Politiques held a competitive examination on the following question, viz. " The ratio of value between the two metals " used as money, and particularly the power of Governments to " maintain between the various metals used as money a ratio of " value other than that resulting from supply and demand." The report of M. Clément Juglar, published in the month of November, 1896, shows that all the four essays submitted for the consideration of the Académie, unanimously agreed in declaring that money, regarded as a metal, is liable to the same fluctuations as other commodities. "An important result," says the report, "has been " obtained, viz. the scientific conclusion, that at no period in the " past has the legal ratio between gold and silver, fixed by Govern- " ments, been maintained." At the same period M. Levasseur, the eminent professor of history, geography and economic statistics at the Collège de France, presented to the "Société Nationale des Agri- culteurs de France" the results of a work of Mr. Powers, who, in the Fifth Biennial Report of the Commissioner of Works of the State of Minnesota (U.S.A.), showed by the investigation of sixteen products, from 1862 to 1895, that the prices of these articles had fluctuated in a varying manner, according to the condition of the local market of the State and the condition of the great inter- national market. As in England, our bankers are sound money men, preferring the public interest to the benefit which they would gain from a fluctuating exchange and from the ebb and flow of both metals under bimetallism. We need only mention MM. Germain and Kleinmann, of the Crédit Lyonnais, Mercet, of the Comptoir National d'Escompte, and Aynard, director of the Banque de France and Member of Parliament for Lyons.

22. **Principles opposed to bimetallists.**—All economists of note have energetically maintained the following principles :—

(1) **It is not the value indicated on a coin that fixes the value of the metal, but it is the value of the metal which fixes the value of the coin.**

(2) **No international agreement, any more than the law of a single State, can accomplish this miracle, viz. to establish a fixed ratio between two variable values.**

(3) **If one or more Governments can impart a fictitious value to silver, they can impart it to**

any other metal, and not only to metal, but
to paper as well.

(4) Even supposing that an agreement, with this
object in view, could be concluded between
several great nations, it would be impossible
to determine the conditions of the liquidation
which would have to follow.

23. However the French Parliament may have allowed itself to
be led away by the illusion of bimetallism in order to palliate the
failure of protection, no Government will be foolish enough even to
ask Parliament to re-establish the free coinage of silver, except by an
international agreement with England and Germany. The manifesto
of the National Bimetallic League formally stated, at the time when
agitation was at its height, that "The fixed ratio between gold and
" silver can only be ensured by means of international bimetallism.
" By 'international bimetallism' we must understand an agreement
" between the principal nations now on the gold standard, including
" England; and by the terms of which agreement the free coinage
" and the unlimited legal tender power would be accorded to both
" gold and silver." Since this manifesto, Russia has changed her
standard, which was paper based on silver, and has adopted a gold
standard; Austria also; Japan has abandoned the silver standard;
the English Government has not been encouraging. These facts
dissipate the illusions of bimetallists. There appear, then,
to be good grounds for assuming that French bimetallists
are now reduced to a state of helplessness.

The Bimetallic Report of the Agricul= tural Commission—A Reply.*

By the Rt. Hon. G. SHAW-LEFEVRE.

1. A MAJORITY of the members of the Agricultural Commission have drawn up a separate report, in which they attribute the depression of agriculture to the appreciation of gold, resulting in part from its reduced production in the few years which succeeded 1873, and in part from the demonetisation of silver by Germany and other Powers which previously had a silver standard, and from the break of the Convention of the Latin States, by which they contend that a parity between silver and gold had been maintained for many years in the ratio of $15\frac{1}{2}$ to 1. They are also of opinion that the continuous fall in the price of silver since 1873 has had the effect of stimulating the export of wheat and other produce from silver-standard countries such as India, that the same effect has been produced by the depreciation of the paper currency of the Argentine Republic, and that the artificial competition thus produced has lowered the price of wheat and other produce in our markets to the detriment of farmers.

They conclude their report with this paragraph :—

* *Issued in November, 1897.*

"We do not suggest that the gold standard should be abandoned
"in this country, but we think that if a conference of the Powers
"was assembled, and that their deliberations resulted in an inter-
"national arrangement for the reopening of the mints abroad and in
"India, and the restoration of silver, either wholly or partially, to the
"position which it filled prior to 1873, it would be of the greatest
"benefit to the industry of agriculture. . . . . We think that if
"an international arrangement for the purpose which we have
"specified was arrived at, the long-continued fall in prices, which is
"the admitted source of agricultural trouble, would be checked, and
"that if there should be any future movement in the course of prices
"they would tend to rise rather than to fall."

2. Although much evidence was taken by the Commission as
to the causes of the great fall of prices since 1873, and the bimetallic
explanation was fully laid before them, and evidence was given in
favour of a general bimetallic arrangement, including this country,
yet **no evidence whatever was given in favour of the limited
proposal now made, and no opportunity was afforded of
examining witnesses as to its feasibility and probable effect.**
Nor was any evidence called for or given of the effect on Indian
finance of this partial measure in the direction of bimetallism.

It must be obvious that the most difficult question of the
effect of reopening the Indian mints, under arrangement with some
other countries, such as France and the United States, was not one
which would have been submitted to a body of men, such as the
signatories of the report in question, who, however competent to
deal with general agricultural questions, are, on their own admission,
without the financial knowledge and experience which would render
their opinions of value on such a question. *

3. Among the members of the Commission were men who have
been strong advocates of bimetallism, such as Mr. Chaplin and Mr.
Everett. It is significant that they have been unable to induce
their colleagues to join in a general recommendation in favour of
bimetallism—*i.e.* for an international arrangement, including our
own country, for the adoption of a double standard of gold and
silver at some fixed ratio. It is most satisfactory to observe
that even these two gentlemen have joined in deprecating any
disturbance of the gold standard in this country. They seem,
however, to be unconscious of the absurdity of recommending to

---

* *See paragraph 64 of the Bimetallic Report.*

other countries a course which they are unable to advise for their own.

One must be pardoned for surmising that the inducement to many of the signatories to this document has been a consciousness that the agricultural classes will consider the recommendations of the main report as "barren and practically useless";* and just as a patient who has lost hope of deriving any benefit from the advice of orthodox practitioners not unfrequently resorts to quack remedies, so these gentlemen, in their perplexity, have turned to those who suggest more or less of bimetallism as a cure for agricultural depression.

4. **There will be general agreement with the report of the Commission that the primary cause of the long-continued depression of agriculture has been the fall of prices of agricultural produce as measured in gold, but there are the strongest objections to the contention of the bimetallic members of it that the main causes of the fall of prices are to be found in currency disturbances, such as the reduced production of gold, or the greater demand for it due to demonetisation of silver, or the stimulation of exports from countries with a silver or paper currency.**

5. These propositions, for which some plausible and specious arguments might be produced a few years ago, have been thoroughly exposed and disproved by recent experience. It is true that the production of gold fell off for a few years, and having at one time—in the six years 1852-57—reached a maximum average of £28,000,000 a year, and having for the fifteen years 1858-72 averaged £25,000,000 a year, fell to an average of £20,000,000 between 1873 and 1888. It is also true that about the year 1873 greater demands for gold arose owing to the demonetisation of silver by Germany, and the termination of the convention of the Latin States for maintaining a parity between gold and silver at 1 to 15½. About the same year also the fall of prices began, which has continued more or less up to the present time; and it not unnaturally appeared to many people that these occurrences were connected together as cause and effect. This deduction, however, has been dispelled by the fact that in 1888 the production of gold again began to rise, and has since risen to a point far above that of the period before 1873. In 1889 it rose to over £25,000,000. In 1893 it was over £32,000,000; in 1894 it was £37,000,000; in 1895, £40,000,000; in 1896 it

---

See paragraph 2 of the Bimetallic Report.

was £41,700,000, and for the current year (1897) it is estimated at £48,000,000.

The extraordinary demands for gold of Germany and other Powers, due to their demonetising silver, have also been satisfied, and all the leading banks and treasuries of Europe have for some time past been overflowing with gold.

If, therefore, the reduced production of gold and the increased demand for it had any immediate and considerable effect on prices between 1873 and 1888, it would seem to follow as a logical consequence that the increased production during the last eight years would long before this have had the opposite effect—namely, of raising prices. But so far from this taking place, the reverse has happened, and prices have continued to fall till a few months ago, in spite of the predictions of those who maintained that there is a close connection between the production of gold and the prices of other commodities.

6. **This recent experience is proof of what the Gold Standard Association has always contended—that there is very little connection between the amount of the annual production of gold and the prices of other commodities measured in gold.** The explanation of this, it has been pointed out, is simple enough — namely, that gold differs essentially from most other commodities from which prices are taken, and which are consumed within a few months of their production, and must annually be renewed again. The annual production of gold, after deducting a certain amount used in trade, is added to the existing great stock of accumulated gold in the world, which is subject to very little wear and tear, which is constantly increasing, and of which the year's production, whether more or less, forms but a small proportion. To whatever extent the quantitative theory be true that prices of other commodities are dependent on the ratio of gold to them, the proposition can only be maintained with reference, not to the yearly product of gold, but to the stock of gold already existing in the world in the form of currency, or bullion easily convertible into currency.

Supposing, for instance, the stock of gold in the world in the form of coin, or available quickly for that purpose, be £1,500,000,000, and that in one year £10,000,000 is added to this stock, and in another year £20,000,000—the ratio by which, on the theory of the quantitative principle, prices are determined is not £10,000,000 at the one time and £20,000,000 at the other, but £1,500,000,000 +

£10,000,000 in the one and £1,500,000,000 + £20,000,000 in the other case—proportions which vary very slightly and which would account for a very minute fall, if any, in the prices of commodities. Even if there should arise an extraordinary demand of £100,000,000 in consequence of the demonetisation of silver, this would have but little permanent effect on prices, as it would be only one-fifteenth of the existing stock of gold, and the annual produce, at the rate of £30,000,000 or £40,000,000, would soon replace it.

7. It is further to be observed that the use of gold has been enormously economised by the use of negotiable instruments, such as cheques and bills of exchange, by banking facilities, and by arrangements such as bankers' clearing houses.

These instruments and facilities, therefore, must be taken into account in estimating the effect of an increased or reduced annual supply of gold, and the effect of any change in the production of or the demand for gold has to be considered, not with reference only to the previous annual supplies, or even to the accumulated stock of gold, but to the stock of gold plus these credit notes of all kinds, which supply the place of gold in the vast mass of commercial transactions, and economise its use.

That prices ultimately have some relation to the quantity of gold in stock in the world is no doubt true, but there is good reason to believe that this ultimate ratio is in a very small degree dependent upon the quantity, more or less, which may be produced year by year.

8. In the Bimetallic Report it is further contended that the prices of all articles, before 1873, were regulated not merely by the quantity of gold in the world but by the quantity of both gold and silver, inasmuch as the arrangements of the Latin States for the free coinage of silver at an agreed ratio to gold, the bimetallic system of the United States, and the silver system of Germany, placed silver on a par with gold as a regulator of prices.

As the value of silver in the world was, twenty-five years ago, not far from that of gold (at the old rate of $15\frac{1}{2}$ to 1), it would appear to follow, if this view be correct, on the quantitative theory, that prices in gold ought to have fallen by about one-half within a short time after the demonetisation of silver about the year 1873, and that when this fall had taken place, gold having been appreciated to this extent, the average previous production would be sufficient to maintain the stock and to keep up prices at the new level.

What occurred, however, was very different. Prices did
not fall within ten years after the demonetisation of silver
in 1873 more than 15 per cent., as compared with the
average of ten years preceding that year, and they have
continued to fall long after the causes alleged for it have
ceased to have effect.

The error involved in the argument of the bimetallists is in
supposing that prices before 1873 were estimated in a double
standard of gold and silver. The effect of the change was to cause
some further demand for gold, and to dispense to some extent with
silver; but the additional demand for gold was small in proportion
to the existing stock, and to the negotiable instruments which
economise its use.

9. As to the contention of the bimetallists that the fall in
price of silver permanently stimulates the exportation of wheat and
other produce from silver-using countries such as India, there
may have been some plausible grounds for attaching importance
to this argument a few years ago, but the experience of later
years has cruelly dealt with it, and has exposed completely its
unsoundness.

The contention that the fall in price of silver has had
a permanent effect in stimulating the export of produce
from India depends mainly on the allegation that prices
in silver of commodities and labour have remained
stationary in that country. This, however, has now been
conclusively disproved. An exhaustive examination of prices
of fifty articles, averaged at numerous centres of production in India
from statistics published by the Indian Government, made for the
first time by Mr. F. J. Atkinson, in a paper published by the Statistical
Society in March, 1897, has proved that the average prices, in
rupees, of commodities in India have risen from the index number of
100 in 1871, to 133 on the average of the six years 1889-95;
and when measured in the value of silver since the closing of the
Indian mints, to 153. If articles of food alone be taken into com
parison, the rise in rupees in the same period has been from 100 to
142, and in silver from 100 to 162. Mr. Atkinson has also shown
that the wages of labourers have risen in the same period in rupees
from 100 to 118, and in silver to 138.

A glance at a table showing the annual export of wheat
from India and the annual price of silver must be sufficient

proof to any unbiassed mind that there is no permanent relation between the fall in price of silver and the increase of exports of wheat from that country. It would be quite as easy, indeed, to construct a plausible theory from the figures that the price of wheat has risen with the fall in value of silver. It is true that for a few years after 1871, when silver was falling from 6od. to 53d. per ounce, the exports of wheat from India rose from 637,000 cwts. to 5,583,000 cwts., but in the following years no relation whatever can be discovered between the fall in price of silver and the increase of exports of wheat. Since 1891 there has been a greater and more rapid fall in the price of silver than in any of the preceding periods —namely, from 45d. per ounce to a minimum of 24d.*; but the quantity of wheat exported from India has been diminishing yearly during this period from 30,303,000 cwts. in 1891 to 6,887,000 cwts. in 1894. The Indian mints were closed to the free coinage of silver in 1893. The Indian exchange, however, continued to fall during 1893 and 1894. In spite of the falling exchange, the exports of Indian wheat steadily decreased during those years. In 1895 exchange rose, and wheat exports, instead of falling, very greatly increased ; thus totally contradicting the argument of the bimetallists as to the connection between wheat exports and exchange. Since 1895 the export of wheat has greatly decreased, but this has been due to drought and famine throughout a great part of India. **The great decrease of exports of wheat while the exchange was falling dispels entirely the argument that the falling exchange acts as a permanent stimulus to the exports of wheat and other produce.**

10. But if this be so, it is impossible that the grower of wheat in this country can, at the present time, be benefited by opening the Indian mints to the coinage of silver, and reverting to a state of things when, according to the bimetallic theory, so much wrong was done to the farmer in this country by a competition stimulated by the fall in price of silver. An examination of the table on the following page, showing the annual production of gold and silver and the prices of wheat and silver for each year since 1870, will be sufficient proof that the price of wheat has neither depended on the annual production of gold nor on the price of silver. Whatever plausible arguments on the subject might have been propounded to this effect a few years ago, they have in both respects been dispelled by the figures of recent years.

* *August, 1897.*

P

	Production of Gold. Ozs.	Production of Silver. Ozs.	Index No. of Price of 45 Articles. Sauerbeck's.	Price of Wheat. Shillings per Quarter.	Price of Silver. Pence per Oz.	Export of Wheat from India. Cwts.
1870 ...	6,270,086	43,051,583	96	47	60	—
1871 ...	5,591,014	63,317,014	100	56	60	637,000
1872 ...	5,591,014	63,317,014	109	57	60	394,000
1873 ...	4,653,675	63,267,187	111	58	59	1,755,000
1874 ...	4,390,031	55,300,781	102	55	58	1,069,000
1875 ...	4,716,563	62,261,719	96	45	56	2,498,000
1876 ...	5,016,488	67,753,125	95	46	53	5,583,000
1877 ...	5,512,196	62,679,916	94	56	55	6,340,000
1878 ...	5,761,114	73,385,451	87	46	52	1,044,000
1879 ...	5,262,174	74,383,495	83	43	51	2,195,000
1880 ...	5,148,880	74,795,273	88	44	52	7,444,000
1881 ...	4,983,742	79,020,872	85	45	51	19,863,000
1882 ...	4,934,086	86,472,091	84	45	51	14,144,000
1883 ...	4,614,588	89,175,023	82	41	50	20,956,000
1884 ...	4,921,169	81,567,801	76	35	50	15,830,000
1885 ...	5,245,572	91,609,959	72	32	48	21,060,000
1886 ...	5,135,679	93,297,290	69	31	45	22,263,000
1887 ...	5,116,861	96,123,586	68	32	44	13,538,000
1888 ...	5,330,775	108,827,606	70	31	42	17,610,000
1889 ...	5,973,790	120,213,611	72	29	42	13,799,000
1890 ...	5,749,306	126,095,062	72	31	47	14,320,000
1891 ...	6,320,194	137,170,919	72	37	45	30,303,000
1892 ...	7,094,266	153,151,762	68	30	39	14,973,000
1893 ...	7,618,811	165,472,621	68	26	35	12,156,000
1894 ...	8,764,362	164,610,394	63	22	29	6,887,000
1895 ...	9,641,337	167,288,729	62	23	29	10,003,000
1896 ...	9,817,991	165,100,887	61	26	30	1,911,000

11. It is equally impossible to admit the contention that the depreciation of paper currency in the Argentine Republic of late years has had a similar effect to that alleged with respect to the depreciation of silver in India, and has stimulated the export of wheat, wool, and meat from that country. If there be any truth in this it would necessarily follow that a government could not confer a greater benefit upon its subjects than by depreciating its currency; for by so doing it would stimulate production and exportation, and would increase imports in the same proportion.

The contention is that the producer pays wages and other charges in depreciated currency, and sells his produce for gold in foreign markets. To whatever extent the producers may temporarily gain by such a process the labourers must lose, for they would receive wages worth less than before in the purchase of other and especially foreign products. All experience, however, is to the effect that adjustments of wages in proportion to the depreciation of currency cannot be very long deferred. It should be recollected, also, that in the Argentine Republic and also in India, the producers of wheat and other agricultural produce are as a general rule a class of farmers working themselves and their families on the land, and employing very few labourers except during the harvest, and that the harvest wages are adjusted to the depreciated currency and form a very small proportion of the cost of production. Further, if the proposition had any basis of truth, it would follow that the reverse action of appreciating the paper currency would have the opposite effect, and would tend to limit the export of produce from such a country as the Argentine Republic.

The following table must show how very little effect the variations in the paper currency and the premium on gold have on the export of wheat, which has continued to increase in spite of the reduced premium of gold.

	1891.	1892.	1893.	1894.	1895
Export of Wheat, cwts.	2,479,000	3,476,000	7,859,000	13,283,000	11,432,000
Gold Premium ...	466	392	362	429	379
Price of Wheat ...	37s.	30·3	26·4	22·10	23·1

12. **What has made the Argentine Republic a most formidable competitor with our farmers in our markets during the last few years has not been the depreciation of its paper currency, but the enormous natural capacities of the country**—the great fertility of its soil, exceeding that of almost any other part of the world; the facility with which the land can be cultivated; its excellent climate; the rapidity with which railways can be, and have been of late years, constructed in a perfectly level country, and the extent to which English capital has been invested for this purpose; and the ready supply of emigrants from the South of Europe, who have been accustomed to a low standard of wages and living. The result of all these advantages is that wheat, wool, and meat can be raised at a lower cost than in other parts of the world. If with these advantages the country

were further blessed with a stable and intelligent Government, with a sound financial system and a fixed standard of money, there can be little doubt that its progress would have been far greater than has been hitherto the case, and that it would have been even a more formidable competitor, as regards quantity and price, with the producers of wheat, wool, and meat in this and other countries.

13. The bimetallists have never attempted to explain how any measures can be devised to prevent such a country as the Argentine Republic from issuing paper money in excess of its metallic reserves, whether gold or silver, or both together, especially as their argument is that the depreciation of the currency and the over-issue of paper must stimulate production, and add therefore to the wealth of the country.

Now that India has closed its mints to the coinage of silver, and Russia and Japan have adopted a gold standard, there are very few parts of the world where a silver standard prevails. In China the copper coin "cash" is the general standard, and is the coin in which wages are paid. In Mexico the silver dollar is the standard, but its exports in no way come into competition with the farm produce of this country.

14. **Another and more serious flaw in the argument of the Bimetallic Report is that it has taken no count of the labour side of the question.** It is admitted by the exponents of the bimetallic theory, such as Professor Foxwell and others, that a fall in prices resulting from the appreciation of gold owing to currency causes, such as its reduced production and the demonetisation of silver, would necessarily involve, after a time, more or less, a corresponding fall in all other values, and especially in the wages of labourers. Professor Foxwell, in his evidence before the Commission, agreed that the reduction of the wages of labourers in harmony with the fall of prices could not be postponed beyond six or seven years.

It must be obvious that when such adjustments have been made, when rents, profits, wages, and prices of all kinds have on the average fallen in the same proportion, all classes of persons employed in agriculture would be in the same relative position as before. The landlord would get less rent, but his income would go as far as before in the purchase of commodities and the payment of wages. The farmer, in the same way, with a reduced profit in money would be as well off as before, for his reduced income would go quite as far in the purchase of his requirements and the payment of rent and wages.

The labourer also would find that his reduced money wages would purchase as much food, drink, and clothing as before the fall of prices; and the relative position of the three classes would ultimately be the same, and no one would have a right to complain, although the process of adjustment might be a difficult one, and might take time, during which some would be gainers and others would be losers.

15. **It is, however, absolutely certain that in agriculture, equally as in other industries of the country, in the twenty-four years which have elapsed since the alleged deficiency of gold commenced, there has been no general adjustment of the wages of labourers in proportion to and consequent upon the fall of prices from the year 1873. On the contrary, money wages generally have risen since the fall of prices began;** and as the fall of prices has been greatest in articles of prime necessity, which form the main consumption of the labouring classes—such as bread, sugar, tea, cheese, the inferior classes of beef and mutton, and cheap clothing and boots—it is certain that, when measured by what the labourers can get for their money, their real remuneration for their work has very considerably improved.

16. The importance of the subject of agricultural labour in connection with the causes and effects of the agricultural depression is so great that it is necessary to deal with it more fully, the more so as the Agricultural Commission have devoted a very small part of their inquiry to it. They give as a reason that the condition of agricultural labourers was fully inquired into by the Royal Commission on Labour, which reported so late as 1894, and they quote with approval the conclusions arrived at in a very full and able report to that Commission by Mr. William Little, who was a member of both Commissions, and who founded his report on inquiries made by numerous sub-commissioners in various parts of the country. The Agricultural Commission appears to have accepted these reports as sufficient and accurate up to the year 1894.

17. What happened, according to these reports, was shortly this:— **In or about 1873, at the very time when prices of produce began rapidly to fall, the money wages of agricultural labourers rose very considerably,** and remained at a high point compared with their previous rates till 1878, when a fall occurred, but not to the point at which they had stood before 1873. Between 1888 and 1892 wages again rose, though not to their highest point between 1873-78. From 1892 there was a fall in wages in some

of the eastern and midland counties, but not to the low level of wages before 1873.

The great rise of wages between 1873-8 was caused mainly by the great migration of labourers from rural districts to the towns, attracted by the high wages due to the great industrial prosperity of 1871-3. This migration of labourers caused not only a rise of wages but compelled the farmers to economise labour in every possible way.

According to Mr. Little, the average rate of agricultural wages throughout the country, exclusive of harvest earnings, was as follows:—

1867-70	...	12s. 3d. per week.
1879-81	...	13s. 9d. „
1892-3	...	13s. 5d. „

The table excludes the period of high wages between 1873-8. Mr. Little says that the average of 1892-3 was taken from 38 typical rural districts, while those for the two other periods were taken from the whole counties, and were not, therefore, fairly comparative, since any county average must include many districts where the influence of town employment is felt, and increases the average of wages.

He concludes that the wages in 1892-3 were somewhat higher than in 1879-81, and, consequently, higher than those in 1867-70, we may presume by about 2s. a week.*

18. Mr. Little very properly did not confine his inquiries to the money wages of labourers, but took into account what the labourers could obtain for their money wages as a truer comparison of their real remuneration at the two periods. He pointed out that the main articles of consumption of labourers—bread, sugar, and tea, the inferior kinds of meat, cheese and butter, and cheap clothing and boots—have been enormously reduced in price since 1873. **The wages, therefore, of labourers go very much further than they did, and their real remuneration is proportionately increased.**

* *In a very elaborate and complete examination of all the statistical information as to the wages of agricultural labourers in England, Mr. A. L. Bowley, in a paper read before the Statistical Society in June, 1895, gives the following as the average ratios, starting with 100 in 1860:—*

1860.	1866.	1870.	1874.	1877.	1880.	1883.	1886.	1891.
100	105	107	130	132	122	117	111	118

The ratios were very different in different parts of the country. Thus in the south midland district and in Yorkshire wages rose from 100 in 1860 to 127 and 126 in 1891, while in the eastern and south-eastern districts they rose only from 100 to 105 and 108.

Another way of estimating the change is this : **Before 1873 two-thirds of the weekly wages of an agricultural labourer were expended in purchasing a sufficiency of bread alone for himself and his family. In 1892-4 less than one-third of his wages sufficed for this purpose.**

It is a matter of common observation that the condition of the agricultural labourers in all parts of the country is very greatly improved as regards food and clothing. Another proof of the improvement of their position is the almost complete cessation of employment of their wives in field labour over the greater part of England and Scotland.

19. Against this it may be said that the number of agricultural labourers has been largely reduced during the last 25 years. It has already been shown that this reduction commenced in 1873, was due to the competition of other employments in the towns, and was the cause of the great rise of wages which then took place. The stream of agricultural labourers to the towns and to employment on railways and in the rural police has since then been continuous. But for this the wages of rural labourers would undoubtedly have fallen in proportion to the fall of prices since 1873.

Farmers have been compelled to meet this drain of labour from the rural districts and the depression caused by low prices by greater economy of labour. The laying down in grass of a large extent of arable land has resulted from this, and has enabled many farmers to reduce their aggregate wages bills though not the rate of wages.

20. It should be added that the Commission report that since 1894 there has been in some of the eastern and midland counties a reduction of wages, and that in some districts work has been more irregular. The statistics compiled and presented by the Labour Department of the Board of Trade enable us accurately to measure what this reduction of wages of agricultural labourers has been. In 1894, out of a total of 756,000 agricultural labourers, there were reported to the Labour Department 107,000 cases in which wages fell, and 22,000 in which they rose. The total net effect of changes was £2,705 per week, equal to 5d. per week on the net decreases of 85,000 men. Wages rose in the northern counties and in Wales, but fell in some of the eastern and midland counties. In Scotland there was no material change. Calculated on the total number of agricultural labourers in England and Wales, the fall per head was only ¾d. per week.

In 1895 there was a net decrease in 57,210 cases of £2,910

per week, or 5¾d. a head, equal to another reduction ¾d. of per week on the total number of labourers. The decrease was again in the eastern, midland, and southern districts. In the northern counties and Wales there was a slight increase.

In 1896 there was a net increase, in 37,000 cases, of £383 per week. The increases were in the eastern and midland districts, and the slight decrease was in the southern districts.

The statistics for 1897 are not yet (November, 1897) to hand, but it is certain that they will show an increase and not a decrease of wages.

The net result of the changes, therefore, in the three years was extremely small, and the decreases which occurred in the eastern and midland districts in the first two years appear to have been, to some extent, reversed in 1896. The report for 1894 speaks of complaints of irregularity of work in some districts in the midland and eastern counties. This was doubtless due to the great drought of 1893, which resulted in much less work in the ensuing winter on arable farms. There was no renewal of these complaints for 1895 and 1896, and we may presume that this difficulty was not generally felt.

21. Mr. Little, in his report, said that out of thirty-eight typical districts there were twenty-seven in which it was reported that the supply of labour was about equal to the demand. In seven districts it was stated that there was a scarcity, and in only three districts was it reported that the supply was in excess of the demand. He added :
" There was universal agreement that if the system of farming had
" remained what it was there would have been a difficulty in finding
" the necessary hands.

" Were it not that the majority of farmers employ decidedly less
" labour than used to be the case, partly on account of the increased
" use of machinery, partly because the character of cultivation has
" been modified and more land has been laid down to grass, and
" partly because the land is less well and carefully tilled than it
" used to be, there would no doubt be a serious deficiency of
" labour.

" It is undoubtedly the opinion of many persons that want of
" employment was the cause of the labourers' migration to the towns,
" but I venture to maintain that the reduction of the working staff of
" farms was the consequence, and not the cause, of migration. The
" agricultural strike in 1873 was no doubt the result of compe-
" tition for the labourer's services by employers engaged in other
" industries."

It is reported that at all the Statute fairs in the country during the present year (1897) there has been a great falling off in the number of farm labourers applying for engagements, and that many farmers have been compelled to offer higher wages. This, again, has been caused by the great activity of trade in the manufacturing districts.

22. It must be obvious, then, that the condition of agricultural labourers has a close relation to that of other wage-earners in the country. If wages rise in manufacturing and mining industries, it means that there is a demand for labour, and men are tempted to leave the rural districts to obtain the better wages in the towns, and this migration of labourers is the cause of higher wages to those who remain on the farms by lessening the supply of labour in proportion to the demand. These higher wages, again, are the cause of greater difficulty to the farmers, and compel them to economise labour by modifying their system of cultivation. On the other hand, if trade is slack in other industries, there is less temptation and opportunity to labourers to leave the rural districts, and wages tend to fall.

The evidence before the Labour Commission showed that the money wages of all labourers employed in manufactures and mines are higher than they were twenty-five years ago; and that, taking into account the fall of prices and what can be obtained for the present money wages, the real remuneration of labour has very considerably increased.

23. During recent years also the returns of the trades unions as to the number of unemployed members of their trades show that a considerable improvement has been taking place, and the number is probably reduced to a minimum, representing men shifting from one employment to another, and not those who cannot obtain employment.

	1893.	1894.	1895.	1896.	1897. (July.)
Percentage of Unemployed	7·5	6·9	5·8	3·4	2·7

The returns of pauperism show also what a great improvement has taken place in the general condition of the people during the last twenty-five years, during which prices have been falling, as the following figures show :—

	Population of England and Wales.	Number of Paupers in thousands.	Percentage of Paupers per thousand.
1870	22,223,000	1,084	48·8
1897	30,717,000	836	27·2

The consumption of food per head of population has increased as follows :—

	Tea.	Sugar.	Meat.
	lbs.	lbs.	lbs.
1876	3·8	47·2	112
1893	5·4	78·9	121·7

24. Between the years 1871 and 1891, the population of Great Britain increased by 6,200,000, and in the six years between 1891 and the present time an addition of at least 1,750,000 must have been made, raising the total increase since 1871 to nearly 8,000,000, representing 1,600,000 families and at least that number of additional working men. **It is certain, therefore, that an additional number of 1,600,000 men have found remunerative employment in other industries—stimulated, doubtless, by the low prices of raw materials.**

However much to be regretted are the depression of agriculture and the falling off in the number of labourers employed on the land, it is impossible to conclude that any hardship has been experienced by the labourers. On the contrary, those who have found employment in other industries have done so, for the most part, of their own free choice, and all have improved their position.

It is equally certain that the 750,000 labourers who have remained on the land have shared in the general improvement, in somewhat better money wages, on the average, than before 1873, and in vastly improved conditions as regards food and clothing in what they have been able to purchase with their wages.

25. The question of the real remuneration of agricultural labourers is of the more importance because it is the key to many other questions connected with the depression of agriculture and the alleged effect of monetary changes. **One of the most striking**

features of the recent economic conditions of agriculture is that the labourers obtain a far larger share of the produce of the land than was the case twenty-five years ago.

It used to be roughly estimated that the land produced three nearly equal profits—the rent, the farmer's profits, and the labourers' wages. The change which has taken place may be illustrated as follows :—Suppose a farm of 100 acres, rented before 1873, at £100 a year; in such case the farmer's profit would be £100 a year, and the labourers' wages also £100—a total of £300, after payment of rates and other expenses of the farm. Since 1873 the receipts from the farm produce have been reduced by one-third. The produce, therefore, is now only £200, and if the labourers' money wages remain the same as before, there is left only £100 to be divided between the landowner's rent and the farmer's profit, instead of £200. To whatever extent the farmer, by altering his system of cultivation and economising labour, can reduce his labour bill, he will add to the proportion which remains for profit and rent.

26. This illustration is fully confirmed by the farmers' accounts which have been published by the Commission. Unfortunately there are very few which go back to the years before 1873. There are however, three farms with an aggregate of 1,636 acres, where the accounts go back to the years 1863–7, with the following results :—

	Rent.	Wages.	Profit.	Total.
	£	£	£	£
1863-7	1,781	1,987	1,344	5,112
1890-4	1,219	2,134	190	3,543

From these figures it is clear that the produce of the farms, after paying rates, manures, &c., brought in thirty per cent. less in the last four years than in 1863–7. Money wages, however, in these accounts have been increased by £147, or seven per cent., and instead of being about one-third of the total, they have been considerably more than one-half. In these cases it would appear that no economy has been effected by a change in the system of cultivation in the number of labourers employed.

In nineteen other farm accounts, which go back only ten or twelve years, the results are as follows :—

	Rent.	Wages.	Profit.	Total.
	£	£	£	£
1882	15,624	16,128	5,306	37,058
1893	11,991	16,518	5,840	34,349

There had doubtless been a considerable reduction of rent and profits before 1882. In 1893 the wages were not far short of the rent and profits combined. The accounts do not show whether there has been any reduction in the number of labourers.

27. **These accounts, then, and the general evidence given to the Agricultural Commission, completely bear out the conclusion arrived at by Mr. Little in his report to the Labour Commission, where he says, "It is no exaggeration "to say that in the last quarter of a century a great "economic revolution, accomplished with little or no aid "from legislation, has transferred to the labourers from "one-third to one-half of the profits which the landowners "and farmers previously received from the cultivation of "the land."**

Great numbers of farmers have been compelled to meet this by changing their system of cultivation so as to economise the number of labourers; but even with these reductions it is clear that wages form a far higher proportion of the outgoings of a farm than twenty-five years ago, and the individual labourer has, on the average, gained at the expense of the landowner's rent and the farmer's profit.

The conclusion which must be forced on the mind of any impartial observer is that the difficulties of the landowner and the farmer, though primarily caused by the fall of prices, have been also in the long run due to the fact that under the existing economic conditions the labourers have been able to obtain a larger share of the net produce of the land, and that it has not been possible for farmers generally to adjust the wages they pay to the fall of prices of their produce, or of the articles which the labourers consume, even if they had desired to do so.

28. It follows also that the small farmers holding pasture farms in the west of England and Scotland and in Wales, who work themselves on their land and employ few or no labourers, have benefited almost as much as the labourers from the low prices of bread, sugar, tea, etc., and they have not felt the rise in price of labour. This

accounts in a great measure for the fact that the small farmers have weathered the difficulties of the last few years better than the larger farmers, and that the rent of small farms, and especially small pasture farms, has fallen much less than that of large farms.

Looking, also, broadly at the condition of the country during the last few years as compared with twenty-five years ago, it follows that the great mass of the people have gained largely by the fall in prices, that the labourers have gained more than any other class, and that the lowest class of labourers, and especially the agricultural labourers, have gained most because the fall in price of articles of primary necessity has been greatest. In higher grades of society, where a smaller part of the income of the family is spent in the main necessaries of life and more in luxuries and in wages, which have risen, there has been little or no gain from low prices. While the real remuneration of labour has increased considerably, profits in trade have been generally reduced, the interest on money has been lowered, and capitalists are prepared to invest their money at a much less rate of interest.

29. It must be admitted that these changes, attended with so much benefit to the labouring people, resulting primarily from low prices, have fallen hardly upon the landed interest. Farmers' profits have been largely reduced, and in many of the corn districts in the east of England have been almost nil. Rent of land, also, has been largely reduced in the eastern and corn-growing districts by an average of over forty per cent., in the districts of mixed husbandry by twenty to thirty per cent., and in the pastoral districts by ten to twenty per cent.

The difficulties of landowners have been increased by the fact that the burthen of fixed charges such as jointures, rent charges, etc., has remained the same. In the case of mortgages, however, although the actual sum charged has remained the same, landowners generally have been able to obtain a reduction of interest from four or four and a half per cent. to three or three and a half per cent., or a reduction of twenty-five per cent. The economic position of reduced prices and higher wages has necessitated a considerable change in the system of cultivation with the object of economising labour. About one and a half million acres of corn land have been laid down in grass, and there has been a reduction in the number of labourers employed by farmers. This, however, has been coincident with greatly improved remuneration to those who continue on

the land; and the labourers who have left have found no difficulty
in obtaining higher wages in other employments.

30. **Of the three classes, then, which form the agricultural community—the landlords, farmers, and labourers—
the labourers, who are by far the most numerous, have
gained very greatly by the fall of prices. The losses and
trials which have been experienced by the other two classes,
and the sympathy we feel for them, must not prevent us
from recognising that the country as a whole has derived
enormous advantages from the low prices of food and of
raw material for our manufactures ; and that the great
mass of labourers, who form nine-tenths of the population,
have secured rather higher money wages, and that their
wages go very much farther than they did, and consequently that they and their families are better fed and
better clothed at a lower price, and have a larger margin
for expenditure in other directions.**

If, then, this diagnosis is accurate, depression of agriculture has
meant greatly reduced profits to the farmers and greatly reduced
rent to landowners, but general improvement in the condition of
the labourers employed on the land and a transfer of a large number
of labourers to other employments, where they have obtained even
higher wages. Just as the depression in agriculture has been due
primarily to the great fall of prices since 1873, so the improvement in
the general condition of all the labouring classes throughout the
country has been due primarily to the same cause.

31. The important question thus arises whether the fall of prices
has been ultimately due mainly to monetary causes, such as the contraction of the gold supply and the demonetisation of silver, or
whether it is due to causes such as the progress of inventions, which,
by making labour more effective, bringing distant countries into very
close connection with our own, and extending the field of production,
might be expected to improve the general condition of workers.

If the fall of prices has been mainly due to the contraction of the
currency, and if no other causes had occurred to affect the general
condition of labourers, we may take it to be certain that long before
this the wages of all labourers, including those of agricultural
labourers, would have been proportionally reduced in adjustment to
the altered ratio of money to commodities, with the result, as we have
already shown, that all classes of the community would be in the
same relative position to one another as before the fall of prices.

We have shown, however, that no such adjustment of wages has taken place. The reverse has occurred, and money wages have risen. It is ridiculous to suppose that the adjustment has been delayed for twenty-five years and is yet to come. We must there-fore conclude that some other cause has been largely affecting labour during the interval, and has resulted in a great increase in the real remuneration of labourers as measured in their articles of consumption. **The question we have to decide is whether the causes for this rise in the remuneration of labour, and the causes for the great fall in prices, are not in the main identically the same.**

32. No one, we believe, of those who have admitted that there has been a great rise in the remuneration of labour during the last twenty-five years has attributed it to any other cause than the pro-gress of inventions, including the great reductions of freight from the districts of production to those of consumption, the opening out of new fields of cultivation, the various inventions for economising labour, making it more productive, and the great accumulation of capital during a period of profound peace throughout the world. No other possible cause for the increase of the real wages of labour has even been suggested.

33. Sir Robert Giffen—who has lent the weight of his authority in his separate memorandum to the Commission of Agriculture to the proposition that the fall of prices was due originally to the contraction of the gold supply, and who claims to have predicted the coming fall in 1870—admits, as appears from his paper, and from his evidence before the Commission, that some other cause has been at work to which the long continuance of the depression has been due. He is fully alive to the fact that wages would necessarily follow suit with prices in any general appreciation of gold, due to its reduced pro-duction or the demonetisation of silver. He predicted in 1870 that a reduction in the rate of wages would necessarily follow a general fall of prices. He admits that this expected reduction of wages has not occurred. He agrees that the real remuneration of wages has increased since 1875, and he estimates this improvement at twenty per cent.*

---

* *Sir Robert Giffen makes the comparison with the year 1875. Between the years 1872 and 1875, however, there was a general rise of wages, especially for agricultural labourers, and if comparison be made with the period before 1872, the rise of remunera-tion to labourers generally, having regard to the fall in price of their main articles of consumption and to the increase of money wages, must be estimated at much higher than 20 per cent, and at not less than 30 to 40 per cent.*

He attributes this to the progress of inventions in the interval, and among the inventions he includes the reduction of freight by land and sea of produce from districts which constitute the principal sources of supply. After stating his views at length as to the appreciation of gold, **Sir Robert Giffen adds:—"All this can be "said without implying any objection to the proposition so "largely supported in the main report, that foreign compe-"tition is the cause of the present agricultural depression, "and that the progress of invention, cheapening of means "of competition, and the like influences are to be regarded "as permanent causes of lower and lower prices."**

34. In his evidence before the Commission he entered more fully into this. He said :—

"I think that the foreign competition, which would have been "felt in any case, has perhaps been felt in an aggravated form owing "to the change in the scale of money prices. If there had been "stationary prices on the average—which might have happened— "then to give the labourer the advantages he now has compared "with the former period, there must have been a considerable rise of "money wages, like what took place between 1850 and 1874, which "would have affected money profits *pro tanto*. . . .

"To put the matter shortly, my view is that in any case foreign "competition must have greatly reduced rents—the real reward of "labour having greatly increased here in the last twenty years; but the "nominal reduction would not have been so great as it has actually "been. Eventually it is of no great importance what the money is. "Everything gets adjusted to the scale in time, though there may be "great perturbations in the transition. But I consider that the real "effect on rents of a rise in the real reward of the labourer is per-"manent, and to that extent, if the foreigner continues able to produce "at present real prices, rents must continue permanently lower, "measured by their purchasing power (and apart from any question of "money), than what they were twenty years ago. To this cause of "change money does not matter. As the real reward of the labourer "has increased, the real reward of other interests in land must be less, "production remaining substantially the same" (*Answer* 18149).

Asked whether he could form any opinion as to the causes of the increased remuneration of labour during the last twenty years, Sir Robert Giffen replied, "Nothing, except that the progress of "invention and the continual accumulation of capital have all been "of advantage to the labourer. It is part of the process of invention "that you have been able to bring. produce from a great distance to "the labourer in this country" (*Answers* 18157–8).

"Undoubtedly foreign competition, looked at in one aspect, is "the cause of the fall in prices, or rather is the cause of the fall of "rents, I should say" (*Answer* 18322).

35. **It may safely be concluded from this that in the opinion of Sir Robert Giffen the ultimate and permanent cause of depression of agriculture, and especially of the reduction of rents, has not been the scarcity of gold, or other currency changes, but the rise in the remuneration of labour, and that this, again, has been due to the progress of invention and the accumulation of capital.**

It appears, then, to follow as a logical consequence that the same causes which account for this rise of the remuneration of labour will also account for the fall of prices of commodities, and that it has been through this fall of prices that the benefit of the inventions referred to have been brought home to the labouring people of this country.

36. I have referred at length to Sir Robert Giffen's views, in part because his authority is relied upon so largely by the majority of his colleagues on the Commission, for their contention that the fall of prices has been due mainly to the demonetisation of silver and other monetary changes, though they have refused to accept his further opinions, to which I have referred, and which are so fatal to their other contentions ; and partly because Sir Robert Giffen has expressed his regret that monometallists, such as our Association consists of, have differed from him on the subject of the scarcity of gold, and has added that, in his view, the weakness of our arguments on this point has been the main reason why the bimetallic agitation has continued so long.* I think it only necessary, in reply to this, to refer Sir Robert Giffen to the use which is made of his own admissions by the bimetallic report ; and, while repeating disagreement with him on the currency question, to point out that his difference with other monometallists is not so material as would appear, in view of his substantial agreement as to the causes of the depression, the causes of the im-

* *Among the Monometallists who have expressed views on these points opposed to those of Sir Robert Giffen are Lord Herschell, Lord Farrer, Lord Playfair, Lord Welby, Sir John Lubbock, Mr. William Fowler, the late Mr. Bertram Currie, and many others ; a weight of authority against whom I know not whom to oppose, except Sir Robert Giffen himself.*

Q

provement in the condition of labour, and as to the insuperable objections to the adoption of bimetallism.

37. It appears further, that the explanation thus given of the fall of prices better fits in with and explains all the other phenomena connected with the present condition of things.

If the fall of prices has been due to a scarcity of gold, it would by this time have shown itself in nearly all commodities and in all countries, with variations due to exceptional circumstances. This has certainly not been the case, for there are numerous and great variations in commodities in different parts of the world. If the fall of prices were due to the progress of invention, etc., it would result that there would be a much greater fall in the prices in the countries of import and consumption than in the countries or districts of production. This is precisely what is the case at the present time as compared with twenty-five years ago.

Comparing the fall of price of wheat, as an illustration, in this country and in the Western States of America, where the cultivation has most extended, and which are now the principal sources of supply in the United States, the following table, prepared by Mr. I. G. Powers, Commissioner of Labour for the State of Minnesota, shows that, while the average price of wheat in the four States of Iowa, Minnesota, Kansas, and Nebraska was maintained between 1871–4 and 1887–90, it fell thirty per cent. at New York and forty per cent. at London, and the difference can only be explained by the reduction in the charges for conveyance.

Years.	Average Gold Price per Bushel.		
	Four States.	New York.	London.
	Cents.	Cents.	Cents.
1871–74	72·6	134·1	176·3
1875–78	68·5	110·5	149·2
1879–82	86·1	125·2	149·6
1883–86	61·6	92·4	113·5
1887–90	70·8	95·3	106·1
1891–94	59·3	83·5	93·0

38. There are very few raw commodities of which England produces enough for its own consumption, and with some excess for export, and which are not much affected therefore by reduced cost of conveyance. The chief of these are coal, salt, fish, straw,

and hay. In none of them, except the last, has there been any substantial reduction of price from the average of a few years before 1873 to the present time. In hay the reduction has been only sixteen per cent., due probably to an increased area of land devoted to it. The greatest reductions of price in our markets have been in articles of great bulk, and which come from very distant places of production—such as wheat, wool, timber ; and in articles of less bulk where there have been exceptional circumstances attending their production, leading to a very great extension of supply—such as sugar, where the system of bounties in connection with the growth of beet sugar on the Continent has considerably increased the supply—and tea, the quantity and price of which have been greatly affected by the vast extension of its cultivation in India and Ceylon. As a general rule, in the case of articles of small bulk where there has not for some exceptional reason been a great increase of supply, such as coffee, tobacco, cocoa, raw pepper, indiarubber, etc., prices have not fallen. **This is a result which is easily to be explained on the hypothesis that progress of invention has been the main cause of the fall of prices, but which is quite unintelligible on the other hypothesis that the fall has been due to monetary causes, such as the scarcity of gold.**

39. While, however, assigning to the progress of invention the main fall of prices of the last twenty-five years, it must not be concluded that all reductions are due to this, and this alone, and that all the recent depression of agriculture has been attributable to the same cause.

For instance, in the years 1894-6 there occurred a great fall in the price of wheat from an average of 30s. per quarter to 20s. But in 1896 there was again a rise to 26s., and in 1897 another rise to 34s. per quarter. It is impossible to explain the fall of price in 1894-6 by either hypothesis which we have referred to. It appears to be abundantly clear that the fall of price in 1894-6 was of an exceptional and temporary character, due to the very abundant harvests of 1894 and 1895 in the United States, the Argentine Republic, and Russia, while the great rise of price in 1897 has been due to deficient crops in the greater part of Europe, and to the famine in India, which has prevented the usual export of wheat from that country.

40. **If, then, the foregoing general explanation of the main cause of the great fall in prices of commodities in**

this country, and also of the greatly increased remuneration of labourers is sound, it also of necessity follows that any attempt to redress what has occurred and to raise prices by altering the currency of this country, either with or without arrangement with other countries, with the object of alleviating agricultural depression by restoring the old proportions which landlords, farmers, and labourers received of the produce of the soil, can and will have no ultimate effect whatever, and cannot produce the desired result. No such measure will reverse the past or impede any future invention in the direction of facilitating production or the transmission of produce. The real remuneration, therefore, of labour cannot be ultimately affected by them. Currency, whether in coin of one kind or another, or in paper, is but the medium of circulation . and exchange by which commodities are transferred from producers to consumers, and cannot ultimately raise or reduce the real wages of labour.

Whether more or less counters are given in exchange for commodities is economically a matter of indifference. The real remuneration of labour is ultimately independent of the currency in which it is nominally paid, and depends on the number of labourers and on the supply of commodities which they require for their sustenance.

41. Supposing that by any monetary changes the prices of wheat and other commodities could be raised all round by one-third. It would necessarily follow that after a time the money wages of labourers would rise in the same proportion. Rent and profits of farmers would also rise in the same ratio, and in the result no one of the three classes would be any better off or any worse off than before the change in money was made. The process of adjustment might indeed be difficult, and pending this process farmers might obtain a somewhat larger share of the produce, and landlords might insist upon a larger payment of rent. Both these gains, however, could only be attained by depriving the labourers for a time of what is their due, and could only be of a temporary character, for the process of adjustment would at once commence and would be completed before long. **The temporary loss would be felt not only by 750,000 agricultural labourers but by 8,000,000 other labourers in Great Britain,** and we might certainly expect considerable discontent during the adjustment due to the increased price of the articles of food. Trade also would be seriously inconvenienced by the sudden and artificial rise in the price of raw materials, and in the interval

before the adjustment of the prices of manufactured goods and
of wages there would be very serious commercial and financial
difficulties.

42. I had, when originally writing this paper, concluded by
some paragraphs commenting on the scheme suggested by the
bimetallic members of the Agricultural Commission in their
separate report for opening the Indian Mints to the free
coinage of silver, in combination with the Governments of other
countries than our own. As proposals of this kind were known
to be before the Government on behalf of the Governments of
France and the United States, it seemed to me to be impossible
to suppose that two Cabinet Ministers could have recommended
them to their colleagues on the Commission, unless they had every
reason to expect that their colleagues in the Cabinet were favourable
in principle to them. The danger of the position, therefore, appeared
to be very serious and imminent. But even while this paper has been
passing through the press (November, 1897) the course of events has
been completely changed in a sense adverse to the bimetallists. The
recent great and continuous fall in the price of silver, and the simultaneous rise in the price of wheat, have not only cut the ground from
under the arguments on which their case largely rested, but have
made it impossible for the Government to give effect to the proposals
of France and the United States. **The Indian Government have
in a most trenchant and weighty despatch refused to be a
party to a scheme which would entirely reverse their
recent remedial measures, and which threatened to over-
whelm them again with financial difficulties**. In view of this,
and of the serious opposition aroused in the City of London, the
Cabinet has been compelled to reject these proposals. The danger,
therefore, has been for the present averted, and it becomes unnecessary to discuss them in detail.

43. It is, however, still worth while to subject to a critical examination the contentions of the bimetallic report on which this rejected
scheme was largely based. The landowners and farmers generally
of this country, during the long period of depression, of greatly
reduced rents and profits, for which everyone must deeply sympathise
with them, have most wisely refrained from joining in the agitation
for tampering with the gold standard, on which so much of our
commercial prosperity and stability rests. It would, I think, be very
unfortunate if they were misled into the belief that they have suffered
from currency disturbances, which might have been obviated if a

remedy had been applied in time, and that a remedy is only now refused to them because of the adverse interests of the Indian Government and of the great commercial and banking community of London.

44. It has been my object, therefore, in this paper to show that, while the fall of prices has been the primary cause of the depression of agriculture, the fall has not been mainly the result either of a contraction of the gold supply, or of the demonetisation of silver, or of an artificial stimulus of exports from countries with silver or paper currencies ; and that any attempt to raise prices artificially by currency changes in this or other countries would not have the desired beneficial effect upon agriculture. It would more probably, by shaking confidence in the credit and commercial stability of countries which attempt it, produce results the very opposite of those which are intended and hoped for.

The Bimetallic Negotiations and their Result.*

By the COMMITTEE OF THE GOLD STANDARD DEFENCE ASSOCIATION.

---

1. For upwards of seventeen years the Bimetallic League has been engaged in an agitation for the adoption of bimetallism by this and other countries. It has hoped thereby to rehabilitate silver, by opening the mints of all countries to its free coinage at a fixed international ratio to gold, and by making it a legal tender for debts equally with gold.

It had never, however, committed itself to the support of a specific scheme; and whenever **challenged on the subject, the principal supporters of the League declined to state what ratio in their opinion should be adopted between silver and gold as the basis of the proposed international arrangement**—whether the old ratio of 15½ to 1, existing before 1873, or the ratio which has existed from time to time since that year in a constantly falling market for silver, and which of late has been about 34 to 1.

2. The Gold Standard Defence Association, on its part—formed for the purpose of defending our existing monetary system against these attacks—has uniformly maintained **the supreme and vital importance to this country of maintaining intact its single gold standard.** It has affirmed that it is impossible, by international arrangement or otherwise, to secure the

* *Issued in February*, 1898.

maintenance of any fixed ratio between the two metals which may be determined on at the outset of any such bimetallic arrangement; and it has shown that the past experience of this and other countries fully confirms this view. It has contended that, in order to appreciate fully the probable effects of any such bimetallic scheme, it is essentially necessary to be informed as to the ratio which it is intended to prescribe between the two metals. It also pointed out that it was all but certain that the Governments of France and the United States, owing to their enormous stocks of silver, acquired at high prices, would not propose or assent to any other ratio than that of about $15\frac{1}{2}$ to 1; and that any attempt to revert to this ratio, and thus to double by one stroke the value of silver in relation to gold, and to produce unknown effects on gold in relation to other commodities, would cause convulsions in the trade of the countries which should attempt it, and consequently of our own also, of a most serious and dangerous character.

3. **In the course of the past summer bimetallists of the United States, France, and our own country conceived the idea of promoting their bimetallic ideas by adopting a scheme which would not in express terms interfere with the gold standard of the United Kingdom.** In furtherance of these views a definite proposal was made to our Government by those of France and the United States that the United States, French, and Indian mints should be reopened to the free coinage of silver, and that our Government, while nominally maintaining the gold standard in the United Kingdom, should give assistance to the bimetallic arrangement between these other powers by measures favouring the use of silver, and therefore increasing the demand for it. **This scheme was based, as we always predicted would be the case, on the establishment on the part of France and the United States of a ratio between silver and gold of $15\frac{1}{2}$ to 1.**

4. The two main features of the scheme were (1) the reopening of the Indian mints to silver only, and the opening of the mints of France and the United States to the free coinage of silver—to be interchangeable with gold at the above ratio; and (2) the substitution of silver for gold in the reserve of the Bank of England to the extent of one-fifth of that reserve, and other measures favouring the use of silver. **This scheme, in its main features, received the favour and support of bimetallists in this country.** No sooner, however, were the details presented in a

practical form, than they created widespread alarm and consternation among commercial classes, and the scheme was finally rejected
by Her Majesty's Government, with very general assent, as
impracticable.

It has served the purpose, however, of showing **how great a
distinction there is between a definite scheme presented for
practical adoption, and the indefinite and plausible generalities on which the Bimetallic League and its supporters
have carried on their agitation for so many years.** In this
view we feel it to be necessary, if only as a warning for
the future, to put on record a narrative of the origin,
progress, and collapse of this scheme.

5. It appears that the scheme had its inception, so far as this
country is concerned, in the great debate on bimetallism in the
House of Commons on March 17th, 1896. That debate was remarkable, on the one hand, for the powerful speech of the Chancellor
of the Exchequer (Sir M. H. Beach), in which he repudiated in the
strongest possible terms any attempt to tamper with the gold standard
of this country ; and, on the other hand, for a no less remarkable
and emphatic statement of the First Lord of the Treasury (Mr.
Arthur Balfour), in which he held out a distinct promise on the
part of the Government to reopen the Indian mints to the free
coinage of silver, in order to facilitate the adoption of bimetallism
by other countries than our own. As there was no attempt to
disguise the difference of principle between these two high authorities on the subject of bimetallism, it may be permitted to us,
without importing party politics, to conclude that their speeches were
the result of contending views in the Cabinet, and that in return for
the concession, on the part of the bimetallic members of it, that no
attempt should be made to interfere with the gold standard of this
country, the monometallic members, on their part, agreed to entertain
a compromise. **The Chancellor of the Exchequer at the close
of his speech, distinguished by its firm insistence on principle and its sound economic views, said:** " If it be possible for
"other nations to be joined in a bimetallic league, or in an agree-
"ment on this matter which seemed good to themselves, I have little
"doubt but that the Indian Government would be prepared to agree
"with us in reopening the Indian mints to the free coinage of silver,
"and that we might endeavour by other minor means to promote the
"increase of silver in coinage to aid in an international agreement on
'this great question. But we can go no further. This great capital

" is the monetary centre of the world. Our trade and commerce are
" probably greater than any other country has ever enjoyed. Our
" wealth is enormous. It arises from investments and enterprise in
" every quarter of the globe, and **the great majority of the men,**
" **able and experienced financiers, who control the working**
" **of this gigantic machine are of opinion that it has been**
" **built up on a gold standard, and that its permanence**
" **depends upon the maintenance of our monetary system.**"

6. In the earlier part of his speech, however, he had thrown the
gravest doubts on the possibility of any such agreement among other
Governments. "We cannot," he said, "alter the gold standard of the
" United Kingdom; but with that reservation we are prepared to do all
" in our power to secure by international agreement a stable monetary
" par of exchange between gold and silver. What are the prospects
" of any such agreement? I fear they are not very brilliant. It will
" be remembered that in the Conference of 1892 the United States
" proposed a bimetallic resolution. It was opposed by Germany, by
" the Scandinavian nations, by Switzerland, and by Austria, who
" declared themselves gold .monometallists. France and the Latin
" Union were only prepared to accept it if Great Britain, Germany,
" Austria, and Russia would join the union; so that the resolu-
" tion fell to the ground, and the vital question of what the ratio
" should be in the event of such an international agreement was
" never even touched."

On the subject of this vital question—the ratio—he said, with
prophetic vision, "I am told that the United States would probably
" desire that the old ratio of 15½ or 16 to 1 should be adopted. In
" **view of the present market price of silver, it seems to me**
" **that to fix any such ratio would be an act of absolute dis-**
" **honesty to creditors.** It would simply mean that kind of
" financial panic with all its possible results to the credit of the
" country which has been in previous debates frequently alluded to
" by some of the highest authorities."

" I have expressed, I think, very frankly my own opinions on this
" important subject to the House, but it is very well known that there
" are some of my colleagues who do not agree with these opinions, and
" who, like my right honourable friend the First Lord of the Treasury
" (Mr. Balfour), are confirmed and pronounced bimetallists. But
" we all agree in this, that we should not be justified in proposing
" or accepting a departure from the gold standard of the United
" Kingdom."

7. The First Lord of the Treasury, in closing the debate, emphasized the conclusion arrived at by the Cabinet as a whole.

"My right honourable friend," said Mr. Balfour, "had a perfect "right to speak as he has spoken. He is a believer in a single "standard, as I am a believer in a double standard. We are abso-"lutely agreed as to the policy to be pursued."

"It appears to me," Mr. Balfour continued, "that the House is "pledged, after the speech of the Chancellor of the Exchequer, to do "as much, or more, for the bimetallic system, and for the rehabili-"tation of silver, as it is in the power of any foreign country to do. "With this resolution we go to foreign nations and tell them that "though you can hardly ask us to make this great change in our habits, "we will do for you as much as you can do for yourselves; **we will** "**make this great contribution to a bimetallic system. We** "**will go back upon the deliberately arranged method of** "**providing a currency for India; we will reopen the Indian** "**mints; we will engage that they shall be kept open,** "and we shall therefore provide for a free coinage of silver within "the limits of the British Empire for a population greater in "number than the populations of Germany, France, and America "put together. I do not think that will be regarded by foreign "nations as a slight contribution to a great problem. I think, on "the contrary, they will feel that in carrying out that great alteration "and smaller changes, which have been accepted by previous Ad-"ministrations, and will be accepted by this Administration, we shall "be contributing our share towards that great object, which, if "foreign nations are willing, can, I believe, be carried into "effect."

8. It will be observed that nothing was said by Mr. Balfour as to the ratio to be fixed between silver and gold in any such arrangement with regard to the opening of the Indian mints. **It is probable, judging by the light of subsequent events, that the Indian Government was not consulted before this wide declaration of policy was made on its behalf. It is certain, at all events, that it did not consent to an arrangement based on a reversion to the old ratio of 15½ to 1.**

9. It was to be expected that, in view of the statements thus made by our Government in the House of Commons, the United States Government, which was pledged at the last Presidential Election to promote an international arrangement for bimetallism,

would respond to it by sending a mission to Europe to negotiate in this direction.

Accordingly, towards the close of 1896, Mr. Wolcott came to Europe to sound the ground, and returned to report to Mr. McKinley the result of his investigations. On the faith, apparently, of this report, Mr. Wolcott and two other Commissioners were sent by the Government of Washington in May last to Europe, with powers to negotiate.

10. **The Commission, thus headed by Senator Wolcott, of the great mining State of Colorado, proceeded first to France, where it won the support of M. Méline, the present Prime Minister.** Towards the close of May last a banquet was held in Paris under the auspices of French bimetallists. M. Méline on that occasion made a speech, in which he described himself as "always a faithful soldier under your flag," and talked of "groans and lamentations which are heard throughout the whole "world of labour." Finally, addressing Mr. Wolcott, he declared that "our support will not be wanting," and he proved as good as his word. Fortified by the active support of the French Ambassador, the American Commissioners opened dealings with our Cabinet in July last, and on the 12th of that month a meeting took place between the envoys and a Committee of the Cabinet consisting of Lord Salisbury, Mr. Balfour, Sir M. H. Beach, and Lord George Hamilton, representing the various Departments interested.

11. **The envoys commenced the proceedings with the request "that England should agree to open English "mints as its contribution to an attempt to restore "bimetallism,"** * **and the ratio at which silver was to be rated to gold was 15½ to 1. In other words, this country was actually to surrender its gold standard and accept unlimited quantities of silver at about double its market price.** It is obvious that this proposal was put forward with the expectation that it would not be accepted, and that it would be withdrawn in favour of a more moderate proposal. It was promptly negatived by the Chancellor of the Exchequer, and then the First Lord of the Treasury (Mr. Balfour) asked whether "it was desired that the subject be discussed upon the

---

* *For this and future quotations, see Commercial Paper, No. 8, 1897 (c.—8,667).*

"basis of something different and less than the opening of Eng-
"lish mints." The bimetallic envoys thereupon produced another
programme, intimating that it was presented "as a list of contributions
"which, among others, England might make towards bimetallism."

12. **This compromise, these "contributions," this catalogue of concessions which, "among others," we were to
make, were as follows:—**

(1) Opening of Indian mints, and repeal of the order making
the sovereign legal tender in India.

(2) Placing one-fifth of the bullion in the Issue Department
of the Bank of England in silver.

(3) (a) Raising the legal tender limit of silver to, say, £10.
(b) Issuing 20s. notes based on silver, which shall be
legal tender. (c) Retirement, gradual or otherwise, of
the 10s. gold pieces, and substitution of paper based on
silver.

(4) Agreement to coin annually £   of silver, or (as an
alternative proposal) to purchase each year £   in
silver at coining value.*

(5) Opening of English mints to coinage of rupees and for
coinage of British dollar, which shall be full tender in
Straits Settlements and other silver standard Colonies,
and tender in the United Kingdom to the limit of
silver legal tender.

(6) Colonial action, and coinage of silver in Egypt.

(7) Something having the general scope of the Huskisson plan.

This proposal in its entirety was based on the adoption by France
and the United States of the ratio of 15¼ to 1.

13. It was stated by Mr. Wolcott that this scheme was founded
on the proceedings in the English House of Commons of March
17th, 1896. He said that a complete and satisfactory preliminary
understanding had been arrived at with the French Government.
When asked as to the ratio, he said that **the French Government preferred the ratio of 15½ to 1, and the United States
Government were inclined to yield this point and accept it
as a proper ratio.**
The Chancellor of the Exchequer suggested that if the Indian

* *At a later stage of the proceedings "the Special Envoys accepted also as important and desirable the proposal (of France) that the English Government should
purchase annually, say, £10,000,000 of silver."*

mints were to be opened England might be held to be interested in the ratio, but the special envoys did not accede to this view, and called attention to the fact that by opening the Indian mints the English Government did not thereby adopt bimetallism in any form.

14. On July 15th there was another meeting of the envoys with the Committee of the Cabinet, at which **the Chancellor of the Exchequer stated definitely that the English Government would not agree to open the English mints to the unlimited coinage of silver,** and that whatever views he and his colleagues might separately hold on the question of bimetallism, he thought he could say they were united upon this point.

In the course of this meeting the French Ambassador stated that the ratio of 15½ to 1 had not been arbitrarily conceived. The men of great scientific worth who had recommended it to the adoption of the Legislative Power had made long and careful preliminary investigations, and they reached the conclusion that the figure 15½ to 1 represented the average ratio of the value of the two precious metals.

It was ultimately arranged that the matter should stand over till the Indian Government had been consulted.

15. **It is to be noted that coming events had already begun to cast their shadow before. In June the Royal Commission on Agriculture made its report,** and the majority of the Commission, including two members of the Cabinet—Mr. Chaplin and Mr. Long—made a separate report, in which they expressed the fear that the agricultural classes might consider the recommendations of the main report "barren and practically useless." They proceeded to attribute the depression of agriculture to monetary causes, the appreciation of gold, the demonetisation of silver, and to the stimulus given to the export of wheat and other produce from India and other silver-standard countries by the great fall in price of silver. They concluded with this paragraph : " **We do not suggest that the** " **gold standard should be abandoned in this country,** but we " think that if a conference of the Powers was assembled, and that " their deliberation resulted in an international arrangement for the " reopening of the mints abroad and in India, and the restoration " of silver, either wholly or partially, to the position which it filled " prior to 1873, it would be of the greatest benefit to the industry of " agriculture."

It is impossible to believe that two Cabinet Ministers would have persuaded their colleagues in the Commission to adopt this suggestion of opening the Indian mints, on which evidence had not been taken, if they had not the best reasons for believing that the Cabinet would adopt this course, and that there was every prospect of its being carried out. .

16. **Apparently the Government, or at least the bi-metallic members of the Government, had no doubt as to the willingness of the Indian Government to accede to the proposed arrangement. The bait held out to the Indian Government of a fixed rate of exchange at a great advance over the then rate was considerable.** The offer was subject to the condition that the ratio to be aimed at by France and the United States was $15\frac{1}{2}$ to 1, and our Government had not apparently at this time considered what would be the effect upon the commerce of India or of the rest of the world of the sudden and enormous artificial increase in the relative value of silver to gold. The Indian Secretary, Lord George Hamilton, forwarded the proposals of the envoys to the Governor-General, with a despatch dated August 5th in which he commended them, and reminded him "that in 1892 the policy "of closing the mints was only recommended by your Excellency's "predecessor in Council on the ground that an international arrange-"ment, similar to that which is now contemplated, was not then "obtainable."

17. **The Government also commenced a negotiation with the Bank of England** for the purpose of obtaining its consent to give effect, if necessary, to the second of the heads of the scheme, that for substituting silver for gold in its reserve to the extent of one-fifth. We do not know as yet the details of this negotiation. But the Governor of the Bank of England wrote a letter to the Chancellor of the Exchequer agreeing on the part of the Bank to this proposal, which was authorised under the Bank Charter Act of 1844, "provided always that the French mint is again open for the "free coinage of silver, and that the prices at which silver is pro-"curable and saleable are satisfactory."

18. Hitherto the details of the negotiation with the Wolcott mission had not transpired ; but when **it became known by an un-official announcement in the *Times* of September 11th that the Bank of England had fallen in with a suggestion from America that it should hold one-fifth of its reserve in silver, there arose at once considerable alarm on the subject in the commercial world.** This was to some extent allayed for a few days by a letter in the

Times of September 13th, from Mr. H. R. Grenfell, one of the senior members of the Bank Court, and one of the leaders of the bimetallist movement, which was generally understood to imply a denial of the whole affair. It demanded on what ground the writer of the remonstrance had presumed to make such an assertion. It proceeded, however, to justify the proposed action by reference to past proceedings; and it was later explained by Mr. Grenfell that he had not intended to deny the fact of an agreement. All doubts on the subject were set at rest on September 16th, at the half-yearly Court of the Bank of England, when the Governor read a letter to the Chancellor of the Exchequer, dated July 29th, in which, with two stipulations, he had assented to the proposal in question. This, taken in connection with Mr. Grenfell's ambiguous letter, gave rise to the suggestion that the Directors of the Bank generally had not been consulted on the matter, and that it was desired to rush the matter through without discussion. However that may have been, there was no hesitation in the expression of public opinion on the subject in the City of London and other centres of the commerce and industry of the country.

19. **When it had come to this, that we were to tamper with the settled policy of the Bank of England, and to enter into negotiations for importing a great volume of silver into our currency, for the benefit of certain interests other than those of the British public, it was too much.**

There was then heard in no uncertain tone the voice of the British Press and of the British people. If this was a compromise, they would have none of it; if this was the "something different and less" of the First Lord of the Treasury, how ruinous must be the total scheme of the greater bimetallism!

20. These considerations powerfully affected the public mind.

The Committee of the London Clearing House Bankers on September 22nd resolved:—"That this meeting entirely dis-"approves of the Bank of England agreeing to exercise the option "permitted by the Act of 1844 of holding one-fifth, or any other "proportion whatever, of silver, as reserve against the circulation "of Bank of England notes."

21. **A memorial extensively signed in the City of London addressed the Chancellor of the Exchequer as follows:—**

"Sir,

"We, the undersigned, are engaged in various Mercantile
"Banking, and Financial enterprises in the City of London of nc
"slight magnitude, and we are therefore deeply interested in all that
"affects the monetary position of the country, the credit of the bank
"note, and the solvency of Banking Institutions.

"We are aware of the visit of the Delegates from the President
"of the United States to this and other countries, but have no
"authoritative information as to the nature of their proposals. From
"the communication of the Governor of the Bank of England to
"yourself lately made public, and from general report, we cannot
"but assume that negotiations of some sort touching the metallic
"currency of this country are proceeding.

"**We feel impelled by a strong sense of duty respectfully**
"**to lay before Her Majesty's Government the following**
"**four considerations, the great importance of which we**
"**trust may be apparent :—**

"1. That no alterations should be introduced affecting the
   "circulating medium of this country, except after full
   "discussion in Parliament and by the public at large, so
   "that the changes proposed may have as ample con-
   "sideration as their importance deserves.

"2. That under no circumstances whatever should the
   "pledges of successive Governments as to the British
   "£ sterling and the single gold standard of this country
   "be set aside, either directly or indirectly ; and that
   "no step should be taken by or with the consent of our
   "Government which has for its object any alteration in
   "the value of that standard.

"3. **That this country alone of the great nations of**
   "**the world, enjoys under her mint regulations a**
   "**coinage system absolutely free from embarrass-**
   "**ments,** internal or external, and we conceive that any
   "departure therefrom in the direction of reliance upon
   "engagements with other countries would be a fatal
   "mistake.

"4. That the mints of India being closed (as to the policy of
   "which we express no opinion), a state of circumstances
   "has arisen in which the greatest caution is necessary,
   "whatever may be the next step which the Indian
   "Government may be advised to take ; but we urge

R

"that no retrograde step be taken except upon as ex-
"haustive an enquiry as that which led up to the
"present position, and then only if Indian interests will
"be primarily benefited thereby.

" We most strongly urge the foregoing considerations upon Her
" Majesty's Government, speaking (as we believe we are justified in
" stating) with some little knowledge of the problems involved and
" of the interests at stake ; and we are prepared, if necessary, to
" give our reasons at length if it be your wish to receive a
" deputation."

Similar remonstrances were forwarded by a large body
of the most influential manufacturers, merchants, and
bankers of Lancashire, and also by the heads of the
Associated Stock Exchanges.

22. The Canadian bankers cabled to London an admirable
survey of the situation. They gave reasons for their conviction that
" silver is entirely unsuitable as a basis for the operations of banking
" and commerce," and proceeded as follows :—" Having, therefore,
" these convictions, the fruit of long experience and observation of
" the conditions of currency matters in various countries, this associa-
" tion must view with much apprehension any measure proposed to
" be taken by financial authorities in the mother country which would
" tend even remotely to the establishment of silver as a basis of
" banking obligation. They express hearty approval of the action of
" the bankers of London in protesting against the holding of silver
" by the Bank of England as part of its reserve, the reserve held by
" that Bank being the ultimate reserve for the whole United Kingdom,
" as such holding must impair to the extent to which it is held the
" ability to maintain the gold standard and give encouragement to
" those who favour the delusive and impracticable theories of bi-
" metallism, and so endanger the great fabric on which the
" banking of Great Britain has rested for generations to the
" incalculable advantage of the world. They finally reiterate
" their conviction that a double standard of value of obliga-
" tion is delusive and impracticable, that of the two standards
" gold is incomparably the most desirable, and that the Dominion
" of Canada having all its obligations, public, private and corporate,
" resting on and being so long and honourably established on this
" most solid basis, any attempt to disturb the same or any measures
" having a tendency in that direction should be met with strenuous
" resistance."

23. This action brought upon the memorialists most unreasoning abuse from bimetallic authorities. Seldom has anything wilder been written than the letter of Professor Foxwell, which was read amid cheers at a bimetallic meeting at Manchester on October 12th. The Professor referred to the petition of the London Bankers—which only asked that the promises of the Government to maintain the gold standard of this country should be fully maintained, and that before anything should be done in the direction of reopening the Indian Mints there should be as full an inquiry as that which led up to the present position—as "the noisy "and irrational clamour of middlemen," actuated by their personal interests, and whose object was "to aggrandise the creditor by "increasing the real value of the money in which his debt is " expressed."

24. In the meantime it became generally known that the Indian Government had been consulted as to the wider and yet more important proposal of the Wolcott Commission that its mints should be thrown open to the coinage of silver.

Lord Farrer, in letters to the *Times,* called attention to this subject. " From the best accessible information," he said, "I believe "the Wolcott Commission to have made a proposal to reopen the "Indian mints to silver, on the · understanding that the United "States and France shall open their mints to silver at the ratio of "$15\frac{1}{2}$ to 1." Lord Farrer pointed out the extreme difficulties and dangers attending the proposal.

His letters were replied to by Lord Aldenham and Mr. H. R. Grenfell, the President and Vice-President of the Bimetallic League, in a letter to the *Times* of October 4th, in which they did not deny or express any doubt as to the information given by Lord Farrer. They accepted practically his statement of facts, and they said :—

" We desire to state that in our opinion the time for academical "discussion has now gone by, and that the question has become one "of practical politics." They added that if the present negotiations were successful there would be no further bimetallic agitation, and they concluded :—"As we believe that the great commercial nations "are fully alive to the dangers which would attend any failure of the "negotiations, we have every reason to hope that this compromise "will be accepted."

25. It is clear that this compromise included not only the opening of the Indian mints, but also the proposal for the partial substitution of silver for gold in the reserve of the Bank of England, and other

R 2

measures for promoting the use of silver in this country. It must also be taken for certain that they were aware that the ratio of 15½ to 1 was the one proposed. Lord Farrer had based his objections largely on this ratio. Lord Aldenham and Mr. Grenfell would have made a reservation on the point if they had seen objection to this ratio. We have it also on the authority of Mr. Herbert Gibbs, another prominent member of the Bimetallic League, and the son of Lord Aldenham, that bimetallists were aware that this ratio was proposed.

"We," he said in a letter to the *Times* of November 6th, "and "no doubt everyone else felt certain that the ratio to be proposed, "in the first instance at all events, would have been 15½ or 16 to 1, "because no other ratio has as yet been discussed in the United "States and France."

26. The organ of the bimetallic movement in the monthly magazines, the *National Review*, was also engaged in writing, in the months of July to October, the strongest possible articles in favour of the so-called compromise, which it assumed had been offered by Mr. Wolcott, and which it asserted would be accepted by the Government. **In an editorial statement in July it was said:—**
"Our readers may take it from us as beyond all doubt "that Lord Salisbury's Government is willing to reopen the "Indian mints in aid of an international settlement of the "monetary problem. They are also willing to make further sub- "stantial contribution towards the rehabilitation of silver by extending "its use in England. By increasing the legal tender of silver, by "making silver the basis for notes, by empowering the Bank of Eng- "land to use silver as a reserve, and in other ways, such as the famous "Huskisson proposals, powerful material assistance and strong moral "support will be given to the object which the United States and "France have in view."

And in August it was said:—"It is now generally recog- "nised, except by the ostriches, that Great Britain's chief contri- "bution to an international settlement of the silver question will "be the reopening of the Indian mints, which all who appreciate "this question regard as a splendid subscription to the common pool."

"Beyond the reopening of the Indian mints the present Govern- "ment are prepared to propose a more extended use of silver in "Great Britain by making it the basis for notes, raising its legal "tender, and making it a part of the bank reserve."

27. It never appears to have entered into the calculations of Lord Aldenham and Mr. Grenfell, or of the Editor of the *National*

Review, that the Indian Government would refuse its sanction to the proposal.

But at the very time when Lord Aldenham and Mr. Grenfell wrote the letter to the *Times* which we have quoted, and when the last of the editorials appeared in the *National Review*, the scheme of the Wolcott Commission had practically received its death-blow at the hands of the Indian Government.

28. **The conclusive despatch in which the Indian Government condemned, root and branch, the proposal to reopen its mints upon the terms suggested was dated September 16th.**

In the course of it the following cogent arguments, among many others, are specially worthy of notice :—

The first result of the suggested measures, if they even temporarily succeed in their object, would be an intense disturbance of Indian trade and industry by the sudden rise in the rate of exchange, which, if the ratio adopted were 15½ to 1, would be a rise from about 16d. to about 23d. the rupee. Such a rise is enough to kill our export trade, for the time at least. If the public were not convinced that the arrangement would have the effect intended, or believed that it would not be permanent, the paralysis of trade and industry would be prolonged and accompanied by acute individual suffering, none of the advantages expected would be attained, and the country would pass through a critical period which would retard its progress for years. How long the crisis would last before normal or stable conditions were restored it is not possible to conjecture. It would be long even if the mercantile and banking community saw that silver was being steadily maintained at the prescribed ratio, while any indication of unsteadiness would greatly prolong the period by giving foundation for doubt. If the doubt should happen to be justified by the results, the position would be disastrous alike to the State, to individuals, and to trade generally. The exchange value of the rupee having risen suddenly, without any intermediate steps, from 16d. to some higher figure, it would fall quite as suddenly to a point far lower than its present level, probably to 9d., or even lower. Such a fall would, apart from other disastrous results, necessitate the imposition of additional taxation to the extent of many crores.

We may here remind your Lordship that such an agreement as is proposed is an infinitely more serious question for India than for either of the other two countries, for it seems clear that practically the whole risk of disaster from failure would fall on India alone. What would happen in each of the three countries if the agreement broke down and came to an end ? France possesses a large stock of gold, and the United States are at present in much the same situation as France, though the stock of that metal is not so large. It may be admitted that if no precautions were taken these gold reserves might disappear under the operation of the agreement, and in that case, if the experiment ultimately failed, the two countries concerned would suffer great loss. But it is inconceivable that precautions would not be taken, at all events so soon as the danger of the depletion of the gold reserves manifested itself, and, therefore, it is probable that no particular change would take place in the monetary system of France or the United States, the only effect of the agreement being a coinage of silver which would terminate with the termination of the agreement. **Thus the whole cost of the failure, if the experiment should fail, would be borne by India.** Here the rupee would rise with great swiftness, it would keep steady for a time, and then, when the collapse came, it would fall headlong. What course could we then adopt to prevent the fluctuation of the exchange value of our standard of value with the fluctuations in the price of silver? We do not think that any remedy would be open to us, for if the Indian mints were reopened to silver now, it would, in our opinion, be practically impossible for the Government of India ever to close them again, and even if they were closed, it would only be after very large additions had been made to the amount of silver in circulation. . . . .

Moreover, it seems to us somewhat unfair to expect that India should, after its struggles and difficulties of the last decade, consider itself on the same plane in the discussion of these projects as France and the United States. India has, since 1893, passed through a period of serious tension and embarrassment alike to trade and to the Government. We are satisfied that, great as have been the troubles which have attended this period of transition, the attainment in the end of the paramount object of stability in exchange is worth more than all the sacrifices made. We believe that our difficulties are now nearly over, and that we shall, in the near future, succeed in establishing a stable exchange at 16d. the rupee by continuing the policy initiated in 1893. . . . .

We have given very careful consideration to the question whether France and the United States are likely, with the help of India, to be able to maintain the relative value of gold and silver permanently, at the ratio they intend to adopt, and have come to the conclusion that while we admit a possibility of the arrangements proposed resulting in the permanent maintenance of the value of gold and silver at the ratio of $15\frac{1}{2}$ to 1, the probability is that they will fail to secure that result, and that it is quite impossible to hold that there is anything approaching a practical certainty of their doing so. . . . .

For these reasons alone, without taking into consideration the objections based on the particular ratio proposed, which we shall separately discuss, we have no hesitation in recommending your Lordship to refuse to give the undertaking desired by the Governments of France and the United States. We are quite clearly of opinion that the interests of India demand that her mints shall not be opened as part of an arrangement to which two or three countries only are parties, and which does not include Great Britain.

We note that the proposals of the Governments of France and the United States are subject to the proviso that they are satisfied that they will receive assistance from other Powers in increasing the demand for silver. We believe that a limited increase of the quantity of silver used as currency will exercise a very trifling influence, if any, in raising the gold price of silver, and that the only assistance from other Powers which can be of any real value would be the addition of other countries to the bimetallic union of France and the United States. . . . .

We believe, however, that whatever inducements are held out to us by other nations, our best policy in monetary matters is to link our system with that of Great Britain. Our commercial connections with that country are far more important than those with all the rest of the world put together, and more than a sixth part of our expenditure is incurred in that country, and measured in its currency. The advantages, which in this respect we gain by following the lead of Great Britain, are not obtained, or not fully obtained, if we become members of a monetary union in which Great Britain takes no part. . . . .

So far, the arguments we have offered, in discussing the chances of success or failure of the arrangement, have been independent of consideration of the precise ratio proposed by France and the United States. We have objected to the arrangement on grounds which apply to it whatever be the ratio adopted, but we must add that our objections are greatly strengthened by the fact that so high a ratio is proposed as $15\frac{1}{2}$ to 1. It seems to us that the difficulty of making the arrangement effective will be immensely increased by the adoption of a ratio differing so widely from the present market ratio. Indeed, even if it could be maintained successfully, we should object to that ratio in the interests of India, and we recommend that your Lordship should, on behalf of India, decline to participate in or do anything to encourage the formation of a union based on that ratio. . . . .

In any case, we are of opinion that the true interests of India demand that any measures for attaining stability in the rate of exchange between gold and silver

should be based upon a rate not greatly differing from 16d. the rupee, and that
any measure which would raise the rupee materially higher than that level involves
great dangers, for which we see no adequate compensations. . . . .
The conditions under which we have had to reply to your Lordship's despatch
preclude our consulting the commercial and banking communities in this country,
although the subject is one in which they are, as we have explained, most closely
interested. It was only after prolonged public discussion, and after a formal
examination by a Committee of experts that the policy of 1893 was adopted ; and
if we thought it our duty to advocate a change in that policy instead of to set
out the strong objections which we see to its abandonment, we would, nevertheless, strongly deprecate any steps of the kind being taken without the
fullest preliminary consideration on the part of the banking and commercial
bodies in this country.
To sum up, our reply to your Lordship's reference is a strong recommendation that you should decline to give the undertaking desired by France
and the United States. Our unanimous and decided opinion is that it would
be most unwise to reopen the mints as part of the proposed arrangements,
especially at a time when we are to all appearances approaching the attainment of stability in exchange by the operation of our own isolated and
independent action.

This crushing despatch, all the more remarkable, inasmuch as
it proceeded from a Government which, but a short time ago, was
theoretically in favour of international bimetallism, must have
reached the Indian Secretary in full within a fortnight.

29. It was stated on the authority of the editor of the *National
Review*, who claimed to be well posted on the subject, that the terms
of this despatch were wholly unexpected by the Government. "The
"India Council in London," he said,* "was, and is, favourable to
"the reopening of the Indian mints, provided foreign mints are re-
"opened. No single member of the British Cabinet expected a hostile
"reply from India." ·'The reply from Calcutta was as unexpected as
"it was inept, and was received with dismay by the British Cabinet."
Mr. Wolcott also, in a speech delivered in the United States Senate
on January 17th of this year, after stating that his proposals were not
volunteered, but made "at the explicit request of the English
"Ministry," added that the refusal of the Indian Government to
re-open their mints "was as much a surprise to the English
"Ministry as a disappointment to us."† However that may be,
there was apparently no hesitation on the part of the Indian
Secretary of State, or of the British Government, in acting upon
it. On October 13th the India Office wrote to the Treasury
stating that **the Secretary of State for India "could not act
"in opposition to the strongly expressed views of the
"Government of India unless he were convinced that the**

* " *The National Review*," *December*, 1897, *p.* 515.
† " *The Times*," *January* 18*th*, 1898.

"proposed scheme is intrinsically sound, and that it would "confer real and lasting advantages upon the Government "and people of India. After most careful consideration, "Lord George Hamilton has arrived at the conclusion that "the scheme does not fulfil those conditions, and that the "criticisms of the Government of India upon it are in the "main well founded." He expressed "concurrence in the request "of the Government of India that Her Majesty's Government will "not assent to the undertaking desired by France and the United "States."

30. The Government upon this lost no time in coming to a conclusion wholly adverse to the scheme, and on October 19th, exactly a fortnight after Lord Aldenham's letter urging that the time for academical discussion had gone by, and that the question had become one of practical politics, Lord Salisbury informed Mr. Hay, the American Ambassador, that Her Majesty's Government were unable to accept the proposals of the Wolcott Commission, so far as concerned the reopening of the Indian mints. "Due consideration," he said, "has "also been given to the remaining proposals, but Her Majesty's "Government do not feel it to be necessary to discuss them at the "present moment. Her Majesty's Government are therefore desirous "to ascertain how far the views of the American and French Govern-"ments are modified by the decision now arrived at, and whether "they desire to proceed further with the negotiations at the present "moment."

31. This closes the correspondence, and there is no sign of any desire on the part of the American Government to reopen the question. It appears that Mr. Wolcott has returned to his country with strong feelings of resentment at having been misled. Especially galling must be the fact that **he has not even been able to obtain a Conference.** Mr. Wolcott complained in his speech in the Senate of the "blind, unreasoning fury of the City of London against any "concessions recognising silver."* He complained not less bitterly of the adverse influences in his own country, especially the statements of New York bankers and, above all, the alleged assertions of the Secretary of the United States Treasury that there was no chance for international bimetallism. These last, he hoped, were fictitious; if not, the official he referred to was "seeking to undermine a mission "appointed and supported by the President." He further attacked the London press for their attitude to the mission, in that "they

* "*The Times*," *January* 18*th*, 1898.

"should have been led to characterise as impertinent proposals
"which had only been made at the request of their own Govern-
"ment." However, hope springs eternal in the human breast, and
Mr. Wolcott appears to think that, in spite of what has occurred,
international bimetallism is not altogether hopeless. He has,
nevertheless, resigned his position on the Commission.

32. There is nothing in the recent Address of Mr. McKinley
(January 27th, 1898) to indicate that the American Government
intend to make any further proposals on the subject. On the
contrary, their action with regard to currency points rather to
internal reforms, with the object of better securing the maintenance
of a gold standard.

**It is from the bimetallists in England that the chief cry
of distress has proceeded. The Bimetallic League, indeed,
has been discreetly and painfully silent,** and has failed to fulfil
the promise, made by its secretary in the *Times* of October 28th last,
to express its opinion on the action of the Government in rejecting
the Wolcott proposals.'

A bimetallic writer, however, in the *National Review* for December,* commenting on the failure of the negotiations, after referring to
Mr. Balfour's speech of March 17, 1896, says, " It appears that these
"hopes have been utterly vain, and that **we have been resting
"in a fool's paradise,"** while the editor actually stigmatised Sir
James Westland, the Financial Member of Council, as being " guilty
of this disastrous document." †

**We are not concerned in disputing the fact that the
bimetallists have been living for years past in a fool's
paradise,** but in view of the most satisfactory conclusion arrived at
by the Government, we are not disposed to join in charges against
them of bad faith to the bimetallists in the earlier stages of the affair.

33. We await, on our part, any further proposals which bimetallists
abroad or at home may propound, with the utmost confidence that
they will prove to be as unsound and impracticable as those which
have been almost universally condemned by public opinion and by
the Government. The moral which we believe will be generally drawn
from the late proceedings is that we have been fully justified in the
past in pressing for a declaration on the part of the bimetallists of
the specific scheme which they favoured and proposed. So long as
they indulged in generalities they could find arguments specious and

* " *The National Review,*" *December,* 1897, *p.* 562.
† Ditto ditto, *p.* 516.

plausible enough to delude the unwary into the belief that bimetallism might be a cure for commercial or agricultural depression; **but so soon as a definite scheme was propounded its difficulties and dangers at once became apparent, and it was admitted almost universally to be impossible. We confidently predict the same will be the result with any future scheme.**

34. We have reason to be well satisfied that three important results have been achieved by the proceedings which we have thus briefly related—the first, that, so far as England is concerned, our gold standard is to be preserved intact; the second, that, so far as other countries are concerned, it has been made clear that neither the United States nor France will propose or accept bimetallism on any other condition than the restoration of the old ratio existing before 1873 of 15½ to 1; the third, that the Indian Government has definitely declined to reopen the Indian mints to the free coinage of silver upon the terms proposed by France and America.

35. We think it will exercise the ingenuity of the bimetallists for a very long time to come to devise any scheme which shall be consistent with these conclusions. **We hope and believe also that what has occurred will show to the British public the danger and folly of relying upon vague generalities, and the necessity for requiring a definite scheme from those who ask us to abandon the long-settled commercial and currency policy of this country.**

THE LATEST PHASE OF THE BIMETALLIC MOVEMENT.*

By the COMMITTEE OF THE GOLD STANDARD DEFENCE ASSOCIATION.

1. THE Committee of the Gold Standard Defence Association, in the leaflet entitled "The Bimetallic Negotiations and their Result," have described very fully the course of events during the autumn of 1897. But it is now desirable to place on record the further proceedings of the bimetallists since that date. It will be remembered that in October last the Bimetallic League declared that it was prepared to express its opinion upon the action of Her Majesty's Government in rejecting the Wolcott proposals. But it was not till March that the promised statement was issued.

2. The statement was chiefly remarkable for the fact that it expressed no opinion upon the important question as to whether Her Majesty's Government were right or wrong in rejecting the Wolcott proposals. Nor did it contain the direct charge of breach of faith against the Government, of which we have heard so much recently, beyond expressing a hope that this country should "restore "the confidence of foreign Governments in the promise of British "Ministers," by taking some steps in the direction of bimetallism; and it appeared, apart from this vague insinuation, to accept with resignation the conclusion arrived at last autumn in respect of those

* *Issued in April,* 1898.

very Wolcott proposals which, as shown in the leaflet on the bi-metallic negotiations, bimetallists had so much responsibility in recommending to the Government and to the country.

3. The Bimetallic League in the statement in question reiterated its general belief in an "International Bimetallic Union including "Great Britain," and still looked for an agreement "under which the "mints of Western Powers, including England, should be open to "both silver and gold at a uniform ratio." It further asked of Her Majesty's Government "why do they not resume negotiations on "another basis"—that is to say, on the basis of a ratio of about 20 to 1. **But considering that only a few months previously Her Majesty's Government, with general approval, declined any scheme of bimetallism for Great Britain altogether, and also endorsed the rejection of the Wolcott proposals by the Indian Government, such suggestions as those now made by the Bimetallic League may be dismissed as not likely to have any influence with Her Majesty's Govern-ment, or with the public at large.**

4. The next step taken by the bimetallists has been to send a deputation to the Treasury. They prepared their way with a manifesto, which accused Her Majesty's Government of breaking their solemn pledges to the country and of disgracing this country in the eyes of the world, and described those who favour our existing monetary system as "selfish and tyrannical" persons. But this manifesto had an effect precisely the opposite of that which they anticipated, for in consequence of its language an audience was denied to them altogether.

5. Nor has this been all. On March 29th a prominent member of the Bimetallic League moved a resolution in the House of Commons, which led to what was to some extent a bimetallic debate. The mover, Mr. Vicary Gibbs, accused the Indian Government of criminal blundering and charged them with "levity, "incapacity, and injustice." In reply the Secretary of State, Lord George Hamilton, declared that it was "quite impossible" to accept the resolution, supported as it was by "more exciting "language than I ever heard before, even in an Irish debate," and moved an amendment, which was unanimously passed.

6. We print in full, in the following pages, the speeches of Lord George Hamilton, Secretary of State for India, and Sir William Harcourt, which wound up the debate. To these we draw atten-tion, not because of their statements as regards Indian currency,

but because of their references to bimetallism. Lord George Hamilton spoke as one believing "theoretically" in bimetallism, and promptly proceeded to point out that such an arrangement was impossible, and that "we have not to deal with individual opinions "but with the opinions of the world." He summarised the situation by saying that, whoever among individuals might favour bimetallism, "the world, unfortunately, does not agree." Sir William Harcourt, who followed, expressed great satisfaction at the "voice "of Balaam that we have heard to-night," and his pleasure that, "better late than never," a bimetallist of so old a standing had himself come to use "the arguments we have been using—we, who "belong to the majority of the world."

7. The following are the speeches* delivered by Lord George Hamilton and Sir William Harcourt, in the House of Commons, on the occasion in question :—

Lord G. Hamilton.—I regret that the exigencies of public business have permitted of only a very short discussion upon this important subject. I think, however, there is still sufficient time to enable me to state very clearly what my views are, and what are the intentions of the Indian Government. Let me in the first place congratulate my hon. friend (Mr. A. Wylie) who has just sat down upon his admirable speech (hear, hear)—a speech which showed real knowledge and grip of the subject, and which was all the more valuable because my hon. friend is largely engaged in trade with India and speaks as a bimetallist, although not as a prejudiced one. The hon. member for Whitechapel (Sir Samuel Montagu) and the hon. member for Cardiff (Mr. J. M. Maclean) have made speeches with which I find but little fault. As far as their demands are concerned, I believe I can satisfy them, for I feel that before any alteration is made in the monetary system of India there should be a thorough and impartial inquiry. I should be sorry to attempt to decide without inquiry upon so controversial and intricate a subject as the monetary system of India. I cannot, however, approve the tone or substance of the speech of my hon. friend (Mr. Vicary Gibbs) who moved this motion. In one respect I must congratulate him. We are discussing the dullest of all subjects—an abstract currency question—and my hon. friend managed to use in his speech more exciting language than I ever heard before, even in an Irish debate or in any debate upon a controversial subject in this House. If my hon. friend succeeds in getting a select committee appointed, and if those who differ from him were to give evidence in similar language, whatever other solution is arrived at I do not think it will be a pacific one. (Laughter.)

8. I was not responsible for the closing of the mints, and my hon. friend wishes to bring those who were responsible before a committee. I have looked most carefully into the history of the matter, and it is my belief that, placed in the circumstances in which they then were—circumstances of very great difficulty—those who were responsible adopted the right course, and I shall not hesitate to say so. (Hear.) It is not an abstract question whether it is right or wrong to close the mints ; we must take into consideration the circumstances with which they had to deal. Believer as I am in bimetallism, having been a convert twenty-five years ago, I had a good deal to do with starting the organisation which has since developed itself. The object of bimetallism is to establish a stable rate of exchange between gold and silver money, and the object of anybody who takes an interest

* *From the " Times " report, March 30th, 1898.*

in Indian finance is to try and bring about that stability of exchange. It is my belief that if that can ever be established so as to induce capitalists to invest their money in India with the knowledge that they will get it back at very much the same rate, I know no bounds to the productive prosperity of India. (Hear, hear.) How is it possible to establish that stability of exchange between England and India? It might be done by an international agreement, and theoretically that would be the best plan, but the world unfortunately does not agree. (Hear, hear.) We have not to deal with individual opinions, but with the opinions of the world. Twenty-five years ago, when the fall in the price of silver took place, largely due to the action of Germany in closing her mints, over a period of seven years, from 1870 to 1877, a certain number of nations demonetised silver and adopted a gold standard, and foremost was Germany. For thirteen years there was a cessation of the movement, but in 1890 it began again, and since then Roumelia, Austro-Hungary, Chi'e, Bulgaria, Russia, and Japan all adopted a gold standard. Now, we must lo)k facts in the face. I believe at this moment there are only two silver-using countries—Mexico and China—and, believing as I do in bimetallism, and not having abandoned the theory, I think it is obvious that we cannot carry out that theory of establishing a stable exchange between England and India.

9. There has been no blame of the Government for rejecting the proposal made in the autumn for reopening the Indian mints. It was obvious to anyone who looked into the matter that the proposal would not obtain the stability it was its object to secure. A Government can give an artificial value to silver in circulation only on one condition—that of keeping restriction on coinage of silver. All nations can open their mints to free coinage, but the value of the coins will be that of the intrinsic value of the metal they contain. The proposition made to us was that the ratio of silver to gold should be 15½ to 1. But the market ratio was 35 to 1, and if the wishes of Governments come into contact with the universal law of supply and demand, that law will prevail, and the ratio of 15½ could not be sustained. If we ever enter into an international arrangement that does not achieve its object we shall be in a worse position than before, for we shall have all the inconveniences of instability of exchange while having tied our hands and fettered our liberty of action. (Hear.)

10. I will go so far as to say—and I speak my own opinion, and I think of everyone connected with the Indian Government—we do not believe that circumstances now exist for entering into an international bimetallic arrangement, because no such arrangement would be worthy of being called international that did not include France, and France would only accept a 15½ ratio. The population of France is 11 per cent. of the total population of Europe, but its currency is 23 per cent. of the total currency of Europe. When that is subdivided, the note circulation is 6½ per cent. of the total circulation of Europe; the gold circulation is 25 per cent., but the silver circulation is 40 per cent. In fact, I believe there is a larger amount of silver in circulation in France than there is in the whole of British India. (Cries of "Oh.") I go by the statement of the Herschell Committee. At any rate, there is this enormous amount of silver at the ratio of 15½ to 1, and I do not believe that France can accept any other ratio. So long as she adheres to that ratio, you cannot enter into an international arrangement which would be a real international arrangement. That, in a nutshell, is the position of the Indian Government; and let the House remember that they did not close their mints until after they saw there was no chance of an international bimetallic arrangement.

11. Another fact which my investigation has brought to my mind very strongly is that I do not believe it is possible for any one nation by its own exertions to rehabilitate silver. America made a tremendous effort in 1890 by the Sherman Act. By that Act the United States Government were compelled annually to buy 54 million ounces of silver, whether the currency of the United States wanted it or not. That 54 million ounces of silver is about 30 or 40 per cent. of the silver production of the whole world. America continued that operation for three years, and at the end of those three years silver was 6d. lower than it was before. (Hear, hear.) That shows clearly that no one country can by its own unaided exertions rehabilitate

the price of silver. Under these conditions what was to be done ? What was the position which the late Government had to face ? I do not want to use language too strong, but India was unquestionably nearing bankruptcy. (Hear, hear.) She could not pay her way, and one of two things was inevitable—either that she would be unable to meet her obligations, or that this country would have had to come to her aid.

12. What is the plea upon which bimetallists have appealed to the working classes of this country ? Is it not that the constant fall in the price of silver raises prices in those countries where silver is the standard, and that in consequence an impetus and bounty is given to the export trade ? But if you open your mints you at once re-establish the bounty system on behalf of the exporter which the closing of the mints has taken away from him, and therefore anybody who has made an appeal as a bimetallist to the working classes of this country to get rid of the bounty which the fall in silver gives to the exporter must vote against the reopening of the mints in India, because, if those mints were opened, that bounty which they have denounced would once more be established. The exporter wants a cheap rupee. Everyone who exports produce from India likes a falling rupee, for the reason that it raises prices. But there is always an interval between the rise in the price of the commodity and the rise in the wages of those who engage in producing the commodity, and the exporter gets the benefit for the time being. (Hear, hear.) It does seem to me absolutely inconsistent in the whole theory and principle of bimetallism that those gentlemen who have been holding up the iniquity of this bounty system should now ask to reopen the mints and re-establish it in full vitality. (Hear, hear.)

13. My hon. friend expressed in very strong language the terrible commercial, monetary, and economic condition of India as it existed at the present time ; and he stated that this had been entirely produced by closing the mints. He only gave one set of figures in support of that statement, and those were in connection with the export of opium to China. No doubt there has been a great falling off in the export of opium to China, but that was always foreseen when the area of opium cultivation in China has, decade after decade, been extending ; and I was glad to think that my hon. friend, with all his industry, was only able to refer to opium as an argument that India has become impoverished under this system of closed mints. I have taken a great deal of trouble to see how far the predictions of those who are opposed to the closing of the mints have been verified. It was stated that the result of the closing of the mints would be to reduce the area of cultivation. The area of cultivation has not diminished in India. The price of staple commodities remains very much the same ; the value of exports has not fallen ; the prices of exported produce have not fallen ; and the prices of imported produce have in-creased. It was predicted that the trade of India with silver-using countries would fall further. So far from that being the case, according to the last returns the volume of trade with silver-using countries was 26 per cent. for the whole of India, whereas previously it was only 24. If I wanted any proof that India was not ruined by the present monetary system, it is given by the extraordinary recuperative power she has exhibited in recovering from one of the greatest disasters that have ever visited any country.

14. No doubt money is dear in India. I do not wish to dogmatise on this point, but it seems to me that dearness of money is not identical with scarcity of currency. I think the dearness of money is caused by want of capital, and the cause of want of capital in India is no doubt due to the sufferings of that country from drought, famine, plague, and war. There is another influence at work. I think one mistake in closing the mints was in trying to fix the rate at which the rupee is converted into gold. The rupee could not rise appreciably above 16d., but could fall below. The result has been a great depletion of money from the banks. What would be the result if the mints were opened ? I have had inquiry made as to what the difference would be between the number of rupees remitted at the present rate in exchange, and the number which would have to be remitted at the market rate of silver at the present moment. That difference amounts to about 15 crores, or £6,000,000 sterling.

The Indian Government must pay its way ; and it could not pay its way in that state of things except by increased taxation. It cannot increase its taxation, and therefore it could not pay its way unless it received help from this country. If additional taxation were put on here, it would be put on those who are subjected to unfair competition in India, and so the community here would get hit right and left. (Hear, hear.)

15. But that is not the only objection. If there were any idea of the mints being opened there would be at once a general disturbance of prices and a continuous fall in the value of the rupee, and a general spirit of apprehension and mistrust would be set up which would be absolutely fatal to the investment of capital and to the development of commerce or trade, or any sustained enterprise anywhere. (Hear, hear.) I cannot conceive what reason anyone can give for arguing that the mints in India should be opened without an international arrangement, except that if the mints in India were opened it is just possible that it might be a stepping-stone to some international arrangement. But I am not prepared myself to make so dangerous an experiment in the hope of the realisation of what I must call a visionary idea. I want it to be distinctly understood that so far as the Indian Government are concerned, both here and in India, we believe that an attempt to open the mints without some international arrangement being come to would be an act of lunacy (hear, hear), and therefore I should be very sorry to be associated in any way with an inquiry which might lead to a reversal of the policy established in 1893. (Cheers.)

16. Now, sir, I quite agree that there should be an impartial inquiry into any proposals the Indian Government send home, and that any such inquiry must be retrospective. The inquiry must not be limited to the scope of the Indian system, but those who conduct it must have the power to investigate the monetary system of England. The body entrusted with the inquiry should not be composed mainly of officials. (Hear, hear.) I think it is most desirable that gentlemen of experience in connection with India whose names carry weight should be asked to participate, and I think they ought certainly to be more in number than the officials. (Hear, hear.) I am prepared to state on behalf of the Government that such shall be the composition and scope of the inquiry into the proposals the Indian Government have sent home, and I am anxious for my own sake that the inquiry should be made as soon as possible. There are many systems in force in different parts of the world, but their success does not depend upon their theoretical perfection, but upon the fact that the people have confidence in them, and I feel that no alteration in the system of India could be accepted with general trust and confidence by the community unless the recommendation was associated with the names of men whose opinions would carry weight with the community at large. It is rather difficult to select gentlemen to take part in such an inquiry. I think we do not want to have extreme controversialists, we do not want to have faddists, because I think nothing is more inconvenient in a case of this kind, where the demand everywhere is that a decision one way or the other should be arrived at—nothing is more undesirable than that such an inquiry as this should be an opportunity for gentlemen of extreme views to fight one another. (Cheers.) At the same time it is desirable that, while we get gentlemen associated with banking and commercial interests, we should try and not put gentlemen on with too direct a personal interest in the exchange one way or the other.

17. Such being the views of her Majesty's Government, I cannot accept the motion of my hon. friend for the reason I have given. It would be quite impossible for me to do so, but I am prepared to move this as a substitution—"That in the opinion of this House it is desirable that a further inquiry be made into the monetary system of India, and into the proposals of the Government of India for the establishment of a gold standard in that country." Of course such a committee would have power to make recommendations. I do not propose to have recourse to a Select Committee, because it is obvious that you have a much wider selection of experts if you do not confine the inquiry to members of this House ; and I do not propose to have recourse to a Royal Commission because a Royal Commission is a somewhat cumbrous form of investigation. But what I would propose is a

committee, not being a departmental committee in the sense of being composed mainly of officials in the India Office, but a committee having all the powers and all the attributes of a Royal Commission, and which is simply put in that shape because that is a handier and I think a more effective instrument of inquiry. (Cheers.) I have stated to the House what the views of the Indian Government are. We cannot assent to the proposal of my hon. friend, and I cannot hold out on behalf of the Government any hope that we shall reverse the policy established in 1893. My hon. friend thinks that the currency system in India can be put on a better footing than that policy ; but I, on the other hand, look forward and hope to be able to consummate the policy which was commenced in 1893. (Cheers.) .

18. **Sir W. Harcourt** (Monmouthshire, W.)—The noble lord was good enough to say that he would leave me some time in which to address the House. That was unnecessary, because he has made a better speech than I could have made in defence of the policy of 1893. There is no doubt what that policy was ; it was an experiment, and a necessary experiment, in the condition in which India was placed. No doubt the Government of India approached that experiment with prepossessions in favour of a different course ; but they have recorded in the despatch their conviction that that policy was right, and that it was better than an international bimetallic policy. (Hear, hear.) Well, that is satisfactory for the Government of India, but still more satisfactory is the voice of Balaam that we have heard to-night (laughter), who confesses that he always has been, and still is, a bimetallist by conviction. I can only express my regret that that speech was not made somewhere about the month of July, 1895 (Opposition cheers and laughter) ; it would have been extremely useful in Lancashire and in the agricultural constituencies. But better late than never ; and I am glad to see that it has carried conviction to the colleague who sits by his side (Mr. Chaplin) (laughter), and to the First Lord of the Treasury. (MR. BALFOUR.—In what respect ?) The arguments which he has used are the arguments we have been using—we, who belong to the majority of the world (laughter)—against the professors for I do not know how many years. But, in spite of all the professors, the world is against the faith that the noble lord still holds.

19. I am delighted to hear that he has vindicated the Government of India against the language, in my opinion absolutely unjustifiable, employed by the mover of this resolution. In his concluding words the hon. member charged the Government of India with levity and incapacity for adopting a policy which I venture to say has been proved by experience to be absolutely necessary to rescue India from impending insolvency, and in that I am supported by the speech of the noble lord who has just sat down. I am not going to trouble the House with arguments about the currency. The sort of speeches we want to hear are not speeches on currency by the professors, but speeches such as we heard from the hon. member for Dumbarton, who spoke with practical knowledge of the questions which have to be decided. The hon. member is the sort of man we want to conduct inquiries of this kind. I do not agree with him, however, that an inquiry would shake the confidence in the Indian Government. I believe the inquiry would establish the soundness of the policy which has been adopted and which I hope will be continued.

20. We have listened to appeals on behalf of the poor people of India, who are said to have been injured by the closing of the mints. That is a most mischievous argument, and it is an untrue one. (Hear, hear.) It has been said that these poor people in the time of famine had to sell their silver ornaments and that they could only get half their value. If anyone is disposed to give in to that mischievous delusion I would ask him to read the most important report written by Mr. O'Conor on the trade of British India. He shows that it is absolutely untrue that these silver ornaments have been sold at reduced prices to the injury and discontent of the poor people of India. That is proved by the fact that silver is being imported into India. Of course, if those ornaments were sold, there would be a plethora of silver in India, and there would be no necessity to import silver into the country. (MR. PARKER SMITH, Lanark, Partick.—Will the right

S

hon. gentleman give us the date of the report?) It is dated 1897, the year of the famine.

21. The noble lord said that no one would condemn the Government for having rejected the proposals which were made to them by the Governments of the United States and France. The noble lord said truly that no international agreement could be made except upon a basis and ratio of 15½ to 1. We have the statement of the Chancellor of the Exchequer, with which I agree, that a proposal of that kind was incompatible with the public interest—that, in view of the present market price of silver, to fix any such ratio would be an act of absolute dishonesty to creditors. It was felt that the opening of the mints at such a ratio would mean the disorganisation and ruin of the whole trade of India.

22. I have heard strong language of condemnation of such a proposal having come from the Governments of the United States and France. Yes, but they were not the authors of the proposal; they were invited to make such a proposal, and very much surprised they were when they found that it was summarily rejected by the Government of India and by the British Government. And why were they surprised? Because in 1896, three years after this measure was adopted which the noble lord says was necessary to save India from bankruptcy, the First Lord of the Treasury pledged himself that the Indian mints should be opened without any reserve whatever in regard to the ratio at which it was to be done. The right hon. gentleman said:—"We will reopen the Indian mints; we will engage that they shall be kept open; and we shall therefore provide for a free coinage of silver within the limits of the British Empire for a population greater in number than the populations of France, Germany, and America put together." This declaration was undoubtedly greatly to the satisfaction of the people of Lancashire. The right hon. gentleman gave the pledge without consulting the Indian Government, and when it was consulted the proposal was absolutely rejected.

23. Then we have the United States making this extraordinary proposal, which was summarily rejected as inconsistent with any honest obligation to the Indian Government. The United States naturally thought that, after the right hon. gentleman's pledge, the proposal would be accepted; and they were extremely astonished at, and they rather resented the violence of, the language used here to describe their proposal. The proposal of the noble lord to-night is perfectly satisfactory. In such a difficult question as the establishment of a gold currency in India there ought to be investigation by experts and practical men. If it could be obtained it would be of great use to this country and to India. I think the substituted motion a very proper one, and I shall give it my support.

INDEX.

---◆◆---

S 2

A SELECTED LIST

OF

CASSELL & COMPANY'S

PUBLICATIONS.

7 G — 5.98

Illustrated, Fine Art, and other Volumes.

Adventure, The World of. Fully Illustrated. Complete in Three Vols. 9s. each.

Adventures in Criticism. By A. T. QUILLER-COUCH. 6s.

Africa and its Explorers, The Story of. By Dr. ROBERT BROWN, F.R.G.S., &c. With about 800 Original Illustrations. *Cheap Edition.* In 4 Vols. 4s. each.

Animal Painting in Water Colours. With Coloured Plates. 5s.

Animals, Popular History of. By HENRY SCHERREN, F.Z.S. With 13 Coloured Plates and other Illustrations. 7s. 6d.

Architectural Drawing. By R. PHENÉ SPIERS. Illustrated. 10s. 6d.

Art, The Magazine of. *Yearly Volume,* 21s. *The Two Half-Yearly Volumes for* 1897 *can also be had,* 10s. 6d. *each.*

Artistic Anatomy. By Prof. M. DUVAL. *Cheap Edition,* 3s. 6d.

Ballads and Songs. By WILLIAM MAKEPEACE THACKERAY. With Original Illustrations by H. M. BROCK. 6s.

Barber, Charles Burton, The Works of. With Forty-one Plates and Portraits, and Introduction by HARRY FURNISS. *Cheap Edition,* 7s. 6d.

Battles of the Nineteenth Century. An entirely New and Original Work, with Several Hundred Illustrations. Complete in Two Vols., 9s. each.

"Belle Sauvage" Library, The. Cloth, 2s. (*A complete list of the volumes post free on application.*)

Beetles, Butterflies, Moths, and other Insects. By A. W. KAPPEL, F.L.S., F.E.S., and W. EGMONT KIRBY. With 12 Coloured Plates. 3s. 6d.

Biographical Dictionary, Cassell's New. Containing Memoirs of the Most Eminent Men and Women of all Ages and Countries. *Cheap Edition,* 3s. 6d.

Birds' Nests, British: How, Where, and When to Find and Identify Them. By R. KEARTON, F.Z.S. With nearly 130 Illustrations of Nests, Eggs, Young, &c., from Photographs by C. KEARTON. 21s.

Birds' Nests, Eggs, and Egg-Collecting. By R. KEARTON, F.Z.S. Illustrated with 22 Coloured Plates of Eggs. *Enlarged Edition.* 5s.

Black Watch, The. The Record of an Historic Regiment. By ARCHIBALD FORBES, LL.D. 6s.

Britain's Roll of Glory; or, the Victoria Cross, its Heroes, and their Valour. By D. H. PARRY. Illustrated. 7s. 6d.

British Ballads. With 300 Original Illustrations. *Cheap Edition.* Two Volumes in One. Cloth, 7s. 6d.

British Battles on Land and Sea. By JAMES GRANT. With about 800 Illustrations. *Cheap Edition.* Four Vols., 3s. 6d. each.

Building World. In Half-Yearly Volumes, 4s. each.

Butterflies and Moths, European. By W. F. KIRBY. With 61 Coloured Plates, 35s.

Canaries and Cage-Birds, The Illustrated Book of. By W. A. BLAKSTON, W. SWAYSLAND, and A. F. WIENER. With 56 Facsimile Coloured Plates. 35s.

Cassell's Magazine. Half-Yearly Volumes, 5s. each; or Yearly Volumes, 8s. each.

Cathedrals, Abbeys, and Churches of England and Wales. Descriptive, Historical, Pictorial. *Popular Edition.* Two Vols. 25s.

Cats and Kittens. By HENRIETTE RONNER. With Portrait and 13 magnificent Full-page Photogravure Plates and numerous Illustrations. 4to, £2 10s.

China Painting. By FLORENCE LEWIS. With Sixteen Coloured Plates, &c. 5s.

Choice Dishes at Small Cost. By A. G. PAYNE. *Cheap Edition,* 1s.

Chums. The Illustrated Paper for Boys. Yearly Volume, 8s.

Cities of the World. Four Vols. Illustrated. 7s. 6d. each.

Civil Service, Guide to Employment in the. *Entirely New Edition.* Paper, 1s.; cloth, 1s. 6d.

Clinical Manuals for Practitioners and Students of Medicine. (*A List of Volumes forwarded post free on application to the Publishers.*)

Cobden Club, Works published for the. (*A Complete List on application.*)

Colour. By Prof. A. H. CHURCH. *New and Enlarged Edition*, 3s. 6d.

Combe, George, The Select Works of. Issued by Authority of the Combe Trustees. *Popular Edition*, 1s. each, net.
The Constitution of Man.   Moral Philosophy.   Science and Religion.
Discussions on Education.   American Notes.

Conning Tower, In a; or, How I Took H.M.S. "Majestic" into Action. By H. O. ARNOLD-FORSTER, M.P. *Cheap Edition.* Illustrated. 6d.

Conquests of the Cross. Edited by EDWIN HODDER. With numerous Original Illustrations. Complete in Three Vols. 9s. each.

Cookery, Cassell's Dictionary of. With about 9,000 Recipes. 5s.

Cookery, A Year's. By PHYLLIS BROWNE. *New and Enlarged Edition*, 3s. 6d.

Cookery Book, Cassell's New Universal. By LIZZIE HERITAGE. With 12 Coloured Plates and other Illustrations. 1,344 pages, strongly bound in leather gilt, 6s.

Cookery, Cassell's Popular. With Four Coloured Plates. Cloth gilt, 2s.

Cookery, Cassell's Shilling. 135th Thousand. 1s.

Cookery, Vegetarian. By A. G. PAYNE. 1s. 6d.

Cooking by Gas, The Art of. By MARIE J. SUGG. Illustrated. Cloth, 2s.

Cottage Gardening. Edited by W. ROBINSON, F.L.S. Illustrated. Half-yearly Vols., 2s. 6d. each.

Countries of the World, The. By Dr. ROBERT BROWN, M.A., F.L.S. With about 750 Illustrations. *Cheap Edition.* Vols. I. to V., 6s. each.

Cyclopædia, Cassell's Concise. With about 600 Illustrations. 5s.

Cyclopædia, Cassell's Miniature. Containing 30,000 Subjects. Cloth, 2s.6d.; half-roxburgh, 4s.

Dictionaries. (For description, see alphabetical letter.) Religion, Biographical, Encyclopædic, Concise Cyclopædia, Miniature Cyclopædia, Mechanical, English, English History, Phrase and Fable, Cookery, Domestic. (French, German, and Latin, see with *Educational Works.*)

Diet and Cookery for Common Ailments. By a Fellow of the Royal College of Physicians and PHYLLIS BROWNE. *Cheap Edition.* 2s. 6d.

Dog, Illustrated Book of the. By VERO SHAW, B.A. With 28 Coloured Plates. Cloth bevelled, 35s.; half-morocco, 45s.

Domestic Dictionary, The. An Encyclopædia for the Household. Cloth, 7s. 6d.

Doré Don Quixote, The. With about 400 Illustrations by GUSTAVE DORÉ. *Cheap Edition.* Cloth, 10s. 6d.

Doré Gallery, The. With 250 Illustrations by GUSTAVE DORÉ. 4to, 42s.

Doré's Dante's Inferno. Illustrated by GUSTAVE DORÉ. *Popular Edition.* With Preface by A. J. BUTLER. Cloth gilt or buckram, 7s. 6d.

Doré's Dante's Purgatory and Paradise. Illustrated by GUSTAVE DORÉ. *Cheap Edition.* 7s. 6d.

Doré's Milton's Paradise Lost. Illustrated by GUSTAVE DORÉ. 4to, 21s. *Popular Edition.* Cloth gilt, or buckram gilt, 7s. 6d.

Earth, Our, and its Story. Edited by Dr. ROBERT BROWN, F.L.S. With 36 Coloured Plates and nearly 800 Wood Engravings. In Three Vols. 9s. each.

Edinburgh, Old and New, Cassell's. With 600 Illustrations. Three Vols. 9s. each; library binding, £1 10s. the set.

Egypt: Descriptive, Historical, and Picturesque. By Prof. G. EBERS. Translated by CLARA BELL, with Notes by SAMUEL BIRCH, LL.D., &c. Two Vols. 42s.

Electric Current, The. How Produced and How Used. By R. MULLINEUX WALMSLEY, D.Sc., &c. Illustrated. 10s. 6d.

Electricity, Practical. By Prof. W. E. AYRTON, F.R.S. *Entirely New and Enlarged Edition.* Completely re-written. Illustrated. 9s.

Electricity in the Service of Man. A Popular and Practical Treatise. With upwards of 950 Illustrations. *New and Cheaper Edition*, 7s. 6d.

Employment for Boys on Leaving School, Guide to. By W. S. BEARD, F.R.G.S. 1s. 6d.

Encyclopædic Dictionary, The. Complete in Fourteen Divisional Vols., 10s. 6d. each; or Seven Vols., half-morocco, 21s. each; half-russia, 25s. each.

England and Wales, Pictorial. With upwards of 320 beautiful illustrations prepared from copyright photographs. 9s. Also an edition on superior paper, bound in half-persian, marble sides, gilt edges and in box, 15s. net.

England, A History of. From the Landing of Julius Cæsar to the Present Day. By H. O. ARNOLD-FORSTER, M.P. Fully Illustrated, 5s.

England, Cassell's Illustrated History of. From the earliest period to the present time. With upwards of 2,000 Illustrations. New Serial issue in Parts, 6d. each.

English Dictionary, Cassell's. Containing Definitions of upwards of 100,000 Words and Phrases. *Cheap Edition*, 3s. 6d. ; *Superior Edition*, 5s.

English History, The Dictionary of. Edited by SIDNEY LOW, B.A., and Prof. F. S. PULLING, M.A., with Contributions by Eminent Writers. *New Edition.* 7s. 6d.

English Literature, Library of. By Prof. H. MORLEY. In 5 Vols. 7s. 6d. each.

English Literature, Morley's First Sketch of. *Revised Edition.* 7s. 6d.

English Literature, The Story of. By ANNA BUCKLAND. 3s. 6d.

English Writers from the Earliest Period to Shakespeare. By HENRY MORLEY. Eleven Vols. 5s. each.

Æsop's Fables. Illustrated by ERNEST GRISET. *Cheap Edition.* Cloth, 3s. 6d. ; bevelled boards, gilt edges, 5s.

Etiquette of Good Society. *New Edition.* Edited and Revised by LADY COLIN CAMPBELL. 1s. ; cloth, 1s. 6d.

Fairy Tales Far and Near. Retold by Q. Illustrated. 3s. 6d.

Fairway Island. By HORACE HUTCHINSON. *Cheap Edition.* 2s. 6d.

Family Doctor, Cassell's. By A MEDICAL MAN. Illustrated, 10s. 6d.

Family Lawyer, Cassell's. An Entirely New and Original Work. By a Barrister-at-Law. 10s 6d.

Fiction, Cassell's Popular Library of. 3s. 6d. each.

Loveday. By A. E. WICKHAM.
Tiny Luttrell. By E. W. Hornung.
The White Shield. By Bertram Mitford.
Tuxter's Little Maid. By G. B. Burgin.
The Hispaniola Plate. (1683–1893.) By John Bloundelle Burton.
Highway of Sorrow. By Hesba Stretton and • • • • • •, a Famous Russian Exile.
King Solomon's Mines. By H. Rider Haggard. (Also People's Edition, 6d.)
The Lights of Sydney. By Lilian Turner.
The Admirable Lady Biddy Fane. By Frank Barrett.
Out of the Jaws of Death. By Frank Barrett.
List, ye Landsmen! A Romance of In-oident. By W. Clark Russell.
Ia: A Love Story. By Q.
The Red Terror: A Story of the Paris Commune. By Edward King.
The Little Squire. By Mrs Henry de la Pasture
Zero, the Slaver. A Romance of Equatorial Africa. By Lawrence Fletcher.
Into the Unknown! A Romance of South Africa. By Lawrence Fletcher.
Mount Desolation. An Australian Romance. By W. Carlton Dawe.
Pomona's Travels. By Frank R. Stockton.

The Reputation of George Saxon. By Morley Roberts.
A Prison Princess. By Major Arthur Griffiths.
Queen's Scarlet, The. By George Manville Fenn.
Capture of the "Estrella," The. A Tale of the Slave Trade. By Commander Claud Harding, R.N.
The Awkward Squads. And other Ulster Stories. By Shan F. Bullock.
A King's Hussar. By Herbert Compton.
A Free-Lance in a Far Land. By Herbert Compton.
Playthings and Parodies. Short Stories. Sketches, &c. By Barry Pain.
Fourteen to One, &c. By Elizabeth Stuart Phelps.
The Medicine Lady. By L. T. Meade.
Father Stafford. By Anthony Hope.
"La Bella," and others. By Egerton Castle.
The Avenger of Blood. By J. Maclaren Cobban.
The Man in Black. By Stanley Weyman.
The Doings of Raffles Haw. By A. Conan Doyle.

Field Naturalist's Handbook, The. By Revs. J. G. WOOD and THEODORE WOOD. *Cheap Edition.* 2s. 6d.

Figuier's Popular Scientific Works. With Several Hundred Illustrations in each. 3s. 6d. each.

The Insect World. | Reptiles and Birds. | The Vegetable World.
The Human Race. | Mammalia. | The Ocean World.
The World before the Deluge.

Flora's Feast. A Masque of Flowers. Penned and Pictured by WALTER CRANE. With 40 pages in Colours. 5s.

Flower Painting, Elementary. With Eight Coloured Plates. 3s.

Flowers, and How to Paint Them. By MAUD NAFTEL. With Coloured Plates. 5s.

Football: the Rugby Union Game. Edited by Rev. F. MARSHALL. Illustrated. *New and Enlarged Edition.* 7s. 6d.

For Glory and Renown. By D. H. PARRY. Illustrated. *Cheap Edition.* 3s. 6d.

Fossil Reptiles, A History of British. By Sir RICHARD OWEN, F.R.S., &c. With 268 Plates. In Four Vols. £12 12s.

Franco-German War, Cassell's History of the. Complete in Two Vols., containing about 500 Illustrations. 9s. each.

Garden Flowers, Familiar. By F. E. HULME, F.L.S., F.S.A. With 200 Full-page Coloured Plates, and Descriptive Text by SHIRLEY HIBBERD. *Cheap Edition* In Five Vols., 3s. 6d. each.

Girl at Cobhurst, The. By FRANK R. STOCKTON. 6s.

Gladstone, The Right Hon. W. E., Cassell's Life of. Profusely Illustrated. 1s.

Gleanings from Popular Authors. With Original Illustrations. *Cheap Edition.* In One Vol., 3s. 6d.

Grace O'Malley, Princess and Pirate. By ROBERT MACHRAY. 6s.

Gulliver's Travels. With 88 Engravings. Cloth, 3s. 6d. ; cloth gilt, 5s.

Gun and its Development, The. By W. W. GREENER. With 500 Illustrations. *Entirely New Edition,* 10s. 6d.

Guns, Modern Shot. By W. W. GREENER. Illustrated. 5s.

Health, The Book of. By Eminent Physicians and Surgeons. Cloth, 21s.

Heavens, The Story of the. By Sir ROBERT STAWELL BALL, LL.D., F.R.S. With Coloured Plates and Wood Engravings. *Popular Edition,* 10s. 6d.

Heroes of Britain in Peace and War. With 300 Original Illustrations. *Cheap Edition.* Complete in One Vol., 3s. 6d.

History, A Foot-note to. Eight Years of Trouble in Samoa. By R. L. STEVENSON. 6s.

Home Life of the Ancient Greeks, The. Translated by ALICE ZIMMERN. Illustrated. *Cheap Edition.* 5s.

Horse, The Book of the. By SAMUEL SIDNEY. With 17 Full-page Collotype Plates of Celebrated Horses of the Day, and numerous other Illustrations. Cloth, 15s.

Horses and Dogs. By O. EERELMAN. With Descriptive Text. Translated from the Dutch by CLARA BELL. With Fifteen Full-page and other Illustrations. 25s. net.

Houghton, Lord : The Life, Letters, and Friendships of Richard Monckton Milnes, First Lord Houghton. By Sir WEMYSS REID. Two Vols. 32s.

Hygiene and Public Health. By B. ARTHUR WHITELEGGE, M.D. Illustrated. *New and Revised Edition.* 7s. 6d.

India, Cassell's History of. In One Vol. *Cheap Edition.* 7s. 6d.

In-door Amusements, Card Games, and Fireside Fun, Cassell's Book of. With numerous Illustrations. *Cheap Edition.* Cloth, 2s.

Iron Pirate, The. By MAX PEMBERTON. Illustrated. 5s.

Khiva, A Ride to. By Col. FRED BURNABY. *New Edition.* Illustrated. 3s. 6d.

King George, In the Days of. By Col. PERCY GROVES. Illustrated. 1s. 6d.

King Solomon's Mines. By H. RIDER HAGGARD. Illustrated. 3s. 6d. *People's Edition.* 6d.

Kronstadt. A New Novel. By MAX PEMBERTON. With 8 Full-page Plates. 6s.

Ladies' Physician, The. By a London Physician. *Cheap Edition, Revised and Enlarged.* 3s. 6d.

Lady's Dressing-Room, The. Translated from the French by Lady COLIN CAMPBELL. *Cheap Edition.* 2s. 6d.

Letts's Diaries and other Time-saving Publications are now published exclusively by CASSELL & COMPANY. (*A List sent post free on application.*)

Little Huguenot, The. *New Edition.* 1s. 6d.

Locomotive Engine, The Biography of a. By HENRY FRITH. 3s. 6d.

Loftus, Lord Augustus, P.C., G.C.B., The Diplomatic Reminiscences of. First Series. With Portrait. Two Vols. 32s. Second Series. Two Vols. 32s.

London, Cassell's Guide to. With Numerous Illustrations. 6d. Cloth, 1s.

London, Greater. By EDWARD WALFORD. Two Vols. With about 400 Illustrations. *Cheap Edition,* 4s. 6d. each. *Library Edition.* Two Vols. £1 the set.

London, Old and New. By WALTER THORNBURY and EDWARD WALFORD. Six Vols.; with about 1,200 Illustrations. *Cheap Ed.,* 4s. 6d. each. *Library Ed.,* £3.

Manchester, Old and New. By WILLIAM ARTHUR SHAW, M.A. With Original Illustrations. Three Vols., 31s. 6d.

Mechanics, The Practical Dictionary of. Three Vols., £3 3s. ; half-morocco, £3 15s. Supplementary Volume, £1 1s. ; or half morocco, £1 5s.

Medical Handbook of Life Assurance. By JAMES EDWARD POLLOCK, M.D., and JAMES CHISHOLM. *New and Revised Edition.* 7s. 6d.

Medicine, Manuals for Students of. (*A List forwarded post free on application.*)

Mesdag, H. W., the Painter of the North Sea. With Etchings and Descriptive Text. By PH. ZILCKEN. The Text translated from the Dutch by CLARA BELL. 36s.

Modern Europe, A History of. By C. A. FYFFE, M.A. *Cheap Edition in One Volume,* 10s. 6d. ; *Library Edition, Illustrated,* 3 vols., 7s. 6d. each.

Music, Illustrated History of. By EMIL NAUMANN. Edited by the Rev Sir F. A. GORE OUSELEY, Bart. Illustrated. Two Vols. 31s. 6d.

National Library, Cassell's. Consisting of 214 Volumes. Paper covers, 3d. ; cloth, 6d. (*A Complete List of the Volumes post free on application.*)

Natural History, Cassell's Concise. By E. PERCEVAL WRIGHT, M.A., M.D., F.L.S. With several Hundred Illustrations. 7s. 6d.

Natural History, Cassell's New. Edited by P. MARTIN DUNCAN, M.B., F.R.S., F.G.S. *Cheap Edition.* With about 2,000 Illusts. Three Double Vols., 6s. each.

Nature and a Camera, With. Being the Adventures and Observations of a Field Naturalist and an Animal Photographer. By RICHARD KEARTON, F.Z.S. Illustrated by a Special Frontispiece, and 180 Pictures from Photographs by CHERRY KEARTON. 21s.

Nature's Wonder-Workers. By KATE R. LOVELL. Illustrated. 2s. 6d.

Nelson, The Life of. By ROBERT SOUTHEY. Illustrated with Eight Plates. 3s. 6d.

New Zealand, Pictorial. With Preface by Sir W. B. PERCEVAL, K.C.M.G. Illust. 6s.

Novels, Popular. Extra crown 8vo, cloth, 6s. each.

Grace O'Malley, Princess and Pirate. By ROBERT MACHRAY.
Cupid's Garden. By ELLEN THORNEYCROFT FOWLER.
A Limited Success. By SARAH PITT.
The Wrothams of Wrotham Court. By FRANCES HEATH FRESHFIELD.
Ill-gotten Gold : A Story of a Great Wrong and a Great Revenge. By W. G. TARBET.
Sentimental Tommy. } By J. M. BARRIE.
The Little Minister.
From the Memoirs of a Minister of France. } By STANLEY WEYMAN.
The Story of Francis Cludde.
Kronstadt.
Puritan's Wife, A. } By MAX PEMBERTON.
The Impregnable City,
The Sea-Wolves.
Young Blood.
My Lord Duke. } By E. W. HORNUNG.
Rogue's March, The.
Spectre Gold. } By HEADON HILL.
By a Hair's-Breadth.
The Girl at Cobhurst.
Story Teller's Pack, A. } By FRANK STOCKTON.
Mrs. Cliff's Yacht.
The Adventures of Captain Horn.
Treasure Island. (Also People's Edition, 6d.)
The Master of Ballantrae.
The Black Arrow. } By ROBERT LOUIS STEVENSON. } Also a *Popular Edition,* 3s. 6d. each.
Kidnapped.
Catriona : A Sequel to "Kidnapped."
Island Nights' Entertainments.
The Wrecker. By ROBERT LOUIS STEVENSON and LLOYD OSBOURNE.
What Cheer ! By W. CLARK RUSSELL.

Nursing for the Home and for the Hospital, A Handbook of. By CATHERINE J. WOOD. *Cheap Edition,* 1s. 6d. ; cloth, 2s.

Nursing of Sick Children, A Handbook for the. By CATHERINE J. WOOD. 2s. 6d.

Our Own Country. With 1,200 Illustrations. *Cheap Edition.* 3 Double Vols. 5s. each.

Painting, The English School of. By ERNEST CHESNEAU. *Cheap Edition,* 3s. 6d.

Paris, Old and New. Illustrated. In Two Vols. 9s. or 10s. 6d. each.

Peoples of the World, The. By Dr. ROBERT BROWN, F.L.S. Complete in Six Vols. With Illustrations. 7s. 6d. each.

Phrase and Fable, Dr. Brewer's Dictionary of. *Entirely New and largely increased Edition.* 10s. 6d. Also in half-morocco, 2 Vols., 15s.

Physiology for Students, Elementary. By ALFRED T. SCHOFIELD, M.D., M.R.C.S. With Two Coloured Plates and numerous Illustrations. *New Edition.* 5s.

Picturesque America. Complete in Four Vols., with 48 Exquisite Steel Plates, and about 800 Original Wood Engravings. £12 12s. the set. *Popular Edition* in Four Vols., price 18s. each.

Picturesque Australasia, Cassell's. With upwards of 1,000 Illustrations. In Four Vols., 7s. 6d. each.

Picturesque Canada. With about 600 Original Illustrations. 2 Vols. £9 9s. the set.

Picturesque Europe. Complete in Five Vols. Each containing 13 Exquisite Steel Plates, from Original Drawings, and nearly 200 Original Illustrations. £21. *Popular Edition.* In Five Vols. 18s. each.

Picturesque Mediterranean, The. With a Series of Magnificent Illustrations from Original Designs by leading Artists of the day. Two Vols. Cloth, £2 2s. each.

Pigeons, Fulton's Book of. Edited by LEWIS WRIGHT. Revised, Enlarged, and Supplemented by the Rev. W. F. LUMLEY. With 50 Full-page Illustrations. *Popular Edition.* In One Vol., 10s. 6d. *Original Edition,* with 50 Coloured Plates and numerous Wood Engravings. 21s.

Planet, The Story of Our. By Prof. BONNEY, F.R.S., &c. With Coloured Plates and Maps and about 100 Illustrations. *Cheap Edition.* 7s. 6d.

Polytechnic Series, The. Practical Illustrated Manuals. (*A List will be sent on application.*)

Portrait Gallery, Cassell's Universal. Containing 240 Portraits of Celebrated Men and Women of the Day. Cloth, 6s.

Portrait Gallery, The Cabinet. Complete in Five Series, each containing 36 Cabinet Photographs of Eminent Men and Women of the day. 15s. each.

Poultry, The Book of. By LEWIS WRIGHT. *Popular Edition.* Illustrated. 10s. 6d.

Poultry, The Illustrated Book of. By LEWIS WRIGHT. With Fifty Exquisite Coloured Plates, and numerous Wood Engravings. *Revised Edition.* Cloth, gilt edges, 21s.

"Punch," The History of. By M. H. SPIELMANN. With nearly 170 Illustrations, Portraits, and Facsimiles. Cloth, 16s.; *Large Paper Edition,* £2 2s. net.

Q's Works, Uniform Edition of. 5s. each.

Dead Man's Rock.	The Astonishing History of Troy Town.
The Splendid Spur.	"I Saw Three Ships," and other Winter's Tales.
The Blue Pavilions.	Noughts and Crosses.
The Delectable Duchy. Stories,	Wandering Heath.
Studies, and Sketches.	

Queen Summer; or, The Tourney of the Lily and the Rose. Penned and Portrayed by WALTER CRANE. With 40 pages in Colours. 6s.

Queen Victoria, The Life and Times of. By ROBERT WILSON. Complete in 2 Vols. With numerous Illustrations. 9s. each.

Queen's Empire, The. First Volume, containing about 300 Splendid Full-page Illustrations. 9s.

Queen's London, The. Containing Exquisite Views of London and its Environs, together with a fine series of Pictures of the Queen's Diamond Jubilee Procession. *Enlarged Edition,* 10s. 6d.

Railway Guides, Official Illustrated. With Illustrations on nearly every page, Maps &c. Paper covers, 1s.; cloth, 2s.

London and North Western Railway.	Great Eastern Railway.
Great Western Railway.	London and South Western Railway.
Midland Railway.	London, Brighton and South Coast Railway.
Great Northern Railway.	South Eastern Railway.

Abridged and Popular Editions of the above Guides can also be obtained. Paper covers. 3d. each.

Railways, Our. Their Origin, Development, Incident, and Romance. By JOHN PENDLETON. Illustrated. 2 Vols., 12s.

Rivers of Great Britain : Descriptive, Historical, Pictorial.
Rivers of the West Coast. With Etching as Frontispiece, and Numerous Illustrations in Text. Royal 4to, 42s.
The Royal River : The Thames from Source to Sea. *Popular Edition,* 16s.
Rivers of the East Coast. With highly-finished Engravings. *Popular Edition* 16s.

Robinson Crusoe. *Cassell's New Fine-Art Edition.* With upwards of 100 Original Illustrations. *Cheap Edition,* 3s. 6d. or 5s.

Rogues of the Fiery Cross. By S. WALKEY. With 16 Full-page Illustrations. 5s.

Ronner, Henriette, The Painter of Cat-Life and Cat-Character. By M. H. SPIELMANN. Containing a Series of beautiful Phototype Illustrations. 12s.

Royal Academy Pictures. With upwards of 200 magnificent reproductions of Pictures in the Royal Academy. 7s. 6d.

Russo-Turkish War, Cassell's History of. With about 400 Illustrations. *New Edition.* In Two Vols., 9s. each.

Sala, George Augustus, The Life and Adventures of. By Himself. *Cheap Edition.* One Vol., 7s. 6d.

Saturday Journal, Cassell's. Illustrated throughout. Yearly Vol., 7s. 6d.

Scarlet and Blue; or, Songs for Soldiers and Sailors. By JOHN FARMER. 5s. Words only, paper, 6d. ; cloth, 9d.

Science for All. Edited by Dr. ROBERT BROWN, M.A., F.L.S., &c. *Cheap Edition.* With over 1,700 Illustrations. Five Vols. 3s. 6d. each.

Science Series, The Century. Consisting of Biographies of Eminent Scientific Men of the present Century. Edited by Sir HENRY ROSCOE, D.C.L., F.R.S., M.P. Crown 8vo, 3s. 6d. each.

> **Michael Faraday, His Life and Work.** By Professor SILVANUS P. THOMPSON, F.R.S
> **Pasteur.** By PERCY FRANKLAND, F.R.S., and Mrs. FRANKLAND.
> **John Dalton and the Rise of Modern Chemistry.** By Sir HENRY E] ROSCOE, F.R.S.
> **Major Rennell, F.R.S., and the Rise of English Geography.** By Sir CLEMENTS R. MARKHAM, C.B., F.R.S., President of the Royal Geographical Society.
> **Justus Von Liebig: His Life and Work.** By W. A. SHENSTONE.
> **The Herschels and Modern Astronomy.** By Miss AGNES M. CLERKE.
> **Charles Lyell and Modern Geology.** By Professor T. G. BONNEY, F.R.S.
> **J. Clerk Maxwell and Modern Physics.** By R. T. GLAZEBROOK, F.R.S.
> **Humphry Davy, Poet and Philosopher.** By T. E. THORPE, F.R.S.
> **Charles Darwin and the Theory of Natural Selection.** By EDWARD B. POULTON, M.A., F.R.S.

Scotland, Picturesque and Traditional. By G. E. EYRE-TODD. 6s.

Sea, The Story of the. An Entirely New and Original Work. Edited by Q. Illustrated. Complete in Two Vols., 9s. each. *Cheap Edition,* 5s. each.

Shaftesbury, The Seventh Earl of, K.G., The Life and Work of. By EDWIN HODDER. Illustrated. *Cheap Edition,* 3s. 6d.

Shakespeare, Cassell's Quarto Edition. Edited by CHARLES and MARY COWDEN CLARKE, and containing about 600 Illustrations by H C SELOUS. Complete in Three Vols., cloth gilt, £3 3s.—Also published in Three separate Vols., in cloth, viz. :—The COMEDIES, 21s.; The HISTORICAL PLAYS, 18s. 6d. ; The TRAGEDIES, 25s.

Shakespeare, The England of. *New Edition.* By E. GOADBY. With Full-page Illustrations. Crown 8vo, 224 pages, 2s. 6d.

Shakespeare, The Plays of. Edited by Prof. HENRY MORLEY. Complete in 13 Vols., cloth, in box, 21s.; also 39 Vols., cloth, in box, 21s.; half-morocco, cloth sides, 42s.

Shakspere, The Leopold. With 400 Illustrations, and an Introduction by F. J. FURNIVALL. *Cheap Edition,* 3s. 6d. Cloth gilt, gilt edges, 5s. ; roxburgh, 7s. 6d.

Shakspere, The Royal. With Exquisite Steel Plates and Wood Engravings. Three Vols. 15s. each.

Sketches, The Art of Making and Using. From the French of G. FRAIPONT. By CLARA BELL. With Fifty Illustrations. 2s. 6d.

Social England. A Record of the Progress of the People. By various Writers. Edited by H. D. TRAILL, D.C.L. Complete in Six Vols. Vols. I. (Revised Ed.), II., and III., 15s. each. Vols. IV. and V., 17s. each. Vol. VI., 18s.

Spectre Gold. A Novel. By HEADON HILL. Illustrated. 6s.

Sports and Pastimes, Cassell's Complete Book of. *Cheap Edition,* 3s. 6d.

Star-Land. By Sir ROBERT STAWELL BALL, LL.D., &c. Illustrated. 6s.

Story of My Life, The. By the Rt. Hon. Sir RICHARD TEMPLE, Bart., G.C.S.I., &c. Two Vols. 21s.

Sun, The Story of the. By Sir ROBERT STAWELL BALL, LL.D., F.R.S., F.R.A.S. With Eight Coloured Plates and other Illustrations. *Cheap Edition,* 10s. 6d.

Taxation, Municipal, at Home and Abroad. By J. J. O'MEARA. 7s. 6d.

Thames, The Tidal. By GRANT ALLEN. With India Proof Impressions of 20 Magnificent Full-page Photogravure Plates, and many other Illustrations, after original drawings by W. L. WYLLIE, A.R.A. *New Edition,* cloth, 42s. net.

Things I have Seen and People I have Known. By G. A. SALA. With Portrait and Autograph. 2 Vols. 21s.

Three Homes, The. By the Very Rev. Dean FARRAR, D.D., F.R.S. *New Edition.* With 8 Full-page Illustrations. 6s.

To the Death. By R. D. CHETWODE. With Four Plates. 5s.

Treatment, The Year-Book of, for 1898. A Critical Review for Practitioners of Medicine and Surgery. Fourteenth Year of Issue. 7s. 6d.

Trees, Familiar. By Prof. G. S. BOULGER, F.L.S., F.G.S. In Two Series. With Forty Coloured Plates in each. 12s. 6d. each.

Uncle Tom's Cabin. By HARRIET BEECHER STOWE. With upwards of 100 Original Illustrations. *Fine Art Memorial Edition.* 7s. 6d.

"Unicode": The Universal Telegraphic Phrase Book. Pocket or Desk Edition. 2s. 6d. each.

United States, Cassell's History of the. By EDMUND OLLIER. With 600 Illustrations. Three Vols. 9s. each.

Universal History, Cassell's Illustrated. With nearly ONE THOUSAND ILLUSTRATIONS. Vol. I. Early and Greek History.—Vol. II. The Roman Period.—Vol. III. The Middle Ages.—Vol. IV. Modern History. 9s. each.

Verses, Wise or Otherwise. By ELLEN THORNEYCROFT FOWLER. 3s. 6d.

War and Peace, Memories and Studies of. By ARCHIBALD FORBES, LL.D. *Original Edition,* 16s. *Cheap Edition,* 6s.

Water-Colour Painting, A Course of. With Twenty-four Coloured Plates by R. P. LEITCH, and full Instructions to the Pupil. 5s.

Westminster Abbey, Annals of. By E. T. BRADLEY (Mrs. A. MURRAY SMITH). Illustrated. With a Preface by the DEAN OF WESTMINSTER. 63s.

Wild Birds, Familiar. By W. SWAYSLAND. Four Series. With 40 Coloured Plates in each. (In sets only, price on application.)

Wild Flowers, Familiar. By F. E. HULME, F.L.S., F.S.A. With 200 Coloured Plates and Descriptive Text. *Cheap Edition.* In Five Vols., 3s. 6d. each.

Wild Flowers Collecting Book. In Six Parts, 4d. each.

Wild Flowers Drawing and Painting Book. In Six Parts. 4d. each.

Windsor Castle, The Governor's Guide to. By the Most Noble the MARQUIS OF LORNE, K.T. Profusely Illustrated. Limp cloth, 1s. Cloth boards, gilt edges. 2s.

World of Wit and Humour, Cassell's New. With New Pictures and New Text. Complete in Two Vols., 6s. each.

With Claymore and Bayonet. By Col. PERCY GROVES. With 8 Plates. 3s. 6d.

Work. The Illustrated Journal for Mechanics. Half-Yearly Vols. 4s. each.

"Work" Handbooks. A Series of Practical Manuals prepared under the Direction of PAUL N. HASLUCK, Editor of *Work.* Illustrated. Cloth, 1s. each.

World of Wonders, The. With 400 Illustrations. *Cheap Edition.* Two Vols., 4s. 6d. each.

Young Blood. A Novel. By E. W. HORNUNG. 6s.

ILLUSTRATED MAGAZINES.

The Quiver. Monthly, 6d.

Cassell's Magazine. Monthly, 6d.

"Little Folks" Magazine. Monthly, 6d.

The Magazine of Art. Monthly, 1s. 4d.

Cassell's Saturday Journal. Weekly, 1d. ; Monthly, 6d.

Chums. The Illustrated Paper for Boys. Weekly, 1d.; Monthly, 6d.

Work. The Journal for Mechanics. Weekly, 1d. ; Monthly, 6d.

Building World. Weekly, 1d. ; Monthly, 6d.

Cottage Gardening. Illustrated. Weekly, ½d. ; Monthly, 3d.

** *Full particulars of* CASSELL & COMPANY'S **Monthly Serial Publications** *will be found in* CASSELL & COMPANY'S COMPLETE CATALOGUE.

Catalogues of CASSELL & COMPANY'S PUBLICATIONS, which may be had at all Booksellers', or will be sent post free on application to the Publishers :—
CASSELL'S COMPLETE CATALOGUE, containing particulars of upwards of One Thousand Volumes.
CASSELL'S CLASSIFIED CATALOGUE, in which their Works are arranged according to price, from *Threepence to Fifty Guineas.*
CASSELL'S EDUCATIONAL CATALOGUE, containing particulars of CASSELL & COMPANY'S Educational Works and Students' Manuals.

CASSELL & COMPANY, LIMITED, *Ludgate Hill, London*

Bibles and Religious Works.

Bible Biographies. Illustrated. 1s. 6d. each.
The Story of Joseph. Its Lessons for To-Day. By the Rev. GEORGE BAINTON.
The Story of Moses and Joshua. By the Rev. J. TELFORD.
The Story of Judges. By the Rev. J. WYCLIFFE GEDGE.
The Story of Samuel and Saul. By the Rev. D. C. TOVEY.
The Story of David. By the Rev. J. WILD.

The Story of Jesus. In Verse. By J. R. MACDUFF, D.D. 1s. 6d.

Bible, Cassell's Illustrated Family. With 900 Illustrations. Leather, gilt edges, £2 10s. ; best full morocco, £3 15s.

Bible, Cassell's Guinea. With 900 Illustrations and Coloured Maps. Royal 4to. Leather, 21s. net. Persian antique, with corners and clasps, 25s. net.

Bible Educator, The. Edited by E. H. PLUMPTRE, D.D. With Illustrations, Maps, &c. Four Vols., cloth, 6s. each.

Bible Dictionary, Cassell's Concise. By the Rev. ROBERT HUNTER, LL.D., Illustrated. 7s. 6d.

Bible Student in the British Museum, The. By the Rev. J. G. KITCHIN, M.A. *Entirely New and Revised Edition*, 1s. 4d.

Bunyan, Cassell's Illustrated. With 200 Original Illustrations. *Cheap Edition*, 3s. 6d.

Bunyan's Pilgrim's Progress. Illustrated. *Cheap Edition*, cloth, 3s. 6d ; cloth gilt, gilt edges, 5s.

Child's Bible, The. With 200 Illustrations. Demy 4to, 830 pp. *150th Thousand.* *Cheap Edition*, 7s. 6d. *Superior Edition*, with 6 Coloured Plates, gilt edges, 10s. 6d.

Child's Life of Christ, The. Complete in One Handsome Volume, with about 200 Original Illustrations. *Cheap Edition*, cloth, 7s. 6d. ; or with 6 Coloured Plates, cloth, gilt edges, 10s. 6d.

Church of England, The. A History for the People. By the Very Rev. H. D. M. SPENCE, D.D., Dean of Gloucester. Illustrated. Vols. I., II., and III., 6s. each.

Church Reform in Spain and Portugal. By the Rev. H. E. NOYES, D.D. Illustrated. 2s. 6d.

Commentary for English Readers. Edited by Bishop ELLICOTT. With Contributions by eminent Scholars and Divines :—
New Testament. *Original Edition.* Three Vols., 21s. each ; or in half-morocco, £4 14s. 6d. the set. *Popular Edition.* Unabridged. Three Vols., 4s. each.
Old Testament. *Original Edition.* Five Vols., 21s. each ; or in half-morocco, £7 17s. 6d. the set. *Popular Edition.* Unabridged. Five Vols., 4s. each.
⁎⁎⁎ *The Complete Set of Eight Volumes in the Popular Edition is supplied at 30s.*

Commentary, The New Testament. Edited by Bishop ELLICOTT. Handy Volume Edition. Suitable for School and General Use.

St. Matthew. 3s. 6d.	Romans. 2s. 6d.	Titus, Philemon, Hebrews, and James. 3s.
St. Mark. 3s.	Corinthians I. and II. 3s.	
St. Luke. 3s. 6d.	Galatians, Ephesians, and	Peter, Jude, and John. 3s.
St. John. 3s. 6d.	Philippians. 3s.	The Revelation. 3s.
The Acts of the Apostles. 3s. 6d.	Colossians, Thessalonians, and Timothy. 3s.	An Introduction to the New Testament. 2s. 6d.

Commentary, The Old Testament. Edited by Bishop ELLICOTT. Handy Volume Edition. Suitable for School and General Use.

Genesis. 3s. 6d.	Leviticus. 3s.	Deuteronomy. 2s. 6d.
Exodus. 3s.	Numbers. 2s. 6d.	

Dictionary of Religion, The. An Encyclopædia of Christian and other Religious Doctrines, Denominations, Sects, Heresies, Ecclesiastical Terms, History, Biography, &c. &c. By the Rev. WILLIAM BENHAM, B.D. *Cheap Edition*, 10s. 6d.

Doré Bible. With 200 Full-page Illustrations by GUSTAVE DORÉ. *Popular Edition.* In One Vol. 15s. Also in leather binding. (*Price on application.*)

Early Days of Christianity, The. By the Very Rev. Dean FARRAR, D.D., F.R.S.
LIBRARY EDITION. Two Vols., 24s. ; morocco, £2 2s.
POPULAR EDITION. In One Vol. ; cloth, gilt edges, 7s. 6d. ; tree-calf, 15s.
CHEAP EDITION. Cloth gilt, 3s. 6d.

Family Prayer-Book, The. Edited by the Rev. Canon GARBETT, M.A., and the Rev. S MARTIN. With Full-page Illustrations. *New Edition.* Cloth, 7s. 6d.

"Graven in the Rock ;" or, the Historical Accuracy of the Bible confirmed by reference to the Assyrian and Egyptian Sculptures in the British Museum and elsewhere. By the Rev. Dr. SAMUEL KINNS, F.R.A.S., &c. &c. Illustrated. *Library Edition*, in Two Volumes, cloth, with top edges gilded, 15s.

"Heart Chords." A Series of Works by Eminent Divines. In cloth, 1s. each.

My Father. By the Right Rev. Ashton Oxenden, late Bishop of Montreal.
My Bible. By the Rt. Rev. W. Boyd Carpenter, Bishop of Ripon.
My Work for God. By the Right Rev. Bishop Cotterill.
My Object in Life. By the Very Rev. Dean Farrar, D.D.
My Aspirations. By the Rev. G. Matheson, D.D.
My Emotional Life. By Preb. Chadwick, D.D.
My Body. By the Rev. Prof. W. G. Blaikie, D.D.
My Soul. By the Rev. P. B. Power, M.A.

My Growth in Divine Life. By the Rev. Prebendary Reynolds, M.A.
My Hereafter. By the Very Rev. Dean Bickersteth.
My Walk with God. By the Very Rev. Dean Montgomery.
My Aids to the Divine Life. By the Very Rev. Dean Boyle.
My Sources of Strength. By the Rev. E. E. Jenkins, M.A.
My Comfort in Sorrow. By Hugh Macmillan, D.D.

Helps to Belief. A Series of Helpful Manuals on the Religious Difficulties of the Day. Edited by the Rev. TEIGNMOUTH SHORE, M.A., Canon of Worcester, 1s. each.

CREATION. By Harvey Goodwin, D.D., late Lord Bishop of Carlisle.
MIRACLES. By the Rev. Brownlow Maitland, M.A.

PRAYER. By the Rev. Canon Shore, M.A.
THE ATONEMENT. By William Connor Magee, D.D., Late Archbishop of York.

Holy Land and the Bible, The. By the REV. CUNNINGHAM GEIKIE, D.D., LL.D. (Edin.). *Cheap Edition*, with 24 Collotype Plates, 12s. 6d.

Life of Christ, The. By the Very Rev. Dean FARRAR, D.D., F.R.S.
CHEAP EDITION. With 16 Full-page Plates. Cloth gilt, 3s. 6d.
POPULAR EDITION. With 16 Full-page Plates. Cloth gilt, gilt edges, 7s. 6d.
LARGE TYPE ILLUSTD. EDITION. Cloth, 7s. 6d. Cloth, full gilt, gilt edges, 10s. 6d.
LIBRARY EDITION. Two Vols. Cloth, 24s. morocco, 42s.

Methodism, Side-Lights on the Conflicts of, During the Second Quarter of the Nineteenth Century, 1827-1852. From the Notes of the Late Rev. JOSEPH FOWLER of the Debates of the Wesleyan Conference. Cloth. 8s.

Moses and Geology; or, the Harmony of the Bible with Science. By the Rev. SAMUEL KINNS, Ph.D., F.R.A.S. Illus. *Library Edition*, 10s. 6d.

New Light on the Bible and the Holy Land. By BASIL T. A. EVETTS, M.A. Illustrated. Cloth, 7s. 6d.

Old and New Testaments, Plain Introductions to the Books of the. Containing Contributions by many Eminent Divines. In Two Vols., 3s. 6d. each.

Plain Introductions to the Books of the Old Testament. 336 pages. Edited by Bishop ELLICOTT. 3s. 6d.

Plain Introductions to the Books of the New Testament. 304 pages. Edited by Bishop ELLICOTT. 3s. 6d.

Protestantism, The History of. By the Rev. J. A. WYLIE, LL.D. Containing upwards of 600 Original Illustrations. Three Vols., 27s.

"Quiver" Yearly Volume, The. With about 600 Original Illustrations and Coloured Frontispiece. 7s. 6d. Also Monthly, 6d.

St. George for England; and other Sermons preached to Children. *Fifth Edition.* By the Rev. T. TEIGNMOUTH SHORE, M.A., Canon of Worcester. 5s.

St. Paul, The Life and Work of. By the Very Rev. Dean FARRAR, D.D., F.R.S.
CHEAP ILLUSTRATED EDITION. 7s. 6d.
CHEAP EDITION. With 16 Full-page Plates, cloth gilt, 3s. 6d.
LIBRARY EDITION. Two Vols., cloth, 24s.; calf, 42s.
ILLUSTRATED EDITION, One Vol., £1 1s.; morocco, £2 2s.
POPULAR EDITION. Cloth, gilt edges, 7s. 6d.

Shortened Church Services and Hymns, suitable for use at Children's Services. Compiled by the Rev. Canon SHORE, *Enlarged Edition.* 1s.

"Six Hundred Years;" or, Historical Sketches of Eminent Men and Women who have more or less come into contact with the Abbey and Church of Holy Trinity, Minories, from 1293 to 1893, and some account of the Incumbents, the Fabric, the Plate, &c. &c. By the Vicar, the Rev. Dr. SAMUEL KINNS, F.R.A.S., &c. &c. With 65 Illustrations. 15s.

"Sunday:" Its Origin, History, and Present Obligation. By the Ven. Archdeacon HESSEY, D.C.L. *Fifth Edition*, 7s. 6d.

Educational Works and Students' Manuals.

Agricultural Text-Books, Cassell's. (The "Downton" Series.) Fully Illustrated. Edited by JOHN WRIGHTSON, Professor of Agriculture. **Soils and Manures.** By J. M. H. MUNRO, D.Sc. (London), F.I.C., F.C.S. 2s. 6d. **Farm Crops.** By Professor WRIGHTSON. 2s. 6d. **Live Stock.** By Professor WRIGHTSON. 2s. 6d.

Alphabet, Cassell's Pictorial. Mounted on Linen, with Rollers. 2s. Mounted with Rollers, and Varnished. 2s. 6d.

Arithmetic :—Howard's Art of Reckoning. By C. F. HOWARD. Paper, 1s. ; cloth, 2s. *Enlarged Edition*, 5s.

Arithmetics, The "Belle Sauvage." By GEORGE RICKS, B.Sc. Lond. With Test Cards. (*List on application.*)

Atlas, Cassell's Popular. Containing 24 Coloured Maps. 1s. 6d.

Blackboard Drawing By W. E. SPARKES. With 52 Full-page Illustrations by the Author. 5s.

Book-Keeping. By THEODORE JONES. FOR SCHOOLS, 2s. ; or cloth, 3s. FOR THE MILLION, 2s. ; or cloth, 3s. Books for Jones's System, Ruled Sets of, 2s.

British Empire Map of the World. New Map for Schools and Institutes. By G. R. PARKIN and J. G. BARTHOLOMEW, F.R.G.S. Mounted on cloth, varnished, and with Rollers or Folded. 25s.

Chemistry, The Public School. By J. H. ANDERSON, M.A. 2s. 6d.

Cookery for Schools. By LIZZIE HERITAGE. 6d.

Dulce Domum. Rhymes and Songs for Children. Edited by JOHN FARMER, Editor of "Gaudeamus," &c. Old Notation and Words, 5s. N.B.—The Words of the Songs in "Dulce Domum" (with the Airs both in Tonic Sol-Fa and Old Notation) can be had in Two Parts, 6d. each.

England, A History of. From the Landing of Julius Cæsar to the Present Day. By H. O. ARNOLD-FORSTER, M.P. Fully Illustrated. 5s.

English Literature, A First Sketch of, from the Earliest Period to the Present Time. By HENRY MORLEY. 7s. 6d.

Euclid, Cassell's. Edited by Prof. WALLACE, M.A. 1s.

Euclid, The First Four Books of. *New Edition.* In paper, 6d. ; cloth, 9d.

French, Cassell's Lessons in. *New and Revised Edition.* Parts I. and II., each 1s. 6d. ; complete, 2s. 6d. Key, 1s. 6d.

French-English and English-French Dictionary. 3s. 6d. or 5s.

French Reader, Cassell's Public School. By GUILLAUME S. CONRAD. 2s. 6d.

Galbraith and Haughton's Scientific Manuals. Astronomy. 5s. Euclid. Books I., II., III. 2s. 6d. Books IV., V., VI. 2s. 6d. Mathematical Tables. 3s. 6d. Mechanics. 3s. 6d. Hydrostatics. 3s. 6d. Algebra. Part I., cloth, 2s. 6d. Complete, 7s 6d. Tides and Tidal Currents, with Tidal Cards, 3s.

Gaudeamus. Songs for Colleges and Schools. Edited by JOHN FARMER. 5s. Words only, paper, 6d. ; cloth, 9d.

Geometry, First Elements of Experimental. By PAUL BERT. Illustrated. 1s. 6d.

German Dictionary, Cassell's. German-English, English-German. *Cheap Edition*, cloth, 3s. 6d. ; half-morocco, 5s.

German Reading, First Lessons in. By A. JÄGST. Illustrated. 1s.

Hand and Eye Training. By GEORGE RICKS, B.Sc., and JOSEPH VAUGHAN. Illustrated. Vol. I. Designing with Coloured Papers. Vol. II. Cardboard Work. 2s. each. Vol. III. Colour Work and Design. 3s.

Hand and Eye Training. By G. RICKS, B.Sc. Two Vols., with 16 Coloured Plates in each. 6s. each. **Cards for Class Use.** Five Sets. 1s. each.

Historical Cartoons, Cassell's Coloured. Size 45 in. × 35 in., 2s. each. Mounted on canvas and varnished, with rollers, 5s. each. (Descriptive pamphlet, 16 pp., 1d.)

Italian Lessons, with Exercises, Cassell's. In One Vol. 2s.

Latin Dictionary, Cassell's. (Latin-English and English-Latin.) 3s. 6d. half morocco, 5s.

Latin Primer, The New. By Prof. J. P. POSTGATE. 2s. 6d.

Latin Primer, The First. By Prof. POSTGATE. 1s.

Latin Prose for Lower Forms. By M. A. BAYFIELD, M.A. 2s. 6d.

Laws of Every-Day Life. For the Use of Schools. By H. O. ARNOLD-FORSTER, M.P. 1s. 6d.

Lessons in Our Laws ; or, Talks at Broadacre Farm. By H. F. LESTER, B.A. In Two Parts. 1s. 6d. each.

Little Folks' History of England. By ISA CRAIG-KNOX. Illustrated. 1s. 6d.

Making of the Home, The. By Mrs. SAMUEL A. BARNETT. 1s. 6d.

Map Building for Schools. A Practical Method of Teaching Geography (England and Wales) By J. H. OVERTON, F.G.S. 6d.

Marlborough·Books:—Arithmetic Examples. 3s. French Exercises. 3s. 6d. French Grammar. 2s. 6d. German Grammar. 3s. 6d.

Mechanics, Applied. By JOHN PERRY, M.E., D.Sc., &c. Illustrated. 7s. 6d.

Mechanics for Young Beginners. By the Rev. J. G. EASTON, M.A. *Cheap Edition,* 2s. 6d.

Mechanics and Machine Design, Numerical Examples in Practical. By R. G. BLAINE, M.E. *New Edition, Revised and Enlarged.* With 79 Illus. 2s. 6d.

Models and Common Objects, How to Draw from. By W. E. SPARKES. Illustrated. 3s.

Models, Common Objects, and Casts of Ornament, How to Shade from. By W. E. SPARKES. With 25 Plates by the Author. 3s.

Natural History Coloured Wall Sheets, Cassell's New. Consisting of 16 subjects. Size, 39 by 31 in. Mounted on rollers and varnished. 3s. each.

Object Lessons from Nature. By Prof. L. C. MIALL, F.L.S., F.G.S. Fully Illustrated. *New and Enlarged Edition.* Two Vols. 1s. 6d. each.

Physiology for Schools. By ALFRED T. SCHOFIELD, M.D., M.R.C.S., &c. Illustrated. 1s. 9d. Three Parts, paper covers, 5d. each ; or cloth limp, 6d. each.

Poetry Readers, Cassell's New. Illustrated. 12 Books. 1d. each. Cloth, 1s. 6d.

Popular Educator, Cassell's. With Revised Text, New Maps, New Coloured Plates, New Type, &c. Complete in Eight Vols., 5s. each.

Readers, Cassell's "Belle Sauvage." An Entirely New Series. Fully Illustrated. Strongly bound in cloth. *(List on application.)*

Reader, The Citizen. By H. O. ARNOLD-FORSTER, M.P. Cloth, 1s. 6d. ; also a Scottish Edition, cloth, 1s. 6d.

Readers, Cassell's Classical. Vol. I., 1s. 8d. ; Vol. II., 2s. 6d.

Reader, The Temperance. By J. DENNIS HIRD. 1s. or 1s. 6d.

Readers, Cassell's "Higher Class." *(List on application.)*

Readers, Cassell's Readable. Illustrated. *(List on application.)*

Readers for Infant Schools, Coloured. Three Books. 4d. each.

Readers, Geographical, Cassell's New. With Numerous Illustrations in each Book. *(List on application.)*

Readers, The Modern Geographical. Illustrated throughout. *(List on application.)*

Readers, The Modern School. Illustrated. *(List on application.)*

Rolit. An entirely novel system of learning French. By J. J. TYLOR. 3s.

Round the Empire. By G. R. PARKIN. With a Preface by the Rt. Hon. the Earl of Rosebery, K.G. Fully Illustrated. 1s. 6d.

Science of Every·Day Life. By J. A. BOWER. Illustrated. 1s.

Sculpture, A Primer of. By E. ROSCOE MULLINS. Illustrated. 2s. 6d.

Shakspere's Plays for School Use. Illustrated. 9 Books. 6d. each.

Spelling, A Complete Manual of. By J. D. MORELL, LL.D. 1s.

Technical Educator, Cassell's. A New Cyclopædia of Technical Education, with Coloured Plates and Engravings. Complete in Six Vols., 3s. 6d. each.

Technical Manuals, Cassell's. Illustrated throughout. 16 Vols., from 2s. to 4s. 6d. *(List free on application.)*

Technology, Manuals of. Edited by Prof. AYRTON, F.R.S., and RICHARD WORMELL, D.Sc., M.A. Illustrated throughout. *(List on application.)*

Things New and Old ; or, Stories from English History. By H. O. ARNOLD-FORSTER, M.P. Fully Illustrated. Strongly bound in cloth. Seven Books from 5d to 1s. 8d.

World of Ours, This. By H. O. ARNOLD-FORSTER, M.P. Fully Illustrated. *Cheap Edition.* 2s. 6d.

Young Citizen, The ; or, Lessons in our Laws. By H. F. LESTER. Fully Illustrated. 2s. 6d.

Books for Young People.

Two Old Ladies, Two Foolish Fairies, and a Tom Cat. The Surprising Adventures of Tuppy and Tue. A New Fairy Story. By MAGGIE BROWNE. With Four Coloured Plates and Illustrations in text. Cloth, 3s. 6d.

Micky Magee's Menagerie; or, Strange Animals and their Doings. By S. H. HAMER. With 8 Coloured Plates and other Illustrations by HARRY NEILSON. Coloured Boards, 1s. 6d.

The Victoria Painting Book for Little Folks. Containing about 300 Illustrations suitable for Colouring, 1s.

"Little Folks" Half-Yearly Volume. Containing 480 pages of Letterpress, with Six Full-page Coloured Plates, and numerous other Pictures printed in Colour. Picture boards, 3s. 6d.; or cloth gilt, gilt edges, 5s.

Bo-Peep. A Treasury for the Little Ones. Yearly Vol. With Original Stories and Verses. Illustrated with Eight Full-page Coloured Plates, and numerous other Pictures printed in Colour. Elegant picture boards, 2s. 6d.; cloth, 3s. 6d.

Beneath the Banner. Being Narratives of Noble Lives and Brave Deeds. By F. J. CROSS. Illustrated. Limp cloth, 1s.; cloth boards, gilt edges, 2s.

Good Morning! Good Night! Morning and Evening Readings for Children, by the Author of "Beneath the Banner." Fully Illustrated. Limp cloth, 1s., or cloth boards, gilt edges, 2s.

Five Stars in a Little Pool. By EDITH CARRINGTON. Illustrated. 3s. 6d.

Merry Girls of England. By L. T. MEADE. 3s. 6d.

Beyond the Blue Mountains. By L. T. MEADE. Illustrated. 5s.

The Cost of a Mistake. By SARAH PITT. Illustrated. *New Edition.* 2s. 6d.

The Peep of Day. Cassell's Illustrated Edition. 2s. 6d.

A Book of Merry Tales. By MAGGIE BROWNE, SHEILA, ISABEL WILSON, and C. L. MATÉAUX. Illustrated. 3s. 6d.

A Sunday Story-Book. By MAGGIE BROWNE, SAM BROWNE, and AUNT ETHEL. Illustrated. 3s. 6d.

Story Poems for Young and Old. By E. DAVENPORT. 3s. 6d.

Pleasant Work for Busy Fingers. By MAGGIE BROWNE. Illustrated. 2s. 6d.

Magic at Home. By Prof. HOFFMAN. Fully Illustrated. A Series of easy and startling Conjuring Tricks for Beginners. Cloth gilt, 3s. 6d.

Little Mother Bunch. By Mrs. MOLESWORTH. Illustrated. *New Edition.* 2s. 6d.

Heroes of Every-Day Life. By LAURA LANE. With about 20 Full-page Illustrations. 256 pages, crown 8vo, cloth, 2s. 6d.

Ships, Sailors, and the Sea. By R. J. CORNEWALL-JONES. Illd. 2s. 6d.

Gift Books for Young People. By Popular Authors. With Four Original Illustrations in each. Cloth gilt, 1s. 6d. each.

The Boy Hunters of Kentucky. By Edward S. Ellis.	Jack Marston's Anchor.
Red Feather: a Tale of the American Frontier. By Edward S. Ellis.	Frank's Life-Battle.
	Major Monk's Motto; or, "Look Before you Leap."
Fritters; or, "It's a Long Lane that has no Turning."	Tim Thomson's Trial; or, "All is not Gold that Glitters."
Trixy; or, "Those who Live in Glass Houses shouldn't throw Stones."	Ursula's Stumbling-Block.
Rhoda's Reward.	Ruth's Life-Work; or,"No Pains, no Gains."
	Uncle William's Charge.

"Golden Mottoes" Series, The. Each Book containing 208 pages, with Four Full-page Original Illustrations. Crown 8vo, cloth gilt, 2s. each.

"Nil Desperandum." By the Rev. F. Langbridge, M.A.	"Honour is my Guide." By Jeanie Hering (Mrs. Adams-Acton).
"Bear and Forbear." By Sarah Pitt.	"Aim at a Sure End." By Emily Searchfield.
"Foremost if I Can." By Helen Atteridge.	"He Conquers who Endures." By the Author of "May Cunningham's Trial." &c.

"Cross and Crown" Series, The. With Four Illustrations in each Book. Crown 8vo, 256 pages, 2s. 6d. each.

Heroes of the Indian Empire; or, Stories of Valour and Victory. By Ernest Foster.	Adam Hepburn's Vow: A Tale of Kirk and Covenant. By Annie S. Swan.
Through Trial to Triumph; or, "The Royal Way." By Madeline Bonavia Hunt.	No. XIII.; or, The Story of the Lost Vestal. A Tale of Early Christian Days. By Emma Marshall.
Strong to Suffer: A Story of the Jews. By E. Wynne.	
By Fire and Sword: A Story of the Huguenots. By Thomas Archer.	Freedom's Sword: A Story of the Days of Wallace and Bruce. By Annie S. Swan.

Albums for Children. Price 3s. 6d. each.

The Album for Home, School, and Play. | Picture Album of All Sorts. Illustrated.
· Set in bold type and illustrated throughout. | The Chit-Chat Album. Illustrated.

"Wanted—a King" Series. *Cheap Edition*. Illustrated. 2s. 6d. each.

Fairy Tales in Other Lands. By Julia Goddard. | Wanted—a King; or, How Merle set the
Robin's Ride. By Ellinor Davenport Adams. | Nursery Rhymes to Rights. By Maggie
| Browne.

"Peeps Abroad" Library. *Cheap Editions*. Cloth gilt, 2s. 6d. each.

Rambles Round London. By C. L. Matéaux. Illustrated. | Wild Adventures in Wild Places. By Dr.
Around and About Old England. By C. L. Matéaux. Illustrated. | Gordon Stables, R.N. Illustrated.
Paws and Claws. By one of the Authors of "Poems Written for a Child." Illustrated. | Modern Explorers. By Thomas Frost. Illustrated. *New and Cheaper Edition.*
Decisive Events in History. By Thomas Archer. With Original Illustrations. | Early Explorers. By Thomas Frost.
The True Robinson Crusoes. | Home Chat with our Young Folks. Illustrated throughout.
Peeps Abroad for Folks at Home. Illustrated throughout. | Jungle, Peak, and Plain. Illustrated throughout.

Three-and-Sixpenny Books for Young People. With Original Illustrations.
Cloth gilt, 3s. 6d. each.

Told Out of School. By A. J. Daniels. | † The White House at Inch Gow. By Sarah Pitt.
† Red Rose and Tiger Lily. By L. T. Meade. | † Polly. By L. T. Meade.
The Romance of Invention. By James Burnley. | † The Palace Beautiful. By L. T. Meade.
† Bashful Fifteen. By L. T. Meade. | "Follow my Leader."
The King's Command. A Story for Girls. By Maggie Symington. | For Fortune and Glory.
| Lost Among White Africans.
† A Sweet Girl Graduate. By L. T. Meade | † A World of Girls. By L. T. Meade.

Books marked thus † can also be had in extra cloth gilt, gilt edges, 5s. each.

Books by Edward S. Ellis. Illustrated. Cloth, 2s. 6d. each.

A Strange Craft and its Wonderful Voyage.
Pontiac, Chief of the Ottawas. A Tale of the Siege of Detroit.
In the Days of the Pioneers.
The Phantom of the River.
Shod with Silence.
The Great Cattle Trail.
The Path in the Ravine.

The Hunters of the Ozark.
The Camp in the Mountains
Ned in the Woods. A Tale of Early Days in the West.
Down the Mississippi.
The Last War Trail.
Ned on the River. A Tale of Indian River Warfare.
Footprints in the Forest.
Up the Tapajos.

Ned in the Block House. A Story of Pioneer Life in Kentucky.
The Young Ranchers.
The Lost Trail.
Camp-Fire and Wigwam.
Lost in the Wilds.
Lost in Samoa. A Tale of Adventure in the Navigator Islands.

Tad; or, "Getting Even" with Him.

Cassell's Picture Story Books. Each containing 60 pages. 6d. each.

Little Talks.
Bright Stars.
Nursery Joys.
Pet's Posy.
Tiny Tales.

Daisy's Story Book.
Dot's Story Book.
A Nest of Stories.
Good-Night Stories.
Chats for Small Chatterers.

Auntie's Stories.
Birdie's Story Book.
Little Chimes.
A Sheaf of Tales.
Dewdrop Stories.

Illustrated Books for the Little Ones. Containing interesting Stories. All
Illustrated. 9d. each.

Bright Tales and Funny Pictures.
Merry Little Tales.
Little Tales for Little People.
Little People and Their Pets.
Tales Told for Sunday.
Sunday Stories for Small People.
Stories and Pictures for Sunday.

Bible Pictures for Boys and Girls.
Firelight Stories.
Sunlight and Shade.
Rub-a-dub Tales.
Fine Feathers and Fluffy Fur.
Scrambles and Scrapes.
Tittle Tattle Tales.
Dumb Friends.
Indoors and Out.
Some Farm Friends.

Those Golden Sands.
Little Mothers and their Children.
Our Pretty Pets.
Our Schoolday Hours.
Creatures Tame.
Creatures Wild.
Up and Down the Garden.
All Sorts of Adventures.
Our Sunday Stories.
Our Holiday Hours.
Wandering Ways.

Shilling Story Books. All Illustrated, and containing Interesting Stories.

Seventeen Cats.
Bunty and the Boys.
The Heir of Elmdale.
Claimed at Last, and Roy's Reward.
Thorns and Tangles.

The Cuckoo in the Robin's Nest.
John's Mistake.
Diamonds in the Sand.
Surly Bob.
The History of Five Little Pitchers.
The Giant's Cradle.

Shag and Doll.
The Cost of Revenge.
Clever Frank.
Among the Redskins.
The Ferryman of Brill.
Harry Maxwell.

Eighteenpenny Story Books. All Illustrated throughout.

Wee Willie Winkie.
Ups and Downs of a Donkey's Life.
Three Wee Ulster Lassies.
Up the Ladder.
Dick's Hero; & other Stories.

The Chip Boy.
Roses from Thorns.
Faith's Father.
By Land and Sea.
Jeff and Leff.
The Young Berringtons.

Tom Morris's Error.
"Through Flood—Through Fire."
The Girl with the Golden Locks.
Stories of the Olden Time.

Library of Wonders. Illustrated Gift-books for Boys. Cloth, 1s. 6d.

Wonders of Animal Instinct.
Wonderful Balloon Ascents.

Wonders of Bodily Strength and Skill.

The "World in Pictures" Series. Illustrated throughout. *Cheap Edition*, 1s. 6d. each.

All the Russias.
Chats about Germany.
Peeps into China.
The Land of Pyramids (Egypt).

The Eastern Wonderland (Japan).
Glimpses of South America.
Round Africa.
The Land of Temples (India).
·The Isles of the Pacific.

Two-Shilling Story Books. All Illustrated.

Two Fourpenny Bits.
Stories of the Tower.
Mr. Burke's Nieces.
The Top of the Ladder:
How to Reach it.

Little Flotsam.
The Children of the Court.
The Four Cats of the Tippertons.
Little Folks' Sunday Book.

Poor Nelly.
Tom Heriot.
Aunt Tabitha's Waifs.
In Mischief Again.
Peggy, and other Tales.

Half-Crown Story Books.

On Board the *Esmeralda*; or, Martin Leigh's Log.
Esther West.
For Queen and King.

Perils Afloat and Brigands Ashore.
Working to Win.
At the South Pole.

Pictures of School Life and Boyhood.

Cassell's Pictorial Scrap Book. In Six Books, each containing 32 pages, 6d. each.

Books for the Little Ones. Fully Illustrated.

The Sunday Scrap Book. With Several Hundred Illustrations. Boards, 3s.6d. cloth, gilt edges, 5s.
Cassell's Robinson Crusoe. With 100 Illustrations. Cloth, 3s. 6d. ; gil edges, 5s.
The New "Little Folks" Painting Book. Containing nearly 350 Outline Illustrations suitable for Colouring. 1s.

The Old Fairy Tales. With Original Illustrations. Cloth, 1s.
Cassell's Swiss Family Robinson. Illustrated. Cloth, 3s. 6d. ; gilt edges, 5s.

The World's Workers. A Series of New and Original Volumes by Popular Authors. With Portraits printed on a tint as Frontispiece. 1s. each.

John Cassell. By G. Holden Pike.
Charles Haddon Spurgeon. By G. Holden Pike.
Dr. Arnold of Rugby. By Rose E. Selfe.
The Earl of Shaftesbury.
Sarah Robinson, Agnes Weston, and Mrs. Meredith.
Thomas A. Edison and Samuel F. B. Morse.
Mrs. Somerville and Mary Carpenter.
General Gordon.
Charles Dickens.
Sir Titus Salt and George Moore.

Dr. Guthrie, Father Mathew, Elihu Burritt, Joseph Livesey.
Sir Henry Havelock and Colin Campbell, Lord Clyde.
Abraham Lincoln.
David Livingstone.
George Müller and Andrew Reed.
Richard Cobden.
Benjamin Franklin.
Handel.
Turner the Artist.
George and Robert Stephenson.

* *The above Works can also be had Three in One Vol., cloth, gilt edges, 3s.*

CASSELL & COMPANY, Limited, Ludgate Hill, London; Paris, New York & Melbourne.

www.ingramcontent.com/pod-product-compliance
Lightning Source LLC
Chambersburg PA
CBHW020241290326

41929CB00045B/1319